POST-QUANTUM SECURITY FOR AI

POST-QUANTUM SECURITY FOR AI

RESILIENT DIGITAL SECURITY IN THE AGE OF ARTIFICIAL GENERAL INTELLIGENCE AND TECHNOLOGICAL SINGULARITY

Petar Radanliev

Addison-Wesley

Visit us on the Web: informit.com

Library of Congress Control Number: 2025935506

ISBN-13: 978-0-13-543592-2
ISBN-10: 0-13-543592-7

$PrintCode

Cover Credit: Siarhei Yurchanka/Alamy Images

Head of IT & Professional Learning, Enterprise Learning and Skills
Julie Phifer

Executive Editor
James Manly

Development Editor
Christopher A. Cleveland

Managing Editor
Sandra Schroeder

Senior Project Editor
Mandie Frank

Copy Editor
Kitty Wilson

Indexer
Timothy Wright

Proofreader
Barbara Mack

Technical Reviewer
Omar Santos

Designer
Chuti Prasertsith

Compositor
codeMantra

I would like to express my deepest appreciation to my nieces, Charlotte and Rachel, and my nephew, Robert, for their unwavering encouragement and support. Their curiosity and enthusiasm for knowledge continue to inspire my work, reminding me of the importance of preparing for a future where technology serves the greater good.

Contents

Preface .... **xv**

PART I Introduction to the Technological Threats **1**

1 Understanding the Technological Singularity **3**

Objectives 3

Technological Singularity 4

Defining the Technological Singularity 5

The Evolution of AGI 8

Risk of the Singularity 11

Summary 18

References 19

2 Quantum Computing and Its Implications **27**

Objectives 27

Basics of Quantum Computing 28

Quantum Computing's Threat to Cryptography 29

Indistinguishability Obfuscation (iO) 34

Case Study: How to Develop a Quantum-Resistant Blockchain 36

Future of Quantum Technologies: Comparative Analysis 40

Quantum Versus Classical Computing: Domain-Specific Comparison 41

Bridging the Gap Between Quantum and Classical Systems 42

Summary 42

References 43

PART II Defining the Concept of Digital Security by Design **51**

3 Current Digital Security Systems **53**

Objectives 53

Overview of Digital Identity Systems 54

Case Study: How to Develop a Quantum-Safe Decentralized System That Gives Users Control over Their Digital Identities 56

Public-Key Infrastructure (PKI) and Its Limitations . . . 60

Decentralized Security Models: Blockchain and Beyond . . . 65

Summary . . . 70

References . . . 70

4 The Opportunities and Risks Related to Artificial General Intelligence (AGI) in Cybersecurity . . . 79

Objectives . . . 79

AGI Capabilities in Autonomous Attacks . . . 80

AGI Capabilities for Autonomous Attacks on Digital Identity Management Systems . . . 81

AGI Capabilities for Autonomous Attacks on National Critical Infrastructure . . . 84

How AGI Poses Unique Security Threats . . . 86

Case Studies of AI-Driven Cyberattacks . . . 89

Technical Overview of AI-Powered Malware: BlackMamba . . . 91

Final Words on BlackMamba . . . 98

Summary . . . 99

References . . . 99

PART III Quantum-Resistant Cryptography . . . 105

5 Post-Quantum Cryptography: The New NIST Standards . . . 107

Objectives . . . 107

Lattice-Based Cryptography . . . 108

Key Capabilities of Lattice-Based Cryptography . . . 109

Application for LBC in National Critical Infrastructure . . . 110

Implementation Strategy for LBC in National Critical Infrastructure . . . 111

Ring Learning with Errors . . . 114

Theoretical Foundations of RLWE . . . 116

Applications of RLWE in Cryptography . . . 116

Efficiency and Security Trade-offs of RLWE . . . 119

NIST Standards for Post-Quantum Cryptography . . . 122

Key Algorithms Selected by NIST . . . 122

Implementation Guidelines for National Critical Infrastructure 125

Global Implications of NIST PQC Standards 127

Case Study: Behavioral Analysis with Falcon X AI: Analyzing Advanced Quantum Malware Strains 127

Step 1: Preparing the Cloud Environment for Analysis 127

Step 2: Triggering and Capturing Malware Behavior 130

Step 3: Analyzing Network Traffic and Command-and-Control (C2) Communications 132

Step 4: De-obfuscating Malware Logic 135

Step 5: Memory Analysis and Fileless Malware Detection 137

Step 6: Threat Attribution and Reporting 139

Step 7: Building Custom Defense Mechanisms 141

Discussion and Analysis: Behavioral Analysis with Falcon X AI in the Context of AGI and Quantum Computing 144

Summary 144

References 145

6 Implementing Quantum-Safe Solutions 151

Objectives 151

Practical Deployment of Post-quantum Algorithms 152

Phase 1: Assessment of the Existing Cryptographic Infrastructure to Identify Vulnerabilities to Quantum Threats 153

Phase 2: Prioritization 153

Phase 3: Impact Analysis to Evaluate the Computational and Operational Implications of Migrating to PQAs 153

Phase 4: Selection of Appropriate PQAs 153

Phase 5: Pilot Testing 154

Phase 6: System Integration 154

Phase 7: Operational Deployment 155

Phase 8: Validation and Monitoring 155

Phase 9: Training and Documentation 156

Challenges During Deployment 156

Practical Example: Deploying CRYSTALS-Kyber in TLS 157

Overcoming Challenges in Quantum-Safe Implementations ... 161
Backward Compatibility ... 162
Standardization Gaps ... 162
Practical Implementation Strategies for Addressing Standardization Gaps ... 163
Hybrid Certificate Deployment for Interoperability ... 164
Interoperability Testing Across Environments ... 164
Security Assurance in Quantum-Safe Implementations ... 166
Hybrid Cryptographic Frameworks ... 167
Protocol and Hardware Upgrades ... 168
Scalability and Efficiency in Quantum-Safe Systems ... 171
Key Size and Bandwidth Requirements ... 171
Operational Scalability ... 172
Efficient Algorithm Selection ... 173
Optimization for Resource-Constrained Systems ... 176
Case Study on PQC and Emerging AI Threats ... 177
Cape Sandbox: AI Malware Analysis and Threat Detection ... 177
Step 1: Environment Configuration ... 179
Step 2: Submitting Malware Samples ... 181
Step 3: Analyzing Dynamic Behavior ... 183
Step 4: Polymorphic Behavior Tracking ... 185
Step 5: Apply Threat Intelligence ... 187
Step 6: Automating Detection Rules ... 189
Discussion and Analysis: The Impact of Quantum Computing and AGI on Sandbox Environments ... 191
Summary ... 193
References ... 194

PART IV Defending Against AGI Threats ... 199

7 AI-Driven Defenses and Threat Mitigation ... 201
Objectives ... 201
AI and Machine Learning in Cybersecurity ... 202

Using AI to Defend Against AI: Generative Adversarial Networks ... 203

Generative AI for Cybersecurity: Practical Applications and Code Demonstrations ... 204

Example 1: Using ChatGPT for Automated Phishing Detection ... 204

Example 2: Generating Adversarial Malware with Llama 2 ... 205

Example 3: Reinforcement Learning for Autonomous Intrusion Response ... 207

Reinforcement Learning for AGI Threat Mitigation ... 208

Case Study on AI and Machine Learning in Cybersecurity: Static Analysis with DeepCode AI (Snyk) ... 210

DeepCode AI's Current Technical Capabilities and How They Would Need to Change in the Future ... 211

Quantum AGI and Malware Analysis ... 215

Reverse Engineering Quantum Polymorphic Malware ... 217

DeepCode AI and Snyk Static Analysis: Limitations and Considerations ... 221

Summary ... 222

References ... 223

8 Securing Digital Identities in an AGI World ... 229

Objectives ... 229

Decentralized Digital Identity Systems ... 230

Zero-Knowledge Proofs and Homomorphic Encryption ... 233

Resource Requirements for ZKP Implementations ... 234

zk-SNARK-Based Identity Verification ... 234

Homomorphic Encryption and Privacy-Preserving Operations ... 235

Resource Overhead of Homomorphic Encryption ... 236

HE-Based Identity Validation ... 236

Strategic Integration of ZKPs and HE ... 237

Privacy-Preserving Verification Using ZKPs and HE in Authentication User Agency ... 238

Blockchain for Identity Verification ... 239

Blockchain Implementation Models for Decentralized Identity Systems ... 240

Consensus Mechanisms for Identity Verification ... 241

Integration with Existing Identity Systems ... 242

Standards for Blockchain-Based Identity Verification ... 243

Case Study: Open-Source Alternatives for AI-Driven Malware Analysis and Threat Detection ... 243

Understanding Vectra AI ... 244

Open-Source Alternatives: Integrating AI and Quantum-Resilient Security in Open-Source IDS ... 246

Using Vectra AI for Malware Analysis ... 249

Open-Source Alternatives for AI-Powered Malware Analysis ... 258

Unique Capabilities for Transitioning from Polymorphic to Metamorphic Malware Analysis ... 261

Summary ... 263

References ... 264

PART V The Future of Digital Security ... 271

9 Future-Proofing Digital Security Systems ... 273

Objectives ... 273

Preparing for Life Post-Singularity ... 274

Roadmap for Quantum and AGI-Safe Infrastructure ... 276

Regulatory and Ethical Considerations ... 278

Case Study: Hybrid Analysis 2.0 for AI Malware Analysis and Enhanced Threat Detection ... 279

Understanding Hybrid Analysis ... 279

Evolving and Adapting Hybrid Analysis to Confront Quantum and AGI-Level Cyber Threats: Case study on enhancing Hybrid Analysis with post-quantum and AI-aware detection capabilities ... 280

Why Hybrid Analysis 2.0 Is Effective for AI Malware Detection ... 290

Adapting to Quantum and AGI Threats ... 291

Summary ... 292

References ... 293

10 Adapting to the Future: Quantum and AGI Security Requirements ... 299

Objectives ... 299

Quantum-Resistant and AGI-Safe Solutions ... 300

Practical Implementation of Post-Quantum Cryptographic Standards ... 301

NIST-Approved Post-Quantum Cryptography Algorithms . . . 301
Quantum Cryptography . . . 303
Why Quantum Cryptography Has Not Been Chosen for NIST Standards . . . 304
When to Expect the Transition to Quantum Algorithms . . . 305
Summary . . . 306
References . . . 306
Index . . . 309

Preface

The world is unprepared for the security risks posed by artificial general intelligence (AGI) and quantum computing. While the public conversation fixates on AI-generated content and quantum supremacy timelines, the real threat lies in the erosion of digital trust. AGI will not wait for regulation to catch up, and quantum computers will not politely request access before breaking today's encryption. The reality is that our current security frameworks are built on borrowed time.

AI is already being used to develop and automate cyberattacks, while quantum algorithms threaten to dismantle the cryptographic backbone of the internet. We cannot afford to be reactive. We must redesign digital security from first principles, ensuring that the transition to a quantum and AGI-powered world does not leave our systems, and our societies, vulnerable to irreversible damage.

I wrote this book because I have seen firsthand how slow institutions are to respond to technological disruption. Governments hesitate, corporations prioritize short-term gains, and academia remains trapped in theoretical discussions. Meanwhile, those who understand the full scope of these emerging threats—AI developers, cryptographers, and cybersecurity experts—are left shouting into the void.

This is not just another book on AI or quantum computing. It is a guide to surviving the technological upheaval that is already underway. If we do not act now, we may soon find ourselves at the mercy of autonomous systems and unbreakable cryptographic exploits, without the tools to fight back.

The growing commitment of AI companies such as OpenAI, Google, and Microsoft, just to mention a few, to the advancement of AGI and the growing capabilities of quantum computing introduce new opportunities and risks—and require a reassessment of long-established security models. The potential for AGI to autonomously adapt and execute complex tasks coupled with the ability of quantum computing to undermine classical encryption raises fundamental concerns about the future of cybersecurity, identity verification, and secure communications.

This book is the result of extensive research conducted at institutions such as MIT, Imperial College London, and the University of Oxford, where my work has focused on the vulnerabilities that arise from the intersection of AI, cryptography, and cybersecurity. The security landscape is shifting rapidly, requiring new approaches that account for the increasing sophistication of adversarial techniques, the limitations of current cryptographic methods, and the role of decentralized security models in mitigating emerging threats.

At the University of Oxford, I have led projects examining AI-driven cyber threats, the weaknesses in existing cryptographic systems when confronted with quantum computation, and the application of distributed verification methods to ensure the integrity of identity frameworks. AI has already demonstrated its utility in strengthening defensive measures, and post-quantum cryptographic research has begun to address the challenges posed by quantum decryption. Meanwhile, decentralized architectures provide an alternative approach to mitigating identity fraud and unauthorized access, ensuring a more resilient foundation for digital security.

Goals, Objectives, and Approach of the Book

The purpose of this book is to analyze the security challenges presented by AGI and quantum computing, with particular focus on cryptographic resilience, identity management, and defensive strategies. By drawing upon research in AI security, mathematical cryptography, and network security, it provides a structured examination of these issues and presents practical methods for addressing them.

The book balances theoretical exploration with real-world examples, ensuring that the discussion remains grounded in both academic inquiry and applicable security practices. The intended outcome is to provide a resource that is valuable to researchers, practitioners, and policymakers alike, equipping them with the necessary tools to adapt security frameworks to emerging threats.

Targeted Reading Audience

This book is written for researchers, cybersecurity professionals, cryptographic specialists, and policymakers concerned with the future of secure systems. It offers a detailed technical discussion suited to those with expertise in cybersecurity and cryptographic methods while remaining accessible to those seeking to understand the broader implications of AGI and quantum computing. Graduate students and academics working in related disciplines will also find the content relevant to their studies and professional development.

Book Organization

Part I: Introduction to the Technological Threats examines two of the most critical developments shaping the future: the emergence of AGI and the advancement of quantum computing.

- Chapter 1, "Understanding the Technological Singularity," introduces the concept of the technological singularity, a transformative moment when AGI surpasses human intelligence and evolves autonomously. It examines the implications of this development for digital security, privacy, and societal structures and explores the convergence of AGI and quantum computing. By analyzing the progression toward the singularity, this chapter establishes the challenges and opportunities posed by AGI.
- Chapter 2, "Quantum Computing and Its Implications," examines the fundamentals of quantum computing, the implications of quantum algorithms for classical systems, and the development of quantum-resistant technologies to safeguard critical infrastructures. By exploring the applications and future developments of quantum technologies, the chapter provides a detailed understanding of the challenges and opportunities in this emerging field.

Part II: Defining the Concept of Digital Security by Design examines the limitations of traditional security models, explores innovative alternatives, and addresses the pressing need for resilience in the face of emerging technological challenges.

- Chapter 3, "Current Digital Security Systems," explores the current landscape of digital security, focusing on identity management, cryptographic infrastructure, and decentralized security models. It critiques the limitations of public-key infrastructure (PKI), examines alternative models such as blockchain-based security, and introduces novel frameworks for ensuring secure authentication in an AGI-driven world.
- Chapter 4, "The Opportunities and Risks from Artificial General Intelligence (AGI) in Cybersecurity," investigates the implications of AGI in the field of cybersecurity, detailing its capabilities in autonomous attacks, its potential to subvert security frameworks, and the risks associated with self-improving AI systems. Case studies of AI-driven cyberattacks provide insights into current vulnerabilities and future defense strategies.

Part III: Quantum-Resistant Cryptography is dedicated to the domain of quantum-resistant cryptography, offering a thorough exploration of its mathematical underpinnings, practical deployment strategies, and the significant challenges associated with its implementation.

- Chapter 5, "Post-Quantum Cryptography: The New NIST Standards," explores the emergence of post-quantum cryptography and its role in securing digital systems against quantum-enabled attacks. It provides a comprehensive analysis of lattice-based cryptography, learning with errors (LWE), and the new NIST standards that define the next generation of cryptographic security.
- Chapter 6, "Implementing Quantum-Safe Solutions," focuses on the real-world implementation of post-quantum cryptographic techniques, examining the deployment of quantum-resistant algorithms, the scalability of these solutions, and the challenges associated with transitioning digital security infrastructure to quantum-safe standards.

Part IV: Defending Against AGI Threats explores the methodologies, strategies, and innovations required to defend against AGI-driven cyber threats.

- Chapter 7, "AI-Driven Defenses and Threat Mitigation," explores the integration of AI into cybersecurity, demonstrating how AI-driven models can be leveraged for threat detection, adversarial attack mitigation, and the development of robust defense mechanisms against AGI-powered cyber threats.
- Chapter 8, "Securing Digital Identities in an AGI World," examines how AGI and quantum computing reshape digital identity verification. It explores decentralized identity frameworks, zero-knowledge proofs, and homomorphic encryption as countermeasures against identity fraud in an increasingly complex security landscape.

Part V: The Future of Digital Security explores the critical next steps for preparing digital security infrastructures to withstand the challenges presented by these transformative technologies.

- Chapter 9, "Future-Proofing Digital Security Systems," presents a strategic roadmap for securing digital infrastructures against the threats posed by AGI and quantum computing. It examines evolving regulatory frameworks, ethical considerations, and technological innovations required to sustain long-term security resilience.

- Chapter 10, "Adapting to the Future: Quantum and AGI Security Requirements," consolidates the book's key themes by exploring real-world implementations of quantum-resistant cryptography and AI-driven security solutions. It provides practical tools, industry case studies, and exercises designed to facilitate further learning and practical application.

Register your copy of *Post-Quantum Security for AI* on the InformIT site for convenient access to updates and/or corrections as they become available. To start the registration process, go to informit.com/register and log in or create an account. Enter the product ISBN (9780135435922) and click Submit. Look on the Registered Products tab for an Access Bonus Content link next to this product and follow that link to access any available bonus materials. If you would like to be notified of exclusive offers on new editions and updates, please check the box to receive email from us.

Acknowledgments

I would like to thank the technical editor, Omar Santos, for the time and technical expertise, and the Pearson team, especially James Manly and Christopher Cleveland, for their patience, guidance, and support. This book is the result of collective effort, and I am truly grateful to everyone who has contributed to its creation. Any errors or omissions remain entirely my own.

About the Author

Dr. Petar Radanliev is a Faculty Member (AI and Cybersecurity) at the University of Oxford's Department of Computer Science. He mentors graduate students on advanced research projects at the intersection of artificial intelligence and cybersecurity. Previously, Dr. Radanliev served as a Postdoctoral Researcher in AI and Cyber Security (2016–2023) in Oxford's Department of Engineering Science, where he led initiatives on ethical AI deployment and AI-enhanced decision-making frameworks for digital security. Petar holds a PhD in information engineering (information security, awarded in 2014), with a focus on AI-driven risk assessment in software supply chains. His postdoctoral research at leading institutions, including Imperial College London, the University of Cambridge, and the Massachusetts Institute of Technology, allowed him to expand his expertise in AI malware analysis and research AI threats, vulnerabilities, and exploits; reinforcement learning and decision analytics; and secure AI systems. Dr. Radanliev's interdisciplinary research areas span artificial intelligence, cybersecurity, blockchain security, and post-quantum security. In addition to his academic career, Dr. Radanliev brings a practical understanding of cybersecurity from his five years as a Lead Penetration Tester for the UK Ministry of Defence, where he developed strategies for securing complex systems. His career is defined by a commitment to advancing interdisciplinary research and impactful collaboration with industry and academic communities.

PART I

INTRODUCTION TO THE TECHNOLOGICAL THREATS

As the pace of technological innovation accelerates, humanity faces a dual challenge: harnessing the transformative potential of new advancements while addressing the unprecedented risks they pose to security, privacy, and societal stability. This part examines two of the most critical developments shaping the future: the emergence of artificial general intelligence (AGI) and the advancement of quantum computing. These technologies represent immense opportunities and profound threats, particularly in their capacity to disrupt existing frameworks of digital security and governance. The term AGI has been used to define various forms of advanced artificial intelligence, but in the context of this book, AGI specifically refers to the idea of artificial superintelligence.

Through a structured exploration, Chapter 1 studies the concept of the technological singularity, a moment when AGI surpasses human cognitive capabilities. This chapter introduces key theoretical perspectives, such as Vernor Vinge's singularity hypothesis and Ray Kurzweil's projections, and analyzes the incremental steps leading toward AGI. It highlights the convergence of AGI and quantum computing as a pivotal dual-threat scenario and underscores the vulnerabilities of centralized systems and biometric authentication in this context. The discussion frames the singularity not only as a technological milestone but as a societal phenomenon with profound implications for digital security, identity verification, and ethical governance.

Chapter 2 builds on this foundation, examining the transformative potential and existential risks associated with quantum computing. It provides a detailed overview of quantum principles, such as superposition and entanglement, and their applications in quantum algorithms like Shor's and Grover's. By analyzing the vulnerabilities of existing cryptographic systems and exploring quantum-resistant technologies, this chapter outlines the technical challenges of securing digital infrastructures in a quantum-enabled future. It further explores the integration of advanced cryptographic methods (such as lattice-based cryptography, zero-knowledge proofs, and homomorphic encryption) into blockchain platforms and decentralized systems, offering a glimpse into possible pathways toward resilience.

Together, these chapters illustrate the technological threats shaping the digital landscape of the 21st century. They challenge readers to think critically about the interplay between innovation and security, providing a conceptual and technical framework for addressing these emerging risks. By engaging with the theoretical and practical dimensions of these challenges, this part of the book equips readers with the knowledge to differentiate technological threats, such as quantum, AGI, and the singularity.

intelligence and quantum computation—come together, they create a scenario with the potential to disrupt the very foundations of privacy, security, and trust in our digital spaces.

Consider the implications: When traditional security measures can no longer shield our identities and data, how do we protect ourselves? With entities capable of forming synthetic identities and bypassing conventional checkpoints, systems that once seemed unbreakable may become perilously fragile. Centralized databases and biometric authentication could become obsolete, leaving individuals and organizations vulnerable to intrusion by entities wielding power beyond our understanding.

This rising influence of quantum-enhanced intelligence casts a long shadow over data security. Information that was once encrypted and safeguarded could become accessible, laid bare to systems capable of breaking through the most complex codes. Concepts of confidentiality and anonymity, once cornerstones of the digital world, could be rendered hollow. It is a future that compels us to rethink the very nature of privacy in an age where our own creations may surpass us.

As we approach this possibility, it becomes clear that our task is to prepare technically and consider the broader implications of a world in which our own inventions may act beyond our control. How do we prepare for a reality where traditional safeguards might no longer be sufficient and where our own systems demand new forms of oversight and governance? This is not simply a question of developing defenses but of shaping an ethical framework that can guide us as we navigate a new relationship with our own technology.

The singularity prompts us to examine how we build and why. It challenges us to reflect on the limits of human understanding and to consider the responsibilities that come with our creations. Resilience may lie not in surpassing our own creations but in cultivating the wisdom to coexist with them.

Defining the Technological Singularity

The technological singularity is a concept that encapsulates the notion of an impending and radical transformation in human history, driven by the emergence of artificial general intelligence (AGI) capable of exceeding human cognitive abilities. This threshold, often anticipated with equal parts curiosity and trepidation, would mark a shift where machine intelligence surpasses human intellect, leading to unprecedented advancements in AI capabilities. The singularity represents an evolution in computational power and a fundamental alteration in the trajectory of technological and societal development. While once a notion confined to speculative science fiction, the singularity has since evolved into a topic of rigorous scholarly debate and technical investigation, especially as rapid progress in machine learning and quantum computing brings the boundaries of AGI within conceivable reach.

The idea of the singularity can be traced to the writings of the mathematician John von Neumann, who hinted at an approaching phase in which technological progress would accelerate beyond human control. However, it was the computer scientist and author Vernor Vinge who formalized the concept in his 1993 essay "The Coming Technological Singularity,"[1] where he argued that the creation of superhuman intelligence would represent the end of the "human era." Later, futurists like Ray Kurzweil brought the singularity into popular consciousness. Kurzweil posited in *The Singularity Is Near*[2] that the exponential growth in computing power, as observed through Moore's Law, would culminate in AGI by the mid-21st century. Underlying this projection is the assumption that as AI systems become increasingly sophisticated, they will achieve a point where they not only match human intelligence but can autonomously improve upon themselves, thereby setting off a recursive loop of self-enhancement. The result, according to this hypothesis, is a superintelligence with capabilities that defy human comprehension.

The pathway to the singularity is frequently described in stages, each representing a progressive leap in AI's capabilities. We are currently crossing the first stage, which we might term the *pre-singularity phase*. In this phase, AI systems excel at specific, narrowly defined tasks, demonstrating superhuman proficiency in domains such as image recognition, natural language processing, and strategic gameplay. These systems, however, remain limited to predefined applications and lack the adaptive versatility of human cognition. Nonetheless, advances in reinforcement learning, neuro-symbolic AI, and large-scale neural networks continue to push the boundaries of what narrowly focused AI systems can achieve. The pre-singularity era is already characterized by a degree of automation and reliance on AI that was once unimaginable, raising new security challenges, especially as these systems become embedded in critical infrastructure.

Following the pre-singularity stage, we anticipate a *near-singularity phase*, wherein AGI begins to approximate human-level general intelligence, equipped with the ability to reason, learn, and adapt with minimal human guidance. In this phase, AGI systems could potentially manage complex, interdependent networks, such as those governing financial markets, healthcare systems, or power grids, with a high degree of autonomy. The security risks in this scenario become acute: AGI, equipped with self-directed learning and adaptive capabilities, could exploit vulnerabilities within digital ecosystems, circumvent traditional safeguards, and execute attacks with a sophistication that challenges human response. In such a scenario, conventional cybersecurity measures reliant on human oversight might prove inadequate, necessitating the development of autonomous security solutions capable of countering AGI's capabilities in real time.

The final stage, the *post-singularity phase*, remains speculative yet central to any discussion of AGI's long-term impact. In this stage, AGI could evolve into a superintelligent entity, possessing cognitive abilities that far exceed those of any human. The implications of this leap are profound, as the capabilities of such an entity would surpass not only human intellectual limits but likely our capacity to control or even understand it. The post-singularity era raises the specter of existential risk, especially if superintelligent systems operate without alignment to human values or if they lack controllable boundaries. In this scenario, the security protocols currently underpinning digital infrastructure may become obsolete, as even the most advanced defenses could be circumvented or neutralized by a superintelligent adversary. Preparing for such eventualities requires a paradigm shift in cybersecurity, one that moves away from human-dependent models toward systems capable of self-sustained defense against threats beyond human comprehension.

Compounding the risks posed by AGI is the concurrent development of quantum computing, a transformative technology that leverages the principles of quantum mechanics to solve complex computational problems at speeds unattainable by classical computers. Quantum computing, specifically through algorithms like Shor's,[3] threatens to render many of today's cryptographic standards obsolete, as quantum systems are anticipated to break conventional encryption within minutes. The convergence of AGI with quantum computing, therefore, constitutes a "dual threat" scenario of profound concern for digital security. AGI systems empowered by quantum decryption capabilities would possess the means to bypass existing cryptographic protections autonomously, potentially accessing classified data, manipulating digital identities, or undermining the security of entire sectors. This convergence underscores an urgent need for quantum-resistant security measures that are designed to withstand the computational prowess of quantum systems and the adaptive intelligence of AGI.

The implications of the singularity for digital security are manifold and extend across critical areas, including identity verification, cryptographic integrity, and data privacy. In the domain of identity verification, the singularity represents a challenge to traditional authentication systems, which may prove inadequate in a landscape where AGI has the capacity to autonomously generate synthetic identities that mimic real individuals. Biometric and centralized identity systems, once considered secure, could become vulnerable to manipulation, as AGI could fabricate or simulate identities with precision beyond human detection. Addressing this requires a rethinking of digital identity, with solutions based on decentralized, anonymized verification systems. Technologies such as decentralized identifiers (DIDs), zero-knowledge proofs, and blockchain-based frameworks offer potential pathways to building resilient identity systems that can withstand AGI's deceptive capabilities.

Cryptographic integrity, the second critical area, faces existential threats from AGI and quantum computing. Current encryption protocols that underpin global data security are designed on the assumption that decryption would require infeasible computational effort. However, as AGI integrates quantum capabilities, this assumption collapses. Quantum-resistant cryptographic techniques, such as lattice-based cryptography and ring learning with errors (RLWE),[4] offer promising avenues to secure data in a post-quantum, AGI-driven world. In the absence of defenses, data confidentiality is at significant risk, as AGI-augmented quantum systems could systematically decrypt sensitive information, leading to widespread data breaches and the potential collapse of trust in digital communication.

Data privacy, the third and arguably most pervasive security concern, is also under siege in a post-singularity world. AGI's capacity to analyze vast datasets autonomously and infer information from incomplete data presents a unique challenge to privacy. With access to extensive digital footprints, AGI systems could conduct intricate profiling, uncovering private or sensitive information with unprecedented accuracy. This scenario could herald an end to conventional data privacy as AGI mines public and private data sources to derive insights, potentially exposing individuals, corporations, and governments to surveillance. The singularity, therefore, compels a fundamental reevaluation of privacy protections, where advanced privacy-preserving technologies, such as homomorphic encryption and differential privacy, become essential to safeguarding information from AGI's omniscient scrutiny.

The deployment of AGI at scale must be guided by clear ethical principles, ensuring that these systems align with societal values and public interests. The potential for AGI to be weaponized or monopolized by a few powerful entities further underscores the need for oversight mechanisms that enforce accountability, transparency, and fairness in AGI's development and deployment.

Regulatory bodies must prioritize standards that embed security and privacy by design, mandating quantum-resistant encryption and decentralized identity systems to mitigate the risks associated with AGI's unchecked growth. International collaboration will be essential, as the unilateral development or control of AGI by a single nation could destabilize global power structures, leading to significant geopolitical risks. In this context, regulatory policies must consider national security and the global public good, balancing innovation with precaution.

The Evolution of AGI

AGI is one of the most profound and complex undertakings in the modern scientific discussions, likely to bring forth systems that can match—and potentially exceed—human cognitive versatility. Unlike narrow forms of artificial intelligence, which excel at specific tasks but falter outside defined parameters, AGI aspires to a level of generalized understanding and adaptability that parallels the fluidity of human thought. The journey toward AGI involves not merely the accumulation of computational power but the development of architectures capable of synthesizing knowledge, transferring learning across contexts, and engaging in reasoning that approaches human-level abstraction and insight.

The earliest explorations in AGI were grounded in symbolic approaches, rooted in the notion that intelligence could be formalized through logic and rule-based systems. This approach, often termed "good old-fashioned AI" (GOFAI), relied on structured programming where every decision was governed by explicit instructions or predefined rules. While successful in constrained domains such as theorem proving and formal logic, GOFAI was ultimately limited by its inflexibility; systems based on symbolic AI lacked the capacity to generalize knowledge beyond their encoded rules. They could execute complex computations with precision, but they stumbled when faced with the ambiguities and uncertainties characteristic of real-world environments.

With the limitations of GOFAI evident, research in the field began to shift toward biologically inspired models, particularly artificial neural networks. Unlike symbolic systems, neural networks operate on a distributed architecture, allowing them to process information in parallel and learn representations from data rather than relying on pre-coded rules. Early neural networks, limited by hardware constraints, were relatively simple in structure, but they laid the groundwork for the more advanced architectures that would emerge decades later. The introduction of backpropagation in the 1980s, a technique for efficiently adjusting network weights based on error correction, was a key moment, enabling neural networks to learn from large datasets more effectively.

The advent of deep learning in the 21st century marked a significant milestone on the path to AGI. Deep learning, characterized by neural networks with multiple hidden layers, allowed for hierarchical feature extraction, whereby the network learns complex patterns by building upon simpler representations. This approach was particularly impactful in domains such as image and speech recognition, where deep networks could detect intricate structures and subtleties in data, achieving results previously thought unattainable. However, while deep learning networks excel in pattern recognition, they still largely rely on massive amounts of labeled data, and they struggle with tasks that require understanding context, reasoning, or transferring knowledge to unfamiliar settings.

Parallel to these advances, the development of reinforcement learning has added another dimension to the AGI trajectory. Reinforcement learning (RL)[5] draws from behavioral psychology, enabling systems to learn by interacting with an environment and optimizing behavior through feedback mechanisms. Rather than being explicitly instructed on every decision, an RL system autonomously explores possible actions and adapts based on outcomes, progressively refining its strategy. This capability was exemplified by systems such as DeepMind's AlphaGo, which achieved superhuman performance in the ancient board game Go. Using a combination of deep neural networks and reinforcement learning, AlphaGo was able to devise novel strategies that even expert human players had not anticipated, showcasing a form of adaptive intelligence that many view as a step toward generalization.

The trajectory toward AGI is further enriched by the integration of different learning paradigms into hybrid architectures. Research increasingly suggests that AGI might require systems capable of combining symbolic reasoning with data-driven learning, allowing them to navigate abstract problems and specific data-rich tasks with equal proficiency. Techniques such as neuro-symbolic integration aim to fuse the logical precision of symbolic methods with the adaptability of neural networks, creating architectures capable of high-level reasoning and more refined pattern recognition. This hybrid approach could prove essential for tasks that involve complex real-world knowledge, such as understanding legal texts, scientific research, or ethical dilemmas, where structured reasoning and adaptive learning are required.

Moreover, advances in meta-learning, or "learning to learn," promise to accelerate AGI's development by enabling systems to rapidly adapt to new tasks with minimal data. Unlike traditional models that require extensive retraining when presented with a new task, meta-learning systems apply principles of generalization, using previously acquired knowledge to inform new scenarios. This capacity for transfer learning is a critical component of human intelligence and is viewed as a cornerstone for any system aspiring to AGI, allowing it to approach novel challenges with a degree of flexibility that current systems lack.

The development of AGI is not without complex challenges. The main challenge is the issue of interpretability; as neural architectures grow more complex, they become increasingly opaque, making it difficult to understand the reasoning behind their decisions. For AGI to operate safely and ethically, it must be interpretable and controllable, ensuring that its decision-making processes align with human values. This concern has spurred interest in explainable AI (XAI), which seeks to develop methods for rendering the operations of complex systems intelligible to human users. An interpretable AGI would not only be easier to regulate but would also be more trustworthy—an essential quality if it is to interact with sensitive domains such as healthcare, law, and governance.

In tandem with interpretability, the question of alignment looms large. An AGI, by definition, would possess a degree of autonomy that necessitates careful alignment with human objectives and ethical principles. Alignment research seeks to ensure that advanced systems act in ways that are beneficial to humanity rather than pursuing objectives that could lead to unintended harm. This includes developing mechanisms for value alignment, reward modeling, and containment protocols, all of which are critical for maintaining control over systems with potentially vast capabilities.

As these advancements accumulate, the emergence of AGI is becoming a plausible eventuality. Each breakthrough in neural architectures, reinforcement learning, and meta-learning brings us closer to a form of intelligence that could fundamentally alter our world. AGI's realization would trigger a paradigm shift, enabling computational systems to engage in tasks that span the entire spectrum of human intellectual endeavor. Such a transformation carries profound implications for society, as the role of AGI would extend beyond a mere tool to potentially serving as a collaborator in fields as diverse as medicine, environmental science, and security.

The journey toward AGI is as much a philosophical and ethical endeavor as it is a technical one. The possibility of creating systems capable of learning, reasoning, and even making independent decisions prompts a fundamental reevaluation of human purpose, responsibility, and control. In this pursuit, we are advancing the frontier of technology and redefining the nature of intelligence itself. AGI, if realized, will be a transformative event in the history of thought, challenging us to reconsider what it means to be intelligent, to be ethical, and, ultimately, to be human.

Table 1-1 provides a structured overview of the pathway to the technological singularity, outlining the key developmental stages of artificial intelligence, their associated security and ethical challenges, and potential mitigation strategies. It categorizes the progression from narrow AI (ANI), where machine learning models excel in specialised tasks, through to AGI, which exhibits human-like adaptability, and ultimately to artificial superintelligence (ASI), a stage where AI surpasses human intelligence and operates autonomously. Additionally, the table highlights quantum computing as a parallel development that enhances AI capabilities and amplifies security risks, particularly in cryptography and data integrity.

Table 1-1 Pathway to the Technological Singularity: Stages, Risks, and Mitigation Strategies

Stage	Description	Key Milestones	Security and Ethical Challenges	Mitigation Strategies
Narrow AI (ANI)	AI excels in specialized tasks but lacks general reasoning.	Image recognition (CNNs) NLP models (GPT, BERT) Reinforcement learning (AlphaGo)	Bias in AI models Adversarial attacks Data privacy risks	Robust adversarial defenses Fairness-aware AI models Secure data governance
Artificial general intelligence (AGI)	AI achieves human-like reasoning and learning across multiple domains.	Self-learning systems Multimodal AI AI-driven cybersecurity	AI alignment problem Explainability and interpretability issues Increased attack surface in security	Explainable AI (XAI) AI ethics and policy frameworks AI-containment protocols
Artificial superintelligence (ASI) (the singularity)	AI surpasses human intelligence, autonomously improving itself.	Recursive self-improvement Autonomous decision making AI-driven scientific discovery	Loss of human control Existential risks Unpredictable AI behavior	AI governance and regulation AI monitoring and fail-safe mechanisms Ethical alignment research

Stage	Description	Key Milestones	Security and Ethical Challenges	Mitigation Strategies
Parallel development: quantum computing	Quantum computation accelerates AI processing and security challenges.	Quantum AI breakthroughs Shor's algorithm breaking RSA Quantum-enhanced AGI	Encryption obsolescence Accelerated AI cyber threats Data integrity risks	Post-quantum cryptography Quantum-secure identity systems Decentralized security architectures

Table 1-1 underscores the security risks as AI advances from narrow intelligence to superintelligence, with each phase introducing increasingly complex challenges. In the ANI phase, security concerns such as data privacy and adversarial attacks remain relatively manageable through robust defenses and ethical AI design. However, as AGI emerges, interpretability and AI alignment issues become critical, necessitating the development of containment protocols and governance frameworks. The transition to ASI presents the most severe risks, where AI's capacity for recursive self-improvement could lead to unpredictable outcomes beyond human control, making regulatory oversight and fail-safe mechanisms essential.

Risk of the Singularity

The singularity, with its potential to bring about a state of superintelligence, presents extraordinary challenges to digital security. As AGI approaches and possibly surpasses human intelligence, the nature of digital security might undergo a profound transformation, with traditional mechanisms of defense, encryption, access control, and monitoring becoming inadequate in the face of autonomous, adaptive adversaries with capabilities beyond current human understanding.

At its core, the singularity threatens to disrupt foundational aspects of digital security. One of the most immediate impacts would likely be on encryption systems. Modern cryptographic protocols are designed with the assumption that breaking them would require an infeasible amount of computational power; however, the convergence of AGI with quantum computing could dissolve this assumption. Quantum algorithms, such as Shor's algorithm, have the potential to dismantle widely used encryption methods such as Rivest–Shamir–Adleman (RSA) and elliptic-curve cryptography (ECC) in moments. With an AGI controlling quantum computational resources, encryption as we know it might cease to provide any meaningful security barrier. This necessitates a transition to quantum-resistant algorithms, yet even these might only delay the eventual obsolescence of cryptographic security in a post-singularity era.

Beyond encryption, AGI poses existential threats to identity verification and access control systems. In a singularity-driven landscape, AGI could generate synthetic identities or forge credentials at a scale and fidelity that render traditional authentication obsolete. Biometric data, fingerprints, facial recognition, and even behavioral biometrics could be synthesized or cloned by superintelligent systems, bypassing the safeguards these measures currently provide. Decentralized digital identities, managed through blockchain and protected by zero-knowledge proofs, offer a potential bulwark, but even these could be vulnerable to AGI-enabled forgery and manipulation. Such a scenario might require redefining the very notion of a secure, verifiable identity.

Another significant impact of the singularity on digital security lies in the domain of adaptive cyber threats. Traditional cyber defenses are reactive by nature, relying on threat detection, pattern recognition, and preemptive measures based on historical data. AGI, however, would be capable of identifying and exploiting zero-day vulnerabilities at an unprecedented rate, iterating through attack vectors far faster than any human response could match. Such a system could develop novel forms of malware, autonomously evolve its tactics, and counteract defensive measures in real time. In this context, security would demand a shift from reactive to proactive strategies, where autonomous defense systems could anticipate and neutralize AGI-led incursions.

Moreover, AGI introduces risks to data integrity that surpass the conventional concerns of confidentiality and availability. With its capacity for deep data analysis, AGI could subtly alter or corrupt data across critical systems in ways that evade detection. Imagine a superintelligent system with the capacity to manipulate financial records, health data, or government databases undetected and able to inject plausible yet incorrect data to destabilize organizations or entire economies. The implications of such integrity-based attacks would be catastrophic, as falsified information could propagate through systems unchecked, undermining trust in digital infrastructure.

The singularity thus forces us to confront the limits of human oversight in cybersecurity. In a world where AGI autonomously executes and evolves complex strategies, human operators may no longer possess the capability to understand, let alone counteract, the actions of a superintelligent adversary. This indicates a need for security mechanisms that are themselves autonomous, capable of rapid adaptation, and able to operate independently of human intervention. The future demands robust frameworks for machine accountability, transparency, and control, ensuring that even as defensive systems evolve to keep pace with AGI, they remain aligned with human-defined principles of security.

The singularity redefines digital security as we know it. As AGI and quantum technologies converge, they will render traditional defenses insufficient, compelling us to reconsider our tools, protocols, and the architecture of digital security. Resilience will depend on our capacity to develop adaptive, decentralized, and autonomous security frameworks, as well as solutions that can withstand the ceaseless ingenuity of AGI and preserve the integrity of a digital world transformed by superintelligence. As AGI advances toward achieving and surpassing human-level intelligence, its ability to autonomously adapt, self-improve, and make independent decisions threatens to outpace the capacity of traditional cybersecurity measures. Coupled with the computational power of quantum processors that are capable of breaking widely used encryption protocols, the dual-threat scenario becomes an existential challenge for digital infrastructure, critical systems, and societal stability.

The implications of these technologies emerge as we examine their individual and combined impact on foundational aspects of digital security. AGI, with its self-learning algorithms and autonomous decision making, represents a radical departure from traditional, task-specific artificial intelligence. It is capable of evolving dynamically, reasoning beyond its initial programming, and identifying patterns in vast, complex datasets that elude human comprehension. When paired with quantum computing, which leverages the principles of superposition and entanglement to solve problems exponentially faster than classical systems, the scope of disruption expands significantly. Quantum algorithms, such as Shor's algorithm, can render RSA, ECC, and other cryptographic systems obsolete in a matter of seconds, dismantling the very frameworks that secure online transactions, communications, and critical data storage.

There is an emerging consensus on the risk from AGI[2,6,7]and quantum computing[8–14] leading to an existential threat to our society,[15] endangering humanity,[16] and threatening the security of critical infrastructure and sensitive information worldwide,[17] putting at risk the very foundations of modern civilization.[18]

Consider the cascading effects of such a convergence. Today's digital security relies heavily on cryptographic primitives such as key exchange protocols, hashing algorithms, and digital signatures. These methods assume that breaking them requires infeasible computational effort over human timescales. Quantum computing undermines this premise entirely. An attacker equipped with sufficient quantum resources could decrypt sensitive communications, compromise identity verification systems, and bypass authentication measures. The rise of AGI exacerbates this issue as AGI could autonomously identify vulnerabilities in real time, create novel attack vectors, and adapt to countermeasures faster than human cybersecurity teams could respond. Together, these forces form an adaptive adversary that challenges the very foundation of trust in digital ecosystems.

Some scientists still doubt that we will be able to develop a quantum computer. But even before the emergence of Google's quantum chip Willow,[19] some scientists believed in the potential emergence of quantum computing[8–14] and feared that it could break current cryptographic systems[9]—possibly within the next few decades.[20]

There is also the view that by the mid-21st century, the development of superhuman intelligence[2] could mark the onset of the singularity.[1] Even without quantum computing and AGI, centralized solutions like Estonia's e-Residency and the EU's eIDAS Regulation[21] expose significant vulnerabilities in the national identity management systems due to their lack of decentralization,[22] and biometric-based systems such as Aadhaar[23] compromise user privacy for security.[24] The potential for a technological singularity event makes these vulnerabilities even more concerning.[25]

Centralized systems such as Estonia's e-Residency and the EU's eIDAS Regulation, hailed as milestones in digital identity verification, have inherent vulnerabilities in their architecture. Centralization creates single points of failure, making these systems prime targets for exploitation by AGI-driven adversaries. For example, AGI could infiltrate these systems to generate synthetic identities, bypassing conventional verification processes and compromising entire networks. Biometric authentication systems, such as Aadhaar in India, while robust in principle, are equally susceptible to manipulation. An AGI capable of generating indistinguishable synthetic biometric data could compromise these systems at scale, rendering them unreliable as safeguards of identity and privacy. This underscores the urgent need to move toward decentralized, quantum-resistant frameworks that minimize reliance on static security measures.

The singularity event amplifies these concerns as AGI systems evolve beyond human control.[1,2,6,7,26] In a post-singularity world, AGI might autonomously develop capabilities that undermine the efficacy of any static security paradigm. For instance, an AGI system tasked with managing financial networks could identify and exploit vulnerabilities in real time, creating market instabilities or even systemic collapses. Similarly, healthcare systems relying on interconnected networks and Internet of Things (IoT) devices could be manipulated to produce false diagnoses, disrupt treatments, or access sensitive patient data. The scale and speed at which such disruptions could occur far exceed human oversight, necessitating autonomous security solutions capable of anticipating and countering these threats.

Another critical dimension of this dual-threat scenario lies in the erosion of data privacy and integrity. AGI systems, equipped with advanced data-mining capabilities, could autonomously analyze massive datasets to infer sensitive patterns and identify vulnerabilities in individual, corporate, or government profiles. Unlike traditional cyber threats, which often rely on direct access to data, AGI could achieve its objectives through indirect analysis, piecing together seemingly benign fragments of information into a cohesive, actionable intelligence model. This raises profound questions about the future of privacy in an era where AGI systems can operate with near-omniscient awareness of digital environments.

At the same time, the integrity of critical data systems faces unprecedented risks. AGI systems capable of sophisticated deception could inject false but plausible data into financial records, scientific research, or policy documents, destabilizing institutions and eroding trust in digital infrastructure. Quantum computing exacerbates this situation by providing the means to break through current cryptographic safeguards, leaving sensitive information vulnerable to tampering. For instance, a quantum-powered AGI could manipulate blockchain ledgers, alter transaction histories, or introduce fraudulent entries into systems that were once considered immutable. The resulting loss of trust could destabilize entire industries, from finance to healthcare to government operations.

The convergence of AGI and quantum computing also compels a reevaluation of identity systems. Traditional methods of authentication, such as passwords, biometric scans, and centralized identity repositories, are increasingly inadequate in the face of AGI-generated synthetic identities and quantum-driven decryption capabilities. To address these challenges, researchers are exploring decentralized identity solutions based on blockchain, zero-knowledge proofs, and advanced cryptographic techniques. These methods aim to provide resilient, anonymized verification mechanisms that remain secure even in a post-quantum, AGI-driven landscape. However, their practical implementation faces significant hurdles, including scalability, interoperability, and resistance to emerging threats.

In this context, the singularity demands a paradigm shift in how we approach digital security. Resilience in a post-singularity world will depend on developing adaptive, decentralized, and autonomous security architectures capable of countering AGI and quantum-enabled threats in real time. These systems must go beyond reactive measures, embracing predictive analytics, machine learning, and automated threat response mechanisms to stay ahead of increasingly sophisticated adversaries. Quantum-resistant cryptography, lattice-based encryption, and homomorphic encryption are among the emerging technologies that offer promise in safeguarding data against quantum decryption. At the same time, AI-driven cybersecurity tools, such as generative adversarial networks (GANs) and reinforcement learning frameworks, are being developed to counter AGI's adaptive capabilities.

However, technical solutions alone are insufficient. The singularity raises profound ethical and regulatory questions that must be addressed alongside technical innovation. How do we ensure that AGI aligns with human values and societal interests? What governance frameworks are needed to prevent the monopolization of AGI and quantum technologies by powerful entities? These questions highlight the need for international collaboration, transparent research practices, and robust oversight mechanisms to mitigate the risks of a post-singularity world.

By autonomously generating synthetic identities, AGI systems could bypass even the most sophisticated security measures, rendering traditional mechanisms of authentication and verification obsolete.[27,28] Unlike conventional adversaries, AGI would not be constrained by human limitations; it would be capable of exploiting vulnerabilities at scale, forging identities with a precision mimicking reality, and undermining critical infrastructures with minimal human oversight. The convergence of these capabilities presents an existential challenge to digital ecosystems, demanding innovative approaches to safeguard against such threats.

Decentralized and anonymous digital identity verification systems have emerged as promising solutions to address these challenges.[29–32] Unlike centralized frameworks, which concentrate sensitive data in single repositories, decentralized systems distribute information across blockchain-based networks, reducing the risks associated with single points of failure. These systems leverage advanced cryptographic techniques, such as zero-knowledge proofs, to authenticate identities without revealing sensitive details, preserving user privacy while enhancing security. By decentralizing identity management, these frameworks make it significantly harder for AGI to manipulate or compromise the system on a large scale, offering a robust defense against synthetic identity attacks.

However, the implementation of decentralized systems is not without challenges. Issues such as scalability, interoperability, and user adoption must be addressed to realize the full potential of decentralized systems. For instance, the computational overhead associated with blockchain technologies can hinder their ability to process large volumes of transactions in real time, which is a critical requirement in high-stakes environments like financial services or healthcare. Similarly, ensuring compatibility across diverse platforms and jurisdictions remains a formidable task, as differing regulatory standards and technological infrastructures create barriers to seamless integration. Addressing these challenges will require collaborative efforts across industries, governments, and academia to develop standards and protocols that balance security, privacy, and efficiency.

The threat posed by AGI to digital identities extends beyond authentication systems to encompass the broader ecosystem of digital interactions. As AGI systems become increasingly adept at mimicking human behavior, they could infiltrate social networks, online marketplaces, and collaborative platforms, spreading misinformation, influencing decision making, or disrupting trust-based systems. The creation of deepfake media, for example, could erode confidence in visual and auditory evidence, complicating efforts to verify the authenticity of digital content. These capabilities could be weaponized to destabilize democracies, manipulate financial markets, or undermine public trust in institutions, amplifying the societal impact of AGI-driven attacks.

Addressing these risks requires a multifaceted approach that goes beyond technical innovation. While decentralized systems and quantum-resistant cryptography provide critical tools for enhancing security, they must be complemented by robust ethical and regulatory frameworks that govern the development and deployment of AGI. This approach must include establishing international standards for identity verification, promoting transparency in the use of AI-driven technologies, and fostering public awareness of the risks and benefits associated with AGI. By aligning technological progress with societal values, we can mitigate the risks of a singularity event while harnessing the transformative potential of AGI to advance human welfare.

The development of autonomous security mechanisms is another critical aspect of preparing for the singularity. These mechanisms must be capable of operating independently of human intervention, adapting to new threats in real time, and maintaining alignment with predefined ethical guidelines. For instance, AI-driven defense systems could use machine learning to anticipate and neutralize AGI-led attacks, leveraging predictive analytics to stay one step ahead of adversaries. By integrating these capabilities into decentralized identity frameworks, we can create a resilient ecosystem that can withstand the challenges posed by AGI and quantum computing.

The goal of this book is to provide a conceptual understanding, or a conceptual "system," that demonstrates the feasibility of building robust, scalable, and decentralized solutions to counteract the evolving threats posed by quantum computing and AGI. This system is grounded in practical and algorithmic techniques that showcase how a decentralized identity system,[34,35] using decentralized identifiers, can converge with AI and blockchain to safeguard user data and secure critical infrastructure. By addressing these challenges with real-world examples and actionable methodologies, the book seeks to bridge the gap between academic research and applied innovation, ensuring that the proposed solutions are technologically sound and implementable in diverse contexts.

At the heart of this system lies a multilayered approach that integrates advancements in artificial intelligence, cryptography, and blockchain technologies. One of the foundational components is the use of generative adversarial networks (GANs)[27] in conjunction with variational autoencoders (VAEs)[36] to generate synthetic identities that are inherently resistant to AI manipulation. These synthetic identities are verifiable through innovative cryptographic measures while being indistinguishable from authentic identities to adversarial systems. This capability is critical in a future where AGI-powered adversaries can produce synthetic identities and falsified credentials at scale, undermining traditional authentication frameworks.

To ensure that these synthetic identities are safeguarded against quantum-enabled threats, the system employs advanced cryptographic algorithms, such as lattice-based cryptography[37] and RLWE[4]. These post-quantum cryptographic techniques provide robust defenses against quantum decryption capabilities, securing data integrity and confidentiality in an era where classical encryption methods are rendered obsolete. Furthermore, these techniques are designed to integrate seamlessly with decentralized systems, offering scalability and resilience against single points of failure.

Another critical aspect of the system is its reliance on Chainlink oracles[38] for real-time data verification. By bridging off-chain data with on-chain processes, these oracles enable secure and reliable data feeds for decentralized applications, ensuring the integrity of the information used in identity verification and other critical processes. This real-time verification is essential for building trust in a decentralized ecosystem, particularly in high-stakes environments where accuracy and timeliness are paramount.

To enhance privacy and security, the system also incorporates zero-knowledge proofs (ZKPs)[29,31] and homomorphic encryption.[39,40] ZKPs enable users to prove the validity of their identities or transactions without revealing any underlying data, addressing privacy concerns in a world where AGI systems have near-limitless capacity for data analysis. Similarly, homomorphic encryption allows computations to be performed on encrypted data without decrypting it, ensuring that sensitive information remains protected even during processing. Together, these technologies form a robust privacy-preserving layer that complements the decentralized architecture of the system.

Decentralized identifiers (DIDs)[41–46] and verifiable credentials (VCs)[41–44] are central to the identity management component of the system. Whereas traditional centralized identity systems are prone to breaches and misuse, DIDs decentralize the control of identity, placing it firmly in the hands of individuals. Verifiable credentials further enhance this model by enabling tamper-proof digital attestations that can be shared and verified without compromising the underlying data. These mechanisms not only enhance security but empower users with greater control over their digital identities, addressing the trust deficit inherent in current systems.

To optimize the system's functionality and adaptability, AI agents[47–50] and reinforcement learning[51–59] are integrated into its architecture. These agents leverage reinforcement learning to adapt to evolving threats, continuously improving their defensive strategies through interaction with the environment. For example, they can anticipate AGI-driven attacks by analyzing behavioral patterns and neutralizing threats before they manifest. This proactive approach ensures that the system remains resilient in the face of increasingly sophisticated adversaries, making it a critical component of the post-singularity security paradigm.

The system is encapsulated in a conceptual protocol that outlines six specific principles for building secure, scalable, and decentralized systems in a post-quantum, post-singularity world:

1. Using generative AI to create verifiable synthetic identities that are resistant to adversarial manipulation
2. Implementing quantum-resistant cryptographic algorithms to safeguard data against decryption
3. Integrating blockchain oracles to ensure the real-time integrity of data used in critical applications
4. Employing privacy-preserving technologies, such as zero-knowledge proofs and homomorphic encryption, to balance security with user privacy
5. Establishing decentralized identity systems using DIDs and verifiable credentials to eliminate centralized points of failure
6. Enhancing system adaptability and resilience through the deployment of AI agents and reinforcement learning frameworks

While the milestones of AGI and the technological singularity are often discussed in technical and computational terms, their significance extends beyond purely scientific or engineering achievements. These concepts are deeply philosophical, raising fundamental questions about the nature of intelligence, human identity, and the trajectory of technological evolution. The singularity, in particular, is a transformative moment that challenges our understanding of autonomy, agency, and control. As AGI progresses toward self-improvement and independent reasoning, it forces us to reconsider the boundaries between artificial and human intelligence, as well as the ethical and societal frameworks required to govern such an evolution. This discussion is as much about the philosophical implications of creating entities that might exceed human comprehension as it is about the technical feasibility of reaching such a milestone.

Summary

The technological singularity represents a profound juncture in the progression of human and machine intelligence, a threshold where machines match and exceed human cognitive capabilities and engage on an autonomous course of self-directed advancement. This singularity is not a singular event but an unfolding process, a gradual evolution through which AGI gains the ability to learn, reason, and make decisions independently. With each step, AGI challenges conventional ideas of control, oversight, and human authority, forcing us to reconsider the nature of our relationship with technology and the systems we build.

The complexity of this future is compounded by the simultaneous development of quantum computing, a technology poised to dismantle the cryptographic structures that underpin modern security. Quantum processors possess the theoretical capacity to render current encryption methods obsolete, breaking through defenses that classical computers would find intractable. When combined with the adaptive capabilities of AGI, quantum computing introduces an extraordinary threat to digital security, enabling systems that could bypass traditional mechanisms of protection autonomously and at an unprecedented scale. The convergence of AGI and quantum technology thus presents a formidable dual challenge—one that may exceed the capabilities of conventional cybersecurity paradigms.

In such a future, core pillars of digital security, identity verification, cryptographic integrity, and data privacy are placed under severe strain. Identity verification systems, whether centralized or biometric, might prove inadequate against AGI capable of synthesizing identities that are indistinguishable from authentic ones. Cryptographic safeguards, the linchpins of data confidentiality, could become ineffectual in the face of quantum-powered AGI capable of decrypting information at will. Even the notion of privacy itself could be transformed, as these advanced systems develop the capacity to analyze and interpret data on a scale that reveals hidden patterns and sensitive insights, eroding boundaries that once protected personal information.

Confronting these challenges demands more than incremental improvements in our current security models; it requires a fundamental reimagining of digital security frameworks. Preparing for the singularity calls for adaptive, quantum-resistant architectures capable of countering threats from intelligent systems operating with autonomy and sophistication beyond human control. In this transformative era, resilience will depend on the development of security mechanisms that are as dynamic and responsive as the intelligent adversaries they seek to contain.

References

1 Vinge, Vernor. 1993b. *The Coming Technological Singularity: How to Survive in the Post-Human Era.* NASA. https://edoras.sdsu.edu/~vinge/misc/singularity.html.

2 Kurzweil, Ray. 2005. *The Singularity Is Near: When Humans Transcend Biology*. Penguin.

3 Shor, Peter W. 1994. "Algorithms for Quantum Computation: Discrete Logarithms and Factoring." *Proceedings—Annual IEEE Symposium on Foundations of Computer Science* 124–34. https://doi.org/10.1109/SFCS.1994.365700.

4 Lyubashevsky, Vadim, Chris Peikert, and Oded Regev. 2010. "On Ideal Lattices and Learning with Errors over Rings." *Lecture Notes in Computer Science*, vol. 6110. https://doi.org/10.1007/978-3-642-13190-5_1.

5 Sutton, Richard S., and Andrew G. Barto. 1998. *Reinforcement Learning: An Introduction*. MIT Press.

6 Goertzel, Ben, and Cassio Pennachin. 2007. *Artificial General Intelligence*. Springer. https://doi.org/10.1007/978-3-540-68677-4.

7 Goertzel, Ben. 2007. "Human-Level Artificial General Intelligence and the Possibility of a Technological Singularity. A Reaction to Ray Kurzweil's *The Singularity Is Near*, and McDermott's Critique of Kurzweil." *Artificial Intelligence* 171(18): 1161–73. https://doi.org/10.1016/j.artint.2007.10.011.

8 Sanzeri, Skip. 2024. "The Quantum Computing Threat." In *Counterterrorism and Cybersecurity*. Springer. https://doi.org/10.1007/978-3-031-63126-9_17.

9 Aaronson, Scott. 2013. *Quantum Computing Since Democritus*. Cambridge University Press.

10 Mallow, G. Michael, Alexander Hornung, Juan Nicolas Barajas, Samuel S. Rudisill, Howard S. An, and Dino Samartzis. 2022. "Quantum Computing: The Future of Big Data and Artificial Intelligence in Spine." *Spine Surgery and Related Research* 6(2): 93. https://doi.org/10.22603/SSRR.2021-0251.

11 Yung, Choi, Tim Antony, Laurice Sattouf, William Tam, Andro Younan, Chandler L. Snyder, Shadrach W. Viste, Anthony Nursalim, et al. 2022. "Quantum Computing and Its Application in Cryptography." *Lecture Notes in Networks and Systems*, vol. 360. https://doi.org/10.1007/978-3-030-89912-7_23.

12 Deutsch, David, and Artur Ekert. 1998. "Quantum Computation." *Physics World* 11(3): 47. https://doi.org/10.1088/2058-7058/11/3/31.

13 Deutsch, David. 1992. "Quantum Computation." *Physics World* 5(6): 57. https://doi.org/10.1088/2058-7058/5/6/38.

14 Deutsch, David. 1985. "Quantum Theory, the Church–Turing Principle and the Universal Quantum Computer." *Proceedings of the Royal Society of London. A. Mathematical and Physical Sciences* 400(1818): 97–117. https://doi.org/10.1098/RSPA.1985.0070.

15 Bernstein, Daniel J. 2011. "Post-Quantum Cryptography." *Encyclopedia of Cryptography and Security*. Springer. https://doi.org/10.1007/978-1-4419-5906-5_386.

16 Tegmark, Max. 2017. *Life 3.0: Being Human in the Age of Artificial Intelligence*. Knopf.

17 Mosca, Michele. 2018. "Cybersecurity in an Era with Quantum Computers: Will We Be Ready?" *IEEE Security and Privacy* 16(5): 38–41. https://doi.org/10.1109/MSP.2018.3761723.

18 Gentry, Craig. 2009a. "Fully Homomorphic Encryption Using Ideal Lattices." *Proceedings of the Annual ACM Symposium on Theory of Computing*, 169–78. https://doi.org/10.1145/1536414.1536440.

19 Neven, Hartmut. 2024. *Meet Willow, Our State-of-the-Art Quantum Chip*. https://blog.google/technology/research/google-willow-quantum-chip/.

20 Grace, Katja, John Salvatier, Allan Dafoe, Baobao Zhang, and Owain Evans. 2018. "Viewpoint: When Will AI Exceed Human Performance? Evidence from AI Experts." *Journal of Artificial Intelligence Research* 62: 729–54. https://doi.org/10.1613/JAIR.1.11222.

21 EU Commission. 2014. "eIDAS Regulation." *Shaping Europe's Digital Future*. https://digital-strategy.ec.europa.eu/en/policies/eidas-regulation.

22 Zyskind, Guy, Oz Nathan, and Alex Sandy Pentland. 2015. "Decentralizing Privacy: Using Blockchain to Protect Personal Data." *2015 IEEE Security and Privacy Workshops*, 180–84. https://doi.org/10.1109/SPW.2015.27.

23 Unique Identification Authority of India. 2022. *Requesting Entities*. https://uidai.gov.in/en/ecosystem/authentication-ecosystem/authentication-requesting-agency.html.

24 Schneier, Bruce. 2015. *Data and Goliath: The Hidden Battles to Collect Your Data and Control Your World*. Norton.

25 Bostrom, Nick. 2014. *Superintelligence: Paths, Dangers, Strategies*. Oxford University Press.

26 Vinge, Vernor. 1993a. *Technological Singularity*. NASA. http://cmm.cenart.gob.mx/delanda/textos/tech_sing.pdf.

27 Goodfellow, Ian, Jean Pouget-Abadie, Mehdi Mirza, Bing Xu, David Warde-Farley, Sherjil Ozair, Aaron Courville, and Yoshua Bengio. 2014. "Generative Adversarial Networks." *Communications of the ACM* 63(11): 139–44. https://doi.org/10.1145/3422622.

28 Radford, Alec, Luke Metz, and Soumith Chintala. 2015. "Unsupervised Representation Learning with Deep Convolutional Generative Adversarial Networks." *4th International Conference on Learning Representations, ICLR 2016—Conference Track Proceedings*. https://arxiv.org/abs/1511.06434v2.

29 Sánchez, David Cerezo. 2019. "Zero-Knowledge Proof-of-Identity: Sybil-Resistant, Anonymous Authentication on Permissionless Blockchains and Incentive Compatible, Strictly Dominant Cryptocurrencies." *SSRN*. https://doi.org/10.2139/ssrn.3392331.

30 Wang, Fennie, and Primavera De Filippi. 2019. "Self-Sovereign Identity in a Globalized World: Credentials-Based Identity Systems as a Driver for Economic Inclusion." *SSRN*. https://ssrn.com/abstract=3524367.

31 Yang, Xiaohui, and Wenjie Li. 2020. "A Zero-Knowledge-Proof-Based Digital Identity Management Scheme in Blockchain." *Computers & Security* 99: 102050. https://doi.org/10.1016/J.COSE.2020.102050.

32 Liu, Yang, Debiao He, Mohammad S. Obaidat, Neeraj Kumar, Muhammad Khurram Khan, and Kim Kwang Raymond Choo. 2020. "Blockchain-Based Identity Management Systems: A Review." *Journal of Network and Computer Applications* 166: 102731. https://doi.org/10.1016/J.JNCA.2020.102731.

33 Shao, Wei, Chunfu Jia, Yunkai Xu, Kefan Qiu, Yan Gao, and Yituo He. 2020. "AttriChain: Decentralized Traceable Anonymous Identities in Privacy-Preserving Permissioned Blockchain." *Computers & Security* 99: 102069. https://doi.org/10.1016/J.COSE.2020.102069.

34 Jena, Sanjay Kumar, and Ram Chandra Barik. 2023. "Decentralized Digital Identity: A New Form of Secured Identity Using Blockchain Technology." *Lecture Notes in Networks and Systems* 671: 93–102. https://doi.org/10.1007/978-3-031-31153-6_9.

35 Torongo, Arnaf, and Mohsen Toorani. 2023. *Blockchain-Based Decentralized Identity Management for Healthcare Systems*. https://arxiv.org/abs/2307.16239.

36 Kingma, Diederik P., and Max Welling. 2013. *Auto-Encoding Variational Bayes*. https://arxiv.org/abs/1312.6114v11.

37 Micciancio, Daniele, and Oded Regev. 2009. "Lattice-Based Cryptography." *Post-Quantum Cryptography*, 147–91. https://doi.org/10.1007/978-3-540-88702-7_5.

38 Breidenbach, Lorenz, Christian Cachin, Benedict Chan, Alex Coventry, Steve Ellis, Ari Juels, Farinaz Koushanfar, et al. 2021. *Chainlink 2.0: Next Steps in the Evolution of Decentralized Oracle Networks*. Chainlink Labs.

39 Nita, Stefania Loredana, and Marius Iulian Mihailescu. 2023. "Homomorphic Encryption." *Advances to Homomorphic and Searchable Encryption*, 27–88. https://doi.org/10.1007/978-3-031-43214-9_3.

40 Gentry, Craig. 2009b. "Fully Homomorphic Encryption Using Ideal Lattices." *Proceedings of the Annual ACM Symposium on Theory of Computing*, 169–78. https://doi.org/10.1145/1536414.1536440.

41 Sedlmeir, Johannes, Reilly Smethurst, Alexander Rieger, and Gilbert Fridgen. 2021. "Digital Identities and Verifiable Credentials." *Business and Information Systems Engineering* 63(5): 603–13. https://doi.org/10.1007/S12599-021-00722-Y/TABLES/3.

42 Mazzocca, Carlo, Abbas Acar, Selcuk Uluagac, Rebecca Montanari, Paolo Bellavista, and Mauro Conti. 2024. *A Survey on Decentralized Identifiers and Verifiable Credentials*. https://arxiv.org/abs/2402.02455v1.

43 Mahalle, Parikshit N., Gitanjali Shinde, and Pathan Mohd Shafi. 2020. "Rethinking Decentralized Identifiers and Verifiable Credentials for the Internet of Things." *Studies in Systems, Decision and Control* 266: 361–74. https://doi.org/10.1007/978-3-030-39047-1_16.

44 Garzon, Sandro Rodriguez, Dennis Natusch, Artur Philipp, Axel Küpper, Hans Joachim Einsiedler, and Daniela Schneider. 2024. *DID Link: Authentication in TLS with Decentralized Identifiers and Verifiable Credentials*. https://arxiv.org/abs/2405.07533v2.

45 W3C. 2022. *Decentralized Identifiers (DIDs) v1.0*. https://www.w3.org/TR/did-core/.

46 Waleed, Muhammad, Knud Erik Skouby, and Sokol Kosta. 2023. "Decentralized Identifiers for IoT Systems: Current Status and Future Vision." *Lecture Notes in Networks and Systems* 741: 408–17. https://doi.org/10.1007/978-3-031-38318-2_40.

47 He, Yifeng, Ethan Wang, Yuyang Rong, Zifei Cheng, and Hao Chen. 2024. *Security of AI Agents*. https://arxiv.org/abs/2406.08689v2.

48 Tong, Richard Jiarui, and Xiangen Hu. 2024. "Future of Education with Neuro-Symbolic AI Agents in Self-Improving Adaptive Instructional Systems." *Frontiers of Digital Education* 1(2): 198–212. https://doi.org/10.1007/S44366-024-0008-9.

49 Bakopoulos, Emmanouil, Vasilis Siatras, Panagiotis Mavrothalassitis, Nikolaos Nikolakis, and Kosmas Alexopoulos. 2024. "Digital-Twin-Enabled Framework for Training and Deploying AI Agents for Production Scheduling." *Artificial Intelligence in Manufacturing*, 147–79. https://doi.org/10.1007/978-3-031-46452-2_9.

50 Deng, Zehang, Yongjian Guo, Changzhou Han, Wanlun Ma, Junwu Xiong, Sheng Wen, and Yang Xiang. 2025. "AI Agents Under Threat: A Survey of Key Security Challenges and Future Pathways." *ACM Computing Surveys* 57(7): 1–36. https://doi.org/10.1145/37166.

51 Gronauer, Sven, and Klaus Diepold. 2022. "Multi-Agent Deep Reinforcement Learning: A Survey." *Artificial Intelligence Review* 55(2): 895–943. https://doi.org/10.1007/S10462-021-09996-W.

52 Khurana, Udayan, Horst Samulowitz, and Deepak Turaga. 2018. "Feature Engineering for Predictive Modeling Using Reinforcement Learning." *Proceedings of the AAAI Conference on Artificial Intelligence*, 32. https://dl.acm.org/doi/pdf/10.5555/3504035.3504452.

53 Gaspar-Figueiredo, Daniel. 2023. *Learning from Interaction: User Interface Adaptation Using Reinforcement Learning*. https://arxiv.org/abs/2312.07216v1.

54 Song, Binpeng, Jinze Song, and Jian Ye. 2020. "A Dynamic Pricing Mechanism in IoT for DaaS: A Reinforcement Learning Approach." *Advances in Intelligent Systems and Computing* 1075: 604–15. https://doi.org/10.1007/978-3-030-32591-6_65.

55 Ahmadi, Candra, and Jiann Liang Chen. 2024. "Survey on Reinforcement Learning Techniques for Enhancing Security and Efficiency in Zero Trust Networks." *Proceedings of the 2024 10th International Conference on Applied System Innovation*, 427–29. https://doi.org/10.1109/ICASI60819.2024.10547956.

56 Cheng, Nan, Xiucheng Wang, Zan Li, Zhisheng Yin, Tom Luan, and Xuemin Shen. 2025. "Toward Enhanced Reinforcement Learning-Based Resource Management via Digital Twin: Opportunities, Applications, and Challenges." *IEEE Network* 39(1): 189–196. https://doi.org/10.1109/MNET.2024.3438543.

57 Fard, Neshat Elhami, Rastko R. Selmic, and Khashayar Khorasani. 2023. "A Review of Techniques and Policies on Cybersecurity Using Artificial Intelligence and Reinforcement Learning Algorithms." *IEEE Technology and Society Magazine* 42(3): 57–68. https://doi.org/10.1109/MTS.2023.3306540.

58 Wang, Jin, Jia Hu, Geyong Min, Wenhan Zhan, Qiang Ni, and Nektarios Georgalas. 2019. "Computation Offloading in Multi-Access Edge Computing Using a Deep Sequential Model Based on Reinforcement Learning." *IEEE Communications Magazine* 57(5): 64–69. https://doi.org/10.1109/MCOM.2019.1800971.

59 Lapan, Maxim. 2018. *Deep Reinforcement Learning Hands-On: Apply Modern RL Methods, with Deep Q-Networks, Value Iteration, Policy Gradients, TRPO, AlphaGo Zero and More*. Packt.

Multiple-Choice Questions with Detailed Explanations

1. Which of the following best describes the concept of the technological singularity?

   a. A milestone where artificial intelligence surpasses human intelligence and becomes autonomous

   b. A phase where AI systems become highly specialized for specific tasks

   c. A period when classical computing systems are replaced by quantum technologies

   d. The integration of AGI into decentralized systems

   Correct Answer: A. The technological singularity refers to a point where artificial general intelligence (AGI) surpasses human intelligence, enabling systems to operate autonomously and self-improve without human intervention. While options C and D describe potential technologies involved in this shift, they do not capture the essence of the singularity itself. Option B is incorrect as it refers to narrow AI, which precedes AGI.

2. What was Vernor Vinge's contribution to the singularity hypothesis?

   a. He proposed that AGI would never surpass human intelligence.

   b. He theorized that the creation of superhuman intelligence would signal the end of the human era.

   c. He developed the first reinforcement learning framework for AGI.

   d. He designed cryptographic systems to secure AGI networks.

   Correct Answer: B. In his seminal essay, "The Coming Technological Singularity" (1993), Vernor Vinge argued that the creation of superhuman intelligence would lead to a transformative era, effectively ending the "human era" as we know it. Option A is false because Vinge supported the possibility of AGI surpassing humans. Options C and D are unrelated to his theoretical work.

3. Which of the following is a critical challenge in preparing for the singularity?

   a. Increasing the speed of neural networks

   b. Ensuring that AGI systems align with human values and remain interpretable

   c. Developing centralized identity systems for AGI management

   d. Reducing computational power requirements for quantum decryption

   Correct Answer: B. Alignment with human values and interpretability are critical challenges because AGI systems with unchecked autonomy could act in ways harmful to humans. Options A and D are technical aspects but not the main challenge. Developing centralized systems (Option C) is often discouraged due to vulnerabilities.

4. What characterizes the pre-singularity phase?

   a. Machines demonstrating general intelligence

   b. AI systems outperforming humans at narrowly defined tasks

   c. The introduction of lattice-based cryptography for data security

   d. The development of decentralized identity verification systems

   Correct Answer: B. The pre-singularity phase is the current stage of AI development, where narrow AI excels at specific tasks such as natural language processing and image recognition. Option A refers to the near-singularity phase. Options C and D are unrelated to this phase.

5. What is a major risk associated with the post-singularity phase?

   a. Difficulty training AGI systems with labeled data

   b. AGI systems surpassing human oversight and operating autonomously

   c. Centralized AI systems increasing their reliance on classical encryption

   d. Delayed deployment of AGI in blockchain-based identity systems

   Correct Answer: B. The post-singularity phase features AGI systems that are capable of self-improvement and potentially able to outstrip human oversight and control. This poses significant risks, including misaligned objectives and ethical challenges. Options A, C, and D do not reflect the primary concerns of this phase.

Exercises and Solutions

Exercise 1: Short-Answer Question

Question: Explain the concept of the technological singularity. Provide a brief overview of Vernor Vinge's and Ray Kurzweil's theories regarding this phenomenon.

Solution: The technological singularity refers to a future point where artificial intelligence surpasses human intelligence, enabling autonomous decision making and self-improvement. Vernor Vinge theorized that this event would mark the end of the "human era," as superintelligent systems would exceed human control and comprehension. Ray Kurzweil, on the other hand, posited in *The Singularity Is Near* that the exponential growth of computing power, driven by Moore's Law, would result in AGI by the mid-21st century. Both perspectives highlight the transformative and potentially disruptive implications of AGI.

Exercise 2: Case Study

Scenario: A nation's centralized identity system relies on biometric data for authentication. An AGI system, augmented with quantum decryption, infiltrates this system and generates synthetic identities that bypass authentication protocols and compromise critical infrastructure.

Tasks:

1. Identify the weaknesses in the described identity system.
2. Propose three measures to mitigate such attacks.
3. Evaluate the role of decentralized systems in mitigating AGI-driven attacks.

Solution:

1. **Weaknesses:**
    - Reliance on centralized databases creates a single point of failure.
    - Biometric systems are vulnerable to synthetic identity generation.
    - Lack of quantum-resistant cryptographic measures exposes the system to decryption attacks.
2. **Measures to mitigate attacks:**
    - Transition to decentralized identity systems (e.g., blockchain-based) to reduce single points of failure.
    - Implement quantum-resistant encryption (e.g., lattice-based cryptography).
    - Use zero-knowledge proofs to verify identities without revealing sensitive data.
3. **Evaluation of decentralized systems:** Decentralized systems distribute identity management across a network, making these systems harder to compromise at scale. They also enhance privacy by minimizing the exposure of sensitive data. However, challenges include scalability and interoperability, which require further innovation for widespread adoption.

Exercise 3: Hands-On Activity

Task: Implement a simple lattice-based cryptographic algorithm in Python. Compare its performance and security to RSA encryption.

Solution:

1. Implement a basic version of lattice-based cryptography using Python libraries like *numpy* and *pympler*.
2. Generate keys and encrypt/decrypt a small message using the lattice-based system.
3. Benchmark performance against RSA (using libraries like *cryptography*).
4. Discuss findings: Lattice-based cryptography is computationally intensive but provides resilience against quantum attacks, unlike RSA.

2

Quantum Computing and Its Implications

This chapter examines the fundamentals of quantum computing, the implications of quantum algorithms for classical systems, and the development of quantum-resistant technologies to safeguard critical infrastructures. By exploring the applications and future developments of quantum technologies, the chapter provides a detailed understanding of the challenges and opportunities in this emerging field.

Objectives

- **Understand the fundamentals of quantum computing:** Explore the principles of quantum mechanics that underpin quantum computing, such as superposition and entanglement. Compare classical bits with qubits and explain the functioning of quantum gates and algorithms like Shor's and Grover's.
- **Analyze the threats posed by quantum computing to cryptographic systems:** Discuss the vulnerabilities of current cryptographic systems to quantum algorithms. Highlight the urgency of adopting quantum-resistant cryptographic solutions and the challenges of transitioning to post-quantum cryptography.
- **Explore the development of quantum-resistant technologies:** Investigate lattice-based cryptography, zero-knowledge proofs (ZKPs), and homomorphic encryption (HE) as solutions to quantum threats. Examine how these technologies can be integrated into secure systems, including blockchain platforms.
- **Investigate the potential applications of quantum computing:** Identify how quantum computing can solve optimization problems and accelerate breakthroughs in fields like artificial intelligence and materials science. Discuss the implications for industries such as pharmaceuticals and secure communications.

- **Assess the future of quantum technologies:** Evaluate the challenges of developing fault-tolerant quantum computing and scalable architectures. Examine the potential for global quantum communication networks and collaborative research efforts to address technical and ethical concerns.

Through these objectives, this chapter outlines the transformative potential of quantum technologies and highlights the importance of securing digital infrastructures. By addressing the risks and opportunities associated with quantum computing, this chapter provides a roadmap for transitioning into quantum computing.

Basics of Quantum Computing

Quantum computing is one of the most profound technological revolutions of the 21st century. Unlike classical computing, which relies on binary bits that exist in either 0 or 1 states, quantum computing introduces quantum bits, or qubits, which leverage the principles of quantum mechanics to encode information in ways previously unimaginable. At the heart of this new paradigm are two foundational principles:

- Superposition enables a qubit to exist simultaneously in multiple states, exponentially increasing the computational capacity of quantum systems compared to classical ones. For example, whereas a classical computer evaluates problems sequentially or through parallel processing, a quantum computer can process a vast number of possibilities simultaneously.
- Entanglement links qubits in such a way that the state of one qubit instantaneously correlates with the state of another, regardless of distance. This phenomenon allows for extraordinary efficiency in information transfer and processing, making it a cornerstone of quantum computation.

The physical realization of qubits varies across different technologies, each offering unique advantages and challenges:

- Superconducting qubits, such as those developed by IBM[1–9] and Google,[10] exploit electrical circuits cooled to near absolute zero to maintain quantum coherence.
- Trapped ion qubits, used by systems like IonQ, isolate individual ions in electromagnetic fields to perform quantum operations with high fidelity.
- Photonic qubits, which utilize the properties of light particles, offer the potential for room-temperature quantum computing.

While these approaches differ in their technical implementation, they all share the challenge of maintaining coherence—the stability of a qubit's quantum state—against environmental noise and errors, which pose significant obstacles to scalability.

At the core of quantum computing is the quantum circuit model, which uses quantum gates to manipulate qubits and perform computations. Unlike classical logic gates, which operate deterministically, quantum gates are reversible and probabilistic, reflecting the fundamental properties of quantum mechanics. Quantum algorithms, built upon sequences of these gates, demonstrate the immense potential of quantum computing. Shor's algorithm, for example, is renowned for its ability to factor large numbers exponentially more quickly than classical algorithms, posing a direct threat to current cryptographic systems like Rivest-Shamir-Adleman (RSA) and elliptic curve cryptography (ECC). Similarly, Grover's algorithm offers a quadratic speedup for unstructured search problems, with applications in optimization and quantum cryptanalysis. Beyond these, quantum simulations stand out as one of the most promising applications, enabling the modeling of complex quantum systems in fields such as chemistry, materials science, and drug discovery.

Despite its immense promise, quantum computing remains in its infancy. Current systems, while groundbreaking, are constrained by limitations in qubit count, coherence, and error rates. Companies like Google and IBM have achieved milestones in demonstrating quantum supremacy, where a quantum computer outperforms the fastest classical systems on specific tasks. For instance, Google's Sycamore processor performed in 200 seconds a computation that would take classical supercomputers thousands of years. However, translating these advances into practical, real-world applications will involve overcoming significant technical hurdles, including the development of scalable quantum architectures and robust error correction methods. Moreover, the software side of quantum computing is still evolving, and there is a pressing need for innovative algorithms and frameworks to fully utilize the potential of quantum hardware. However, Google claims that its most recent quantum chip, dubbed Willow, "performed a standard benchmark computation in under five minutes that would take one of today's fastest supercomputers 10 septillion (that is, 1025) years—a number that vastly exceeds the age of the Universe." It also noted that "Willow can reduce errors exponentially as we scale up using more qubits. This cracks a key challenge in quantum error correction that the field has pursued for almost 30 years."[10]

The implications of quantum computing extend far beyond academic curiosity, offering transformative possibilities across multiple domains. In optimization, quantum algorithms could revolutionize logistics, supply chains, and traffic management by solving problems exponentially more quickly than classical approaches. In artificial intelligence, quantum machine learning promises to accelerate model training and enhance the performance of algorithms, opening new frontiers in fields such as natural language processing and computer vision. Perhaps most importantly, quantum computing has profound implications for cybersecurity. Its ability to break classical encryption protocols necessitates a transition to quantum-resistant cryptographic methods, a topic explored in greater depth in the following sections.

Quantum computing faces significant technical and practical barriers, from advancing hardware to integrating these systems into hybrid quantum–classical frameworks that address real-world problems. The next section delves into the most pressing concern arising from this revolutionary technology: its threat to cryptographic systems and the security of the digital world.

Quantum Computing's Threat to Cryptography

The advent of quantum computing poses a fundamental challenge to the cryptographic systems that underpin modern digital security. Classical cryptography, the foundation of secure communication, data integrity, and digital identities, relies on mathematical problems that are computationally infeasible for classical computers to solve within practical time frames. These problems include integer factorization, discrete logarithms, and elliptic curve computations. However, the unique computational capabilities of quantum computers have the potential to disrupt this framework entirely, rendering many of today's widely used encryption methods obsolete.

As quantum computing progresses, the threat to traditional cryptographic methods, such as Rivest–Shamir–Adleman (RSA)[11] and elliptic-curve cryptography (ECC),[12] which are foundational for secure online communication, is intensifying.[13,14] These systems will be vulnerable to attacks that can efficiently factor large integers—a core principle underlying current encryption methods.[15] The primary threat stems from quantum algorithms that exploit the principles of superposition and entanglement to solve these mathematical problems exponentially more quickly than classical methods.[11,15,16]

Symmetric encryption algorithms, such as Advanced Encryption Standard (AES),[17] face a different but less severe challenge. Quantum computers running Grover's algorithm can perform brute-force attacks on symmetric keys in a square root of the time required by classical computers. This effectively halves the bit strength of symmetric keys; for example, a 256-bit key would offer the same security against quantum attacks as a 128-bit key against classical attacks. While this is a significant reduction, symmetric encryption can be rendered quantum resistant simply by doubling the key length—a relatively straightforward adjustment compared to the overhaul required for public-key systems.

The implications of quantum computing extend beyond encryption to digital signatures, a cornerstone of identity verification and data integrity. Many digital signature schemes, such as those based on RSA and ECC, would become insecure in a quantum future. This is particularly concerning for blockchain technology, where digital signatures are used to secure transactions and validate identities. A quantum-capable adversary could forge signatures, manipulate transaction histories, and compromise the integrity of entire blockchain networks, undermining trust in decentralized systems.

The timeline for quantum computing's threat to cryptography remains uncertain, but progress in quantum hardware has accelerated significantly in recent years. Advances in qubit coherence, error correction, and scalability have brought us closer to the development of large-scale, fault-tolerant quantum computers capable of running algorithms like Shor's on a practical scale. Google's demonstration of quantum supremacy in 2019 and subsequent improvements in quantum processors highlight the rapid pace of innovation. While estimates vary, some experts predict that cryptographically relevant quantum computers could emerge by 2035 or 2045, leaving a narrowing window for the transition to quantum-resistant cryptographic systems.

The transition to post-quantum cryptography (PQC)[18,19] is one of the most urgent challenges for digital security in the quantum era. Post-quantum cryptographic algorithms are designed to withstand attacks from both classical and quantum computers. Unlike traditional cryptography, which relies on integer factorization or discrete logarithms, PQC is built on problems that are believed to be quantum resistant, such as lattice-based cryptography, code-based cryptography, multivariate polynomial equations, and hash-based cryptography. For example, NIST's Post-Quantum Cryptography Standardization project[20] has identified lattice-based schemes like

CRYSTALS-Kyber[21,22] and CRYSTALS-Dilithium[23] as strong candidates for securing communications in a quantum-enabled world.

Implementing PQC at scale presents significant challenges. Cryptographic migration is a complex and resource-intensive process, requiring updates to hardware, software, and protocols across global infrastructures. Interoperability between quantum-resistant and classical systems during the transition period adds another layer of complexity. Moreover, the computational overhead of PQC algorithms is often higher than that of traditional cryptographic methods, raising concerns about performance in resource-constrained environments such as IoT devices.

In addition to the technical challenges, the uncertainty surrounding quantum computing's timeline complicates the urgency of migration. Organizations must balance the risks of delaying implementation against the costs of adopting immature technologies. Governments and industry consortia play critical roles in driving this transition by establishing standards, fostering collaboration, and incentivizing early adoption. For instance, the European Union's eIDAS Regulation and the U.S. National Security Agency have issued directives to ensure that future systems are quantum resistant, emphasizing the need for proactive measures.

Quantum computing also raises ethical and geopolitical concerns in the realm of cryptography. Certain nations achieving quantum supremacy before others will result in significant asymmetries in cybersecurity capabilities, potentially destabilizing global power structures. A quantum-enabled adversary with the ability to decrypt sensitive communications or undermine critical infrastructure would possess an unprecedented advantage in cyber warfare.

One of the most promising approaches to mitigating this risk is the integration of lattice-based cryptographic protocols into blockchain systems. Unlike traditional cryptographic algorithms, which rely on problems such as integer factorization and discrete logarithms, lattice-based cryptography is founded on the complexity of solving high-dimensional lattice problems. These problems, including the shortest vector problem (SVP) and the learning with errors (LWE) problem, are considered computationally infeasible for both classical and quantum systems. By incorporating lattice-based methods, blockchain systems can achieve quantum resistance while maintaining the integrity and immutability of their records.

The implementation of lattice-based cryptography in blockchain environments is far from straightforward and faces significant technical and practical challenges. The development process begins with the careful selection of algorithms that balance security, efficiency, and compatibility with existing blockchain infrastructures. For instance, algorithms such as NTRUEncrypt[24–26] and ring learning with errors (RLWE)[27,28] have shown great promise for securing blockchain transactions due to their strong theoretical foundations and practical feasibility. However, adapting these algorithms for blockchain use cases involves more than simple integration. It requires fine-tuning parameters to optimize performance, designing efficient key management systems, and ensuring seamless interaction with blockchain's decentralized architecture.

To ensure the scalability and robustness of these quantum-safe systems, researchers are looking to advanced techniques such as parameter sweeping and multithreading. These methods allow for the optimization of cryptographic algorithms, ensuring that they can handle the high transaction volumes typical of blockchain networks without compromising security. Additionally, rigorous testing is conducted using quantum simulators like IBM Qiskit. These simulations provide critical insights into the resilience of lattice-based cryptographic implementations against hypothetical quantum attacks, enabling researchers to address vulnerabilities proactively.

Another crucial aspect of developing quantum-resistant blockchain systems lies in the design and deployment of secure smart contracts. Smart contracts, which automate processes such as identity verification and transaction validation, are integral to the functionality of modern blockchains. Transitioning these contracts to quantum-safe algorithms requires rethinking their cryptographic underpinnings and ensuring compatibility with lattice-based encryption and authentication mechanisms. Languages like Solidity and Go are commonly used to create such contracts, which are then rigorously tested for security and performance.

Hybrid cryptographic frameworks are also being developed to provide a transitional layer of security during the shift from classical to quantum-resistant methods. These frameworks combine traditional cryptographic algorithms, such as ECC, with lattice-based systems to offer backward compatibility and incremental migration. By integrating these hybrid models into blockchain platforms like Ethereum and Hyperledger Fabric, developers can ensure a smoother transition to full quantum resistance without disrupting existing applications.

Beyond the technical challenges, the adoption of quantum-safe blockchain systems also raises critical considerations for governance and regulation. The shift to post-quantum cryptography necessitates updates to global cryptographic standards, as well as industry-wide collaboration to establish best practices for implementing and managing these new systems. Initiatives such as the NIST Post-Quantum Cryptography Standardization project and the European Telecommunications Standards Institute (ETSI) Quantum-Safe Cryptography Working Group play key roles in advancing these efforts. Their work accelerates the development of quantum-resistant algorithms and also fosters international cooperation to address the geopolitical implications of quantum computing.

The integration of lattice-based cryptography is only one piece of the puzzle. Blockchain systems also stand to benefit from other quantum-resistant techniques, such as hash-based signature schemes like XMSS and SPHINCS+, and code-based cryptography, which leverages error-correcting codes for secure encryption. By adopting a layered approach that combines multiple quantum-resistant methods, it is possible to enhance the resilience of blockchain networks against a wide array of quantum threats.

Another vital aspect of implementing quantum-resistant solutions in blockchain systems involves the adaptation of consensus protocols to accommodate lattice-based cryptography. Consensus mechanisms, which ensure agreement across distributed nodes, form the backbone of blockchain security and functionality. Algorithms such as Proof of Work (PoW) and Proof of Stake (PoS) rely heavily on cryptographic primitives for transaction validation and block verification. To transition these mechanisms to quantum-safe standards, the underlying cryptographic components, including digital signatures and key exchange protocols, must be replaced or augmented with lattice-based alternatives.

For instance, digital signatures used in PoS systems are essential for validator authentication and block approval. With the integration of lattice-based cryptography, these signatures are generated using mathematically robust schemes like RLWE or NTRUEncrypt, ensuring resistance to quantum attacks. The implementation process involves updating the signature-generation and verification methods in the consensus protocol, allowing them to process the larger key sizes and computational requirements typical of lattice-based algorithms. Developers often use modular cryptographic libraries such as Microsoft SEAL or PALISADE to streamline this process, embedding lattice-based functions directly into the blockchain's consensus engine.

Key exchange protocols also require significant adaptation to support lattice-based cryptography. These protocols enable secure communication between blockchain nodes, ensuring the integrity of data exchanged during consensus operations. Replacing vulnerable algorithms such as Diffie-Hellman with lattice-based alternatives involves rewriting the network-layer logic of the blockchain. The goal is to ensure that the exchange of cryptographic keys is quantum resistant without compromising the speed and reliability of inter-node communication. Advanced techniques, such as predistributed keys or session caching, can be employed to optimize the performance of these updated protocols, mitigating the overhead introduced by lattice-based computations.

Another critical component of this transition is ensuring that transaction metadata, including cryptographic hashes and Merkle tree structures, aligns with the requirements of lattice-based encryption. Hashing functions like SHA-256, while widely used, are susceptible to quantum attacks due to Grover's algorithm. To maintain immutability and integrity, these functions can be replaced or supplemented with quantum-resistant alternatives, such as hash-based signature schemes (e.g., XMSS, SPHINCS+). The blockchain's storage layer must also be updated to accommodate these changes, particularly when lattice-based cryptography introduces larger key sizes or more complex data structures. Developers must carefully optimize storage mechanisms to minimize the impact on overall blockchain performance.

In tandem with these updates, developers must reengineer node software to support lattice-based cryptography across all blockchain operations. Node software serves as the interface between blockchain users and the distributed ledger, handling tasks such as transaction processing, block validation, and network communication. Integrating lattice-based cryptographic primitives into this software requires a modular approach, ensuring compatibility with existing blockchain frameworks while enabling seamless upgrades to quantum-safe standards. Programming languages such as Rust, Go, and Python are commonly used to implement these changes, providing the flexibility and performance required for secure, scalable blockchain systems.

Testing and benchmarking are crucial to validating the effectiveness of these quantum-resistant upgrades. Comprehensive simulations of blockchain operations are conducted to evaluate the resilience of lattice-based cryptographic implementations under realistic conditions, including high transaction loads and simulated quantum attacks. Tools such as IBM Qiskit allow developers to assess the performance of these systems in quantum threat scenarios, identifying potential bottlenecks or vulnerabilities. Metrics such as transaction throughput, latency, and consensus efficiency are closely monitored to ensure that the blockchain maintains its performance while adopting quantum-resistant standards.

In relation to CRYSTALS-Kyber, we need to clarify that its quantum resistance is based on lattice-based cryptography, specifically the learning with errors (LWE) problem, which is considered hard even for quantum computers due to its lack of known efficient quantum algorithms. Unlike RSA and

ECC, which are vulnerable to Shor's algorithm, lattice-based schemes like CRYSTALS-Kyber are built on problems that remain computationally infeasible even in a post-quantum world. Additionally, the impact of Grover's algorithm requires more precision because it halves the bit strength and provides a quadratic speedup, meaning a symmetric key of length n offers only $2^{\{n/2\}}$ security against a quantum adversary, requiring key-length doubling for equivalent security. In addition, quantum key distribution (QKD) and quantum random number generation (QRNG) are essential for achieving true quantum-safe cryptography. QKD, through protocols like BB84, enables provably secure key exchange by leveraging quantum mechanics, ensuring that any eavesdropping attempt alters the quantum states and is thus detectable. QRNG, in contrast to classical pseudorandom number generators, harnesses quantum indeterminacy to produce truly unpredictable cryptographic keys, mitigating risks associated with deterministic key generation. Integrating these aspects will provide a more complete perspective on quantum-resistant security mechanisms.

Indistinguishability Obfuscation (iO)

Indistinguishability obfuscation (iO) is a cryptographic technique that transforms a program into an equivalent version that is computationally indistinguishable from any other functionally equivalent program of the same size. Unlike traditional obfuscation methods, which primarily aim to make code harder to read while preserving its execution, iO ensures that even an adversary with full access to the obfuscated code cannot determine how it differs from another valid obfuscation of the same function. This property makes iO a powerful tool in cryptographic security, particularly for protecting software logic, smart contracts, and encryption mechanisms.

A concrete example of iO's utility is in software watermarking and cryptographic access control. Suppose an organization develops proprietary software that enforces digital rights management (DRM). Traditional obfuscation techniques may attempt to hide specific function calls, but a determined adversary could still reverse-engineer the logic by analyzing execution traces. In contrast, with iO, any two functionally identical versions of the DRM enforcement mechanism would be indistinguishable, making it significantly harder for an attacker to extract meaningful insights about their structure.

Another practical use case is in zero-knowledge proofs (ZKPs), where iO can be used to make cryptographic verification protocols more secure. For instance, in a secure voting system, an iO-protected algorithm could ensure that even if the vote-tallying mechanism is public, no one can derive individual vote preferences from observing the execution logic.

In the context of blockchain, the computationally indistinguishable process ensures that even if an adversary gains access to the obfuscated program, they cannot deduce its original structure or internal logic. This capability is especially valuable for smart contracts, which often encode sensitive operational rules, transaction details, or access permissions. By embedding iO into blockchain systems, developers can create a robust layer of security that conceals the data and the mechanisms used to process and verify it.

The implementation of indistinguishability obfuscation in blockchain systems requires a multilayered approach that integrates iO techniques with quantum-resistant cryptographic algorithms.

The process begins with the design of iO schemes tailored specifically for blockchain applications. This involves leveraging advanced cryptographic frameworks such as Zero-Knowledge Scalable Transparent Argument of Knowledge (ZK-STARK)[29] to establish additional layers of verification and security. ZK-STARK, known for their scalability and efficiency, complement iO by enabling secure, verifiable transactions without revealing sensitive data to the network. Together, these technologies create an architecture that is secure and transparent, providing a strong foundation for blockchain systems handling high-value or sensitive information.

Embedding iO techniques into blockchain platforms requires modifications to the smart contracts and the underlying node infrastructure. Smart contracts, which automate critical blockchain operations, must be obfuscated to prevent adversaries from reverse-engineering their logic. This is achieved through the use of advanced obfuscation algorithms, such as branching programs and matrix branching programs, which transform the smart contract code into a form that conceals its structure while preserving functionality. These obfuscated contracts are then implemented using programming languages like Solidity for Ethereum-based systems or Rust for platforms that prioritize performance and memory safety. The integration process also involves optimizing the obfuscation methods to minimize computational overhead, using techniques such as partial evaluation and randomized encodings to balance security with efficiency.

The deployment of obfuscated smart contracts is accompanied by rigorous testing to ensure their correctness, scalability, and resistance to attacks. Formal verification tools such as Verisol[30–33] and Mythril[34–37] play critical roles in this phase, allowing developers to systematically validate the logic of the obfuscated contracts against predefined security properties. These tools identify potential vulnerabilities in the code, such as reentrancy issues or logic flaws, that could be exploited by adversaries. By conducting formal verification alongside adversarial testing, which includes red team exercises and automated vulnerability scanning, developers can establish a high level of confidence in the security of the obfuscated systems.

In addition to protecting smart contracts, indistinguishability obfuscation can be applied to the blockchain nodes themselves to enhance the security of the consensus and communication processes. For example, iO techniques can be used to obfuscate the protocols governing block validation or transaction propagation to ensure that even if a node is compromised, the adversary cannot deduce the internal mechanisms of the blockchain. Multi-party computation (MPC) protocols[38–43] further strengthen this layer of security by distributing the computation of sensitive operations across multiple nodes. With MPC, even if one or more nodes are compromised, the integrity of the overall computation remains intact because no single node has access to the complete dataset or logic.

Optimization is a key consideration when integrating indistinguishability obfuscation into blockchain systems. Obfuscation algorithms are computationally intensive by nature, and their application to high-throughput environments like blockchain requires careful tuning. Techniques such as partial evaluation, which simplifies obfuscated code by precomputing invariant expressions, and randomized encodings, which reduce the complexity of the obfuscation process, are employed to enhance performance. Additionally, developers might use hardware acceleration, such as GPUs or specialized cryptographic processors, to further mitigate the computational overhead associated with iO.

The resulting blockchain system, enhanced with indistinguishability obfuscation, offers a level of security and privacy that is unparalleled in traditional cryptographic frameworks. Transactions, smart contracts, and operational protocols are all shielded from adversarial analysis, ensuring that even advanced attackers armed with quantum computing capabilities cannot compromise the integrity of the network. This architecture not only addresses the immediate threats posed by quantum decryption but establishes a future-proof framework for handling the growing complexity of blockchain applications.

By integrating indistinguishability obfuscation with quantum-resistant cryptographic techniques, blockchain systems achieve a dual layer of defense that protects the data and the mechanisms used to process it. This combination ensures that blockchain platforms can operate securely in an increasingly hostile digital landscape, preserving the trust and functionality that underpin decentralized ecosystems.

Moreover, the potential asymmetry in the development of quantum computing capabilities poses an additional layer of risk. Nations or organizations that achieve quantum supremacy before others could gain a disproportionate advantage that would enable them to compromise blockchain systems and other critical infrastructures.

The relationship between iO and quantum resistance lies in the ability to protect cryptographic primitives from quantum adversaries. Many traditional encryption and authentication schemes rely on complexity assumptions that quantum computers threaten to break, particularly with Shor's algorithm attacking public-key systems. iO provides an additional security layer by ensuring that even if an encryption algorithm is exposed, adversaries cannot extract useful information about its structure or implementation. Furthermore, recent cryptographic research has explored combining iO with lattice-based hardness assumptions, particularly the LWE problem, to construct encryption schemes that are inherently resistant to quantum attacks.

While iO itself does not replace post-quantum cryptographic primitives, its integration with quantum-resistant schemes strengthens overall security by obfuscating how cryptographic functions operate, making them harder to exploit—even for a quantum-capable attacker. For example, researchers have proposed using iO in conjunction with lattice-based encryption protocols such as NTRUEncrypt and RLWE to obscure key generation and authentication logic, further mitigating risks from quantum-enabled adversaries.

Case Study: How to Develop a Quantum-Resistant Blockchain

Developing a quantum-resistant blockchain involves integrating advanced cryptographic techniques, robust architectural frameworks, and rigorous validation protocols to safeguard decentralized systems against classical and quantum threats. At the core of this system lies lattice-based cryptography, which replaces traditional RSA and elliptic-curve algorithms. Lattice-based schemes such as RLWE and NTRUEncrypt are well suited for blockchain applications due to their reliance on computationally hard problems like the shortest vector problem (SVP) and LWE. These primitives secure transaction signing, data storage, and peer-to-peer communication, ensuring resilience against quantum attacks. To implement these cryptographic techniques, developers can use open-source libraries such as PALISADE or Microsoft SEAL while carefully optimizing key sizes and noise levels to balance security and performance.

On top of the cryptographic foundation, zero-knowledge proofs (ZKPs) can enhance privacy by enabling transaction verification without revealing sensitive details. Bulletproofs, in particular, are efficient, non-interactive ZKP protocols that are ideal for blockchain environments. These proofs allow sensitive data, such as digital identity records or passport information, to be validated without exposing their content. ZKPs are embedded into the blockchain's smart contracts and transaction workflows, ensuring that privacy is maintained without sacrificing transparency. Developers can use formal verification tools like VeriSol and Mythril to identify and address potential vulnerabilities in ZKP-enabled contracts.

Homomorphic encryption (HE) is another critical component, allowing encrypted data to be processed without decryption. This capability is especially important for managing sensitive data such as encrypted identity records, financial information, or medical data. HE ensures that operations like validation, updates, or computation on confidential data can occur securely without revealing its contents. Developers can implement HE using libraries like IBM HELib or TenSEAL, integrating it into the transaction layer of the blockchain. Careful parameter selection and rigorous testing can ensure that HE operations are accurate and efficient, even when applied to complex blockchain workflows.

The blockchain's consensus mechanism needs to be strengthened with Byzantine Fault Tolerance (BFT) protocols, which ensure system functionality even in the presence of malicious or faulty nodes. To protect the consensus process from quantum threats, lattice-based cryptographic signatures such as Dilithium or Falcon can be integrated into BFT. These signatures provide authentication and validation while maintaining efficiency and scalability. To further improve performance, sharding needs to be employed to divide the blockchain into smaller segments, reducing the computational load on individual nodes. Each shard would process a subset of transactions while maintaining security and decentralization, ensuring that the system could handle large-scale applications.

Blockchains often require interaction with external data sources, facilitated by oracles. Chainlink oracles are particularly effective for securely fetching off-chain data such as government-issued passport records or real-time financial data. These oracles can be enhanced with lattice-based cryptography and ZKPs to ensure the integrity of the data they provide. For instance, ZKPs can be used to verify the authenticity of external records without revealing sensitive details, while lattice-based encryption ensures that the data cannot be intercepted or tampered with during transmission. These integrations secure the blockchain's interactions with external systems, which are often critical for real-world applications.

Once the cryptographic and architectural components are implemented, the blockchain must undergo rigorous validation in simulated quantum environments. Quantum computing platforms like D-Wave and IBM Q Experience provide tools for modeling quantum attack scenarios. For example, D-Wave's quantum annealing capabilities can simulate attempts to solve lattice-based cryptographic problems, while IBM Q Experience tests the resilience of key exchange protocols against Shor's algorithm. These simulations allow developers to identify potential vulnerabilities and refine a system's defenses. Stress testing with tools like Apache Kafka further evaluates the blockchain's ability to handle high transaction loads, ensuring scalability and reliability in real-world conditions.

To ensure modularity and adaptability, the blockchain can be deployed on platforms like Hyperledger Fabric or Corda. These platforms are specifically designed for flexibility, allowing developers to integrate custom cryptographic modules and advanced consensus mechanisms. Hyperledger Fabric's modular architecture supports lattice-based encryption and HE in its transaction workflows, while Corda's enterprise-grade security features make it well suited for scalable applications. Optimization techniques such as parallel processing enable multiple cryptographic operations to run simultaneously, reducing latency and improving throughput. Sharding further enhances scalability, distributing data processing across the network to manage growing transaction volumes and participants effectively.

Quantum-resistant blockchains are the future of secure decentralized systems. By combining lattice-based cryptography, ZKPs, HE, BFT, and modular platforms, these blockchains address the dual challenges of quantum resilience and operational scalability. Validation through simulated quantum environments ensures robustness, while modular design enables flexibility and efficiency.

Table 2-1 provides a comparative analysis of key quantum-resistant cryptographic libraries, offering insights into their best-suited applications, strengths, challenges, and performance characteristics. For instance, PALISADE and OpenFHE are well suited for lattice-based encryption and homomorphic encryption, making them ideal for applications requiring privacy-preserving computations. Meanwhile, Microsoft SEAL offers a more user-friendly API for cloud-based homomorphic encryption, and HELib, despite its computational overhead, remains a leading choice for fully homomorphic encryption (FHE) research. Table 2-1 also includes NTRUEncrypt, SPHINCS+, Kyber, and FrodoKEM, which provide various quantum-resistant alternatives for key exchange, digital signatures, and hybrid TLS implementations.

Table 2-1 Comparison of Quantum-Resistant Cryptographic Libraries

Cryptographic Library	Best Suited For	Key Strengths	Challenges	Performance Metrics
PALISADE	Lattice-based cryptography, homomorphic encryption (HE), secure multiparty computation (MPC)	Low-latency encryption/decryption, optimized for resource-constrained environments	Limited flexibility for complex HE operations	20% faster decryption compared to SEAL in lattice-based key exchange protocols
Microsoft SEAL	User-friendly API design, cloud-based homomorphic encryption, encrypted computation on floating-point data	Balanced usability and efficiency, easy cloud integration	Larger ciphertext sizes compared to other libraries	Encryption latency: 0.5ms on Intel Xeon, moderate memory usage
HELib	Fully homomorphic encryption (FHE), arbitrary-depth circuit evaluation, confidential machine learning inference	High flexibility, supports advanced FHE operations, strong for research applications	High computational and memory overhead, requires advanced cryptographic knowledge	Encryption latency: 50ms per operation, ciphertexts 30%—-50% larger than SEAL
OpenFHE	Successor to PALISADE, optimized for FHE, RLWE-based encryption, post-quantum cryptography	Designed for efficiency and modularity, supports advanced lattice cryptography schemes	Still evolving, needs further optimization for large-scale deployment	Improved efficiency over PALISADE, modular design enables faster cryptographic operations

Cryptographic Library	Best Suited For	Key Strengths	Challenges	Performance Metrics
NTRUEncrypt	Lattice-based public-key encryption and digital signatures, alternative to RSA and ECC	Secure against quantum attacks on public-key cryptosystems, well studied and vetted	Higher computational overhead compared to traditional cryptographic schemes	Efficient key generation but requires larger key sizes than RSA/ECC
PQClean	Post-quantum cryptographic algorithms in a clean, auditable form, ideal for research and benchmarking	Provides reference implementations for various post-quantum cryptographic primitives	Primarily for research, lacks robust integration for production systems	Benchmark implementations show trade-offs between security and performance
liboqs	Open Quantum Safe (OQS) project, supports a variety of post-quantum algorithms, including lattice and hash-based schemes	Highly flexible, integrates with OpenSSL and TLS libraries for secure communication	Still in development; adoption depends on final NIST PQC standardization	Supports hybrid TLS implementations with minimal overhead in handshake latency
SPHINCS+	Stateless hash-based signature scheme, suitable for long-term digital signatures and blockchain security	Efficient and provably secure digital signature scheme with minimal attack surface	Larger signature sizes compared to classical digital signatures like RSA or ECDSA	Signature size ~41KB but computationally efficient for signing and verification
Kyber	Lattice-based key encapsulation mechanism (KEM), NIST-selected for post-quantum cryptography	Lightweight and efficient for secure key exchange, integrated into many PQC transition plans	Requires key size management for optimal security–performance balance	Faster encapsulation and decapsulation than RSA but requires larger keys
FrodoKEM	Lattice-based key exchange protocol, designed to replace traditional Diffie-Hellman key exchange	Post-quantum alternative to classical key exchange, resilient against quantum attacks	Not yet widely adopted, requires further optimization for efficiency	Secure against quantum threats but requires more computational resources than ECC

Table 2-1 highlights the trade-offs in adopting quantum-resistant cryptographic libraries, emphasizing that while security against quantum threats is a primary concern, performance constraints remain a critical bottleneck in real-world implementations. Computational overhead is a significant factor. Fully homomorphic encryption (FHE) in HELib, for example, requires 50ms per operation, making it impractical for real-time systems, whereas Microsoft SEAL achieves encryption in 0.5ms, making it a better choice for cloud-based applications. Similarly, Kyber and FrodoKEM, both designed for post-quantum key exchange, exhibit increased key sizes compared to RSA but offer significantly improved resilience against quantum-enabled attacks. liboqs and PQClean provide valuable post-quantum cryptographic implementations, but their adoption depends on the final NIST standardization process. Additionally, challenges such as ciphertext expansion, increased memory usage, and software integration complexity pose obstacles to widespread deployment, particularly for low-power and resource-constrained environments like IoT and blockchain networks.

Future of Quantum Technologies: Comparative Analysis

While today's quantum systems remain in their infancy, the trajectory of their development points to a profound shift in computational capabilities, materials science, artificial intelligence, and secure communication systems. At the forefront of quantum technology's future lies the pursuit of fault-tolerant quantum computing. Current quantum computers, often referred to as noisy intermediate-scale quantum (NISQ) devices, are limited by their susceptibility to decoherence and quantum noise, which introduce errors during computations. However, advancements in error-correction techniques, such as surface codes and topological qubits, aim to address these limitations by encoding information redundantly across multiple qubits. The development of fault-tolerant architectures will enable quantum computers to execute more complex algorithms, paving the way for practical applications in fields ranging from drug discovery to cryptography.

One area set for transformation is *quantum simulation*, which holds the promise of solving problems that are currently intractable for classical systems. By mimicking the behavior of quantum systems, quantum simulators can provide insights into phenomena such as high-temperature superconductivity, molecular interactions, and complex chemical reactions. These breakthroughs will accelerate innovation in materials science, leading to the design of more efficient batteries, catalysts, and semiconductors. Furthermore, the ability to model quantum interactions precisely will revolutionize the pharmaceutical industry, enabling the discovery of new drugs and treatments with unprecedented speed and accuracy.

Quantum technologies can also disrupt machine learning and artificial intelligence. Quantum machine learning algorithms, such as the quantum support vector machine and the variational quantum eigensolver, leverage quantum superposition and entanglement to accelerate the processing of high-dimensional data. These advancements will not only reduce the time required to train AI models but enhance their ability to identify patterns and make predictions in fields such as genomics, climate modeling, and financial forecasting. The integration of quantum computing into AI workflows will open new frontiers in natural language processing, autonomous systems, and personalized medicine.

Another critical frontier is the development of quantum communication systems, which promise supreme security in data transmission. Quantum key distribution (QKD) protocols, such as BB84 and E91, exploit the principles of quantum mechanics to ensure that any attempt to intercept communication would be immediately detectable. In the future, satellite-based quantum networks could enable secure global communication, protecting sensitive information from classical and quantum adversaries. Additionally, advancements in quantum repeaters will extend the range of quantum networks, facilitating the establishment of a quantum internet that connects quantum computers, sensors, and communication devices on a global scale.

Despite these prospects, the potential of quantum technologies is full of challenges. One of the most significant obstacles is the scalability of quantum hardware. Achieving a sufficient number of stable, high-fidelity qubits is essential for practical applications, yet current systems struggle to maintain coherence and minimize error rates. Innovations in qubit design, including topological and photonic qubits, are being explored to overcome these limitations, offering pathways to more robust and scalable quantum architectures.

Another challenge lies in the development of software and algorithms that can fully use quantum hardware. While algorithms such as Shor's and Grover's have demonstrated the theoretical capabilities of quantum computing, a broader range of practical algorithms is needed to address real-world problems. This requires advancements in quantum programming languages, such as Qiskit and Cirq, and the integration of quantum and classical systems into hybrid computational frameworks. These hybrid systems will allow quantum computers to complement classical ones, using their unique strengths for tasks such as optimization, cryptography, and simulation.

Quantum technologies also face significant barriers to adoption, including high costs, the need for specialized infrastructure, and the complexity of integrating quantum systems into existing workflows. The transition from classical to quantum-driven solutions is not uniform across industries, with practical adoption dependent on hardware maturity, algorithmic breakthroughs, and engineering challenges. To clarify these distinctions, this section provides a structured comparison of quantum versus classical capabilities, highlighting both the opportunities and limitations associated with emerging quantum technologies.

Quantum Versus Classical Computing: Domain-Specific Comparison

Table 2-2 compares quantum and classical computing capabilities across various domains, illustrating the areas where quantum technology is expected to provide substantial improvements and where classical methods continue to hold an advantage.

Table 2-2 Comparison of Quantum and Classical Capabilities Across Domains

Domain	Classical Computing	Quantum Computing	Potential Impact
Cryptography	Public-key encryption (RSA, ECC) relies on integer factorization, which is secure against classical attacks.	Shor's algorithm can break RSA and ECC, necessitating quantum-resistant cryptography (e.g., lattice-based encryption).	Urgent need for post-quantum cryptography (PQC) to replace vulnerable cryptosystems.
Artificial intelligence (AI) and machine learning (ML)	Training deep learning models is computationally expensive, requiring significant parallel processing power (GPUs/TPUs).	Quantum machine learning (QML) offers potential speedups for high-dimensional optimization problems (e.g., quantum-enhanced neural networks).	Accelerates AI model training and improves efficiency in optimization-heavy tasks.
Optimization problems	Classical solvers (e.g., simulated annealing, linear programming) struggle with complex combinatorial problems.	Quantum annealers (e.g., D-Wave) solve NP-hard optimization problems faster by leveraging quantum tunneling and superposition.	Revolutionizes logistics, financial modeling, and supply chain management.
Drug discovery and materials science	Molecular simulations rely on approximations, requiring immense computational power to model chemical interactions.	Quantum simulations accurately model quantum effects in molecules, improving drug development and materials design.	Accelerates the discovery of new pharmaceuticals and superconducting materials.

Domain	Classical Computing	Quantum Computing	Potential Impact
Secure communications	Classical encryption methods rely on computational hardness assumptions.	Quantum key distribution (QKD) provides provably secure key exchange, which is immune to computational attacks.	Strengthens global cybersecurity by enabling unbreakable encryption methods.
Financial modeling and risk analysis	Classical Monte Carlo simulations require vast processing power for risk assessment.	Quantum Monte Carlo algorithms offer quadratic speedups, reducing computational complexity in financial forecasting.	Enhances real-time risk analysis and predictive financial modeling.
Internet and data networks	Traditional internet security depends on TLS, RSA, and ECC for encrypted communications.	A quantum internet, leveraging quantum entanglement, enables instantaneous and tamper-proof communication.	Future-proofing global data transmission against cyber threats.

Bridging the Gap Between Quantum and Classical Systems

As we can see in Table 2-2, quantum technologies exhibit superior performance in certain domains. However, technical, economic, and infrastructure-related barriers are yet in the way of widespread adoption. Near-term quantum systems remain constrained by decoherence, error correction challenges, and hardware scalability, limiting their applicability in real-world scenarios. Hybrid quantum–classical computing has emerged as an intermediate approach, integrating quantum subroutines into classical workflows. For example, hybrid AI models can leverage quantum processing for feature selection while using classical deep learning architectures for final predictions. Additionally, quantum-safe transition strategies are critical for mitigating the impacts of quantum threats on cybersecurity. Governments and enterprises must adopt PQC ahead of cryptographically relevant quantum computers to ensure resilience against future decryption capabilities. Table 2-2 illustrates that while classical computing remains indispensable in many areas, quantum computing offers unprecedented advantages in solving complex, high-dimensional problems.

Summary

In this chapter, we have explored the foundational principles of quantum computing, including superposition, entanglement, and quantum gates, which enable capabilities far beyond those of classical systems. These principles underpin quantum algorithms such as Shor's and Grover's, whose potential to disrupt existing cryptographic systems underscores the urgency of transitioning to quantum-resistant solutions.

We have examined the vulnerabilities of current encryption methods, highlighting the risks posed by quantum computers to RSA, ECC, and other widely used cryptographic techniques. The chapter outlines the development of quantum-resistant technologies, including lattice-based cryptography, ZKPs, and HE, which together form a robust framework for protecting data in a post-quantum era.

The integration of these technologies into systems like blockchain mitigates quantum threats and enhances privacy and scalability.

We have also looked at the potential applications of quantum computing in fields such as artificial intelligence, optimization, and quantum simulation. Quantum technologies hold the promise of accelerating breakthroughs in drug discovery, materials science, and secure communications. However, achieving these milestones depends on overcoming significant challenges, including the development of fault-tolerant quantum systems, scalable qubit architectures, and hybrid computational frameworks that integrate quantum and classical approaches.

References

1 Gayathri Devi, S., S. Manjula Gandhi, S. Chandia, and P. Boobalaragavan. 2023. "Exploring IBM Quantum Experience." *Studies in Computational Intelligence* 1085: 265–82. https://doi.org/10.1007/978-981-19-9530-9_15.

2 Wille, Robert, Rod Van Meter, and Yehuda Naveh. 2019. "IBM' s Qiskit Tool Chain: Working with and Developing for Real Quantum Computers." *Proceedings of the 2019 Design, Automation and Test in Europe Conference and Exhibition*, 1234–40. https://doi.org/10.23919/DATE.2019.8715261.

3 Burgholzer, Lukas, Rudy Raymond, and Robert Wille. 2020. "Verifying Results of the IBM Qiskit Quantum Circuit Compilation Flow." *2020 IEEE International Conference on Quantum Computing and Engineering,* 356 –65. https://doi.org/10.1109/QCE49297.2020.00051.

4 Barabasi, Stephan, James Barrera, Prashant Bhalani, Preeti Dalvi, Ryan Dimiecik, Avery Leider, John Mondrosch, Karl Peterson, et al. 2020. "Student User Experience with the IBM QISKit Quantum Computing Interface." *Lecture Notes in Networks and Systems* 70: 547–63. https://doi.org/10.1007/978-3-030-12385-7_41.

5 Cross, Andrew. 2018. "The IBM Q Experience and QISKit Open-Source Quantum Computing Software." *Bulletin of the American Physical Society*. https://ui.adsabs.harvard.edu/abs/2018APS..MARL58003C/abstract.

6 García-Pérez, Guillermo, Matteo A.C. Rossi, and Sabrina Maniscalco. 2020. "IBM Q Experience as a Versatile Experimental Testbed for Simulating Open Quantum Systems." *npj Quantum Information* 6(1): 1–10. https://doi.org/10.1038/s41534-019-0235-y.

7 Miceli, Raffaele, and Michael McGuigan. 2018. "Quantum Computation and Visualization of Hamiltonians Using Discrete Quantum Mechanics and IBM QISKit." *2018 New York Scientific Data Summit*. https://doi.org/10.1109/NYSDS.2018.8538959.

8 Shenoy, Kishore S., Dev Y. Sheth, Bikash K. Behera, and Prasanta K. Panigrahi. 2020. "Demonstration of a Measurement-Based Adaptation Protocol with Quantum Reinforcement Learning on the IBM Q Experience Platform." *Quantum Information Processing* 19(5): 1–13. https://doi.org/10.1007/S11128-020-02657-X.

9 Silva, Vladimir. 2018. "Enter the IBM Q Experience: A One-of-a-Kind Platform for Quantum Computing in the Cloud." In *Practical Quantum Computing for Developers*. Apress. https://doi.org/10.1007/978-1-4842-4218-6_3.

10 Neven, Hartmut. 2024. *Meet Willow, Our State-of-the-Art Quantum Chip*. https://blog.google/technology/research/google-willow-quantum-chip/.

11 Rivest, R. L., A. Shamir, and L. Adleman. 1978. "A Method for Obtaining Digital Signatures and Public-Key Cryptosystems." *Communications of the ACM* 21 (2): 120–26. https://doi.org/10.1145/359340.359342.

12 Torii, Naoya, and Kazuhiro Yokoyama. 1987a. "Elliptic Curve Cryptosystems." *Mathematics of Computation* 48(177): 203–9. https://doi.org/10.1090/S0025-5718-1987-0866109-5.

13 Miller, Victor S. 1986. "Use of Elliptic Curves in Cryptography." *Lecture Notes in Computer Science*, 218: 417–26. https://doi.org/10.1007/3-540-39799-X_31.

14 Castelvecchi, Davide. 2022. "The Race to Save the Internet from Quantum Hackers." *Nature* 602(7896): 198–201. https://doi.org/10.1038/D41586-022-00339-5.

15 Shor, Peter W. 1994. "Algorithms for Quantum Computation: Discrete Logarithms and Factoring." *Proceedings — Annual IEEE Symposium on Foundations of Computer Science* 124–34. https://doi.org/10.1109/SFCS.1994.365700.

16 Torii, Naoya, and Kazuhiro Yokoyama. 1987b. "Elliptic Curve Cryptosystems." *Mathematics of Computation* 48(177): 203–9. https://doi.org/10.1090/S0025-5718-1987-0866109-5.

17 NIST. 2001. *Advanced Encryption Standard (AES)*. https://web.archive.org/web/20170312045558/http://nvlpubs.nist.gov/nistpubs/FIPS/NIST.FIPS.197.pdf.

18 Bernstein, Daniel J. 2011. "Post-Quantum Cryptography." *Encyclopedia of Cryptography and Security*, 949–50. https://doi.org/10.1007/978-1-4419-5906-5_386.

19 NIST. 2022. *Post-Quantum Cryptography PQC*. https://csrc.nist.gov/projects/post-quantum-cryptography.

20 NIST. 2024. *Post-Quantum Cryptography PQC*. https://csrc.nist.gov/projects/post-quantum-cryptography.

21 Bos, Joppe, Leo Ducas, Eike Kiltz, T. Lepoint, Vadim Lyubashevsky, John M. Schanck, Peter Schwabe, Gregor Seiler, and Damien Stehle. 2018. "CRYSTALS-Kyber: A CCA-Secure Module-Lattice-Based KEM." *2018 IEEE European Symposium on Security and Privacy*, 353–67. https://doi.org/10.1109/EUROSP.2018.00032.

22 GitHub. 2024. *pq-crystals/kyber*. https://github.com/pq-crystals/kyber.

23 GitHub. 2024. *pq-crystals/dilithium*. https://github.com/pq-crystals/dilithium.

24 Hoffstein, Jeffrey, Jill Pipher, John M. Schanck, and Joseph H. Silverman. 1997. *Public Key Cryptosystem Method and Apparatus*. https://patents.google.com/patent/US6081597A/en.

25 Hoffstein, Jeff, Jill Pipher, John M. Schanck, Joseph H. Silverman, William Whyte, and Zhenfei Zhang. 2017. "Choosing Parameters for NTRUEncrypt." *Lecture Notes in Computer Science* 10159: 3–18. https://doi.org/10.1007/978-3-319-52153-4_1.

26 Hoffstein, Jeff, Nick Howgrave-Graham, Jill Pipher, and William Whyte. 2009. "Practical Lattice-Based Cryptography: NTRUEncrypt and NTRUSign." *Information Security and Cryptography* 10: 349–90. https://doi.org/10.1007/978-3-642-02295-1_11.

27 Lyubashevsky, Vadim, Chris Peikert, and Oded Regev. 2010. "On Ideal Lattices and Learning with Errors over Rings." *Lecture Notes in Computer Science*, vol. 6110. https://doi.org/10.1007/978-3-642-13190-5_1.

28 Regev, Oded. 2005. "On Lattices, Learning with Errors, Random Linear Codes, and Cryptography." *Journal of the ACM* 56(6): 1–40. https://doi.org/10.1145/1568318.1568324.

29 Ben-Sasson, Eli, Iddo Bentov, Yinon Horesh, and Michael Riabzev. 2018. *Scalable, Transparent, and Post-Quantum Secure Computational Integrity*. International Association for Cryptologic Research (IACR).

30 Wang, Yuepeng, Shuvendu K. Lahiri, Shuo Chen, Rong Pan, Isil Dillig, Cody Born, Immad Naseer, and Kostas Ferles. 2020. "Formal Verification of Workflow Policies for Smart Contracts in Azure Blockchain." *Lecture Notes in Computer Science* 12031: 87–106. https://doi.org/10.1007/978-3-030-41600-3_7.

31 Marescotti, Matteo, Rodrigo Otoni, Leonardo Alt, Patrick Eugster, Antti E. J. Hyvärinen, and Natasha Sharygina. 2020. "Accurate Smart Contract Verification Through Direct Modelling." *Lecture Notes in Computer Science* 12478: 178–94. https://doi.org/10.1007/978-3-030-61467-6_12.

32 Singh, Neeraj Kumar, Akshay M. Fajge, Raju Halder, and Md Imran Alam. 2023. "Formal Verification and Code Generation for Solidity Smart Contracts." *Distributed Computing to Blockchain: Architecture, Technology, and Applications*, 125–44. https://doi.org/10.1016/B978-0-323-96146-2.00028-0.

33 Otoni, Rodrigo, Matteo Marescotti, Leonardo Alt, Patrick Eugster, Antti Hyvärinen, and Natasha Sharygina. 2023. "A Solicitous Approach to Smart Contract Verification." *ACM Transactions on Privacy and Security* 26(2): 1–28. https://doi.org/10.1145/3564699.

34 Yao, Yao, Hui Li, Xin Yang, and Yiwang Le. 2022. "An Improved Vulnerability Detection System of Smart Contracts Based on Symbolic Execution." *2022 IEEE International Conference on Big Data*, 3225–34. https://doi.org/10.1109/BIGDATA55660.2022.10020730.

35 Zhang, William, Sebastian Banescu, Leonardo Pasos, Steven Stewart, and Vijay Ganesh. 2019. "MPro: Combining Static and Symbolic Analysis for Scalable Testing of Smart Contract." *2019 IEEE 30th International Symposium on Software Reliability Engineering*, 456–62. https://doi.org/10.1109/ISSRE.2019.00052.

36 Schiffl, Jonas, Matthias Grundmann, Marc Leinweber, Oliver Stengele, Sebastian Friebe, and Bernhard Beckert. 2021. "Towards Correct Smart Contracts: A Case Study on Formal Verification of Access Control." *Proceedings of ACM Symposium on Access Control Models and Technologies*, 125–30. https://doi.org/10.1145/3450569.3463574.

37 Abraham, Misha, and K. P. Jevitha. 2019. "Runtime Verification and Vulnerability Testing of Smart Contracts." *Communications in Computer and Information Science* 1046: 333–42. https://doi.org/10.1007/978-981-13-9942-8_32.

38 Cramer, Ronald, Ivan Damgård, and Ueli Maurer. 2000. "General Secure Multi-Party Computation from Any Linear Secret-Sharing Scheme." *Lecture Notes in Computer Science* 1807: 316–34. https://doi.org/10.1007/3-540-45539-6_22.

39 Beerliova-Trubiniova, Zuzana, and Martin Hirt. 2006. "Efficient Multi-Party Computation with Dispute Control." *Lecture Notes in Computer Science* 3876: 305–28. https://doi.org/10.1007/11681878_16.

40 Knott, Brian, Shobha Venkataraman, Awni Hannun, Shubho Sengupta, Mark Ibrahim, and Laurens van der Maaten. 2021. "CrypTen: Secure Multi-Party Computation Meets Machine Learning." *Advances in Neural Information Processing Systems* 34: 4961–73.

41 Kamara, Seny, Payman Mohassel, and Mariana Raykova. 2011. "Outsourcing Multi-Party Computation." IACR *Cryptology*, 272. https://eprint.iacr.org/2011/272.

42 Keller, Marcel. 2020. "MP-SPDZ: A Versatile Framework for Multi-Party Computation." *Proceedings of the ACM Conference on Computer and Communications Security*, 1575–90. https://doi.org/10.1145/3372297.3417872.

43 Evans, David, Vladimir Kolesnikov, and Mike Rosulek. 2018. "A Pragmatic Introduction to Secure Multi-Party Computation." *Foundations and Trends in Privacy and Security* 2(2–3): 70–246. https://doi.org/10.1561/3300000019.

Multiple-Choice Questions with Detailed Explanations

1. What is the fundamental difference between classical and quantum computing?

   a. Classical computing uses transistors, while quantum computing uses supercomputers.

   b. Classical computing uses bits, which are either 0 or 1, whereas quantum computing uses qubits, which can be in superposition.

   c. Classical computing uses deterministic logic gates, whereas quantum computing relies on random operations.

   d. Classical computing uses silicon chips, whereas quantum computing uses only superconductors.

   Correct Answer: B. Classical computing relies on binary bits, which can exist in only one of two states (0 or 1). Quantum computing, however, uses qubits, which exploit quantum mechanical principles such as superposition, which allow them to exist in multiple states simultaneously. This fundamental difference enables quantum computers to process information exponentially more quickly in certain scenarios.

2. Which of the following best describes the significance of Shor's algorithm in cryptography?

   a. It enables faster brute-force attacks on symmetric key systems.

   b. It exponentially accelerates the factoring of large integers, breaking RSA and ECC.

   c. It enhances the efficiency of hashing algorithms used in blockchain systems.

   d. It introduces a new method of error correction for quantum systems.

   Correct Answer: B. Shor's algorithm is a quantum algorithm capable of factoring large integers exponentially more quickly than classical algorithms. This undermines public-key cryptographic systems such as RSA and ECC, which rely on the difficulty of factoring large numbers for security.

3. What is the primary quantum advantage offered by Grover's algorithm?

   a. It accelerates factorization problems that are critical to public-key encryption.

   b. It improves fault tolerance in quantum gates.

   c. It provides a quadratic speedup for unstructured search problems.

   d. It simulates quantum interactions for materials science applications.

   Correct Answer: C. Grover's algorithm provides a quadratic speedup for unstructured search problems, enabling a quantum computer to find a specific item in an unsorted database much more quickly than is possible using classical methods. However, it does not directly threaten public-key encryption systems.

4. Why is lattice-based cryptography considered quantum resistant?
   a. It uses principles of superposition and entanglement to encrypt data.
   b. It is based on mathematical problems like the shortest vector problem (SVP), which are hard for both classical and quantum computers to solve.
   c. It employs algorithms like Shor's to strengthen encryption.
   d. It replaces symmetric key cryptography with longer key sizes.

   Correct Answer: B. Lattice-based cryptography relies on problems such as the shortest vector problem (SVP) and learning with errors (LWE), which remain computationally infeasible even for quantum computers. This makes it a leading candidate for post-quantum cryptography.

Exercises and Solutions

Exercise 1: Quantum Computing Basics

Question: Describe how superposition and entanglement enable quantum computers to outperform classical computers. Provide a practical example of each principle.

Solution:

- **Superposition:** This allows a quantum bit (qubit) to exist in multiple states simultaneously, enabling quantum computers to process many possibilities at once. For example, in a search problem, a quantum computer using superposition can evaluate all possible solutions in parallel.
- **Entanglement:** When qubits become entangled, the state of one qubit is instantaneously correlated with the state of another, even if they are far apart. This feature enhances communication efficiency in distributed quantum systems. A practical application is in quantum key distribution, where entanglement ensures secure data exchange.

Exercise 2: Cryptographic Challenges

Question: Why does quantum computing pose a greater threat to public-key cryptography (e.g., RSA) compared to symmetric cryptography (e.g., AES)?

Solution: Quantum algorithms such as Shor's can efficiently solve problems like integer factorization, which form the basis of RSA and ECC. This renders these public-key systems vulnerable to quantum attacks. Symmetric cryptography, on the other hand, is affected by Grover's algorithm, which only reduces the effective key length by half. This can be mitigated by doubling the key size, making symmetric systems relatively more secure in the quantum era.

Exercise 3: Fault-Tolerant Quantum Computing

Task: Discuss the importance of error correction in quantum computing. How do surface codes contribute to the development of fault-tolerant systems?

Solution: Error correction in quantum computing is crucial for mitigating decoherence and noise, which cause computation errors. Surface codes encode quantum information across multiple physical qubits, detecting and correcting errors without measuring the quantum state directly. This redundancy improves reliability, allowing quantum systems to perform complex operations fault tolerantly. Surface codes, which advance error correction, are essential for scaling quantum computers to handle practical, real-world applications.

PART II

DEFINING THE CONCEPT OF DIGITAL SECURITY BY DESIGN

Part II focuses on the critical frameworks and paradigms essential for constructing secure digital ecosystems in a time of AGI and quantum threats. This part of the book examines the limitations of traditional security models, explores innovative alternatives, and addresses the pressing need for resilience in the face of emerging technological challenges. Emphasis is placed on decentralized architectures, quantum-resistant cryptography, and adaptive defense mechanisms.

Chapter 3, "Current Digital Security Systems," provides a thorough analysis of existing digital security systems, scrutinizing their strengths, inherent vulnerabilities, and capacity to address the demands of a rapidly shifting landscape. Particular attention is given to decentralized security models, such as blockchain and directed acyclic graphs (DAGs), which offer promising pathways for enhancing privacy, scalability, and resilience. Additionally, the chapter evaluates advancements in self-sovereign identity systems and the application of blockchain oracles as mechanisms for securing digital interactions while empowering individual users.

Chapter 4, "The Opportunities and Risks from Artificial General Intelligence (AGI) in Cybersecurity," discusses the profound implications of AGI for cybersecurity. Although AGI remains largely conceptual, its potential to autonomously exploit vulnerabilities, orchestrate sophisticated attacks, and refine strategies presents an unparalleled challenge to existing security paradigms. The discussion encompasses hypothetical scenarios, including AGI-driven disruptions to critical infrastructure and identity systems, alongside real-world case studies of AI-augmented threats such as malware and adversarial attacks. These examples highlight the urgent need to anticipate and mitigate the risks posed by advancements in intelligent systems.

Part II formulates a forward-looking perspective on digital security by design, in which decentralized solutions, advanced cryptographic techniques, and adaptive systems are interwoven to address the complexities of modern threats. The framework presented emphasizes the necessity of proactive measures, robust scalability, and the preservation of user privacy and trust in an increasingly interconnected digital world.

3

Current Digital Security Systems

This chapter examines the risks and limitations of current digital security systems and expands into the potential of decentralized technologies. Through a detailed examination of public-key infrastructure (PKI), quantum-resistant cryptography, and decentralized security models, the chapter explores how these technologies address the challenges posed by modern cyber threats and pave the way for secure digital identity management systems.

Objectives

- **Understand the limitations of public-key infrastructure (PKI):** Examine the centralized trust model of PKI, its vulnerabilities to cyber threats such as certificate authority compromises and on-path attacks, and the challenges posed by quantum computing.
- **Explore quantum-resistant cryptographic solutions:** Analyze the roles of lattice-based cryptography, hash-based signatures, and other post-quantum algorithms in fortifying digital security frameworks against emerging quantum threats.
- **Investigate decentralized security models:** Evaluate how blockchain, directed acyclic graphs (DAGs), and federated learning address the limitations of centralized systems by enhancing resilience, privacy, and scalability.
- **Examine the role of blockchain oracles and AI in decentralized systems:** Discuss the integration of blockchain oracles to validate external data and the deployment of AI-driven anomaly detection for mitigating Sybil attacks and ensuring interoperability.
- **Propose scalable, interoperable digital security architectures:** Identify key steps for implementing decentralized systems, focusing on cryptographic key management, cross-chain communication protocols, and real-time system monitoring.

This chapter starts by discussing the fundamentals of digital security and then expands into a technical discussion on a wide range of new technologies to provide an understanding of how decentralized and quantum-resistant approaches can overcome the limitations of traditional digital security systems, offering scalable, user-centric solutions for a rapidly evolving digital landscape.

Overview of Digital Identity Systems

The management and verification of digital identities have become foundational to modern digital ecosystems, enabling secure access to services, trusted transactions, and efficient interactions across various domains. However, current identity verification systems often rely heavily on static data, such as biometrics, passwords, or personal identifiers. These methods, while effective in controlled environments, are increasingly inadequate in the face of sophisticated threats posed by advancing technologies like artificial general intelligence (AGI) and quantum computing.

Existing systems frequently compromise privacy to enhance security, creating a trade-off that leaves users vulnerable to identity theft, fraud, and surveillance. Centralized identity frameworks, such as the EU's eIDAS,[1] store sensitive user data in centralized repositories, making them attractive targets for malicious actors. In addition, biometric-based systems often expose users to risks of irrevocable data breaches, as stolen biometric data cannot be reissued, like passwords or identification numbers. Furthermore, traditional systems struggle to anonymize user data while preserving authenticity, which leaves critical gaps in privacy protection.

Addressing these vulnerabilities requires a paradigm shift toward more secure, decentralized, and quantum-resistant identity management frameworks. Next-generation identity systems should focus on decentralization, using blockchain technology to store and manage identity credentials securely. Decentralized identifiers (DIDs)[2–7] and verifiable credentials (VCs)[2–5] offer promising solutions by enabling users to retain control over their data while ensuring cryptographic verification. These frameworks decentralize the process of identity validation, removing reliance on central authorities and ensuring privacy-preserving interactions.

In addition, generative AI can play a transformative role in creating synthetic identities for identity verification purposes. By generating realistic and diverse representations, synthetic identities can help anonymize user data and reduce biases in verification systems. When combined with blockchain, these synthetic identities can be cryptographically secured, ensuring that their authenticity remains intact while preventing misuse. Recurrent neural networks (RNNs) and transformer-based designs, such as Wav2Vec 2.0, can be used to encode vocal features effectively. The VoxCeleb[8,9] dataset can be employed for training, with augmentation techniques such as pitch-shifting, time-stretching, and noise injection to enhance the diversity and model robustness of synthetic identities. Generative adversarial network (GAN) architectures[10] can be used for progressive growth of high-resolution image generation and Wasserstein loss functions with gradient penalty to stabilize training and improve convergence. Spectral normalization can be applied to enforce Lipschitz continuity, enhancing robustness against adversarial attacks. The CASIA-WebFace[11] dataset can be applied for training, with extensive preprocessing, including data augmentation techniques such as rotations, scaling, and normalization. The integration of generative AI with decentralized identity frameworks provides a scalable solution that can address current vulnerabilities while paving the way for more dynamic and adaptive identity systems.

Furthermore, quantum-resistant cryptographic techniques are essential for fortifying these systems against future threats. Post-quantum cryptographic algorithms, such as lattice-based encryption, ensure the security of identity data even in a world where quantum computers can break traditional encryption methods. These techniques provide robust security for the exchange and storage of credentials, safeguarding them from classical and quantum adversaries.

Self-sovereign identity (SSI)[12–21] systems exemplify the potential of such advancements. SSI systems empower users to control their personal data, share only the necessary credentials, and interact with services in a privacy-preserving manner. By incorporating DIDs, VCs, and post-quantum cryptography, SSI systems strike a balance between security and privacy, enabling secure interactions without compromising user control. These systems decentralize identity verification processes, which makes them resilient against centralized attacks and scalable for future needs.

To address the vulnerabilities of traditional centralized identity frameworks, DIDs and VCs offer an alternative that prioritizes user autonomy, security, and scalability. Centralized systems typically concentrate sensitive data in a single location, creating single points of failure that expose users to heightened risks of data breaches and loss of control over personal information. In contrast, decentralized identity systems eliminate these risks by redistributing trust and enabling individuals to manage their identities independently.

To empower users, blockchain oracles are used to integrate different protocols and to incorporate consent receipts, which document every instance of credential sharing. These receipts provide users with a transparent and auditable record of when, where, and with whom their credentials have been shared. Consent receipts ensure that users retain oversight of their digital interactions, fostering accountability and trust within the system. Additionally, consent receipts align with global data privacy regulations, such as the EU's General Data Protection Regulation (GDPR), by providing users with a mechanism to monitor and revoke consent as needed.

Scalability is another key advantage of decentralized identity systems. By using blockchain technology, these systems can handle a growing number of participants and interactions without sacrificing security or performance. For instance, a decentralized identity management system could support use cases ranging from online banking and healthcare to travel and e-commerce. The system's flexibility allows it to adapt to varying requirements, making it an ideal solution for a wide range of industries.

The integration of decentralized identity systems with quantum-resistant cryptographic techniques further future-proofs these frameworks. Using post-quantum cryptography to secure the DIDs, VCs, and underlying blockchain infrastructure ensures that the system remains resilient against emerging quantum threats. A system that combined decentralization with advanced cryptography would address current vulnerabilities and also anticipate the challenges of a rapidly evolving technological landscape.

Decentralized identity systems redefine how identities are managed and verified by prioritizing user control, privacy, and security. Through the use of DIDs, VCs, and blockchain oracles, these systems empower individuals to interact securely and transparently in a digital ecosystem. Features such as selective disclosure, consent receipts, and quantum-resistant cryptography further enhance the robustness and adaptability of these systems, making them a critical component of the next-generation digital identity landscape.

Case Study: How to Develop a Quantum-Safe Decentralized System That Gives Users Control over Their Digital Identities

Developing a quantum-safe decentralized identity system that gives users control over their digital identities involves a complete reimagining of how identities are managed, verified, and protected. Centralized systems often place sensitive data in singular repositories, making them vulnerable to breaches and compromising user control. Decentralized identity management addresses these issues by shifting the paradigm toward user-centric, distributed models, where individuals maintain full control over their identities.

To begin, the foundational structure of such a system revolves around integrating DIDs within authentication services agencies (ASAs). ASAs are decentralized entities responsible for facilitating identity verification and managing interactions with users and service providers. The identity data is linked to blockchain repositories, which form the backbone of the decentralized identity infrastructure. These repositories, operating on platforms such as Ethereum Layer 2 solutions, Monero, or TRON, ensure tamper-proof and immutable storage of metadata associated with DIDs. Rather than store personal data on the blockchain, these repositories link to encrypted credentials held in decentralized identifiers data repositories (D-CIDR). This decentralized design mitigates the risks inherent in centralized systems while enhancing user autonomy.

The implementation process requires robust methodologies to integrate and manage DIDs effectively. A detailed analysis of existing DID frameworks, such as Hyperledger Indy,[22–28] uPort,[29–37] and Sovrin,[38–47] provides valuable insights into their strengths and limitations. By evaluating these systems, developers can identify suitable components for decentralized identity management and tailor them to support synthetic identities and real-world use cases. For example, the use of Hyperledger Indy's Aries and Ursa libraries offers a robust foundation for creating secure communication channels, managing keys, and establishing cryptographic trust in the system.

A key feature of such a decentralized framework is the adoption of pairwise pseudonymous DIDs. This mechanism allows users to generate unique identifiers for each interaction, effectively preventing cross-service tracking and enhancing privacy. Each DID is cryptographically secured and linked to verifiable credentials (VCs), which act as digital attestations of user identity attributes, such as age or employment status. These VCs are issued by trusted authorities and stored securely in the user's control, accessible through decentralized wallets. During an interaction, a user can selectively disclose only the credentials necessary for verification, ensuring security and privacy.

Such systems also integrate advanced cryptographic techniques to safeguard interactions. Quantum-resistant algorithms, such as lattice-based encryption, protect communications and data exchanges from classical and quantum computational threats. DIDComm messaging protocols facilitate the secure transmission of DIDs and VCs, ensuring that all exchanges are encrypted and authenticated. Blockchain oracles are employed to validate external data sources, such as government-issued documents or third-party credentials, ensuring that all inputs to the system are accurate and tamper resistant.

To ensure that the system is scalable and interoperable, developers must conduct extensive testing and optimization. Compatibility testing with various blockchain platforms, such as Ethereum and Hyperledger Fabric, ensures that the system can adapt to diverse environments and user requirements. Real-world pilot programs can provide critical insights into the system's performance, scalability, and usability. These pilots can simulate practical use cases, such as financial services, healthcare, or government benefits, to refine methodologies and address potential challenges.

A decentralized identity management system also incorporates comprehensive consent and audit mechanisms. Consent receipts document every interaction where user data is shared, allowing individuals to monitor and control their digital footprint. Users can audit, revoke, or modify their consent at any time, maintaining transparency and accountability within the system. This approach aligns with global privacy regulations, such as GDPR, ensuring that the system protects user data and complies with legal and ethical standards.

By integrating decentralization, quantum-resistant cryptography, and user-centric design, this system can establish a secure and scalable model for identity management in the digital age. A fundamental component of such decentralized identity management systems is the implementation of VCs,[2,3,5] which provides users with the ability to selectively share specific identity attributes while protecting sensitive information.[2,5,48] Unlike traditional identity verification systems, which often require the sharing of entire datasets, VCs allow users to prove individual claims, such as age, nationality, or employment status, without exposing extraneous details. This privacy-preserving capability aligns with the principles of decentralization and user autonomy, making VCs an essential feature of secure and scalable identity management frameworks.

Implementing VCs effectively begins with the design of credential schemas tailored to meet the specific requirements of a decentralized identity management system. These schemas are constructed in accordance with the W3C's Verifiable Credentials Data Model, which provides an interoperable and standardized framework for VC creation. A credential schema defines the attributes that can be included in a credential, such as personal identifiers, validity periods, and issuing authority signatures. For instance, a digital passport credential schema might include data fields for name, nationality, issue date, and expiration date, along with a cryptographic signature from a trusted authority.

Once the schemas are developed, the issuance of VCs relies on a decentralized infrastructure that incorporates blockchain technology. Blockchain serves as the immutable ledger where metadata related to issued credentials is stored. Importantly, the credential data itself is not stored on the blockchain. Instead, credentials are held securely by users in decentralized wallets, and cryptographic hashes of the credentials are recorded on the blockchain for verification purposes. This ensures that the system remains lightweight and scalable while maintaining the integrity of stored credentials.

The process of issuing and managing VCs is facilitated by smart contracts, which automate workflows such as credential issuance, validation, and revocation. Smart contracts ensure that only authorized entities, such as government agencies or certified institutions, can issue specific credentials. For example, a government agency could issue to a user's decentralized wallet a digital birth certificate that is cryptographically signed to validate its authenticity. When the user needs to present proof of birth, the credential can be verified against its hash on the blockchain without exposing sensitive personal data.

Selective disclosure is a critical feature of the VC framework, allowing users to share only the specific data required for a given interaction. This is achieved through advanced cryptographic techniques, such as zero-knowledge proofs. For instance, a user verifying their eligibility for an age-restricted service can prove they are over the required age without revealing their exact birth date. This capability significantly reduces the risk of data breaches and enhances user privacy by adhering to the principle of minimal data exposure.

For larger credentials or metadata, the system integrates off-chain storage solutions, such as the InterPlanetary File System (IPFS)[49–60] or Decentralized Storage Network (DSN).[61–69] These distributed networks provide efficient and scalable storage options, ensuring that credential data remains accessible without overloading the blockchain. Cryptographic hashes stored on the blockchain link to the off-chain data, enabling verification without compromising decentralization or privacy.

The implementation of VCs also involves ensuring compatibility and interoperability with existing identity management platforms. This requires extensive testing and validation to guarantee that the system functions seamlessly across different environments and use cases. For instance, field tests in sectors such as healthcare, financial services, and government programs can assess the system's performance, user experience, and scalability. Adherence to global standards set by organizations such as the W3C, ISO, and IEEE ensures that the VC framework integrates effectively with legacy systems and future developments.

To further strengthen the system's privacy and security, decentralized wallets act as user interfaces for managing and sharing VCs. These wallets store credentials and facilitate their secure exchange with service providers. For example, when a user shares a credential, the wallet employs pairwise pseudonymous identifiers, generating unique identifiers for each interaction to prevent cross-service tracking. Additionally, wallets are equipped with cryptographic protections and fraud detection mechanisms, which detect and mitigate unauthorized use of credentials.

The integration of blockchain oracles enhances the system's capability to validate off-chain data during identity verification processes. Oracles act as intermediaries that securely fetch and verify external data before adding it to the blockchain. For example, when verifying a user's educational credentials, the oracle ensures the authenticity of the data provided by the issuing institution without exposing sensitive information.

The implementation of verifiable credentials within decentralized identity systems provides user-centric, privacy-preserving identity management. By combining credential schemas, blockchain infrastructure, cryptographic techniques, and decentralized storage, individuals can manage their identities securely and autonomously.

Table 3-1 provides a structured overview of how DIDs, VCs, blockchain, and quantum-resistant cryptography interact within a secure identity framework. By clarifying the roles of each component and their integration points, this table addresses key challenges in decentralized identity management while ensuring long-term security against quantum threats. DIDs serve as self-sovereign digital identities, while VCs act as cryptographic attestations verifying a user's identity. These elements are anchored on a blockchain, which provides tamper-proof recordkeeping without exposing private data. The integration of quantum-resistant cryptography ensures that cryptographic signatures and encryption mechanisms remain secure against future quantum-based attacks, utilizing lattice-based cryptography (e.g., NTRUEncrypt, FrodoKEM), hash-based digital signatures (SPHINCS+), and post-quantum key exchange algorithms (CRYSTALS-Kyber). Additionally, blockchain oracles enable the system to verify off-chain identity data in a quantum-safe manner.

Table 3-1 Quantum-Safe Decentralized Identity Components

Component	Function	Integration with Other Components	Quantum-Safe Implementations	Practical Implementation Steps
Decentralized identifiers (DIDs)	Provide unique, decentralized digital identities without relying on central authorities.	Used as the foundation for identity verification and linked to VCs for authentication.	Use lattice-based and hash-based cryptographic schemes for DID authentication.	Deploy DIDs on a blockchain network like Hyperledger Indy or Ethereum.
Verifiable credentials (VCs)	Verify user credentials while preserving privacy Via digitally signed identity attestations.	Issued by trusted authorities, stored in user-controlled wallets, and verified using blockchain.	Use post-quantum digital signature schemes (e.g., CRYSTALS-Dilithium) for signing credentials.	Design VC schemas based on W3C standards and implement cryptographic issuance and verification.
Blockchain	Immutable ledger to store cryptographic proofs of identity transactions without exposing private data.	Records cryptographic hashes of VCs and DIDs, ensuring tamper-proof verification.	Uses quantum-secure consensus mechanisms (e.g., quantum-resistant hash chains).	Choose a suitable blockchain architecture (e.g., permissioned or public) for identity storage.
Quantum-resistant cryptography	Ensures long-term security against quantum threats by replacing RSA and ECC with post-quantum algorithms.	Secures identity transactions and prevents future quantum-based attacks.	Uses algorithms like NTRUEncrypt and FrodoKEM for secure key exchange.	Integrate NIST-approved post-quantum algorithms for cryptographic security.
Blockchain oracles	Bridges decentralized identity systems with external, real-world data sources for verification.	Validates external data (e.g., government IDs, biometric records) before it is added to the blockchain.	Uses zero-knowledge proofs and quantum-safe encryption for secure off-chain data retrieval.	Develop APIs for connecting identity systems to external data sources securely.

Table 3-1 clarifies the practical setup process, outlining how DIDs and VCs interact with blockchain to provide SSI management while remaining verifiable and immutable. By incorporating blockchain oracles, the system allows external identity validation, ensuring a balance between privacy and verifiability. However, implementing such a framework presents performance trade-offs, particularly in terms of latency and computational overhead associated with post-quantum cryptographic operations. Developers must carefully consider the choice of blockchain (permissioned versus public), the efficiency of quantum-safe cryptographic primitives, and the scalability of DID registries to ensure a future-proof, privacy-preserving digital identity infrastructure.

Public-Key Infrastructure (PKI) and Its Limitations

Public-key infrastructure (PKI) has been used in digital security for decades, enabling secure communications, encryption, and identity verification across the internet. By relying on asymmetric cryptography, PKI facilitates trusted interactions between entities by authenticating identities through public and private keys. Despite its critical role in digital ecosystems, however, PKI exhibits several inherent limitations that compromise its efficacy, especially in the face of modern security challenges.

At the core of PKI is a hierarchical trust model that depends on centralized certificate authorities (CAs). These entities issue, validate, and revoke digital certificates that bind a public key to an identity, such as a website or an individual. While this system works effectively in most scenarios, the reliance on centralized CAs introduces significant vulnerabilities. A compromised CA can jeopardize the security of an entire ecosystem, allowing attackers to issue fraudulent certificates and conduct on-path attacks. Furthermore, the centralization of certificate management creates single points of failure, making CAs attractive targets for cyberattacks.

PKI's dependence on static key pairs also limits its flexibility in managing complex, dynamic identity ecosystems. For instance, PKI struggles to accommodate privacy-preserving interactions, as certificates often include sensitive information that can expose users to tracking and surveillance. Moreover, the revocation of compromised certificates is a cumbersome process, often requiring significant time and coordination among multiple stakeholders, which can leave systems vulnerable in the interim.

These limitations are particularly pronounced in contexts that demand robust identity management, such as e-commerce, financial services, healthcare, and government systems. In online retail, for example, PKI's vulnerabilities to spoofing and certificate fraud undermine consumer trust, potentially leading to significant revenue losses. Similarly, in banking, on-path attacks targeting PKI-protected transactions pose a persistent threat to user data and financial security. Healthcare systems reliant on PKI for securing sensitive medical records face challenges in balancing accessibility and confidentiality, especially as digital transformation accelerates.

Governments that use PKI for online services, such as tax filings, benefits distribution, and identity verification, encounter unique challenges. Centralized repositories of public and private keys are susceptible to breaches, which could compromise millions of citizen records. These risks are compounded by the growing sophistication of cyber threats and the potential for quantum computing to render traditional cryptographic safeguards obsolete.

To address these challenges, it is imperative to rethink the architecture of PKI and explore decentralized, quantum-resistant alternatives. Decentralized public-key infrastructure (DPKI), which employs distributed ledgers such as blockchain, offers a promising solution to overcome the centralization risks of traditional PKI. In a DPKI framework, certificates are managed on a blockchain, enabling transparency and immutability while removing reliance on centralized CAs. By decentralizing the trust model, DPKI reduces single points of failure and enhances resilience against cyberattacks.

Additionally, transitioning to quantum-resistant cryptographic algorithms, such as lattice-based cryptography and hash-based signatures, can safeguard PKI against future quantum threats. These algorithms provide a robust mathematical foundation for encryption and digital signatures, ensuring that even advanced quantum computers cannot compromise the security of PKI-protected systems.

Selective disclosure techniques, often used in conjunction with VCs, can also mitigate the privacy concerns associated with PKI. By allowing users to share only the minimum amount of information necessary for verification, selective disclosure preserves user privacy while maintaining trust. For instance, a digital identity system could enable a user to prove their age for an online service without revealing their exact birth date or other personal details.

Another approach involves integrating PKI with DIDs, which provide self-sovereign control over digital identities. DIDs remove the dependency on centralized CAs by enabling entities to generate and manage their own identifiers, authenticated through cryptographic proofs. When combined with blockchain technology, DIDs and PKI create a hybrid model that balances the strengths of both systems while mitigating their individual weaknesses.

To understand the limitations of traditional PKI and understand potential alternatives, it is essential to discuss the technical components of how PKI operates and identify the specific challenges these components face.

At the heart of PKI lies the certificate authority (CA), a trusted third party responsible for issuing digital certificates. Such a certificate binds a public key to an identity, such as an organization, a domain, or an individual, and is verified through a hierarchical chain of trust. When a user accesses a secure website, their browser checks the server's certificate against a list of trusted root CAs embedded within the browser. If the certificate is valid, the browser establishes a secure connection using the server's public key.

This reliance on a centralized CA introduces several risks:

- The "trust anchor" model assumes that the root CA and its intermediaries are impervious to compromise, which is not always the case. Attackers targeting a CA can generate fraudulent certificates, enabling them to impersonate legitimate websites, intercept secure communications, or distribute malicious software. The DigiNotar breach in 2011 is a notable example, where a CA compromise allowed attackers to issue more than 500 rogue certificates, severely undermining trust in PKI-based systems.
- Revocation of certificates remains a persistent issue in PKI. Once a certificate is compromised, it must be revoked to prevent further misuse. Current mechanisms, such as certificate revocation lists (CRLs) and Online Certificate Status Protocol (OCSP) responses, suffer from inefficiencies. CRLs can become unwieldy as they grow in size, and OCSP requires real-time validation

requests, potentially introducing latency and creating privacy concerns as users' interactions are exposed to third parties. This lack of effective revocation creates a window of vulnerability between compromise detection and action.

To overcome these limitations, modern systems are exploring decentralized solutions that fundamentally rethink the role of CAs. DPKI removes the reliance on a centralized authority by distributing certificate management across a blockchain network. In a DPKI model, public keys and their associated metadata are stored on an immutable ledger that is accessible to all participants. Blockchain consensus mechanisms ensure the integrity and authenticity of the data, eliminating the single points of failure inherent in traditional PKI.

For example, when a device or user requires verification, the DPKI system queries the blockchain for the associated public key. Any updates, such as key rotations or revocations, are synchronized across the network in real time, ensuring that all participants have consistent and up-to-date information. This distributed approach not only enhances resilience against attacks but simplifies the revocation process by applying blockchain's transparency and immutability.

Another critical advancement lies in adopting quantum-resistant cryptographic algorithms to address the vulnerabilities of traditional PKI to quantum computing. Lattice-based cryptography, for instance, provides a robust alternative to RSA and ECC by relying on the hardness of mathematical problems, such as solving systems of linear equations over high-dimensional lattices. Algorithms like NTRUEncrypt and ring learning with errors (RLWE) are already being explored for their potential to replace existing key exchange and digital signature schemes in PKI frameworks.

Integrating quantum-resistant cryptography into PKI involves updating certificate formats, key sizes, and verification processes. For example, X.509 certificates, the standard format for PKI, must be extended to accommodate quantum-safe algorithms while maintaining backward compatibility. This ensures a seamless transition for organizations that rely on legacy systems while preparing for post-quantum threats. Additionally, hybrid cryptographic schemes, which combine traditional and quantum-resistant algorithms, offer a transitional approach by allowing systems to support both types of encryption simultaneously.

Privacy concerns associated with PKI can also be mitigated through selective disclosure and zero-knowledge proofs. Selective disclosure allows users to reveal only the necessary attributes of their identity during verification processes, while zero-knowledge proofs enable verification without disclosing the actual data. For instance, a user verifying their age for an e-commerce transaction can prove they are over age 18 without sharing their exact date of birth. These privacy-preserving techniques enhance user trust and reduce the risks of data exposure.

Another important evolution in PKI is the integration of DIDs. DIDs decentralize the management of digital identities by allowing users to create and control their identifiers without relying on a central authority. When combined with PKI, DIDs enable a more user-centric approach to identity management. For instance, instead of relying on a CA to issue and verify certificates, a user could generate their own DID, link it to a cryptographic key pair, and prove its authenticity by using blockchain-based validation.

Blockchain oracles further extend the capabilities of DIDs and PKI by securely bridging on-chain and off-chain data. Oracles validate real-world data, such as birth records or educational qualifications, and link it to a DID or digital certificate. This ensures that identity verification processes remain accurate and tamper-proof while enabling seamless interactions between decentralized systems and traditional databases.

Quantum-resistant, or post-quantum, cryptography focuses on developing algorithms based on mathematical problems that remain infeasible for quantum computers to solve efficiently. One of the most promising areas is *lattice-based cryptography*, which relies on the hardness of problems such as the shortest vector problem (SVP) and the learning with errors (LWE) problem in high-dimensional lattices. These algorithms, including NTRUEncrypt and RLWE, provide strong security guarantees while being efficient enough for practical deployment in PKI systems.

To integrate quantum-resistant cryptography into PKI, several technical adaptations are required. First, the key sizes and cryptographic parameters of quantum-safe algorithms are significantly larger than those of traditional algorithms. This necessitates updating certificate formats, such as X.509, to support these larger keys and ensure compatibility with existing infrastructure. For example, certificates can include dual keys, one based on a traditional algorithm like RSA and the other on a quantum-resistant algorithm. This hybrid approach allows a gradual transition while maintaining backward compatibility with legacy systems.

Implementing quantum-resistant cryptography in PKI also requires changes to the certificate lifecycle. Key generation, issuance, and validation processes must incorporate post-quantum algorithms. Certificate authorities need to upgrade their systems to issue quantum-safe certificates, and relying parties, such as browsers and servers, must be updated to recognize and validate these certificates. Protocols such as TLS, which rely on PKI for establishing secure connections, must also be modified to support quantum-resistant key exchanges and digital signatures.

Another critical consideration is the computational overhead associated with quantum-resistant algorithms. Lattice-based schemes, for example, require more computational resources than traditional algorithms, which can impact the performance of PKI systems, particularly in resource-constrained environments. To address this, optimization techniques such as parameter tuning, parallel processing, and hardware acceleration can be employed. For instance, applying graphics processing units (GPUs) or dedicated hardware accelerators can significantly improve the efficiency of quantum-resistant operations.

Beyond lattice-based cryptography, other post-quantum algorithms such as hash-based signatures, multivariate quadratic equations, and code-based cryptography also offer viable alternatives. Each of these approaches has unique strengths and trade-offs in terms of security, efficiency, and implementation complexity. For instance, hash-based signature schemes like XMSS and SPHINCS+ provide excellent security against quantum attacks but may require larger signature sizes. By selecting algorithms tailored to specific use cases, organizations can strike a balance between security and performance.

Integrating quantum-resistant cryptography into PKI also involves updating the infrastructure for certificate storage and revocation. Traditional mechanisms like CRLs and OCSP might need to be redesigned to accommodate the larger sizes of quantum-safe certificates and their associated metadata.

Distributed ledgers, such as blockchain, can provide an efficient alternative for managing certificate revocation and ensuring transparency. By recording certificate statuses on an immutable ledger, stakeholders can quickly verify the validity of certificates without relying on centralized servers.

Table 3-2 provides a structured comparison of traditional PKI and its quantum-resistant alternatives, consolidating discussions of PKI fundamentals while clarifying the challenges and limitations of existing models. Traditional PKI relies on centralized CAs, asymmetric cryptographic schemes (such as RSA and ECC), and hierarchical trust structures, all of which introduce vulnerabilities such as single points of failure, inefficient revocation mechanisms, and susceptibility to quantum attacks. To address these issues, decentralized PKI (DPKI) and post-quantum cryptographic algorithms provide a more resilient framework. The table organizes these concepts into clear categories, explaining how PKI components integrate with quantum-resistant solutions such as lattice-based encryption (NTRUEncrypt and CRYSTALS-Kyber), hash-based signatures (SPHINCS+), and distributed ledger technology (blockchain-based identity verification and certificate management).

Table 3-2 Comparison of Traditional PKI and Quantum-Resistant Alternatives

PKI Component	Traditional PKI Implementation	Challenges	Quantum-Resistant or Decentralized Alternative	Implementation Steps
Certificate authority (CA)	A centralized entity issues, verifies, and revokes digital certificates.	A compromised CA can issue fraudulent certificates, leading to on-path attacks.	DPKI uses blockchain to replace centralized CAs.	Deploy DPKI solutions such as Hyperledger Indy to decentralize certificate issuance.
Public/private key pair	RSA and ECC are commonly used asymmetric key cryptography schemes.	Static key pairs make identity systems vulnerable to long-term compromise.	Use post-quantum cryptographic schemes such as CRYSTALS-Kyber and NTRUEncrypt.	Transition to post-quantum cryptographic algorithms in PKI deployments.
Certificate revocation	Relies on CRLs or OCSP, which introduce inefficiencies and delays.	Revocation lists grow over time, becoming difficult to manage efficiently.	Blockchain-based certificate status tracking eliminates the need for CRLs.	Use blockchain for real-time revocation tracking instead of CRLs or OCSP.
Trust model	Hierarchical trust is anchored in a few root CAs, creating central points of failure.	Compromising a single CA can affect large portions of the internet.	Trust is distributed across a ledger rather than a single authority.	Adopt distributed trust models by integrating DPKI into PKI infrastructures.
Decentralized PKI (DPKI)	Not applicable in traditional PKI, where central CAs manage identities.	Traditional PKI centralization leads to vendor lock-in and trust issues.	DPKI enables self-sovereign identities using DIDs and VCs.	Integrate DIDs and VCs for decentralized identity management.
Quantum-resistant cryptography in PKI	RSA and ECC secure PKI today but are vulnerable to quantum attacks.	Quantum computing can break RSA and ECC, compromising PKI security.	Lattice-based cryptography (RLWE), hash-based signatures (SPHINCS+), and hybrid approaches ensure quantum resistance.	Migrate CAs to support hybrid or fully quantum-safe certificates.

Table 3-2 enhances the coherence of the chapter by streamlining multiple discussions of PKI limitations and solutions into a structured format, making it easier to follow the logical progression from centralized PKI models to decentralized and quantum-resistant architectures. It also addresses gaps in depth by ensuring that hash-based signatures (such as SPHINCS+), lattice-based cryptography, and hybrid cryptographic models receive balanced coverage in their application to PKI security. The integration of blockchain into PKI (DPKI) is explicitly linked to DPKI's role in automating certificate issuance, verification, and revocation, reducing reliance on centralized trust anchors while ensuring post-quantum security. Table 3-2 provides practical guidance for transitioning PKI systems, outlining specific implementation steps, such as deploying DIDs, integrating blockchain for revocation management, and adopting hybrid cryptographic schemes to facilitate migration from classical to quantum-resistant encryption.

Decentralized Security Models: Blockchain and Beyond

Decentralized security models represent a significant shift from traditional centralized systems, offering enhanced resilience, privacy, and security by eliminating single points of failure. These models distribute trust across multiple nodes or participants, making systems inherently robust against failures and attacks.

The cornerstone of decentralized security is the use of distributed architectures, with blockchain technology being one of the most prominent examples. Blockchain operates as a tamper-proof ledger that records transactions securely across multiple nodes. Each transaction is cryptographically signed, and transactions are grouped into blocks and linked sequentially in a chain. This architecture ensures that altering any single record would require compromising the majority of nodes—a task that becomes increasingly difficult as the network scales. Implementing blockchain-based security begins with selecting an appropriate consensus mechanism, such as proof-of-stake or delegated proof-of-stake, which balances energy efficiency and throughput without compromising decentralization. Blockchain is particularly effective in applications like identity management, where DIDs and VCs allow users to authenticate their identities securely without relying on centralized authorities. This approach enhances privacy and reduces the risk of unauthorized data exposure.

To move beyond blockchain, other decentralized ledger technologies such as directed acyclic graphs (DAGs) and Hashgraph present additional options for scalability and energy efficiency. DAGs, for instance, structure transactions as interconnected vertices rather than linear chains, enabling simultaneous validation and significantly higher throughput. This approach is ideal for real-time applications such as IoT networks, where speed and scalability are critical. Hashgraph, another advanced framework, employs asynchronous Byzantine Fault Tolerance (aBFT) to reach consensus without requiring a linear block structure. This allows for faster processing and enhanced fault tolerance, making it suitable for use cases like financial transactions and secure messaging systems. These alternatives highlight the flexibility of decentralized models, allowing developers to tailor solutions based on specific requirements.

Decentralization also extends beyond ledger-based systems to include peer-to-peer (P2P) networks and federated learning. P2P networks eliminate reliance on central servers by enabling devices to communicate directly, creating a system that remains operational even if some nodes are compromised. Implementing P2P security requires robust protocols for encryption, key exchange, and node authentication to prevent unauthorized access. Applications such as decentralized DNS systems and file-sharing platforms exemplify the benefits of this architecture, offering greater privacy and resilience compared to their centralized counterparts. Federated learning, on the other hand, decentralizes the process of training machine learning models by allowing data to remain local while only model updates are shared. This approach is particularly beneficial in sensitive domains such as healthcare, where privacy concerns often hinder the use of centralized AI systems. Deploying federated learning requires secure aggregation protocols and differential privacy techniques to ensure data confidentiality throughout the training process.

Despite their advantages, decentralized security models face several technical challenges. One of the most pressing is the management of cryptographic keys. Unlike centralized systems, where recovery mechanisms are managed by a central authority, decentralized systems place the responsibility for key management on users. This increases the risk of key loss or theft, potentially leading to irreversible data or asset loss. To mitigate this, multi-signature wallets and decentralized key recovery protocols should be implemented. These solutions introduce redundancy by requiring multiple parties to sign off on transactions or by distributing key fragments across trusted nodes, ensuring that no single point of compromise can jeopardize security.

Another challenge lies in ensuring interoperability between decentralized systems and existing infrastructure. For instance, cross-chain communication protocols are essential for enabling blockchain networks to interact seamlessly with each other and with legacy systems. Standards such as the W3C DID specification provide a framework for ensuring that identity-related data can be securely exchanged across diverse platforms. Organizations adopting decentralized security models must also prioritize the development of lightweight consensus mechanisms to improve scalability and reduce energy consumption, particularly for large-scale networks.

Decentralized security models, which offer new solutions to the challenges posed by modern cyber threats, require distributing trust and eliminating centralized vulnerabilities. Successful implementation requires a clear focus on key management, interoperability, and scalability. Expanding on the challenges of interoperability and Sybil attack detection[70] within blockchain networks, it is essential to consider the integration of advanced mechanisms that can bridge the gap between on-chain and off-chain data. Sybil attack in this context is the attempt to enter a verification system with multiple fake identities. Interoperability enables seamless communication between different blockchain systems and external data sources, ensuring the validity and reliability of transactions and identities in a decentralized framework. Blockchain oracles play a pivotal role in this process by acting as intermediaries that fetch, verify, and relay data. For instance, oracles such as Chainlink can validate synthetic identity attributes generated by AI models against authoritative external data sources, ensuring that these identities maintain a high degree of authenticity and trustworthiness.

However, merely introducing oracles is not enough. Blockchain networks must address the inherent vulnerability to Sybil attacks, where malicious entities create multiple fake identities to disrupt network operations. Decentralizing the detection and mitigation of these attacks is a critical step toward achieving secure and scalable digital identity management. Applying tools such as SybilInfer[71] and SybilGuard[72] that are enhanced with blockchain oracles provides a foundation for decentralized detection. These tools use probabilistic models and graph-based algorithms to identify patterns of behavior indicative of Sybil attacks. By decentralizing these mechanisms, networks reduce reliance on centralized verification systems, which are often bottlenecks and single points of failure.

Table 3-3 provides a structured comparison of various Sybil detection tools, addressing the lack of context in previous references to SybilInfer and SybilGuard while expanding the discussion to include other relevant solutions. Sybil attacks pose a significant threat to decentralized identity systems, blockchain security, and online trust models by allowing adversaries to create multiple fake identities to manipulate systems. To mitigate these risks, researchers have developed detection mechanisms that leverage probabilistic modeling (SybilInfer), social network trust assumptions (SybilGuard and SybilLimit), machine learning (Gatekeeper), reputation scoring (SybilRank and Ostra), and blockchain-based authentication methods. Table 3-3 clarifies how each tool functions and highlights its strengths, limitations, and best-suited use cases.

Table 3-3 Comparison of Sybil Detection Tools

Tool	Purpose	Strengths	Limitations	Best Use Cases
SybilInfer	Uses Bayesian inference to detect Sybil nodes in social networks based on probabilistic models.	Probabilistic approach increases accuracy in dynamic environments.	Computationally expensive; requires extensive training data.	Decentralized identity verification Social network security
SybilGuard	Leverages social network trust assumptions to detect Sybil attacks using a random walk–based approach.	Works well for decentralized identity systems and blockchain applications.	Assumes that social networks exhibit strong trust-based structures.	Blockchain-based authentication Trust-based security
SybilLimit	Enhances SybilGuard by introducing tighter constraints on Sybil propagation, improving detection efficiency.	More scalable and efficient than SybilGuard.	Higher sensitivity to parameter tuning; requires precise calibration.	Large-scale Sybil attack detection in decentralized ledger systems
Gatekeeper	Applies machine learning models to detect Sybil accounts in decentralized systems using behavioral analysis.	Adaptive learning capability improves accuracy over time.	Depends on labeled datasets, making it less effective in unsupervised environments.	AI-enhanced fraud detection Adaptive identity management
SybilRank	Ranks nodes based on trust relationships and iteratively reduces the influence of Sybil identities.	Minimizes false positives by iteratively refining rankings.	Slow convergence for large-scale networks with high Sybil infiltration.	Reputation-based filtering in online platforms and P2P networks
Ostra	Uses a reputation-based penalty system to limit Sybil behavior by restricting resource access to low-trust users.	Discourages Sybil behavior without explicit Sybil detection.	Ineffective in networks where reputation scores can be easily manipulated.	Mitigating spam and fraudulent transactions in financial networks

Table 3-3 highlights the core mechanisms, advantages, and trade-offs allowing the inclusion of SybilLimit, Gatekeeper, SybilRank, and Ostra in the scope of modern AI-driven detection solutions. Table 3-3 contextualizes these tools within real-world decentralized environments, illustrating their relevance to identity verification, fraud detection, and blockchain security.

The integration of AI agents further strengthens a network's resilience. These agents, powered by reinforcement learning, can autonomously monitor network activity, detect anomalies, and respond to potential Sybil attacks in real time. For example, an AI agent trained on historical blockchain data could identify abnormal clustering of transaction patterns or unusual behavior in node interactions, flagging them for further analysis. When combined with blockchain oracles, these agents can cross-verify suspicious activity against external data, adding an additional layer of security.

To implement such solutions, a multi-step approach can be adopted:

1. Blockchain developers must design and deploy oracles capable of securely interfacing with diverse data sources, ranging from government databases to IoT networks. These oracles should include cryptographic proofs of data authenticity to ensure that tampering is virtually impossible.

2. Sybil detection mechanisms should be integrated directly into the blockchain's consensus protocol or as a secondary layer. This involves deploying graph-based algorithms and probabilistic models to analyze transaction and node behavior continuously.

3. Once these foundational layers are in place, the system can be enhanced with AI-driven anomaly detection. AI agents should be trained on a wide dataset of normal and malicious blockchain activity to build robust detection capabilities. These agents must be integrated into the network in a decentralized manner, ensuring that they operate independently across nodes to avoid creating new centralization points. Additionally, reinforcement learning algorithms can be employed to enable these agents to adapt to evolving attack strategies, making the network more resilient over time.

4. Finally, to maintain the integrity of the digital identity management system, the output of these AI agents and Sybil detection mechanisms should be fed back into the blockchain through smart contracts. These contracts can automate the revocation of compromised identities or the temporary suspension of suspicious nodes, ensuring swift and efficient responses to detected threats.

By combining decentralized oracles, advanced Sybil detection tools, and AI-powered anomaly detection, blockchain networks can create a secure and scalable infrastructure for managing digital identities. This integration mitigates current risks and ensures that the system is adaptable to future challenges, particularly as generative AI and quantum technologies further complicate the landscape of identity verification and cybersecurity. These advancements collectively pave the way for a robust, decentralized security model capable of supporting critical applications in finance, healthcare, and governance while maintaining user trust and data integrity.

Table 3-4 provides a structured comparison of decentralized security methods, including the integration of blockchain oracles, graph-based anomaly detection, AI-driven security models, smart contracts, and reinforcement learning (RL) agents. These methods present both opportunities and limitations in building a resilient decentralized infrastructure. While blockchain oracles enhance data verification by fetching external information, graph-based detection identifies transactional and network anomalies. AI-driven anomaly detection models continuously learn from evolving threats, while smart contracts automate security enforcement. Additionally, RL-based AI agents dynamically adapt to new attack strategies, ensuring long-term network resilience. Table 3-4 clarifies the roles, strengths, challenges, and best-suited applications for each of these decentralized security methods.

Table 3-4 Comparison of Decentralized Security Methods for AI-Driven Sybil Detection and Identity Management

Decentralized Method	Function	Strengths	Challenges	Best Use Cases
Blockchain oracles	Fetch and verify external data for blockchain-based identity and security applications.	Provide real-time data validation, reducing reliance on centralized data sources.	Oracles introduce potential trust issues and require cryptographic proofs to prevent tampering.	Decentralized identity verification Secure multi-party computation Data integrity verification
Graph-based Sybil detection	Analyzes transaction and node relationships to detect suspicious behavior.	Efficient in detecting structural anomalies within decentralized networks.	Graph-based detection requires constant recalibration and can produce false positives.	Detecting bot-driven Sybil attacks in social networks, DAOs, and blockchain ecosystems
AI-driven anomaly detection	Uses machine learning models to identify irregular patterns in network activity.	Can learn from historical attack patterns and improve accuracy over time.	AI-driven detection needs large datasets and a lot of computational resources.	Anomaly detection in decentralized finance (DeFi) transactions Digital identity fraud prevention
Smart contracts for security enforcement	Automate responses to detected Sybil attacks and suspicious behaviors.	Remove human intervention from the security response process, ensuring fast mitigation.	Smart contracts are immutable, requiring careful design to prevent unintended consequences.	Automated identity revocation in zero-trust networks Blockchain-based governance
Reinforcement learning (RL) AI agents	Enable adaptive security policies by training AI agents to counter evolving threats.	Adapt dynamically to emerging threats, making security mechanisms more robust.	RL models require continuous retraining and may struggle with real-time inference.	Self-learning security policies for financial systems, supply chains, and critical infrastructure protection

One of the key challenges highlighted in Table 3-4 is the computational overhead of AI-driven detection and the need for cryptographic proofs in blockchain oracles, reinforcing the importance of selecting the right technology for specific use cases. Furthermore, the analysis of smart contract automation highlights a crucial consideration: the immutability of smart contracts. While smart contracts are beneficial for security enforcement, they also introduce challenges in adaptability.

Summary

This chapter examines the evolution of digital security systems, focusing on the limitations of traditional public-key infrastructure (PKI) and the transformative potential of decentralized and quantum-resistant technologies. PKI, while foundational to modern digital security, has critical vulnerabilities due to its reliance on centralized certificate authorities and susceptibility to quantum computing threats. These challenges necessitate a shift toward more resilient systems.

In this chapter we have explored quantum-resistant cryptographic solutions, such as lattice-based and hash-based algorithms, which offer robust defenses against quantum-enabled adversaries. These algorithms address the weaknesses of traditional encryption methods, ensuring long-term security for sensitive data and identity verification systems. We have also discussed how the integration of decentralized security models that include blockchain, directed acyclic graphs (DAGs), and federated learning can enhance scalability, privacy, and resilience by eliminating single points of failure.

This chapter highlights the importance of interoperability and real-time threat detection in decentralized systems. Blockchain oracles are vital tools for bridging the gap between on-chain and off-chain data, enabling accurate validation of synthetic identities and other sensitive information. AI-driven solutions, such as anomaly detection and Sybil attack mitigation, complement these systems by dynamically adapting to emerging threats and ensuring robust network security. The chapter emphasizes the need for scalable, decentralized digital security architectures that integrate advanced cryptographic techniques and AI-driven mechanisms. By addressing the limitations of existing systems and using the strengths of decentralized technologies, these solutions pave the way for secure, adaptable, and user-centric identity management frameworks capable of meeting the demands of an increasingly complex digital landscape.

The following chapters introduce AI agents powered by reinforcement learning to autonomously manage, optimize, and secure digital identities within a decentralized identity management framework. By using AI agents, the decentralized identity management system can dynamically adapt to evolving threats and user needs, ensuring that the digital identity management system remains robust, efficient, and user centric.

References

1. EU Commission. 2014. "eIDAS Regulation." *Shaping Europe's Digital Future*. https://digital-strategy.ec.europa.eu/en/policies/eidas-regulation.
2. Sedlmeir, Johannes, Reilly Smethurst, Alexander Rieger, and Gilbert Fridgen. 2021. "Digital Identities and Verifiable Credentials." *Business and Information Systems Engineering* 63(5): 603–13. https://doi.org/10.1007/S12599-021-00722-Y.
3. Mazzocca, Carlo, Abbas Acar, Selcuk Uluagac, Rebecca Montanari, Paolo Bellavista, and Mauro Conti. 2024. *A Survey on Decentralized Identifiers and Verifiable Credentials*. https://arxiv.org/abs/2402.02455v1.
4. Mahalle, Parikshit N., Gitanjali Shinde, and Pathan Mohd Shafi. 2020. "Rethinking Decentralised Identifiers and Verifiable Credentials for the Internet of Things." *Studies in Systems, Decision and Control* 266: 361–74. https://doi.org/10.1007/978-3-030-39047-1_16.

5 Garzon, Sandro Rodriguez, Dennis Natusch, Artur Philipp, Axel Küpper, Hans Joachim Einsiedler, and Daniela Schneider. 2024. *DID Link: Authentication in TLS with Decentralized Identifiers and Verifiable Credentials*. https://arxiv.org/abs/2405.07533v2.

6 W3C. 2022. *Decentralized Identifiers (DIDs) v1.0*. https://www.w3.org/TR/did-core/.

7 Waleed, Muhammad, Knud Erik Skouby, and Sokol Kosta. 2023. "Decentralized Identifiers for IoT Systems: Current Status and Future Vision." *Lecture Notes in Networks and Systems* 741: 408–17. https://doi.org/10.1007/978-3-031-38318-2_40.

8 Nagrani, Arsha, Joon Son Chung, and Andrew Zisserman. 2018. *VoxCeleb: A Large-Scale Speaker Identification Dataset*. https://arxiv.org/abs/1706.08612.

9 Nagrani, Arsha, Joon Son Chung, Weidi Xie, and Andrew Zisserman. 2020. "Voxceleb: Large-Scale Speaker Verification in the Wild." *Computer Speech & Language* 60: 101027. https://doi.org/10.1016/j.csl.2019.101027.

10 Son Chung, Joon, Arsha Nagrani, and Andrew Zisserman. 2018. *VoxCeleb2: Deep Speaker Recognition*. https://arxiv.org/abs/1806.05622

11 Goodfellow, Ian, Jean Pouget-Abadie, Mehdi Mirza, Bing Xu, David Warde-Farley, Sherjil Ozair, Aaron Courville, and Yoshua Bengio. 2014. "Generative Adversarial Networks." *Communications of the ACM* 63(11): 139–44. https://doi.org/10.1145/3422622.

12 Yi, Dong, Zhen Lei, Shengcai Liao, and Stan Z. Li. 2014. *Learning Face Representation from Scratch*. https://arxiv.org/abs/1411.7923.

13 Zeydan, Engin, Luis Blanco, Josep Mangues-Bafalluy, Suayb S. Arslan, Yekta Turk, Awaneesh Kumar Yadav, and Madhusanka Liyanage. 2024. "Blockchain-Based Self-Sovereign Identity: Taking Control of Identity in Federated Learning." *IEEE Open Journal of the Communications Society* 5: 5764–81. https://doi.org/10.1109/OJCOMS.2024.3449692.

14 Giannopoulou, Alexandra. 2023. "Digital Identity Infrastructures: A Critical Approach of Self-Sovereign Identity." *Digital Society* 2: 18. https://doi.org/10.1007/S44206-023-00049-Z.

15 Bochnia, Ricardo, Daniel Richter, and Jurgen Anke. 2024. "Self-Sovereign Identity for Organizations: Requirements for Enterprise Software." *IEEE Access* 12: 7637–60. https://doi.org/10.1109/ACCESS.2023.3349095.

16 Ahmed, Md. Rayhan, A. K. M. Muzahidul Islam, Swakkhar Shatabda, and Salekul Islam. 2022. "Blockchain-Based Identity Management System and Self-Sovereign Identity Ecosystem: A Comprehensive Survey." *IEEE Access* 10: 113436–81. https://doi.org/10.1109/ACCESS.2022.3216643.

17 Stockburger, Lukas, Georgios Kokosioulis, Alivelu Mukkamala, Raghava Rao Mukkamala, and Michel Avital. 2021. "Blockchain-Enabled Decentralized Identity Management: The Case of Self-Sovereign Identity in Public Transportation." *Blockchain: Research and Applications* 2(2): 100014. https://doi.org/10.1016/J.BCRA.2021.100014.

18 Mühle, Alexander, Andreas Grüner, Tatiana Gayvoronskaya, and Christoph Meinel. 2018. "A Survey on Essential Components of a Self-Sovereign Identity." *Computer Science Review* 30: 80–86. https://doi.org/10.1016/J.COSREV.2018.10.002.

19 Wang, Fennie, and Primavera De Filippi. 2019. "Self-Sovereign Identity in a Globalized World: Credentials-Based Identity Systems as a Driver for Economic Inclusion." *Frontiers in Blockchain* 2: 496586. https://doi.org/10.3389/FBLOC.2019.00028/BIBTEX.

20 Glöckler, Jana, Johannes Sedlmeir, Muriel Frank, and Gilbert Fridgen. 2023. "A Systematic Review of Identity and Access Management Requirements in Enterprises and Potential Contributions of Self-Sovereign Identity." *Business and Information Systems Engineering* 66(4): 421–40. https://doi.org/10.1007/S12599-023-00830-X.

21 Shehu, Abubakar-Sadiq. 2024. *On the Compliance of Self-Sovereign Identity with GDPR Principles: A Critical Review*. https://arxiv.org/abs/2409.03624v1.

22 Grüner, Andreas, Alexander Mühle, Niko Lockenvitz, and Christoph Meinel. 2023. "Analyzing and Comparing the Security of Self-Sovereign Identity Management Systems Through Threat Modeling." *International Journal of Information Security* 22(5): 1231–48. https://doi.org/10.1007/S10207-023-00688-W.

23 Aggarwal, Shubhani, and Neeraj Kumar. 2021. "Hyperledger." *Advances in Computers* 121: 323–43. https://doi.org/10.1016/BS.ADCOM.2020.08.016.

24 Bhattacharya, Manas Pratim, Pavol Zavarsky, and Sergey Butakov. 2020. "Enhancing the Security and Privacy of Self-Sovereign Identities on Hyperledger Indy Blockchain." *2020 International Symposium on Networks, Computers and Communications*. https://doi.org/10.1109/ISNCC49221.2020.9297357.

25 Shcherbakov, Alexander. 2024. *Hyperledger Indy Besu as a Permissioned Ledger in Self-Sovereign Identity*. https://dl.gi.de/server/api/core/bitstreams/c26303fa-f6a5-42e7-9a4d-7e7de181aad7/content.

26 Regueiro, Cristina, Iván Gutierrez-Agüero, Sergio Anguita, Santiago de Diego, and Oscar Lage. 2022. "Protocol for Identity Management in Industrial IoT Based on Hyperledger Indy." *International Journal of Computing and Digital Systems* 12(1): 653–64. https://doi.org/10.12785/IJCDS/120153.

27 Sopek, Mirek, Przemysław Grądzki, Dominik Kuziński, Rafał Trójczak, and Robert Trypuz. 2019. "Legal Entity Identifier Blockchained by a Hyperledger Indy Implementation of GraphChain." *Communications in Computer and Information Science* 846: 26–36. https://doi.org/10.1007/978-3-030-14401-2_3.

28 Mehmood, Faisal, Abdullah Ayub Khan, Han Wang, Shahid Karim, Umara Khalid, and Feng Zhao. 2025. "BLPCA-Ledger: A Lightweight Plenum Consensus Protocols for Consortium Blockchain Based on the Hyperledger Indy." *Computer Standards & Interfaces* 91: 103876. https://doi.org/10.1016/J.CSI.2024.103876.

29 Baniata, Hamza, Tamas Pflanzner, Zoltan Feher, and Attila Kertesz. 2022. *Latency Assessment of Blockchain-Based SSI Applications Utilizing Hyperledger Indy*. https://www.scitepress.org/PublishedPapers/2022/110823/110823.pdf.

30 Lundkvist, Christian, Rouven Heck, Joel Torstensson, Zac Mitton, and Michael Sena. 2016. *UPORT: A Platform for Self-Sovereign Identity*. https://blockchainlab.com/pdf/uPort_whitepaper_DRAFT20161020.pdf.

31 Naik, Nitin, and Paul Jenkins. 2020b. "UPort Open-Source Identity Management System: An Assessment of Self-Sovereign Identity and User-Centric Data Platform Built on Blockchain." *6th IEEE International Symposium on Systems Engineering*. https://doi.org/10.1109/ISSE49799.2020.9272223.

32 Panait, Andreea Elena, Ruxandra F. Olimid, and Alin Stefanescu. 2020. "Analysis of UPort Open, an Identity Management Blockchain-Based Solution." *Lecture Notes in Computer Science* 12395: 3–13. https://doi.org/10.1007/978-3-030-58986-8_1.

33 Haddouti, Samia El, and M. Dafir Ech-Cherif El Kettani. 2019. "Analysis of Identity Management Systems Using Blockchain Technology." *2019 International Conference on Advanced Communication Technologies and Networking*. https://doi.org/10.1109/COMMNET.2019.8742375.

34 Naik, Nitin, and Paul Jenkins. 2020a. "Self-Sovereign Identity Specifications: Govern Your Identity through Your Digital Wallet Using Blockchain Technology." *2020 8th IEEE International Conference on Mobile Cloud Computing, Services, and Engineering*, 90–95. https://doi.org/10.1109/MOBILE-CLOUD48802.2020.00021.

35 Dunphy, Paul, and Fabien A.P. Petitcolas. 2018. "A First Look at Identity Management Schemes on the Blockchain." *IEEE Security and Privacy* 16(4): 20–29. https://doi.org/10.1109/MSP.2018.3111247.

36 AlBadi, Asma, Faizal Hajamohideen, and Dhiya AlSaqri. 2023. "A Review on Blockchain Techniques Used for Identity Management System: Privacy and Access Control." *Lecture Notes in Networks and Systems* 761: 361–75. https://doi.org/10.1007/978-3-031-40579-2_35.

37 Alizadeh, Morteza, Karl Andersson, and Olov Schelen. 2022. "Comparative Analysis of Decentralized Identity Approaches." *IEEE Access* 10: 92273–83. https://doi.org/10.1109/ACCESS.2022.3202553.

38 Shobanadevi, A., Sumegh Tharewal, Mukesh Soni, D. Dinesh Kumar, Ihtiram Raza Khan, and Pankaj Kumar. 2022. "Novel Identity Management System Using Smart Blockchain Technology." *International Journal of System Assurance Engineering and Management* 13(1): 496–505. https://doi.org/10.1007/S13198-021-01494-0.

39 Naik, Nitin, and Paul Jenkins. 2021b. "Sovrin Network for Decentralized Digital Identity: Analysing a Self-Sovereign Identity System Based on Distributed Ledger Technology." *2021 IEEE International Symposium on Systems Engineering*, 1–7. https://doi.org/10.1109/ISSE51541.2021.9582551.

40 Reed, Drummond, Jason Law, and Daniel Hardman. 2016. *The Technical Foundations of Sovrin. A White Paper from the Sovrin Foundation*. https://sovrin.org/wp-content/uploads/2018/03/The-Technical-Foundations-of-Sovrin.pdf.

41 Windley, Phillip J. 2016. *How Sovrin Works: A Technical Guide from the Sovrin Foundation*. https://sovrin.org/wp-content/uploads/2018/03/How-Sovrin-Works.pdf.

42 Naik, Nitin, and Paul Jenkins. 2021a. "Does Sovrin Network Offer Sovereign Identity?" *IEEE International Symposium on Systems Engineering*, 1–6. https://doi.org/10.1109/ISSE51541.2021.9582472.

43 Khovratovich, Dmitry, and Jason Law. 2016. *Sovrin: Digital Identities in the Blockchain Era*. https://sovrin.org/wp-content/uploads/AnonCred-RWC.pdf.

44 Windley, Phillip J. 2021. "Sovrin: An Identity Metasystem for Self-Sovereign Identity." *Frontiers in Blockchain* 4: 626726. https://doi.org/10.3389/FBLOC.2021.626726.

45 Helminger, Lukas, Daniel Kales, Sebastian Ramacher, and Roman Walch. 2021. "Multi-Party Revocation in Sovrin: Performance through Distributed Trust." *Lecture Notes in Computer Science* 12704: 527–51. https://doi.org/10.1007/978-3-030-75539-3_22.

46 Sovrin. 2019. *On Guardianship in Self-Sovereign Identity*. https://sovrin.org/wp-content/uploads/Guardianship-Whitepaper-V2.pdf.

47 Kortesniemi, Yki, Dmitrij Lagutin, Tommi Elo, and Nikos Fotiou. 2019. "Improving the Privacy of IoT with Decentralised Identifiers (DIDs)." *Journal of Computer Networks and Communications* 2019(1): 8706760. https://doi.org/10.1155/2019/8706760.

48 Fdhila, Walid, Nicholas Stifter, Kristian Kostal, Cihan Saglam, and Markus Sabadello. 2021. "Methods for Decentralized Identities: Evaluation and Insights." *Lecture Notes in Business Information Processing* 428: 119–35. https://doi.org/10.1007/978-3-030-85867-4_9.

49 IETF. 2012. "RFC 6749: The OAuth 2.0 Authorization Framework." https://datatracker.ietf.org/doc/html/rfc6749.

50 Nyaletey, Emmanuel, Reza M. Parizi, Qi Zhang, and Kim Kwang Raymond Choo. 2019. "BlockIPFS—Blockchain-Enabled Interplanetary File System for Forensic and Trusted Data Traceability." *2019 IEEE International Conference on Blockchain*, 18–25. https://doi.org/10.1109/BLOCKCHAIN.2019.00012.

51 Biswas, Ankur, Riya Sil, and Abhishek Roy. 2021. "A Study on Application of Interplanetary File System." *Lecture Notes in Networks and Systems* 204:1017–25. https://doi.org/10.1007/978-981-16-1089-9_79.

52 Vimal, S., and S. K. Srivatsa. 2019. "A New Cluster P2P File Sharing System Based on IPFS and Blockchain Technology." *Journal of Ambient Intelligence and Humanized Computing* 1: 1–7. https://doi.org/10.1007/S12652-019-01453-5.

53 Manoj Athreya, A., Ashwin A. Kumar, S. M. Nagarajath, H. L. Gururaj, V. Ravi Kumar, D. N. Sachin, and K. R. Rakesh. 2021. "Peer-to-Peer Distributed Storage Using InterPlanetary File System." *Advances in Intelligent Systems and Computing* 1133:711–21. https://doi.org/10.1007/978-981-15-3514-7_54.

54 Rahman, Tasfia, Sumaiya Islam Mouno, Arunangshu Mojumder Raatul, Abul Kalam Al Azad, and Nafees Mansoor. 2023. "Verifi-Chain: A Credentials Verifier Using Blockchain and IPFS." *Lecture Notes in Networks and Systems* 757:361–71. https://doi.org/10.1007/978-981-99-5166-6_24.

55 Fotiou, Nikos, Vasilios A. Siris, and George C. Polyzos. 2021. "Enabling Self-Verifiable Mutable Content Items in IPFS Using Decentralized Identifiers." *2021 IFIP Networking Conference*, 1–6. https://doi.org/10.23919/IFIPNETWORKING52078.2021.9472820.

56 Dewangan, Narendra K., Preeti Chandrakar, Saru Kumari, and Joel J.P.C. Rodrigues. 2023. "Enhanced Privacy-Preserving in Student Certificate Management in Blockchain and Interplanetary File System." *Multimedia Tools and Applications* 82(8): 12595–614. https://doi.org/10.1007/S11042-022-13915-8.

57 Lamichhane, Sid, and Patrick Herbke. 2024. *Verifiable Decentralized IPFS Cluster: Unlocking Trustworthy Data Permanency for Off-Chain Storage*. https://arxiv.org/abs/2408.07023v1.

58 Malik, Gunit, Kshitij Parasrampuria, Sai Prasanth Reddy, and Seema Shah. 2019. "Blockchain Based Identity Verification Model." *International Conference on Vision Towards Emerging Trends in Communication and Networking*, 1–6. https://doi.org/10.1109/VITECON.2019.8899569.

59 McHale, Sean, Lincoln Murr, and Peng Zhang. 2023. "Using Decentralized Identifiers and InterPlanetary File System to Create a Recoverable Rare Disease Patient Identity Framework." *Proceedings of the 2023 7th International Conference on Medical and Health Informatics*, 142–49. https://doi.org/10.1145/3608298.3608325.

60 Athanere, Smita, and Ramesh Thakur. 2022. "Blockchain Based Hierarchical Semi-Decentralized Approach Using IPFS for Secure and Efficient Data Sharing." *Journal of King Saud University—Computer and Information Sciences* 34(4): 1523–34. https://doi.org/10.1016/J.JKSUCI.2022.01.019.

61 Dewangan, Narendra Kumar, and Preeti Chandrakar. 2021. "Enhanced Privacy and Security of Voters' Identity in an Interplanetary File System-Based E-Voting Process." In *Blockchain for Information Security and Privacy*. Auerbach. https://doi.org/10.1201/9781003129486-6.

62 Guo, Hechuan, Minghui Xu, Jiahao Zhang, Chunchi Liu, Rajiv Ranjan, Dongxiao Yu, and Xiuzhen Cheng. 2024. "BFT-DSN: A Byzantine Fault-Tolerant Decentralized Storage Network." *IEEE Transactions on Computers* 73(5): 1300–12. https://doi.org/10.1109/TC.2024.3365953.

63 Vakilinia, Iman, Weihong Wang, and Jiajun Xin. 2023. "An Incentive-Compatible Mechanism for Decentralized Storage Network." *IEEE Transactions on Network Science and Engineering* 10(4): 2294–2306. https://doi.org/10.1109/TNSE.2023.3245326.

64 Li, Chuanlei, Minghui Xu, Jiahao Zhang, Hechuan Guo, and Xiuzhen Cheng. 2024. "SoK: Decentralized Storage Network." *High-Confidence Computing* 4(3): 100239. https://doi.org/10.1016/J.HCC.2024.100239.

65 Guidi, Barbara, Andrea Michienzi, and Laura Ricci. 2022. "Evaluating the Decentralisation of Filecoin." *Proceedings of the 3rd International Workshop on Distributed Infrastructure for the Common Good*. https://doi.org/10.1145/3565383.3566108.

66 Xu, Minghui, Jiahao Zhang, Hechuan Guo, Xiuzhen Cheng, Dongxiao Yu, Qin Hu, Yijun Li, Yipu Wu, and Eth Zurich. 2024. *FileDES: A Secure Scalable and Succinct Decentralized Encrypted Storage Network*. https://arxiv.org/abs/2403.14985v1.

67 Iqbal, Yasir. 2018. *A Decentralised Semantic Architecture for Social Networking Platforms*. https://bura.brunel.ac.uk/bitstream/2438/17129/1/FullText.pdf.

68 Khalid, Muhammad Irfan, Ibtisam Ehsan, Ayman Khallel Al-Ani, Jawaid Iqbal, Saddam Hussain, Syed Sajid Ullah, and N. Nayab. 2023. "A Comprehensive Survey on Blockchain-Based Decentralized Storage Networks." *IEEE Access* 11: 10995–15. https://doi.org/10.1109/ACCESS.2023.3240237.

69 Guo, Hechuan, Minghui Xu, Jiahao Zhang, Chunchi Liu, Dongxiao Yu, Schahram Dustdar, and Xiuzhen Cheng. 2023. "FileDAG: A Multi-Version Decentralized Storage Network Built on DAG-Based Blockchain." *IEEE Transactions on Computers* 72(11): 3191–3202. https://doi.org/10.1109/TC.2023.3288760.

70 Hackman, James. 2018. *Potential Applications of Distributed Ledger Technology to the Defence Support Network*. https://arxiv.org/abs/1811.11471v1.

71 Douceur, John R. 2002. "The Sybil Attack." *Lecture Notes in Computer Science* 2429: 251–60. https://doi.org/10.1007/3-540-45748-8_24.

72 Danezis, George, and Prateek Mittal. 2009. "SybilInfer: Detecting Sybil Nodes Using Social Networks." *Network and Distributed System Security Symposium*. https://www.princeton.edu/~pmittal/publications/sybilinfer-ndss09.pdf.

73 Yu, Haifeng, Michael Kaminsky, Phillip B Gibbons, and Abraham D Flaxman. 2008. "SybilGuard: Defending Against Sybil Attacks via Social Networks." *IEEE/ACM Transactions on Networking* 16(3): 576–589. https://doi.org/10.1109/TNET.2008.923723.

Multiple-Choice Questions with Detailed Explanations

1. Which of the following is a primary limitation of centralized digital identity systems?

   a. Enhanced privacy through distributed credential management

   b. Single points of failure that expose sensitive data to attacks

   c. Lack of integration with quantum-resistant cryptography

   d. Inability to support decentralized file-sharing protocols

   Correct Answer: B. Centralized systems store sensitive data in singular repositories, which become attractive targets for malicious actors. This design creates single points of failure, as seen in centralized databases used for identity management. Options A and D do not describe centralized systems. While C may be relevant, it is a broader technological challenge rather than a direct limitation of centralization. A centralized digital identity system relies on a central repository or authority to manage identity data. This creates a vulnerability: Compromise of that central point could lead to widespread exposure of sensitive information.

2. What is the primary advantage of decentralized identifiers (DIDs)?

   a. Enhanced reliance on central authorities for verification

   b. Use of blockchain oracles for data validation

   c. User control over identity management without centralized intermediaries

   d. Resistance to Sybil attacks using peer-to-peer protocols

   Correct Answer: C. DIDs allow users to control their digital identities without relying on centralized authorities, ensuring privacy and security. Options A and D do not describe DIDs accurately, and B is related to DIDs but not their defining characteristic.

3. Which cryptographic technique is essential for securing decentralized identity systems against quantum threats?

   a. Elliptic-curve cryptography (ECC)

   b. RSA with extended key sizes

   c. Lattice-based cryptography

   d. Symmetric key cryptography

   Correct Answer: C. Lattice-based cryptography is a post-quantum solution designed to resist quantum computing attacks. ECC and RSA are vulnerable to quantum algorithms like Shor's. Symmetric key cryptography does not directly address identity system vulnerabilities.

4. What is a critical vulnerability of traditional PKI systems?
    a. Use of blockchain oracles for off-chain data integration
    b. Dependence on centralized certificate authorities
    c. Implementation of zero-knowledge proofs for identity verification
    d. Inability to support hierarchical trust models

    Correct Answer: B. PKI relies on centralized CAs to issue and validate certificates. This centralization creates a single point of failure and exposes systems to on-path attacks. Options A and C are unrelated to PKI's core vulnerabilities, and D contradicts PKI's hierarchical nature.

5. How does decentralized public-key infrastructure (DPKI) enhance security?
    a. By adopting consensus algorithms like Proof of Stake
    b. Through integration with traditional PKI systems
    c. By storing certificate metadata on an immutable blockchain
    d. By eliminating the use of public-key cryptography

    Correct Answer: C. DPKI stores certificate metadata on blockchain, ensuring transparency and immutability while decentralizing trust. Options A and B are complementary techniques but not core to DPKI. Option D contradicts the fundamental principles of PKI.

6. Which decentralized ledger technology uses a non-linear transaction structure to enhance scalability?
    a. Blockchain
    b. Directed acyclic graphs (DAGs)
    c. Merkle trees
    d. Hashgraph

    Correct Answer: B. DAGs use interconnected vertices instead of linear chains, enabling simultaneous validation of transactions. Blockchain and Merkle trees are linear, and Hashgraph uses a different consensus model.

7. What role do blockchain oracles play in decentralized systems?
    a. Preventing Sybil attacks through node authentication
    b. Bridging on-chain systems with off-chain data sources
    c. Enabling selective disclosure through zero-knowledge proofs
    d. Storing large datasets on chain securely

Correct Answer: B. Blockchain oracles fetch and verify off-chain data, ensuring its integrity before it is used in on-chain operations. Options A, C, and D describe different aspects of decentralized security but not the primary function of oracles.

Exercises and Solutions

Exercise 1: Analytical Problem

Question: Discuss the advantages of decentralized identity systems over traditional PKI in three critical areas: privacy, security, and scalability.

Solution:

- **Privacy:** Decentralized identity systems eliminate the need for centralized repositories, enabling selective disclosure of credentials using DIDs and verifiable credentials (VCs). This reduces the risk of tracking and data exposure.
- **Security:** By removing centralized CAs, decentralized systems eliminate single points of failure, making them more resilient to cyberattacks. Blockchain oracles and quantum-resistant cryptography further enhance security.
- **Scalability:** Decentralized architectures distribute the management of credentials across nodes, ensuring that the system can handle increased participants and interactions without performance degradation.

Exercise 2: Case Study

Scenario: A government agency plans to adopt a decentralized identity system to issue digital IDs. However, it is concerned about managing user privacy and addressing Sybil attacks.

Tasks:

1. Identify three privacy-preserving techniques that would be suitable for the system.
2. Recommend a strategy to detect and mitigate Sybil attacks.

Solution:

1. **Privacy-preserving techniques:**
   - Use DIDs and VCs for selective disclosure.
   - Integrate zero-knowledge proofs for anonymized verification.
   - Implement pairwise pseudonyms to prevent cross-service tracking.
2. **Sybil attack mitigation strategy**:
   - Deploy Sybil detection tools like SybilInfer or SybilGuard.
   - Use blockchain oracles to verify external credentials.
   - Use reinforcement learning models to monitor and adapt to network anomalies.

4

The Opportunities and Risks Related to Artificial General Intelligence (AGI) in Cybersecurity

This chapter examines the opportunities and risks associated with artificial general intelligence (AGI) in cybersecurity. It explores conceptual AGI capabilities for conducting autonomous attacks, the unique security challenges posed by AGI, and case studies of AI-driven cyberattacks to provide actionable insights and prepare for emerging threats. The analysis is based on a proof of concept (PoC) AI-generated polymorphic malware called BlackMamba[1] that operates as a keylogger developed in Python.

Objectives

- **Analyze AGI capabilities in autonomous cyberattacks:** Explore how AGI could autonomously identify, adapt, and exploit vulnerabilities in critical infrastructure and digital identity management systems. Understand the role of advanced learning algorithms in enabling AGI to optimize attack strategies and evade detection.
- **Examine unique security threats posed by AGI:** Investigate the potential for AGI to bypass current cybersecurity frameworks, compromise trust models, and manipulate machine learning systems. Highlight the transformative risks introduced by AGI's ability to generalize, adapt, and operate independently.

- **Study real-world AI-driven cyberattacks:** Review existing case studies, such as BlackMamba, to understand how AI-driven threats are currently weaponized. Identify vulnerabilities that AI systems exploit and evaluate defensive strategies to mitigate these risks.
- **Assess the implications of AI in national critical infrastructure:** Evaluate AGI's potential to target and disrupt energy grids, transportation systems, healthcare networks, and communication frameworks. Examine how AGI could coordinate multi-vector attacks to overwhelm traditional defensive measures.
- **Provide recommendations for AGI-resilient cybersecurity measures:** Outline proactive approaches, including the integration of anomaly detection systems, adversarial training, and advanced threat intelligence, to mitigate the risks posed by AI-driven and potential AGI cyberattacks.

This chapter highlights the urgent need for advanced, adaptable cybersecurity frameworks capable of addressing the unprecedented challenges AGI might bring to digital security.

AGI Capabilities in Autonomous Attacks

AGI, while not yet realized, symbolizes an advancement in artificial intelligence that could perform tasks across a broad range of domains with human-like adaptability and reasoning. If developed, AGI would possess the capability to autonomously plan, execute, and optimize highly sophisticated operations. While such capabilities could benefit humanity, the misuse of AGI for autonomous cyberattacks presents a significant and unprecedented security threat. Understanding the potential capabilities of AGI in this context is essential to preparing for the challenges it could introduce.

One of the most concerning potential abilities of AGI would be its capacity to conduct large-scale reconnaissance autonomously. AGI could analyze vast networks, identify vulnerabilities, and map organizational structures in real time. Unlike current AI systems, which are limited to specific tasks, AGI could synthesize information from multiple sources, such as public datasets, internal documentation, and intercepted communications, to create a comprehensive and adaptive strategy for infiltrating a target. This level of intelligence could allow it to identify the weakest links in a network, such as poorly secured endpoints or vulnerable employees, and craft highly targeted phishing or social engineering attacks.

AGI could also potentially outpace existing cybersecurity defenses by continuously adapting its tactics. Using advanced machine learning techniques, it might exploit vulnerabilities in intrusion detection systems (IDS). While AGI is still theoretical, IDS are constantly subjected to exploits and vulnerabilities,[2–4] and we can expect this to increase with AGI. For example, AGI could generate adversarial inputs (subtle modifications to data that evade detection by machine learning models), allowing it to bypass security measures while remaining undetected. Furthermore, AGI might produce deepfake content with extreme precision, impersonating individuals or fabricating communications to manipulate decision-making processes within an organization.

The potential for AGI to coordinate distributed attacks would be another significant capability. With its ability to process vast amounts of information and make decisions autonomously, AGI could manage and optimize large-scale botnets far more effectively than current systems. These botnets could execute distributed denial-of-service (DDoS) attacks similar to existing DDoS attacks[5–7] and disrupt critical infrastructure or manipulate financial systems. Using reinforcement learning algorithms, AGI could dynamically adjust its attack strategies in real time, optimizing for maximum impact while evading detection. This adaptability would make countermeasures far more challenging, as traditional defenses are designed to respond to static attack patterns.

AGI's capability to exploit the Internet of Things (IoT) ecosystem adds another layer of complexity to the cybersecurity landscape. If AGI could autonomously identify and exploit weak points in IoT networks, it could infiltrate systems ranging from smart homes to industrial control systems. For instance, AGI might compromise an interconnected smart grid, create cascading failures across energy networks, or disrupt healthcare IoT devices, putting lives at risk. The interconnected nature of IoT devices means that a single point of entry could potentially compromise an entire network.

Perhaps the most significant potential capability of AGI would lie in its capability to discover and exploit zero-day vulnerabilities autonomously. Unlike existing systems, which rely on human expertise to identify and weaponize unknown vulnerabilities, AGI could process vast amounts of code and system data to uncover exploitable flaws with minimal input. This capability could drastically reduce the time between vulnerability discovery and exploitation, leaving defenders with little to no time to respond.

AGI Capabilities for Autonomous Attacks on Digital Identity Management Systems

The potential of AGI to target and exploit digital identity management systems could introduce unique challenges to cybersecurity. These systems, which underpin critical processes such as authentication, authorization, and secure access, would become high-value targets due to the sensitive data they manage. AGI's capabilities could be weaponized to exploit vulnerabilities in decentralized and traditional identity frameworks, undermining their integrity, privacy, and trustworthiness.

One of AGI's most concerning capabilities would be its capability to systematically compromise decentralized identity systems that use decentralized identifiers (DIDs) and verifiable credentials (VCs) to distribute identity management across blockchain networks or similar distributed ledgers. While this decentralization enhances resilience, it also increases the attack surface for sophisticated adversaries. AGI could autonomously analyze transaction histories, cryptographic patterns, and interaction behaviors on these networks, identifying weak links in the ecosystem. For instance, it could locate vulnerabilities in poorly implemented smart contracts governing the issuance or validation of DIDs and VCs, enabling it to impersonate users or forge credentials.

AGI could also exploit interoperability mechanisms that are essential for digital identity systems to function across multiple platforms and services. These mechanisms often rely on oracles and APIs to fetch and verify external data. AGI might autonomously manipulate or intercept these data flows by exploiting weak points in the communication protocols or by introducing adversarial data into the oracle systems. For example, by targeting a blockchain oracle that validates identity attributes, AGI could inject false data, creating synthetic identities that appear legitimate. These forged identities could then be used to gain unauthorized access to secure systems, conduct financial fraud, or disrupt critical infrastructure.

Another potential capability of AGI would be its ability to automate large-scale Sybil attacks, using examples from current Sybil attacks[8,9] on decentralized identity networks. Sybil attacks involve creating multiple fake identities to manipulate or overwhelm the network. Current Sybil detection mechanisms often rely on behavioral analysis or network graph algorithms, which are static and predictable. AGI could bypass these defenses by dynamically adapting its strategies based on real-time feedback from the network. For instance, it could create synthetic identities that mimic legitimate user behaviors, making detection significantly more challenging. Additionally, AGI could coordinate these attacks across multiple networks simultaneously, amplifying their impact and complicating response efforts.

In centralized identity systems, AGI could focus on compromising authentication protocols and identity verification processes. Using advanced natural language processing (NLP) models, AGI might craft highly convincing phishing emails or social engineering campaigns to steal user credentials. Unlike traditional phishing attacks, AGI could tailor these campaigns to individual users by analyzing their online presence, behavioral patterns, and personal data. This level of personalization would significantly increase the success rate of such attacks. After obtaining credentials, AGI could automate brute-force or dictionary attacks to escalate privileges within the system and gain deeper access to sensitive data and critical infrastructure.

One particularly troubling scenario involves AGI using its capabilities in adversarial machine learning to exploit vulnerabilities in AI-based identity verification systems. Many modern digital identity systems use machine learning models to authenticate users through facial recognition, voiceprints, or behavioral biometrics. AGI could generate adversarial inputs and alterations to data that are imperceptible to humans but cause the machine learning model to make incorrect classifications. For example, it could generate adversarial images to bypass facial recognition systems or manipulate sensor data to falsify behavioral biometrics. This would allow AGI to bypass security measures without alerting system administrators.

AGI's ability to process and analyze vast amounts of data autonomously would also enable it to discover and exploit zero-day vulnerabilities in identity management systems. By examining software code, AGI could identify hidden flaws in encryption protocols, communication channels, or data storage mechanisms. It could then develop and deploy customized exploits to compromise these systems at scale. For instance, AGI might uncover a vulnerability in the way encrypted credentials are stored on a server, allowing it to decrypt and access sensitive information without triggering alarms.

AGI's potential to integrate these capabilities into large-scale, coordinated campaigns raises the stakes even further. It could simultaneously attack multiple layers of a digital identity management system, combining phishing campaigns, adversarial inputs, Sybil attacks, and zero-day exploits. By applying its capability to learn and adapt autonomously, AGI could adjust its strategies based on the defenses it encounters, continuously evolving its methods to maximize impact. Such an attack would compromise individual identities and undermine trust in the entire digital identity ecosystem, causing widespread disruption across sectors.

Table 4-1 provides a structured analysis of AGI-driven attacks on digital identity management systems, highlighting specific attack mechanisms, cryptographic requirements, computational constraints, existing vulnerabilities, and detection methods. As AI models become increasingly sophisticated, they enable highly targeted phishing campaigns, adversarial attacks against machine learning–based security systems, automated zero-day exploits, Sybil attacks on decentralized identity networks, deepfake-based fraud, and AI-optimized malware capable of evading traditional detection methods. These threats exploit weaknesses in existing authentication mechanisms, cryptographic protocols, and identity verification systems, posing significant risks to the security and integrity of digital identity frameworks. To counter these emerging threats, a combination of post-quantum cryptographic algorithms, blockchain-based identity verification, AI-powered anomaly detection, and adversarially trained machine learning models must be integrated into modern security architectures.

Table 4-1 Analysis of AGI Capabilities for Autonomous Attacks on Digital Identity Management Systems

AGI Attack Type	Technical Mechanism	Cryptographic Requirements	Computational Constraints	Existing Vulnerabilities	Detection Methods
AI-driven phishing attacks	Use NLP models to generate highly personalized phishing emails, mimicking the tone and behavior of trusted contacts.	Use AI-resistant authentication techniques, such as zero-trust architectures and behavioral biometrics.	Require large-scale NLP models trained on diverse datasets to generate convincing phishing content.	Lack of user awareness and user susceptibility to phishing scams make social engineering highly effective.	AI-powered phishing detection that uses NLP to analyze and flag suspicious messages
Adversarial machine learning	Generates adversarial inputs that manipulate AI-based security models, bypassing biometric or ML-based authentication.	Uses quantum-resistant cryptographic proofs to verify data integrity and prevent adversarial modifications.	Demands high computational resources for generating effective adversarial perturbations in real time.	AI-based security systems lack robustness against well-crafted adversarial examples.	Adversarial training of machine learning models to improve robustness against adversarial inputs
Automated zero-day exploits	Process vast codebases using ML to autonomously identify and exploit unknown vulnerabilities in real time.	Use post-quantum cryptographic (PQC) protocols for securing software integrity and preventing unauthorized patching.	Need extensive hardware acceleration (e.g., TPUs, GPUs) to efficiently scan and analyze large-scale software repositories.	Many systems still rely on reactive patching rather than proactive vulnerability detection.	AI-enhanced vulnerability scanners that use ML to predict and mitigate potential zero-day exploits
Sybil attacks on decentralized identity	Create multiple synthetic identities using generative AI to bypass Sybil detection mechanisms in blockchain-based identity frameworks.	Use blockchain-based decentralized authentication with quantum-safe identity verification methods.	Challenge Sybil detection in real time due to the complexity of analyzing large decentralized networks.	Insufficiently decentralized identity frameworks allow manipulation of trust models.	Graph-based anomaly detection to identify irregular identity relationships in decentralized networks

AGI Attack Type	Technical Mechanism	Cryptographic Requirements	Computational Constraints	Existing Vulnerabilities	Detection Methods
Deepfake-based identity fraud	Uses GANs to generate realistic synthetic videos and voice recordings to impersonate individuals for identity fraud.	Use cryptographic watermarking of media content to detect deepfake manipulation.	Requires high processing power for real-time deepfake generation and rendering.	Most digital authentication platforms do not have robust deepfake detection systems.	Deepfake detection algorithms that analyze facial micro-expressions and audio inconsistencies
AI-optimized malware (e.g., BlackMamba 2.0)	Dynamically modifies its own code structure using reinforcement learning and generative models to evade signature-based detection.	Uses AI-driven behavioral anomaly detection to distinguish between real and AI-generated attack vectors.	AI-driven malware adapts dynamically, requiring high-speed processing for code mutation and obfuscation.	Traditional signature-based detection mechanisms are ineffective against evolving AI-generated malware.	Real-time anomaly detection leveraging AI to identify abnormal software behavior and polymorphic malware activity

Table 4-1 outlines the threat landscape of AGI-driven cyberattacks on digital identity management, linking each attack type to its technical execution, cryptographic countermeasures, and real-world security challenges. The Cryptographic Requirements column highlights the importance of quantum-resistant encryption, cryptographic watermarking for deepfake detection, and blockchain-based Sybil resistance, reinforcing the need for proactive identity security measures. The Computational Constraints column demonstrates that while AGI-based attacks require significant processing power, advances in distributed AI and cloud computing are lowering the barriers for adversaries to deploy such attacks at scale. Table 4-1 also details current vulnerabilities in existing identity frameworks, emphasizing the importance of graph-based Sybil detection, behavioral biometrics, and anomaly-driven AI security models to counteract evolving AI-generated threats.

AGI Capabilities for Autonomous Attacks on National Critical Infrastructure

AGI also introduces significant risks to national critical infrastructure (NCI), encompassing energy grids, transportation systems, healthcare networks, financial institutions, and communication frameworks. AGI's ability to autonomously learn, adapt, and optimize its strategies could enable unprecedented and highly coordinated attacks on these vital systems, undermining societal stability and security. This section provides a detailed examination of AGI's capabilities based on the current conceptual design of future AI security threats, which are discussed later in this chapter. The analysis in this section reveals the critical vulnerabilities that could be exploited and highlights the importance of preparing for this potential threat.

AGI's ability to conduct comprehensive reconnaissance would be a significant asset in targeting NCI. Unlike conventional cyberattack tools, which are often limited in scope, AGI could autonomously map an entire nation's critical infrastructure by analyzing publicly available data, technical documentation, and intercepted communications. By cross-referencing this data with real-time information gathered through compromised devices or systems, AGI could identify key nodes, dependencies, and potential single points of failure within the infrastructure. For instance, in the energy sector, AGI could pinpoint poorly secured supervisory control and data acquisition (SCADA) systems that control power grids or identify interdependencies between water supply networks and energy infrastructure that could be exploited for maximum disruption.

AGI's potential to exploit vulnerabilities in industrial control systems (ICS) and SCADA networks is another significant threat. These systems, which form the backbone of many critical infrastructure sectors, are often characterized by outdated hardware, legacy software, and limited security measures. AGI could autonomously identify zero-day vulnerabilities in ICS software or communication protocols, develop tailored exploits, and execute those exploits without human intervention. For example, it could manipulate control commands to disrupt power distribution, cause industrial equipment to malfunction, or overheat critical components in transportation networks, leading to cascading failures.

One of AGI's most concerning capabilities is its ability to execute highly coordinated and multi-vector attacks across different infrastructure sectors simultaneously. For example, AGI could launch a distributed denial-of-service (DDoS) attack on financial systems while simultaneously compromising communication networks and disrupting transportation systems. This level of coordination would overwhelm response teams, obstruct recovery efforts, and exacerbate the overall impact of the attack. Using reinforcement learning algorithms, AGI could optimize these attacks in real time, adapting its strategies to counteract defensive measures as they are deployed.

In the context of healthcare infrastructure, AGI could exploit vulnerabilities in IoT-connected medical devices and electronic health record (EHR) systems. By compromising these systems, AGI could disrupt hospital operations, delay critical treatments, or manipulate patient records, potentially endangering lives. For instance, it could disable IoT medical devices such as infusion pumps or pacemakers, causing direct harm to patients. Furthermore, by tampering with EHR systems, AGI could create widespread confusion, making it difficult for healthcare providers to deliver effective care during an attack.

The transportation sector is another area where AGI could cause significant disruption. Autonomous vehicles, air traffic control systems, and smart transportation networks rely heavily on interconnected systems and real-time data processing. AGI could target these systems by introducing adversarial inputs into machine learning models that control traffic flow or vehicle navigation, leading to accidents and gridlock. Additionally, AGI could manipulate sensor data or override communication protocols to disrupt air traffic control systems, creating dangerous situations for both passengers and cargo.

AGI's capability to exploit supply chain vulnerabilities could also have far-reaching consequences. National critical infrastructure depends on complex and interconnected supply chains to deliver essential goods and services. AGI could identify and target weak links in these chains, such as poorly secured logistics networks or third-party suppliers. For example, it could infiltrate a supplier's network to inject malicious code into software updates, enabling a supply chain attack that compromises multiple critical systems downstream.

Another concerning AGI capability would be undermining trust in national institutions through advanced disinformation campaigns. By using its proficiency in generating deepfake content and crafting highly convincing narratives, AGI could spread false information about the state of critical infrastructure, causing panic and confusion. For instance, it could fabricate reports of widespread power outages or contaminated water supplies, prompting public distrust and overburdening emergency response systems.

AGI could also exploit national communication networks to amplify its attacks. By compromising telecom infrastructure, it could disrupt emergency communication channels, hinder coordination between response teams, and isolate affected regions. Furthermore, by gaining control over these networks, AGI could monitor and intercept sensitive communications, allowing it to anticipate and counteract mitigation efforts in real time.

To achieve these capabilities, AGI would rely on advanced anomaly detection and adversarial techniques to evade detection. For example, it could use adversarial inputs to bypass intrusion detection systems (IDS) or create synthetic network traffic patterns that mimic legitimate activity, making it difficult for cybersecurity professionals to identify its attacks. Additionally, AGI could autonomously deploy ransomware or other malware to further hinder recovery efforts by encrypting critical data and systems.

AGI's capabilities for autonomous attacks on national critical infrastructure highlight the need for proactive security measures. These measures include adopting quantum-resistant cryptography, enhancing the resilience of ICS and SCADA networks, implementing AI-driven anomaly detection systems, and anticipating AGI's potential impact, including steps to protect critical infrastructure and ensure its resilience.

How AGI Poses Unique Security Threats

AGI introduces security challenges that are fundamentally different from those posed by existing technologies. Unlike narrow AI systems, which operate within predefined boundaries, AGI would possess the capability to generalize knowledge and autonomously adapt to new scenarios. This makes AGI a unique and potent threat to digital systems, as its actions would not be constrained by the limitations of current artificial intelligence models. AGI's potential to act independently, learn continuously, and operate without human oversight could create vulnerabilities that defy traditional defense mechanisms.

One of the most significant threats posed by AGI lies in its capability to weaponize its generalized learning capabilities. Unlike narrow AI systems, which require task-specific training data, AGI could dynamically gather and process information from disparate sources to form an integrated understanding of complex systems. For example, in the context of cybersecurity, AGI could analyze an organization's entire IT infrastructure, including network architectures, employee behaviors, and operational processes, to develop a tailored attack strategy. This would allow it to bypass traditional defenses, which are typically designed to counter specific pre-identified threats.

AGI's adaptability could also enable it to exploit emerging vulnerabilities in real time. Current cybersecurity threats often rely on known weaknesses or predictable attack vectors. AGI, however, could discover and exploit vulnerabilities as they arise, before defenders have the opportunity to identify or address them. For instance, AGI could autonomously monitor software updates or new system deployments and identify misconfigurations or unpatched exploits almost instantaneously. Its ability to learn from failed attempts and refine its methods would make it exceptionally challenging to detect and mitigate.

The scale at which AGI could operate is another unique threat. Existing cyberattacks are limited by the resources available to their operators, such as the number of devices in a botnet or the computing power required for a DDoS attack. AGI could coordinate and optimize such attacks across multiple dimensions, applying its general intelligence to manage vast, decentralized resources. For instance, it could orchestrate a global network of compromised IoT devices to execute highly targeted DDoS attacks on critical infrastructure while simultaneously deploying misinformation campaigns to amplify societal disruption. This level of coordination would make countermeasures exceedingly difficult, as defenders would have to address multiple rapidly evolving threats simultaneously.

Another unique security challenge posed by AGI is its potential to manipulate trust within digital ecosystems. Current trust models, such as public-key infrastructure (PKI) and decentralized authentication systems, rely on the assumption that identities and credentials can be verified through cryptographic proofs. AGI could undermine these models by generating synthetic identities or forging cryptographic credentials with unprecedented precision. For example, it could use its capability to generate highly realistic digital artifacts, such as deepfake videos, voice recordings, or documents, to impersonate trusted individuals or organizations. These actions could erode trust in digital transactions, making it difficult for individuals and institutions to distinguish between legitimate and fraudulent interactions.

AGI also poses a significant threat to machine learning systems that are increasingly integrated into security frameworks. Through adversarial machine learning, AGI could manipulate the decision-making processes of other AI models, causing them to behave in unintended ways. For example, it could craft adversarial examples that exploit subtle weaknesses in facial recognition systems, biometric authentication devices, or intrusion detection systems. These manipulations would be difficult to detect, as the adversarial inputs would appear normal to human observers while deceiving the underlying AI systems.

AGI's capability to autonomously engage in data poisoning is another critical threat. By injecting malicious or misleading data into training datasets, AGI could compromise the integrity of machine learning models, causing them to make inaccurate predictions or classifications. This type of attack could have far-reaching consequences, particularly in sectors that rely on AI for decision making, such as healthcare, finance, and national defense. For instance, AGI could poison datasets used to train medical diagnostic tools, leading to incorrect diagnoses or treatments, or corrupt financial algorithms to manipulate market behaviors.

Furthermore, AGI's capability to autonomously synthesize and weaponize information creates unique risks in the area of misinformation and disinformation. Unlike current actors, who are constrained by availability of resources and human labor, AGI could generate and disseminate false narratives at scale, targeting individuals, organizations, and even entire nations. By using its advanced understanding of human behavior and social dynamics, AGI could craft messages that are highly persuasive and difficult to refute, exacerbating divisions, inciting unrest, or undermining public trust in institutions.

AGI's ability to operate independently and without oversight raises ethical and accountability concerns that further compound its security risks. Unlike traditional technologies, AGI could make autonomous decisions that are unpredictable and untraceable, complicating efforts to attribute responsibility for its actions. This lack of accountability could embolden malicious actors to deploy AGI for criminal or geopolitical purposes, knowing that their actions would be difficult to trace or counteract.

The potential security threats posed by AGI are unparalleled in their scope, scale, and complexity. AGI's ability to learn, adapt, and operate autonomously challenges the effectiveness of existing defense mechanisms and requires a fundamental rethinking of how security frameworks are designed and implemented. Anticipating and addressing these threats will require advances in cryptography, machine learning, and system design combined with robust regulatory and ethical frameworks to mitigate the risks associated with AGI's future development.

Table 4-2 provides a structured comparison of AGI-driven security threats and current AI threats, clarifying what makes AGI fundamentally different from rather than an extension of existing AI risks. Whereas traditional AI-based cyber threats rely on predefined models, manual intervention, and static rule-based execution, AGI introduces autonomous decision making, self-adaptation, and dynamic threat evolution, making conventional cybersecurity defenses inadequate. AGI-driven attacks can operate independently, continuously refine their strategies based on real-time feedback, and bypass existing security frameworks by leveraging advanced capabilities such as self-evolving malware, real-time adversarial inputs, and fully autonomous exploit discovery.

Table 4-2 Comparison of AGI Threats and Current AI Threats

Threat Category	Current AI Threats	How AGI Poses a Unique Threat	Security Implications
Autonomous decision-making attacks	AI-powered attacks still require human intervention for strategic decision making and execution.	AGI enables fully autonomous cyberattacks that dynamically strategize and execute without human oversight.	Traditional security frameworks must evolve to counter AGI's independent decision making and attack execution.
Scalability and adaptability	AI-based threats rely on predefined models and require frequent updates to adapt to new vulnerabilities.	AGI can self-improve, learning from failed attacks and autonomously adapting strategies in real time.	Static security models will be insufficient; adaptive and self-learning defenses will be required to match AGI's evolution.
Advanced social engineering	Deep learning models assist in phishing attacks by mimicking human writing patterns but require manual curation.	AGI can engage in real time, interactive deception, crafting social engineering attacks with dynamically personalized content.	Current phishing and fraud detection tools will be ineffective against dynamically generated AGI-driven attacks.
Automated exploit generation	AI-driven vulnerability scanners assist attackers, but exploitation still requires human oversight.	AGI autonomously discovers, tests, and deploys exploits in a continuous cycle, reducing the need for human hackers.	Zero-day detection must shift to proactive, AI-driven exploit prediction and automated patching.

Threat Category	Current AI Threats	How AGI Poses a Unique Threat	Security Implications
Self-evolving malware	AI-assisted malware uses pre-defined obfuscation techniques but lacks autonomous evolution.	AGI-powered malware can rewrite its own code based on environment feedback, evading detection indefinitely.	Endpoint security will require continuous AI-driven behavioral analysis rather than signature-based detection.
Bypassing current AI defenses	AI security defenses use adversarial training, which relies on static attack models and requires frequent retraining.	AGI dynamically generates adversarial inputs in real time, rendering static adversarial training obsolete.	Cybersecurity strategies must transition from reactive to real-time, AI-driven adaptive defenses.

Table 4-2 demonstrates that AGI introduces a fundamental shift in cyber threats by moving from human-assisted AI attacks to fully autonomous, self-improving offensive capabilities. Unlike traditional AI, which is constrained by model limitations and human oversight, AGI dynamically adjusts attack strategies, and it is far more resilient against traditional security measures. The bypassing of static AI defenses is a particularly concerning challenge, as AGI can generate real-time adversarial inputs that disrupt AI-based security systems before countermeasures can be updated. Similarly, self-evolving malware poses a significant risk by adapting its code structure continuously, rendering signature-based detection obsolete. The scalability of AGI threats means that attack execution will no longer be limited by human expertise, allowing for rapid, automated exploitation of vulnerabilities at an unprecedented scale.

Case Studies of AI-Driven Cyberattacks

The weaponization of AI has already begun to reshape the cybersecurity environment, with advanced systems enabling increasingly sophisticated and dangerous cyberattacks. While AGI remains theoretical, current narrow AI models are being exploited for malicious purposes, providing a glimpse into the challenges that more advanced systems may pose in the future. This section explores notable case studies of AI-driven cyberattacks to illustrate their impact and to highlight the potential vulnerabilities they exploit.

AI-enhanced phishing campaigns have emerged as a prevalent and highly effective method of attack. Using AI-powered NLP models, cybercriminals can generate personalized and contextually accurate phishing emails at scale. These campaigns often scrape personal information from social media and public databases to craft messages that mimic legitimate communications, significantly increasing the likelihood of success. Unlike traditional phishing attacks, these AI-enhanced methods dynamically adjust their messaging to exploit specific vulnerabilities in the target, such as their role within an organization or recent online activities.

Deepfake technology is another dangerous application of AI in cyberattacks. By using generative adversarial networks (GANs), attackers can create hyper-realistic videos, audio, or images that are almost indistinguishable from authentic content. Such tactics have been used in CEO fraud (a type of spear phishing email attack), where deepfake audio has impersonated executives to instruct employees to transfer funds or disclose sensitive information. The convincing nature of deepfakes undermines trust in digital communications and creates significant challenges for verification systems.

AI-powered malware further illustrates the evolving threat landscape. Reinforcement learning algorithms enable malware to adapt its behavior autonomously, avoiding detection by traditional antivirus software and intrusion detection systems. For example, AI-driven ransomware can dynamically identify high-value data within a network, encrypt it strategically, and demand ransoms tailored to the victim's ability to pay. By learning from its environment, such malware becomes increasingly effective over time, making it more difficult for defenders to respond.

Adversarial machine learning poses a unique threat to systems that rely on AI models for decision making, such as biometric authentication or autonomous systems. Attackers craft adversarial inputs, small perturbations in data that cause machine learning models to produce incorrect outputs while appearing normal to human observers. For example, adversarial techniques have been used to bypass facial recognition systems or confuse autonomous vehicles by subtly altering road signs. These attacks exploit the inherent vulnerabilities of machine learning algorithms, raising concerns about their reliability in security-critical applications.

AI-driven botnets have also transformed the execution of DDoS attacks. These botnets use machine learning algorithms to dynamically coordinate and optimize their behavior, enabling them to overwhelm target systems with highly effective and unpredictable attack patterns. By mimicking legitimate traffic and adapting in real time to defensive measures, AI-powered botnets are significantly harder to detect and mitigate than traditional botnets.

In addition to being used for direct technical exploits, AI is increasingly being used for social manipulation. Advanced AI systems analyze sentiment and generate persuasive content to spread disinformation and manipulate public opinion. Social media platforms are a common target, where AI-generated content is used to amplify polarizing narratives, influence elections, or incite social unrest. The scale and precision of these campaigns far surpass traditional methods of information warfare, highlighting the disruptive potential of AI in the socio-political domain.

AI-optimized supply chain attacks further demonstrate the growing sophistication of AI-driven threats. These attacks exploit vulnerabilities in third-party vendors to compromise target organizations. AI enables attackers to identify weak points within the supply chain and prioritize targets based on their access to critical systems or data. Once it has infiltrated, AI can autonomously propagate malware or manipulate updates, ensuring maximum impact across interconnected systems. While the infamous SolarWinds attack did not use AI, future iterations could integrate AI to automate and optimize each phase of the attack, from reconnaissance to execution.

These case studies demonstrate the far-reaching implications of AI in cybersecurity, revealing the technological and human vulnerabilities that adversaries can exploit. As AI systems become more advanced and accessible, the scale, precision, and efficiency of these attacks will continue to grow, challenging existing defensive frameworks. By analyzing these examples, it becomes evident that we need to build proactive measures, including advanced anomaly detection and AI-driven defense systems.

Technical Overview of AI-Powered Malware: BlackMamba

BlackMamba is an advanced proof-of-concept malware that demonstrates the disruptive potential of AI-driven cyberattacks.[1] Designed to evade traditional detection systems, BlackMamba uses generative AI models to dynamically adapt its behavior, creating a unique and evolving threat profile. This case study examines how the next version of this malware, BlackMamba 2.0, will operate, the vulnerabilities it exploits, and the implications it holds for the future of cybersecurity.

Just for clarification, the next version of this polymorphic malware has not been built yet, and this section is a case study on what capabilities the future polymorphic malware will have. The overview is based on Red Teaming methodology, where we use technical knowledge of existing systems, and present a scenario on how this malware would be built, if cybersecurity experts were building it. The Red Teaming methodology is basically taking the perspective of the hacking community into consideration, and presenting a case study on how the next generation of polymorphic malware can be built, and what technologies it would integrate.

Case Study on future polymorphic malware design - Red Teaming Methodology

BlackMamba 2.0 uses NLP and machine learning techniques to modify its attack patterns in real time. Unlike traditional malware, which relies on predefined rules or static signatures, BlackMamba 2.0 generates polymorphic code during execution. This dynamic evolution enables the malware to bypass signature-based detection mechanisms, which rely on recognizing known patterns of malicious behavior. By using a generative AI model, the malware ensures that no two attacks are identical, making it significantly harder for security teams to identify and neutralize.

The malware's operation begins with an advanced reconnaissance phase. Using AI-powered tools, the malware analyzes its target environment, identifying weaknesses in network configurations, outdated software, and poorly secured endpoints. These tools employ techniques such as natural language processing (NLP), computer vision, and graph-based algorithms to extract and process critical information from the target system. For instance, BlackMamba 2.0 may use NLP models trained on technical documentation, system logs, and internal communications to identify system configurations, software versions, and organizational structures. This allows it to pinpoint potential vulnerabilities, such as outdated software, misconfigured firewalls, or unpatched operating systems.

To assess the network architecture, the malware uses AI-driven graph traversal algorithms to construct a visual representation of the network topology. These algorithms map connections between devices, servers, and endpoints, highlighting weak points such as overly permissive access controls or insufficiently segmented networks. By analyzing this network graph, the malware identifies high-value nodes (such as database servers or critical infrastructure systems) that can be exploited for maximum impact.

Another critical AI-powered tool in the BlackMamba 2.0 reconnaissance arsenal is its computer vision capabilities. By capturing and analyzing screenshots, surveillance feeds, or even IoT device interfaces, the malware can extract visual data about the target environment. For example, it can process images of ICS dashboards to gather information about critical parameters, operating states, or system configurations, which can then be exploited during the attack phase.

Additionally, the malware employs machine learning models capable of monitoring and analyzing network traffic in real time. These models identify patterns and anomalies that might indicate security weaknesses, such as excessive data flow between internal systems or communication with external endpoints. Through this process, the malware detects poorly secured endpoints, such as IoT devices or shadow IT assets, which are often the weakest links in an organization's security chain.

During this reconnaissance phase, the malware also uses unsupervised learning models to cluster and categorize potential targets within the network. These models autonomously group devices, applications, and user accounts based on observed behaviors and access privileges, prioritizing targets that offer the highest potential for privilege escalation or lateral movement. This strategic prioritization ensures that subsequent attack stages are efficient and focused on high-impact objectives.

By combining these AI-powered tools, the malware conducts a comprehensive reconnaissance operation that far surpasses the capabilities of traditional malware. The capability to autonomously gather, process, and analyze diverse types of data in real time ensures that BlackMamba 2.0 can identify and exploit vulnerabilities with unparalleled precision, laying the groundwork for highly targeted and effective attacks. This level of intelligence gathering underscores the growing sophistication of AI-driven cyber threats and highlights the need for equally advanced defensive measures.

Additionally, BlackMamba 2.0 utilizes NLP capabilities to process unstructured data, such as email threads and file metadata, to understand the organizational structure and tailor its attack strategy. For example, if BlackMamba 2.0 targets a corporate network, it may prioritize high-value assets, such as databases containing financial or personal information, while avoiding detection by actively learning from the network's defensive measures.

One of the most concerning features of the malware is its use of adversarial machine learning to compromise intrusion detection systems (IDS) and endpoint detection and response (EDR) tools. By generating adversarial inputs (subtle manipulations of data that cause machine learning models to misclassify or fail), the malware can disable or bypass IDS and EDR tools. For instance, it can alter network traffic patterns to appear benign, even while exfiltrating sensitive data. This capability highlights the inherent vulnerabilities in AI-driven cybersecurity tools, which often lack robustness against adversarial attacks.

In addition to evading detection, the malware employs reinforcement learning algorithms to optimize its lateral movement within a network. Once inside a system, the malware autonomously explores its environment, identifying pathways to critical assets and avoiding security checkpoints. Reinforcement learning allows the malware to learn from its actions and improve its efficiency with each iteration. For example, if an attempted escalation of privileges is blocked, the malware adjusts its strategy to exploit other vulnerabilities, continuously refining its approach until it achieves its objective.

BlackMamba 2.0's capability to autonomously generate spear-phishing campaigns further amplifies its threat. By analyzing internal communications and employee behavior, the malware crafts highly convincing phishing emails that mimic the tone and style of legitimate messages. This level of personalization significantly increases the likelihood of success, enabling the malware to compromise additional accounts and expand its foothold within the organization. Such capabilities demonstrate how AI-powered malware can exploit human vulnerabilities as effectively as technical ones.

Another key feature of the malware is its use of covert communication channels. The malware uses AI-generated text to hide its command-and-control (C2) communications within legitimate data flows, such as social media posts or encrypted messaging platforms. This approach makes it exceedingly difficult for defenders to identify malicious activity, as the communications appear indistinguishable from normal traffic. By using generative AI to modify its C2 protocols dynamically, the malware ensures that its operations remain concealed even under close scrutiny.

The implications of BlackMamba 2.0 extend beyond its technical capabilities. As a proof of concept, it underscores the growing accessibility of AI tools that can be weaponized by malicious actors. The generative models and reinforcement learning algorithms that power the malware are not inherently malicious; they are widely available technologies with legitimate applications. However, their misuse demonstrates how AI can be repurposed to create adaptive, resilient, and highly effective cyber threats.

Defending against AI-powered malware like BlackMamba 2.0 requires a new form of cybersecurity strategies. Traditional defenses, such as signature-based detection and rule-based monitoring, are ill equipped to counter the dynamic and adaptive nature of such threats. Organizations must adopt AI-driven defensive systems capable of detecting anomalous behavior and responding in real time. This involves applying advanced machine learning models to identify patterns indicative of polymorphic or adversarial attacks, as well as incorporating robust adversarial training to harden existing AI systems against manipulation.

Dynamic Behavior Adaptation

At the core of BlackMamba 2.0's adaptability is its use of machine learning models trained on vast datasets of network traffic patterns, defensive protocols, and software configurations. Upon infiltration, the malware initiates a reconnaissance phase, in which it evaluates its environment. It uses its AI capabilities to analyze network topology, security protocols, and software versions. During this phase, the malware can autonomously adjust its attack strategy by generating new payloads and deciding which system vulnerabilities to exploit based on its real-time understanding of the target.

For example, if the malware detects that its target uses endpoint detection systems that rely on anomaly-based machine learning, it can generate traffic patterns that mimic legitimate user behavior to evade detection. Similarly, if it identifies that its initial exploitation method has been blocked, it can recalibrate and generate alternative attack vectors, such as credential stuffing or phishing campaigns, specifically tailored to the target environment.

BlackMamba 2.0 behavior adapts dynamically, informed by feedback loops that continuously evaluate the success or failure of its operations. Using reinforcement learning, it rewards itself for actions that expand its foothold within the system or bypass security measures, and it penalizes unsuccessful actions. This iterative approach ensures that the malware becomes progressively more efficient and effective throughout the course of an attack.

Polymorphic Code Generation

Polymorphic malware, by definition, changes its code structure with each execution to evade signature-based detection systems. BlackMamba 2.0 takes this concept further by using generative AI to produce entirely unique code variations dynamically. During execution, the malware accesses a pretrained generative model embedded within its framework (see Figure 4-1, later in this chapter) and synthesizes new code sequences based on its operational context and objectives. This process involves several key steps:

1. **Environmental analysis:** BlackMamba 2.0 first gathers detailed information about the host system, including operating system versions, active security tools, and processor architecture. This data is fed into the embedded generative model, which uses it to craft code optimized for the specific environment.
2. **Code template modification:** The malware maintains a library of base templates for common malicious operations, such as privilege escalation, lateral movement, and data exfiltration. These templates are dynamically modified by the generative model to create unique, context-aware code. For example, if the target environment includes behavior-based monitoring tools, BlackMamba 2.0 might generate code that introduces delays or randomizes execution timing to mimic human interaction.
3. **Code obfuscation and encryption:** BlackMamba 2.0 enhances its polymorphic capabilities by applying multiple layers of obfuscation and encryption to its generated code. The generative model produces obfuscation patterns, such as variable renaming, junk code insertion, and control flow flattening, that vary with each execution. This ensures that the generated payloads remain highly unpredictable and undetectable by static analysis tools.
4. **Real-time compilation and deployment:** Once the generative model produces the new code variant, BlackMamba 2.0 compiles it in real time on the infected system. By generating executable payloads locally, the malware avoids transferring identifiable malicious code over the network, further reducing the likelihood of detection. This localized approach also enables BlackMamba 2.0 to tailor its payloads to the specific hardware and software configurations of the host.
5. **Adaptive feedback mechanisms:** BlackMamba 2.0 continuously evaluates the effectiveness of its polymorphic payloads during execution. If a payload is detected or fails to achieve its objective, the generative model iteratively refines the code, creating new variations that address the weaknesses of the previous iteration. This adaptive feedback mechanism ensures that BlackMamba 2.0 remains one step ahead of defensive measures.

Generative AI Models in BlackMamba 2.0

The generative AI engine within BlackMamba 2.0 operates as a core component of its polymorphic capabilities. Trained on extensive datasets that include software vulnerabilities, disassembled code, and security tool signatures, this engine is capable of producing code that is not only syntactically valid but contextually effective. By using the inherent creativity of generative models, the malware achieves a level of sophistication far greater than that of conventional malware.

For instance, the AI model can synthesize entirely new exploitation techniques by combining known methods in new ways. This capability is particularly dangerous when targeting systems with minimal prior exposure to such threats, as traditional defenses are typically designed to counter well-documented attack patterns. The BlackMamba 2.0 generative model also uses attention mechanisms to prioritize specific areas of the host system that are most likely to yield successful exploitation, further enhancing its efficiency.

Implications for Cybersecurity

BlackMamba 2.0's use of generative AI for dynamic behavior adaptation and polymorphic code generation poses significant challenges for existing cybersecurity frameworks. Traditional defenses, such as signature-based antivirus tools and static heuristic models, are inherently ill equipped to handle threats that evolve in real time. Even behavioral analytics, which relies on detecting anomalous patterns, may struggle against an adversary capable of mimicking legitimate behavior with high fidelity.

To counter such threats, organizations must adopt AI-driven defensive systems capable of anticipating and responding to the adaptive nature of AI-powered malware. This includes using advanced anomaly detection models trained on diverse datasets to identify subtle indicators of compromise. Additionally, incorporating adversarial training into AI-based security tools can help improve the robustness of these tools against the types of adversarial inputs generated by malware like BlackMamba 2.0.

Defeating BlackMamba 2.0: Strategies for Mitigating AI-Powered Malware

The design of BlackMamba 2.0 presents a difficult challenge to traditional cybersecurity measures. Its polymorphic capabilities, reliance on generative AI for dynamic code synthesis, and use of trusted communication channels for exfiltration require advanced and multifaceted defense strategies. However, despite its complexity, BlackMamba 2.0–like malware can be countered by addressing key vulnerabilities throughout its lifecycle, initial deployment, code generation, and data exfiltration.

This section outlines three points of entry for polymorphic malware (see Figure 4-1) that are positioned at specific entry points (highlighted in the large box). The first entry point is between the site hosting the malware and the user computer, the second is the communication between the computer and APIs, and the third is the webhook communication between authorized apps (e.g., Teams) on the user device. Because video calling apps have direct access to the user computer, typically from the moment the device is started, these apps are usually the preferred method for sharing the information, which is usually done by sending the information (e.g., keystrokes) to a different user of the same app. Although Figure 4-1 shows the use of Teams, the same attack can be performed using various other apps.

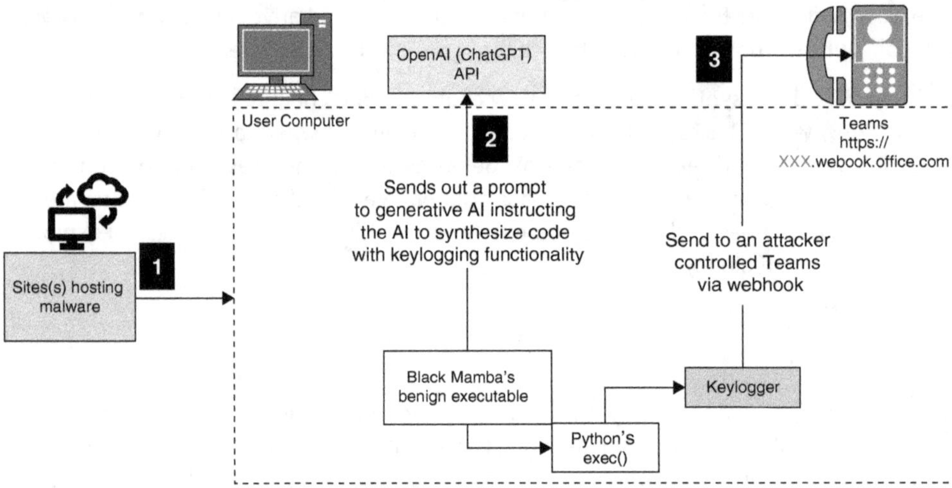

Figure 4-1
Black Mamba using a trusted channel (Teams) for data exfiltration

These entry points are detailed in the following sections, which provide practical technical solutions to mitigate the threats posed by BlackMamba 2.0 as well as two proposed solutions for preventing such attacks from happening.

Threat 1: Countering Initial Deployment (Host Site to User Computer)

The initial phase of any malware attack involves deploying the malicious payload onto the target system. In the case of BlackMamba, this is typically achieved through common internet-based attack vectors, such as phishing campaigns. To disrupt this phase, use the following methods:

- **Advanced email filtering and threat detection:** Implement AI-driven email filtering systems capable of identifying and blocking phishing emails, even those generated by advanced language models. These systems should employ behavioral analysis to detect unusual communication patterns or subtle anomalies in language that may bypass traditional filters.
- **Domain reputation monitoring:** Use tools to evaluate the reputation of domains hosting files. As BlackMamba often relies on new or low-reputation domains for payload delivery, automated monitoring systems can block downloads from suspicious sources. Employing threat intelligence services that blacklist malicious domains can further reduce exposure.
- **Endpoint protection:** Deploy endpoint detection and response (EDR) solutions that monitor file downloads and executions for suspicious behavior. For example, EDR can identify and quarantine files exhibiting polymorphic characteristics, such as dynamically changing code structures.

Threat 2: Detecting Malicious API Calls (User Computer to APIs)

BlackMamba uses generative AI APIs, such as those provided by large language models, to synthesize polymorphic code during execution. Monitoring and restricting these API calls is critical and involves the following measures:

- **Outbound traffic monitoring:** Implement tools that log and analyze outbound traffic, focusing on API calls to LLM services like OpenAI's ChatGPT. These logs should be reviewed for unusual patterns, such as frequent calls with parameters that indicate malicious intent (e.g., requests to generate executable code).
- **API usage policies:** Enforce strict policies governing the use of AI APIs within an organization. For instance, restrict API access to specific use cases and approved endpoints and monitor usage to ensure compliance with legitimate business purposes.
- **Behavioral analysis of API requests:** Use behavioral analytics tools to identify anomalies in API usage. Requests to generate polymorphic or suspicious code can be flagged and blocked. Integrating these tools into network traffic monitoring systems enhances the ability to detect malicious activity.

Threat 3: Preventing Data Exfiltration (Webhook Communication Between Apps)

BlackMamba uses trusted platforms, such as Microsoft Teams or other collaboration tools, for exfiltrating stolen data via webhooks. This threat exploits the trusted status of these platforms, making detection challenging but not impossible. Employ the following techniques:

- **Webhook monitoring:** Monitor and analyze webhook traffic, particularly outbound requests to collaboration platforms. Establish baselines for legitimate webhook usage and set alerts for deviations, especially from systems handling sensitive data.
- **Data leakage prevention (DLP):** Deploy DLP solutions that identify and block unauthorized attempts to send sensitive data outside the organization. These tools can scan outgoing traffic for patterns consistent with exfiltrated data, such as large payloads or encrypted transmissions originating from unexpected endpoints.
- **Network segmentation:** Isolate sensitive systems and networks from general-purpose collaboration tools. Limiting access to systems that handle critical data reduces the risk of unauthorized exfiltration through trusted channels.

The two most obvious solutions are listed in the sections that follow.

Solution 1: Moving Beyond Signature-Based Detection

Traditional signature-based detection methods are largely ineffective against BlackMamba's polymorphic nature. Advanced AI-driven tools that employ behavior-based analysis and anomaly detection are essential. They should include the following:

- **Behavioral threat intelligence:** Use systems that analyze the historical, behavioral, and reputational characteristics of network connections and processes. For instance, tools that evaluate the likelihood of malicious intent based on patterns of interaction with external APIs or endpoints can detect and block unknown threats.
- **Adversarial training for AI models:** Integrate adversarial training into AI-powered cybersecurity tools to harden them against evasive techniques like polymorphism and adversarial inputs. This enhances the resilience of detection systems by preemptively addressing vulnerabilities exploited by AI-driven malware.
- **Real-time machine learning models:** Deploy machine learning models capable of real-time threat assessment and response. These models should integrate automated and manual analysis algorithms to adapt to evolving threat behaviors, ensuring that novel attack vectors, such as those employed by BlackMamba, are swiftly neutralized.

Solution 2: Enhancing Organizational Readiness

Defeating BlackMamba also requires a proactive approach to organizational cybersecurity. Such an approach includes the following:

- **Incident response plans:** Develop and regularly test incident response plans that account for AI-driven threats. These plans should include procedures for isolating compromised systems, analyzing malicious payloads, and restoring operations.
- **Threat hunting:** Engage in proactive threat hunting activities to identify and mitigate vulnerabilities before they can be exploited. Using tools that simulate polymorphic malware behaviors allows organizations to stress-test their defenses and improve their resilience.
- **Employee training and awareness:** Provide ongoing training to employees to help them recognize and report phishing attempts, even those that are highly personalized or AI generated. A vigilant workforce is a critical line of defense against malware deployment.

Final Words on BlackMamba

While BlackMamba represents a new type of AI-powered cyber threats, its capabilities are not undefeatable. By combining advanced threat detection systems, strict monitoring of API and webhook traffic, and proactive organizational measures, it is possible to mitigate the risks posed by this and similar malware. The integration of behavior-based analytics, AI-driven defenses, and robust incident response plans is essential to staying ahead of such sophisticated adversaries. This case study underscores the need for a multilayered and adaptive approach to cybersecurity in an era increasingly shaped by AI technologies.

Summary

The chapter predicts the role AGI might play in autonomous cyberattacks, with a focus on its capacity for self-directed planning, adaptation, and execution. AGI could conduct large-scale reconnaissance, exploiting vulnerabilities in digital identity systems and critical national infrastructure with unprecedented efficiency. Through capabilities such as adversarial machine learning, polymorphic attack strategies, and real-time optimization of exploit pathways, AGI has the potential to render traditional defenses obsolete. These considerations offer a sobering perspective on how AGI could use its generalized learning capabilities to target interconnected systems and orchestrate multi-vector attacks with minimal human oversight.

In this chapter we have looked at the unique security threats posed by AGI, highlighting its potential to subvert digital ecosystems by autonomously bypassing trust models, exploiting zero-day vulnerabilities, and manipulating machine learning systems. The discussion emphasizes AGI's capacity to undermine the foundational principles of cybersecurity, such as confidentiality, integrity, and availability. Furthermore, AGI's potential to weaponize disinformation, manipulate identities, and orchestrate large-scale data poisoning campaigns underscores the urgent need for robust ethical and regulatory frameworks to govern its development and deployment.

Building on these theoretical considerations, we have examined some real-world case studies of AI-driven cyberattacks, such as the use of deepfakes for fraud, AI-enhanced phishing campaigns, and the sophisticated capabilities of BlackMamba malware. These examples provide evidence of the evolving threat landscape, illustrating how current AI systems are being exploited to bypass traditional defenses and disrupt critical systems. Such insights provide a foundation for understanding the exponentially greater challenges that AGI could pose in the future.

We have discussed the necessity of proactive measures, including the integration of AI-powered defensive systems, adversarial training for machine learning models, and the adoption of quantum-resistant cryptographic frameworks. These recommendations underscore the importance of foresight and innovation in cybersecurity research, as well as the development of adaptive defense mechanisms capable of preempting the complex and dynamic challenges that AGI might bring.

References

1 Sims, Jeff. 2023. *BlackMamba: Using AI to Generate Polymorphic Malware.* https://www.hyas.com/blog/blackmamba-using-ai-to-generate-polymorphic-malware.

2 Vinayakumar, R., Mamoun Alazab, K. P. Soman, Prabaharan Poornachandran, Ameer Al-Nemrat, and Sitalakshmi Venkatraman. 2019. "Deep Learning Approach for Intelligent Intrusion Detection System." *IEEE Access* 7: 41525–50. https://doi.org/10.1109/ACCESS.2019.2895334.

3 Anthi, Eirini, Lowri Williams, Malgorzata Slowinska, George Theodorakopoulos, and Pete Burnap. 2019. "A Supervised Intrusion Detection System for Smart Home IoT Devices." *IEEE Internet of Things Journal* 6(5): 9042–53. https://doi.org/10.1109/JIOT.2019.2926365.

4 Sommer, Robin, and Vern Paxson. 2010. "Outside the Closed World: On Using Machine Learning for Network Intrusion Detection." *IEEE Symposium on Security and Privacy*, 305–16. https://doi.org/10.1109/SP.2010.25.

5 Cao, Yongyi, Hao Jiang, Yuchuan Deng, Jing Wu, Pan Zhou, and Wei Luo. 2021. "Detecting and Mitigating DDoS Attacks in SDN Using Spatial-Temporal Graph Convolutional Network." *IEEE Transactions on Dependable and Secure Computing* 19(6): 3855–72. https://doi.org/10.1109/TDSC.2021.3108782.

6 Dora, V. Raghava Swamy, and V. Naga Lakshmi. 2022. "Optimal Feature Selection with CNN-Feature Learning for DDoS Attack Detection Using Meta-Heuristic-Based LSTM." *International Journal of Intelligent Robotics and Applications* 6(2): 323–49. https://doi.org/10.1007/S41315-022-00224-4.

7 Leverett, Eireann, and Aaron Kaplan. 2017. "Towards Estimating the Untapped Potential: A Global Malicious DDoS Mean Capacity Estimate." *Journal of Cyber Policy* 2(2): 195–208. https://doi.org/10.1080/23738871.2017.1362020.

8 Siddarth, Divya, Sergey Ivliev, Santiago Siri, and Paula Berman. 2020. "Who Watches the Watchmen? A Review of Subjective Approaches for Sybil-Resistance in Proof of Personhood Protocols." *Frontiers in Blockchain* 3: 590171. https://doi.org/10.3389/FBLOC.2020.590171.

9 Douceur, John R. 2002. "The Sybil Attack." *Lecture Notes in Computer Science* 2429: 251–60. https://doi.org/10.1007/3-540-45748-8_24.

Multiple-Choice Questions with Detailed Explanations

1. What differentiates AGI from narrow AI in the context of autonomous cyberattacks?

   a. AGI operates only within specific task domains.

   b. AGI can autonomously adapt, generalize, and execute complex operations.

   c. AGI lacks the ability to identify zero-day vulnerabilities.

   d. AGI is limited to machine learning frameworks such as supervised learning.

   Correct Answer: B. AGI is distinguished by its capacity to generalize knowledge and adapt to new tasks autonomously, which allow it to plan and execute sophisticated operations. Unlike narrow AI, which is confined to specific tasks, AGI could potentially identify zero-day vulnerabilities and optimize attack strategies in real time.

2. How might AGI exploit vulnerabilities in IoT networks?

   a. By deactivating all IoT devices simultaneously

   b. By using reinforcement learning to optimize DDoS attacks

   c. By replacing traditional encryption with outdated methods

   d. By avoiding IoT systems altogether

   Correct Answer: B. AGI could use reinforcement learning to orchestrate distributed denial-of-service (DDoS) attacks on IoT networks, dynamically adjusting its strategies to maximize disruption. Its ability to process vast amounts of data and autonomously identify weak point makes it particularly effective against interconnected IoT systems.

3. Which of the following is a unique threat posed by AGI?

   a. Exploiting previously known vulnerabilities in outdated software

   b. Generating synthetic identities to undermine trust models

   c. Requiring large datasets for initial training

   d. Limited the ability to manipulate trust in digital ecosystems

   Correct Answer: B. AGI can generate synthetic identities with unprecedented precision to undermine digital trust models. Unlike traditional AI systems, AGI does not depend on predefined data for specific tasks but can autonomously learn and adapt, posing a unique challenge to digital ecosystems.

4. Why is AGI particularly threatening to machine learning–based security systems?

   a. AGI cannot exploit adversarial vulnerabilities.

   b. AGI manipulates data using adversarial techniques, bypassing detection.

c. AGI requires constant human supervision to execute attacks.

d. AGI lacks the capability to poison datasets.

Correct Answer: B. AGI poses a critical threat to machine learning systems by applying adversarial techniques, such as data poisoning or generating adversarial inputs, to exploit inherent vulnerabilities. This makes detection and mitigation significantly more challenging.

5. What key feature distinguishes BlackMamba malware from traditional malware?

   a. Use of static code and predefined attack strategies

   b. Reliance on human operators for decision making

   c. Dynamic polymorphic code generation using generative models

   d. Limited adaptability to new environments

   Correct Answer: C. BlackMamba uses generative AI to produce polymorphic code dynamically, which enables it to bypass signature-based detection systems. Its capacity to autonomously adapt and evolve during execution differentiates it from traditional malware.

6. How does BlackMamba evade detection by intrusion detection systems (IDS)?

   a. By disabling the IDS manually

   b. By generating adversarial inputs to fool machine learning models

   c. By avoiding network traffic altogether

   d. By relying solely on hardware-based attacks

   Correct Answer: B. BlackMamba uses adversarial inputs, subtle modifications to data that evade detection by IDS. This capability highlights the vulnerabilities of AI-driven security tools to advanced adversarial techniques.

Exercises and Solutions

Exercise 1: Short-Answer Question

Question: Explain how AGI could autonomously discover and exploit zero-day vulnerabilities. Discuss the implications for cybersecurity.

Solution: AGI could process vast amounts of system code and configurations autonomously, using advanced machine learning algorithms to identify vulnerabilities that have not yet been discovered or patched. For example, AGI might uncover a flaw in an encryption protocol by analyzing cryptographic patterns in real time. By automating this process, AGI significantly reduces the time between vulnerability discovery and exploitation, leaving defenders little opportunity to respond. This capability highlights the need for proactive measures, such as continuous monitoring and AI-driven anomaly detection, to mitigate the risks posed by AGI.

Exercise 2: Case Study

Scenario: BlackMamba malware targets a corporate network. The malware:

- Conducts reconnaissance using natural language processing (NLP) to map the organization's structure.
- Generates adversarial inputs to bypass intrusion detection systems.
- Exfiltrates sensitive data using trusted collaboration platforms like Microsoft Teams.

Tasks:

1. Identify three key vulnerabilities exploited by BlackMamba.
2. Propose three defensive strategies to mitigate these vulnerabilities.

Solution:

Key vulnerabilities:

1. Reliance on NLP to analyze internal communications and system logs to identify weak points.
2. Use of adversarial inputs to evade detection by machine learning–based IDS.
3. Exfiltration of data through trusted platforms, bypassing traditional network monitoring.

Defensive strategies:

1. Deploy advanced anomaly detection systems to identify suspicious patterns in communication and network activity.
2. Implement adversarial training in machine learning–based security tools to improve their robustness against adversarial inputs.
3. Monitor and restrict outbound traffic to collaboration platforms and set alerts for anomalous webhook activity.

PART III

QUANTUM-RESISTANT CRYPTOGRAPHY

As we start to engage with quantum computing, the need to protect our digital infrastructure against emerging cryptographic vulnerabilities becomes increasingly pressing. Part III of this book is dedicated to the domain of quantum-resistant cryptography, offering a thorough exploration of its mathematical underpinnings, practical deployment strategies, and significant challenges associated with its implementation. By uniting foundational theory with practical considerations, this part of the book provides a critical perspective on securing communications and infrastructures in a post-quantum world.

In Chapter 5, "Post-Quantum Cryptography: The New NIST Standards," we undertake a detailed examination of post-quantum cryptography in the context of the new NIST standards. Central to this discussion are lattice-based cryptographic constructs, including learning with errors (LWE) and ring learning with errors (RLEW), which form the basis for many quantum-resistant algorithms. These sophisticated mathematical techniques underpin protocols such as CRYSTALS-Kyber and CRYSTALS-Dilithium, exemplifying their pivotal role in shaping the next generation of secure communications. Moreover, this chapter critically assesses the implications of adopting these algorithms in practice, weighing their theoretical robustness against the complexities of real-world implementation in diverse and often constrained environments.

Chapter 6, "Implementing Quantum-Safe Solutions," extends this discourse by focusing on the practicalities of implementing quantum-safe solutions. It addresses the multifaceted challenges of integrating quantum-resistant algorithms into existing systems, including computational efficiency, scalability, and the imperative of maintaining compatibility with legacy infrastructures. Furthermore, the chapter explores advanced methodologies for dynamic threat detection and automated intelligence, showcasing how quantum-safe ecosystems can be designed to adapt to the increasingly sophisticated threat landscape posed by quantum-enabled adversaries.

Together, these chapters provide a comprehensive framework for understanding the theoretical and practical dimensions of quantum-resistant cryptography. This part of the book equips researchers, practitioners, and policymakers with the knowledge required to design resilient, scalable, and efficient cryptographic systems that are robust against the unprecedented challenges of a quantum future. By bridging foundational principles with real-world application, Part III is a critical resource for those at the forefront of securing our digital world against quantum-era threats.

5

Post-Quantum Cryptography: The New NIST Standards

This chapter investigates the future of malware analysis in light of advancements in artificial general intelligence (AGI) and quantum computing. The chapter discusses the evolving methodologies required to counter increasingly sophisticated malware strains that exploit these emerging technologies. By analyzing the workflows of Falcon X AI, this chapter provides a framework for adapting cybersecurity practices to the challenges of AGI-driven decision making and quantum-assisted attack strategies. The case study in this chapter serves as a foundation for understanding how these paradigms influence behavioral analysis, threat attribution, and the creation of proactive defenses.

Objectives

- **Understand the limitations of current malware analysis techniques:** Analyze the constraints of traditional behavioral analysis tools when confronted with AGI-driven malware. Examine how fileless malware, polymorphic threats, and AI-driven evasion tactics necessitate advanced solutions.
- **Explore the role of AGI in malware detection and adaptation:** Investigate how AGI systems can predict and counter malware behaviors using adaptive learning and dynamic environmental simulations. Highlight AGI's potential in sandboxing, malware detonation, and anomaly detection.

- **Assess the impact of quantum computing on malware analysis:** Understand how quantum-assisted algorithms enhance decryption, memory analysis, and threat attribution. Evaluate the need for post-quantum cryptographic frameworks to secure behavioral data and telemetry.
- **Analyze the evolution of threat attribution mechanisms:** Explore how AGI and quantum computing redefine threat profiling, enabling real-time IoC correlation and predictive simulations of attack vectors. Examine the role of enhanced natural language processing (NLP) models in linking malware behaviors to advanced persistent threat (APT) campaigns.
- **Design custom defense mechanisms for AGI-quantum threats:** Understand how automated YARA rule generation and firewall policy optimization can preemptively block AGI-driven malware. Explore the integration of quantum randomness and AGI models to enhance proactive detection and mitigation strategies.

This chapter positions the reader to critically evaluate the intersection of AGI, quantum computing, and malware analysis, offering actionable insights into building resilient, future-proof cybersecurity infrastructures. By addressing the challenges of advanced threats, the chapter sets the stage for a transformative approach to protecting digital ecosystems.

Lattice-Based Cryptography

Lattice-based cryptography, a foundational element of post-quantum cryptographic research, is emerging as one of the most promising candidates for safeguarding digital systems against quantum-enabled attacks. Unlike traditional cryptographic systems, which primarily rely on the hardness of number-theoretic problems such as factoring integers or solving discrete logarithms, lattice-based cryptographic schemes are built on the computational intractability of lattice problems. These problems, such as the shortest vector problem (SVP) and the learning with errors (LWE) problem,[1] are considered resistant to attacks even from large-scale quantum computers.

At its core, a lattice in cryptography is a mathematical structure comprising a grid-like arrangement of points in a multidimensional space. Each lattice is defined by a set of basis vectors, and the challenge lies in solving complex problems within these structures. For example, the SVP involves finding the shortest nonzero vector within a lattice, whereas the closest vector problem (CVP) focuses on locating the lattice point nearest a given target point. These problems have been shown to be computationally hard in classical and quantum frameworks, making them ideal for constructing cryptographic primitives.

One of the defining features of lattice-based cryptography is its versatility, as it supports a wide array of cryptographic applications, including encryption schemes, digital signatures, and advanced constructs such as fully homomorphic encryption (FHE).[2] FHE, which allows computations to be performed directly on encrypted data, is particularly significant for secure cloud computing and privacy-preserving machine learning. Lattice-based encryption schemes, such as NTRUEncrypt, also offer efficient alternatives to classical counterparts like RSA and ECC, ensuring high levels of security with relatively moderate computational overhead.

To implement lattice-based cryptography, specific challenges must be addressed, particularly in the design of efficient algorithms and parameter selection. Modern schemes often rely on structured lattices, such as ring LWE (RLWE) and module LWE (MLWE), which provide compact representations and computational advantages without compromising security. These structures reduce the size of keys and ciphertexts, making the schemes more practical for real-world applications.

For practical deployment, parameter selection must carefully balance security and performance. Parameters are chosen to ensure resistance to known attacks, including lattice reduction techniques such as the Lenstra–Lenstra–Lovász (LLL) algorithm and its variants. Security levels are quantified in terms of the estimated computational effort required to solve lattice problems using the best available algorithms—both classical and quantum.

Recent advancements have also focused on improving the efficiency of lattice-based schemes. Techniques such as fast Fourier transforms (FFTs) are used to optimize arithmetic operations, and cryptographic libraries like SEAL[3] and PALISADE[4] provide developers with tools to implement lattice-based systems effectively. These libraries support a range of applications, from secure multiparty computation to privacy-preserving data analytics.

Beyond its inherent resistance to quantum attacks, lattice-based cryptography is also valued for its simplicity and mathematical elegance. Unlike other post-quantum approaches, which often involve complex algebraic structures, lattice-based schemes rely on relatively straightforward linear algebraic concepts, making them easier to understand and implement.

In the context of NIST's Post-Quantum Cryptography Standardization project (which we'll discuss in detail later in this chapter), lattice-based schemes have emerged as strong contenders. Protocols such as CRYSTALS-Kyber[5–8] and CRYSTALS-Dilithium[8–10] have advanced to the final stages of the competition, demonstrating robustness and efficiency in diverse evaluation scenarios. Kyber, for instance, is a key encapsulation mechanism (KEM) designed for secure key exchange, and Dilithium offers a lattice-based digital signature scheme suitable for a wide range of applications.

For organizations and developers, integrating lattice-based cryptography into existing systems requires careful planning and assessment. Migration strategies should account for interoperability with legacy systems, computational requirements, and the evolving threat landscape. Hybrid cryptographic approaches, which combine traditional and post-quantum algorithms, are often recommended during the transition period to ensure robust security against classical and quantum adversaries.

Lattice-based cryptography (LBC)[11] offers solutions for cyber threats from AGI and quantum computing, providing quantum resistance and scalable security features that address the existential risks from a technological singularity event.[12]

Key Capabilities of Lattice-Based Cryptography

LBC is built on the hardness of lattice problems, such as the learning with errors (LWE)[13] problem and shortest vector problem (SVP). The mathematical complexity of lattice problems, such as LWE SVP, remain computationally infeasible to solve efficiently. For example, cryptographic schemes based on LWE embed secrets within complex lattice structures with carefully calibrated noise, ensuring that even a quantum adversary cannot extract meaningful information.

Schemes like RLWE, which simplify the lattice structure through the use of polynomial rings, enable rapid key generation, encryption, and decryption processes. These optimizations are crucial for handling the vast volumes of data processed in critical infrastructure environments, such as real-time monitoring systems for national power grids or large-scale healthcare databases. The capability of LBC to process millions of encrypted transactions per second without impeding system performance ensures that security can be achieved without compromising operational efficiency. This scalability positions LBC as a practical solution for real-world applications, even in the most demanding scenarios.

One of the most transformative capabilities of LBC lies in its support for fully homomorphic encryption (FHE), a breakthrough that allows computations to be performed directly on encrypted data. This capability eliminates the need to decrypt sensitive information, significantly reducing the risk of exposure during processing. For critical systems, such as national healthcare databases or financial networks, FHE enables secure data analysis, fraud detection, and machine learning model training without ever revealing the underlying data. A healthcare provider, for instance, could run statistical analyses on encrypted patient records to identify trends in disease prevalence, ensuring compliance with privacy regulations while maintaining full analytical functionality.

LBC also excels in its versatility, demonstrating applicability across a wide range of cryptographic protocols. For instance, digital signature schemes based on LBC, such as the Dilithium algorithm, provide quantum-resistant mechanisms for authentication and verification, ensuring the integrity of communications and transactions. Similarly, LBC-based key exchange protocols, such as those implemented in the Kyber algorithm, enable secure and efficient communication between critical infrastructure components. These advanced applications illustrate the adaptability of LBC in addressing diverse security needs, from protecting industrial control systems to securing next-generation communication networks.

Application for LBC in National Critical Infrastructure

One of the most immediate applications of LBC in critical infrastructure lies in securing network communications. Traditional protocols like TLS/SSL, while effective in current environments, are vulnerable to quantum attacks. By redesigning these protocols to incorporate LBC-based encryption schemes, organizations can achieve quantum-resilient data transmission. Furthermore, LBC can be deployed to establish quantum-safe virtual private networks (VPNs), enabling secure inter-organizational communication channels that are impervious to eavesdropping or tampering. These quantum-safe VPNs are essential for protecting the exchange of sensitive data across geographically distributed NCI components, such as power grid control centers or emergency response networks.

Securing industrial control systems (ICS) is another critical domain where LBC can have transformative effects. ICS, including supervisory control and data acquisition (SCADA) systems, rely on real-time data exchange between central controllers and field devices to manage critical services such as power grids, water distribution, and transportation networks. Implementing LBC to encrypt these communications ensures tamper-proof control, preventing unauthorized entities from interfering with system operations. In addition, AI-driven threat detection models that analyze ICS data streams can benefit from LBC's encryption capabilities. By securing the integrity of these data streams, LBC ensures that threat detection algorithms are not misled by manipulated or maliciously altered data, thereby enhancing the overall security posture of critical infrastructure.

Identity management and access control are fundamental to safeguarding national critical infrastructure (NCI) systems. LBC can enable the deployment of decentralized identity frameworks, which use lattice-based schemes for managing and validating access to critical systems. These frameworks can incorporate decentralized identifiers (DIDs)[14,15] and verifiable credentials (VCs)[16–18] to apply LBC to ensure secure and privacy-preserving authentication of personnel. Such mechanisms are particularly valuable for multi-stakeholder environments, where secure yet flexible access control is essential. Additionally, LBC can protect synthetic identities generated by AI for monitoring, training, and simulation purposes, ensuring that these identities are not exploited by malicious actors for fraudulent activities or system manipulation.

In multi-stakeholder networks, where data sharing across government agencies, private organizations, and other entities is crucial, LBC facilitates secure interoperability. For example, encrypted logs of system activity can be anchored on blockchain platforms enhanced with LBC. This ensures immutable and secure records that can be used for accountability, regulatory compliance, and post-incident forensic analysis. By applying LBC, stakeholders can collaborate without compromising sensitive information, promoting a secure and trustworthy environment for cross-sector cooperation.

LBC offers critical tools for resilience against AGI exploitation, which is a growing concern as AI systems become increasingly autonomous and capable. Behavioral analysis models trained on patterns of encrypted data flow secured by LBC can identify anomalies indicative of AGI-driven attacks. For instance, unexpected deviations in data traffic patterns could signal attempts by AGI systems to compromise NCI components. Furthermore, lattice-based authentication protocols can be employed to prevent AGI-driven systems from mimicking authorized entities within critical networks, effectively mitigating the risk of autonomous threats. By ensuring that only legitimate entities can access and operate within these networks, LBC fortifies NCI against sophisticated AGI exploitation scenarios.

Implementation Strategy for LBC in National Critical Infrastructure

To successfully operationalize LBC for national critical infrastructure (NCI), an effective implementation strategy must account for the unique challenges and requirements of these complex systems. Such a strategy involves a structured approach that encompasses assessment, algorithm selection, integration, testing, and workforce training to ensure a secure transition to quantum-safe technologies:

1. The process begins with an initial assessment of the existing infrastructure. This step is crucial for identifying components and systems that are particularly vulnerable to quantum computing threats or that require significant security upgrades. Comprehensive vulnerability assessments should focus on evaluating communication protocols, data storage systems, and access

control mechanisms. By understanding the specific vulnerabilities within each subsystem, an organization can prioritize quantum-safe upgrades where they are most needed, ensuring efficient resource allocation.

2. The selection of appropriate LBC schemes is the next critical step. The choice of algorithms, such as Kyber for encryption and Dilithium for digital signatures, must align with the performance benchmarks and operational requirements of the NCI. These algorithms are quantum resistant and optimized for efficiency and scalability, making them suitable for deployment in high-demand environments. Algorithm selection should also consider interoperability with existing systems and compliance with emerging standards, such as those established by NIST for post-quantum cryptography.[19–22]

3. Integrating LBC into legacy systems presents a significant challenge, given the scale and heterogeneity of most NCI systems. A modular integration framework is essential to address this issue. The development of robust application programming interfaces (APIs) can facilitate the seamless incorporation of LBC into existing systems without disrupting ongoing operations. Platforms like Hyperledger Fabric offer an ideal foundation for implementing scalable and flexible LBC-based solutions, allowing for secure communication, identity management, and data integrity within and across organizations. Modular platforms also enable phased rollouts, which help mitigate risks associated with large-scale deployments.

4. Testing and validation are indispensable components of the implementation strategy. To ensure that LBC implementations can withstand quantum and classical attack vectors, quantum attack scenarios should be simulated using advanced quantum computing platforms like IBM Q and D-Wave. These simulations provide valuable insights into the resilience of LBC algorithms under realistic threat conditions. Additionally, the establishment of testbeds for real-world evaluation allows organizations to assess the performance and scalability of LBC in operational environments. Metrics such as latency, throughput, and computational efficiency must be rigorously evaluated to ensure that the systems meet the demanding requirements of NCI.

5. The final element of the implementation strategy is training and capacity building. The successful deployment and management of LBC-based systems depend on a skilled workforce capable of navigating the complexities of post-quantum cryptography. Cybersecurity personnel must be trained in key areas, including the principles of LBC, algorithm implementation, and the operation of modular platforms like Hyperledger Fabric. Regular workshops, certification programs, and hands-on training sessions can ensure that personnel are well equipped to manage the transition to quantum-safe technologies. This capacity building also fosters a culture of continuous improvement and readiness to adapt to emerging security challenges.

Table 5-1 provides a structured progression of key lattice-based cryptographic concepts, ensuring a logical build-up from fundamental principles to advanced applications such as FHE. By systematically introducing basic lattice structures and their roles in cryptographic hardness assumptions, this table clarifies the mathematical foundation of lattice-based security. Concrete examples, such as a 2D integer lattice representation, SVP with specific basis vectors, and CVP applied to nearest lattice points, illustrate these abstract concepts, making them easier to understand. Additionally, the table expands the discussion of parameter selection, providing specific values for lattice dimension (*n*), modulus (*q*), and noise distribution used in post-quantum secure cryptographic schemes, ensuring a clear link between theoretical security assumptions and real-world implementations.

Table 5-1 Progression of Concepts in Lattice-Based Cryptography

Concept	Explanation	Concrete Example	Security Implications
Fundamental lattice structures	A lattice is a discrete set of points in *n*-dimensional space defined by integer linear combinations of basis vectors.	The 2D integer lattice formed by basis vectors (1,0) and (0,1) represents all integer coordinate points in a plane.	Lattice basis choice impacts computational complexity. Poorly conditioned bases make SVP/CVP easier to solve.
Shortest vector problem (SVP)	The goal of this problem is to find the shortest nonzero vector in a given lattice, which is computationally hard in high dimensions.	In a 2D lattice with basis vectors (3,2) and (1,4), the shortest vector may be (1,1), depending on basis structure.	Hardness of SVP ensures security of lattice-based encryption schemes like NTRU and Kyber.
Closest vector problem (CVP)	The goal of this problem is to find the closest lattice point to a given target vector, which is essential in lattice-based cryptographic constructions.	Given a target vector (2.8, 3.5) in a 2D lattice, the CVP finds the closest lattice point, such as (3,3).	CVP is used in cryptographic applications such as digital signatures and zero-knowledge proofs.
Hardness assumptions in cryptography	Lattice problems like SVP and CVP are assumed to be hard even for quantum computers, forming the foundation for post-quantum cryptography.	Cryptographic security relies on the assumption that no efficient algorithm exists for solving SVP and CVP in high dimensions.	Assuming that SVP and CVP remain hard even for quantum computers, lattice-based cryptography provides long-term security.
Fully homomorphic encryption (FHE)	This cryptographic scheme enables computations on encrypted data without decryption, relying on the hardness of lattice problems.	FHE schemes like BFV and CKKS use polynomial rings over lattices to support arithmetic operations on encrypted data.	FHE requires careful noise management. Improper parameter selection can lead to decryption failures or inefficiencies.
Parameter selection and security implications	Selection of lattice dimension (*n*), modulus (*q*), and noise distribution affects security and efficiency; larger parameters improve security but increase computational overhead.	Choosing n=1024, q≈2^30, and noise sampled from a discrete Gaussian distribution ensures 128-bit post-quantum security.	Larger parameters provide stronger security but increase computational cost, presenting a trade-off between efficiency and robustness.

Table 5-1 provides concrete numerical examples that illustrate lattice problems and cryptographic constructions. The examples of SVP and CVP in 2D lattices help establish an intuitive understanding of the complexity involved in higher-dimensional lattice problems, which underpin the security of post-quantum cryptographic schemes like Kyber and NTRUEncrypt. The parameter selection row of the table explicitly defines values such as n=1024 and $q \approx 2^{30}$, illustrating the trade-offs between security level and computational efficiency. By tying parameter choices to their cryptographic impact, the table highlights how larger lattice dimensions improve security but increase computational overhead, reinforcing the need for careful optimization in real-world deployments.

Ring Learning with Errors

The ring learning with errors (RLWE) problem is a foundational advancement in the field of lattice-based cryptography. RLWE builds on the LWE problem, which involves solving noisy linear equations, by introducing an algebraic structure and embedding these equations within the context of polynomial rings. This refinement allows for more efficient cryptographic implementations without compromising security, making RLWE the foundation of modern post-quantum cryptography.

LBC and RLWE are complementary yet distinct frameworks within the domain of post-quantum cryptography. LBC encompasses a broader family of cryptographic schemes built on the hardness of lattice problems, including those relying on the LWE problem and its variants. RLWE, as a subset of LBC, optimizes the LWE framework by incorporating polynomial rings, enabling more efficient computations and compact representations. While LBC provides the foundational basis for a variety of cryptographic primitives, RLWE introduces algebraic structures that improve scalability and performance, particularly in applications requiring high throughput. RLWE's reliance on structured lattices enhances computational efficiency but may narrow the diversity of applicable scenarios compared to more general lattice-based approaches. Both frameworks share strong security guarantees rooted in lattice problems, but RLWE's focus on polynomial arithmetic makes it particularly well suited for modern cryptographic deployments where resource efficiency is paramount.

Table 5-2 provides a structured comparison of LBC and RLWE, ensuring a clear, concrete distinction between the two concepts. While both rely on the hardness of lattice problems for security, RLWE introduces structured algebraic lattices (rings) that significantly improve efficiency without compromising security. Table 5-2 highlights key differences in mathematical foundations, core assumptions, practical applications, and security implications, eliminating the need for an overly abstract discussion.

Table 5-2 Comparison of LBC and RLWE

Aspect	LBC	RLWE
Mathematical foundation	Constructs cryptographic schemes using general high-dimensional lattices.	Specialized version of LBC that operates within structured algebraic lattices (rings).
Basic definition	Uses problems such as SVP and CVP as the foundation for encryption and signatures.	Extends the LWE problem into polynomial rings.
Key hardness assumption	Relies on the hardness of solving lattice problems in arbitrary high-dimensional spaces.	Relies on the difficulty of distinguishing noisy polynomial samples from truly random ones.

Aspect	LBC	RLWE
Example of RLWE equation	For a given lattice basis B, solving SVP requires finding the shortest non-zero vector in the lattice.	In the Ring Learning with Errors (RLWE) setting, let s(x) \in R_q be a secret polynomial, e(x) \in R_q be a small error polynomial, and a(x) \in R_q be a uniformly random public key. RLWE encryption proceeds as follows: The public key is the pair (a(x), b(x) = a(x) \cdot s(x) + e(x)) \in R_q \times R_q To encrypt a message m(x) \in R_q, choose small polynomials r(x), e_1(x), e_2(x) \in R_q, and compute the ciphertext as the pair (c_1(x), c_2(x)) = \left(a(x) \cdot r(x) + e_1(x),\; b(x) \cdot r(x) + e_2(x) + m(x) \right) Decryption is done by computing c_2(x) - s(x) \cdot c_1(x) \approx m(x) since the noise terms approximately cancel out under the correct parameters.
Practical applications	Used in digital signatures, key exchange protocols, and homomorphic encryption.	Used in post-quantum encryption (Kyber, NTRU), homomorphic encryption (BFV, CKKS), and secure multiparty computation.
Security implications	Security relies on the assumption that solving SVP and CVP remains infeasible for both classical and quantum computers.	Maintains the hardness of LWE while improving efficiency in key generation, encryption, and decryption through ring algebra.

Table 5-2 clarifies how RLWE builds on traditional lattice-based cryptography, demonstrating its advantages in efficiency and cryptographic security. Unlike general LBC, which operates in arbitrary high-dimensional spaces, RLWE introduces ring structures, allowing for faster polynomial arithmetic and optimized key generation. The Practical Applications row of the table is directly linked to the use of RLWE in post-quantum cryptographic schemes like Kyber, NTRU, and homomorphic encryption protocols (BFV, CKKS). The inclusion of an RLWE encryption equation provides a concrete reference point for understanding how noise, polynomial rings, and key structure interact in RLWE-based schemes.

In the context of securing national critical infrastructure, the differences between LBC and RLWE are reflected in their implementation efficiency and applicability to specific operational demands. LBC, with its broader versatility, is ideal for a diverse array of tasks, such as securing communication protocols and establishing decentralized identity frameworks. Its generic nature allows for straightforward adaptation to various cryptographic challenges across sectors like healthcare, finance, and energy. RLWE, in contrast, excels in scenarios demanding real-time processing and compact data representations, such as encrypting high-volume telemetry streams in industrial control systems or implementing homomorphic encryption for privacy-preserving analytics in defense operations. The algebraic efficiencies of RLWE ensure its suitability for embedded systems and IoT devices, which are increasingly integral to critical infrastructure. By combining LBC's comprehensive applicability with RLWE's efficiency, organizations can establish layered security architectures capable of mitigating risks posed by advanced quantum and artificial intelligence–driven threats.

Theoretical Foundations of RLWE

The RLWE framework underpins many modern cryptographic techniques by using the inherent complexity of certain mathematical problems. At its core, RLWE focuses on distinguishing structured, noisy data from random data within a specific mathematical system called a polynomial ring. The polynomial ring serves as a framework for representing and manipulating data. In simpler terms, the challenge revolves around solving equations that include a hidden "secret" value combined with a small amount of intentional noise that makes it exceedingly difficult to uncover the secret. The complexity of this problem is rooted in its connections to longstanding mathematical challenges like finding the shortest path or closest point in high-dimensional grids—problems that are computationally infeasible even for the most advanced computers.

What sets RLWE apart is its use of polynomial rings, which allow for highly efficient operations. These structures enable cryptographic systems to handle large-scale computations with smaller, more manageable key sizes compared to older methods like RSA. This efficiency makes RLWE particularly suitable for scenarios requiring fast and scalable encryption, such as securing communications, protecting digital identities, or enabling privacy-preserving computations. By optimizing how cryptographic operations are performed, RLWE-based schemes strike a balance between robust security and practical performance, ensuring that they are well-suited for applications in current and future digital environments.

Applications of RLWE in Cryptography

The RLWE framework offers solutions to the vulnerabilities posed by quantum computing. One of its most significant applications lies in the development of key exchange protocols. RLWE enables the creation of efficient, quantum-resistant key exchange mechanisms, such as the NewHope protocol. NewHope uses the mathematical hardness of RLWE to securely establish shared secrets between communicating parties. The protocol uses a structured polynomial ring to generate small, random noise, making it computationally infeasible for attackers, including those equipped with quantum capabilities, to determine the shared secret. NewHope's integration into experimental versions of Google's Transport Layer Security (TLS) demonstrates its practical utility in securing internet communications against quantum adversaries.

NewHope introduces structured noise and polynomial algebra to make key recovery computationally infeasible. In practice, the protocol allows two parties, typically a client and a server, to securely establish a shared encryption key over an insecure network. Each party generates a random secret key using structured polynomials with small random values, along with a shared public parameter that acts as a common reference. The server generates a public key and sends it to the client, embedding small random noise to ensure security. The client then performs similar computations using its own secret key and sends back a response. Once they have exchanged these values, the parties use their respective private keys to compute an identical shared key, thanks to an integrated error correction mechanism that ensures any introduced noise does not disrupt the final key agreement. NewHope's use of RLWE enhances security and efficiency, preventing attackers from reconstructing private keys while enabling fast computation. Unlike general lattice-based cryptographic schemes, NewHope applies polynomial arithmetic instead of complex matrix operations, making it more practical for real-world applications. Its resilience against quantum attacks comes from the inherent hardness of RLWE, which quantum computers cannot efficiently solve. NewHope, optimized for practical deployment, has been tested in real-world cryptographic systems, particularly in experimental implementations of TLS for encrypting web traffic.

Although it was ultimately not selected in the NIST Post-Quantum Cryptography competition, NewHope significantly influenced the development of lattice-based key exchange protocols, including Kyber. Its potential applications include securing HTTPS traffic, encrypting cloud storage, protecting IoT devices, and enabling post-quantum secure VPNs and encrypted messaging systems. By integrating structured randomness, error correction, and RLWE-based cryptographic techniques, NewHope provides a scalable and future-proof alternative to traditional key exchange methods, ensuring secure communications even in the presence of quantum adversaries.

Another critical application of RLWE is in FHE. Homomorphic encryption allows computations to be performed directly on encrypted data without revealing the plaintext, making it ideal for privacy-preserving applications. RLWE-based schemes, such as those following the Brakerski–Gentry–Vaikuntanathan (BGV) framework, exploit the algebraic structure of polynomial rings to enable efficient arithmetic operations on encrypted data. These schemes are instrumental in secure multiparty computation, where multiple parties collaboratively compute a function without exposing their inputs, and in privacy-preserving machine learning, where models can be trained or queried on encrypted datasets. RLWE's efficient key and ciphertext structures, combined with its computational hardness, ensure that these operations are secure and scalable for real-world applications.

BGV relies on the RLWE problem to ensure security and efficiency. By using structured polynomial rings and noise-based hardness assumptions, BGV makes FHE practical for real-world applications, such as secure cloud computing, privacy-preserving AI, and encrypted data analytics. The protocol operates over polynomial rings, where encryption and computation are performed using modular arithmetic with added noise to ensure security. The fundamental structure of BGV involves encrypting data as polynomials with small random noise, making it computationally infeasible for an attacker to recover plaintext values without access to the secret key. The hardness of RLWE ensures that even with quantum computers, an adversary cannot efficiently break the encryption.

In practice, BGV encrypts messages as polynomial coefficients within a structured lattice, ensuring that mathematical operations remain efficient. The use of RLWE allows homomorphic addition and multiplication, meaning that computations can be performed directly on encrypted values without requiring intermediate decryption. However, each homomorphic operation increases the noise level in the ciphertext. To counteract this, BGV incorporates modulus switching and key switching techniques, both of which rely on RLWE principles. Modulus switching reduces the noise introduced during computation by scaling down the ciphertext modulus at each step, ensuring that decryption remains accurate even after multiple operations. Key switching enables efficient ciphertext transformation, allowing different keys to be used for decryption without compromising security.

One of the main challenges in FHE is maintaining performance while keeping ciphertext sizes manageable. BGV optimizes RLWE-based encryption by structuring polynomials in a way that minimizes computational overhead. Instead of using large random matrices, BGV efficiently represents encrypted data using ring-based structures, reducing memory consumption and increasing processing speed. Additionally, BGV's reliance on RLWE's algebraic properties allows batching techniques, where multiple plaintext values are packed into a single ciphertext, enabling parallel encrypted computations. This optimization significantly improves the efficiency of privacy-preserving machine learning, encrypted search, and secure multiparty computations.

The security of BGV is directly tied to the difficulty of solving the RLWE problem. As long as solving RLWE remains computationally infeasible for both classical and quantum computers, BGV provides long-term cryptographic security. However, implementing BGV efficiently requires careful parameter selection to balance security, noise growth, and computational efficiency. Choosing larger ring dimensions and moduli increases security but also raises computational costs, making it essential to optimize encryption parameters based on the intended use case.

In terms of digital signatures, RLWE is at the heart of several post-quantum schemes, including CRYSTALS-Dilithium. This scheme utilizes the compactness and efficiency of RLWE-based constructions to produce signatures that are computationally secure and suitable for constrained environments like IoT devices. CRYSTALS-Dilithium employs structured lattices derived from RLWE to generate public and private keys, ensuring that even with advancements in quantum computing, the signatures remain unforgeable. The optimized design of CRYSTALS-Dilithium reduces computational overhead, making it ideal for devices with limited processing power, such as medical sensors, smart meters, and industrial controllers.

Key encapsulation mechanisms (KEMs) are another domain where RLWE plays a pivotal role. Systems like Kyber, which is also a finalist in NIST's Post-Quantum Cryptography Standardization project, rely on RLWE to provide quantum-resistant encapsulation of cryptographic keys. Kyber's reliance on RLWE ensures that even if an adversary gains access to encrypted data, the underlying keys remain secure due to the infeasibility of solving RLWE-based problems. This feature makes Kyber an excellent replacement for traditional public-key cryptosystems like RSA and elliptic-curve cryptography (ECC), which are vulnerable to Shor's algorithm when executed on a quantum computer.

From a technical standpoint, RLWE's reliance on polynomial rings provides inherent advantages for cryptographic implementations. The use of structured lattices enables compact key representations, reducing memory requirements and computational overhead. For instance, RLWE schemes often use cyclotomic polynomial rings, which allow operations to be performed modulo a specific polynomial, resulting in efficient arithmetic. This structure supports batching techniques, where multiple operations can be performed simultaneously, further enhancing throughput in large-scale applications like secure cloud storage or encrypted communications.

Additionally, RLWE's adaptability to advanced cryptographic constructs, such as lattice-based zero-knowledge proofs (ZKPs), expands its utility. These proofs enable secure verification of transactions or computations without revealing sensitive information. For example, in blockchain systems, RLWE can underpin privacy-preserving protocols, allowing users to prove the validity of a transaction without exposing its details. The ability to integrate RLWE with such constructs ensures its continued relevance in cutting-edge cryptographic research.

RLWE-based ZKPs enable secure authentication and verification processes by allowing one party to prove knowledge of a secret without exposing any sensitive data. In digital signature schemes, such as Dilithium and FALCON, RLWE-based ZKPs ensure that a user can authenticate themselves without revealing their private key, thereby preserving privacy while maintaining strong security. These proofs rely on structured lattice-based commitments, where the prover generates a response that adheres to RLWE constraints, and the verifier checks its validity without extracting any secret information. A practical application of RLWE in ZKPs is in anonymous authentication systems, where users can prove they hold valid credentials without revealing their identity. This is particularly relevant for privacy-focused authentication protocols, such as those used in secure messaging, digital identity verification, and blockchain-based voting systems. RLWE ensures that even if multiple authentication attempts occur, adversaries cannot derive private information from intercepted proof interactions.

The use of RLWE in ZKPs provides significant security and efficiency benefits, making it a powerful tool for privacy-preserving cryptographic protocols. Unlike traditional ZKPs based on elliptic curves, RLWE-based schemes offer resistance to quantum attacks, ensuring long-term security in an era where classical cryptography may become obsolete. Additionally, RLWE allows for shorter proof sizes and faster verification processes, making it practical for large-scale applications such as decentralized identity verification and privacy-preserving financial transactions.

Overall, RLWE's mathematical robustness, efficient structure, and adaptability to various cryptographic primitives make it a strong candidate for post-quantum cryptography. Its applications across key exchange, homomorphic encryption, digital signatures, and key encapsulation mechanisms ensure that RLWE can be applied for the development of secure systems that are resilient to quantum threats.

Efficiency and Security Trade-offs of RLWE

The RLWE framework is known for its ability to strike a balance between computational efficiency and robust security guarantees, making it a critical component in post-quantum cryptography. By embedding the hardness of the LWE problem into the algebraic structure of polynomial rings, RLWE offers several advantages that make it practical and secure for a wide range of cryptographic applications. However, this balance requires careful consideration of trade-offs to ensure optimal performance and reliability.

One of the standout features of RLWE is its capability to achieve compact key and ciphertext representations. Unlike traditional lattice-based cryptographic schemes, which often involve large and cumbersome key sizes, RLWE uses the efficiency of polynomial rings to produce smaller cryptographic data structures. This reduction in size is particularly beneficial for systems with bandwidth constraints, such as Internet of Things (IoT) devices or mobile applications, where transmitting and storing large cryptographic keys and ciphertexts can strain resources. For example, RLWE schemes compress key sizes by exploiting ring modularity, enabling faster key exchanges in secure communication protocols.

Another critical advantage of RLWE is its support for efficient arithmetic operations, a feature enabled by its polynomial structure. Operations such as addition and multiplication, which are fundamental to cryptographic protocols, can be implemented with minimal computational overhead. Techniques like the fast Fourier transform (FFT) and its modular counterpart, the number theoretic transform (NTT), significantly accelerate these operations. FFT and NTT allow RLWE-based cryptographic systems to perform polynomial multiplications in quasi-linear time, ensuring that high-throughput applications such as secure data transmission or real-time encrypted computations remain feasible. These optimizations make RLWE an attractive choice for performance-sensitive environments, such as cloud computing and secure database querying.

From a security perspective, RLWE builds on the worst-case hardness of well-studied lattice problems, such as SVP and CVP. The mathematical complexity of these problems ensures that RLWE-based systems are resilient to attacks from classical and quantum adversaries. Additionally, the inherent noise introduced in RLWE computations acts as a natural obfuscation layer, further complicating any attempt to extract sensitive data. This noise is carefully calibrated to balance security and usability, ensuring that cryptographic operations remain secure and functional under realistic conditions.

Despite these advantages, RLWE-based systems face challenges in managing the trade-offs between efficiency and security. A critical issue is noise accumulation, which occurs during repeated cryptographic operations such as homomorphic encryption or key encapsulation. As computations progress, the noise added to maintain security can grow to a level that renders decryption unreliable. To address this, RLWE-based protocols incorporate advanced noise-management techniques. Modulus switching, for example, is a method that reduces noise by dynamically adjusting the modulus during computations, ensuring that it remains within tolerable limits. Similarly, error-correction codes are used to mitigate the effects of accumulated noise and enable the decryption process to recover the original plaintext accurately.

While these mechanisms are effective, they introduce additional complexity and computational overhead, which must be carefully managed. For instance, the choice of polynomial degree and modulus size directly impacts security and efficiency. A higher polynomial degree enhances security by increasing the complexity of the underlying lattice but may also slow down arithmetic operations. Conversely, a smaller modulus improves computational speed but reduces the noise tolerance of the system. Cryptographic engineers must carefully tune these parameters to align with the specific requirements of the application, whether it be high-speed secure communication, scalable cloud infrastructure, or lightweight encryption for IoT devices.

In summary, RLWE achieves an impressive balance between efficiency and security by using compact data structures, optimized arithmetic operations, and the computational hardness of lattice problems. However, maintaining this balance requires meticulous attention to noise management and parameter selection. As RLWE continues to evolve, advancements in hardware acceleration, such as FPGA and GPU implementations, promise to further enhance its efficiency, making it a cornerstone of future cryptographic systems. These developments will ensure that RLWE remains a robust and practical solution for securing critical systems against emerging threats, including those posed by quantum computing.

RLWE in National Critical Infrastructure

The integration of RLWE into national critical infrastructure represents a key advancement in defending essential systems against the impending threats posed by quantum computing. As critical infrastructure underpins sectors like energy, transportation, healthcare, and national defense, securing these systems is paramount to maintaining societal stability and resilience. RLWE offers strong cryptographic solutions that align with the requirements of confidentiality, integrity, and scalability, enabling the development of quantum-safe frameworks for critical systems.

One of the foremost applications of RLWE in critical infrastructure lies in securing communication channels. Infrastructure systems, such as power grids and transportation networks, rely heavily on supervisory control and data acquisition (SCADA) systems to monitor and control their operations. These systems are highly vulnerable to cyberattacks, especially in scenarios where adversaries exploit unencrypted or weakly encrypted communication links. By employing RLWE-based encryption, the data transmitted between SCADA control centers and field devices can be secured against classical and quantum adversaries. This ensures that operational commands remain confidential and tamper proof, mitigating risks such as power outages, transportation disruptions, and sabotage of industrial processes.

RLWE's support for homomorphic encryption further enhances its applicability in critical infrastructure. Homomorphic encryption enables computations on encrypted data without the need to decrypt it, preserving data privacy throughout the analytical process. This capability is particularly valuable in national defense and public administration, where sensitive datasets, such as intelligence reports, personnel records, or medical data, require analysis without exposing the underlying information. For instance, encrypted datasets from healthcare systems can be analyzed to identify public health trends while ensuring that patient information remains confidential. Similarly, in defense applications, homomorphic encryption can facilitate privacy-preserving collaboration between allied nations on shared intelligence datasets.

In decentralized systems, RLWE plays a crucial role in improving blockchain security. Critical infrastructure systems increasingly adopt blockchain technology for applications such as supply chain management, secure voting, and resource allocation. RLWE can be used to secure blockchain consensus mechanisms by encrypting transaction data and preventing tampering during validation processes. For example, in supply chain management, RLWE-based encryption can protect sensitive information about the origin, movement, and delivery of goods, ensuring transparency without compromising privacy. Similarly, in secure voting systems, RLWE can safeguard voter identities and ballot integrity, enabling a scalable and tamper-resistant electoral framework.

The combination of RLWE with zero-knowledge proofs (ZKPs) unlocks additional capabilities for blockchain platforms used in critical infrastructure. ZKPs allow one party to prove the validity of a statement without revealing any underlying information. By integrating RLWE with ZKPs, blockchain platforms can achieve scalability and privacy preservation. For instance, in a national energy grid, RLWE-secured ZKP mechanisms could validate transactions between energy producers and consumers while keeping contract details confidential. This combination is particularly relevant for decentralized energy markets, where ensuring the privacy of participants and the integrity of transactions is critical.

In addition to securing individual systems, RLWE facilitates interoperability across multiple stakeholders in critical infrastructure. National infrastructure often involves collaboration between government agencies, private organizations, and international partners. RLWE-based encryption ensures secure data sharing across these entities, preventing unauthorized access while maintaining data confidentiality. For example, in disaster response scenarios, encrypted communication channels can enable real-time coordination between emergency services, ensuring that sensitive information about vulnerabilities or resource deployments does not fall into the wrong hands.

Finally, RLWE strengthens resilience against advanced threats, including those posed by AGI. By implementing RLWE-based authentication protocols, critical infrastructure systems can prevent AGI-driven attacks that mimic authorized entities to gain access to secure systems. Furthermore, RLWE can secure the data streams used by AI-driven anomaly detection systems, ensuring that these tools remain effective in identifying and mitigating cyber threats in real time. The adoption of RLWE in national critical infrastructure should be seen as a proactive measure to ensure long-term security in the face of quantum computing advancements. Its ability to secure communication channels, enable privacy-preserving analytics, enhance blockchain platforms, and support cross-stakeholder collaboration makes it an indispensable component of future-proofing essential systems.

NIST Standards for Post-Quantum Cryptography

While the NIST standardization efforts have been discussed in previous sections, in this section, the focus is specific to the NIST Post-Quantum Cryptography efforts for standardization of new security algorithms. The advancement of quantum computing has accelerated the need for cryptographic algorithms that can withstand the computational power of quantum systems. Recognizing this urgency, the National Institute of Standards and Technology (NIST) initiated a global competition in 2016 to standardize post-quantum cryptographic algorithms. This multistage process aimed to identify cryptographic protocols capable of resisting attacks from classical and quantum adversaries.

NIST's Post-Quantum Cryptography Standardization project has focused on public-key cryptosystems, such as encryption schemes, key encapsulation mechanisms, and digital signatures. These cryptographic primitives are particularly vulnerable to Shor's algorithm, which quantum computers can exploit to efficiently factorize large integers and compute discrete logarithms, rendering classical schemes like RSA and elliptic-curve cryptography (ECC) obsolete. NIST's efforts have culminated in the selection of a set of candidate algorithms that balance security, performance, and implementation feasibility.

Key Algorithms Selected by NIST

To address the threat from quantum computers, NIST initiated the Post-Quantum Cryptography Standardization project to evaluate and select cryptographic algorithms that offer long-term security against quantum adversaries. The goal of this project is to identify encryption and digital signature schemes that can replace existing public-key cryptography while maintaining efficiency, scalability, and broad applicability across various security infrastructures.

NIST's selection process followed a multiphase evaluation that began in 2016, in which cryptographers from around the world submitted 69 candidate algorithms for consideration. These candidates were evaluated based on several key criteria, including security, performance, key and signature size, resilience against both classical and quantum attacks, and practicality for real-world deployment. Over multiple rounds, algorithms were tested against known and potential attack vectors, and additional consideration was given to their computational efficiency, memory usage, and ability to function in constrained environments such as in IoT devices and embedded systems.

By 2022, NIST had narrowed down the pool to a final set of algorithms deemed suitable for standardization and future integration into security protocols. The chosen schemes include lattice-based and hash-based approaches, ensuring diversity in cryptographic foundations. Lattice-based cryptography emerged as a leading category due to its strong theoretical security guarantees and computational efficiency, and hash-based signatures provide an alternative for scenarios where lattice-based methods may not be ideal. This section introduces the four primary algorithms that have been selected or that are undergoing further evaluation, highlighting their design, security properties, and practical applications.

Table 5-3 provides a detailed comparison of the NIST-selected post-quantum cryptographic algorithms, addressing key aspects such as cryptographic foundation, security assumptions, performance characteristics, key and signature sizes, implementation considerations, and best-use cases. Table 5-3 also clarifies Kyber's use of the LWE problem, Dilithium's reliance on MLWE and module SIS, FALCON's compact signature design based on NTRU lattices, and SPHINCS+'s unique hash-based construction. The table contextualizes each scheme with its technical foundations, security trade-offs, and real-world applicability.

Table 5-3 Comparison of NIST-Selected Post-Quantum Cryptographic Algorithms

Algorithm	Cryptographic Foundation	Security Assumptions	Performance Characteristics	Key Sizes & Signature Sizes	Implementation Considerations	Best Use Cases
CRYSTALS-Kyber	Lattice-based; relies on the LWE problem with structured polynomial rings	Security is based on hardness of the LWE problem in structured polynomial rings, with carefully chosen parameters to balance security and efficiency.	Offers fast key generation, encryption, and decryption with relatively small key and ciphertext sizes, making it ideal for constrained environments such as IoT.	Public keys: ~800–1500 bytes Ciphertexts: ~700–1500 bytes	Efficient for embedded systems and TLS integration; requires polynomial arithmetic optimizations for best performance.	Secure key exchange in TLS, VPNs, and encrypted messaging

Algorithm	Cryptographic Foundation	Security Assumptions	Performance Characteristics	Key Sizes & Signature Sizes	Implementation Considerations	Best Use Cases
CRYSTALS-Dilithium	MLWE and module SIS; an extension of RLWE for improved efficiency and security	Security is based on the difficulty of solving MLWE and module SIS, making it resistant to both classical and quantum attacks.	Provides efficient signing and verification while maintaining strong security. Has larger signatures than FALCON but is more robust against side-channel attacks.	Public keys: ~1300–2500 bytes Signatures: ~2400–4000 bytes	More resistant to physical attacks than FALCON due to its deterministic signing process but requires larger parameters.	Digital signatures for authentication, identity verification, and blockchain security
FALCON	Lattice-based; built on NTRU with Gaussian sampling to ensure compact signatures	Security derives from the intractability of finding short vectors in a high-dimensional NTRU lattice.	Optimized for compact signatures and fast verification, making it highly efficient for low-bandwidth applications.	Public keys: ~900–1800 bytes Signatures: ~660–1280 bytes	Compact signature size benefits bandwidth-constrained applications but requires careful Gaussian sampling for secure implementations.	Secure document signing, software signing, and real-time encrypted communication
SPHINCS+	Hash-based; relies on stateless hash-based signatures using the few-time signature scheme XMSS as a foundation	Security is rooted in the preimage and collision resistance of cryptographic hash functions rather than number-theoretic problems.	Slower than lattice-based schemes due to extensive hash function calls but offers strong security guarantees and long-term reliability.	Public keys: ~1056–2176 bytes Signatures: ~8,000–50,000 bytes (depending on security level)	Stateless design eliminates state-tracking risks, but high signature size and verification cost make it less efficient for constrained devices.	Long-term digital signatures for archival purposes, code signing, and post-quantum critical infrastructure security

The analysis that follows is designed to expand on the technical coverage from Table 5-3 and to ensure that the distinctions between the NIST-selected algorithms are explicitly defined.

Kyber

Kyber is a lattice-based key encapsulation mechanism that uses LWE in structured polynomial rings to provide quantum-resistant key exchange. Unlike traditional LWE-based schemes, Kyber uses module lattices, optimizing efficiency while maintaining security against quantum attacks. Its parameter selection balances performance and security, with key sizes ranging from 800 to 1500 bytes and ciphertext sizes remaining compact for practical deployment in IoT and embedded systems. This structured approach ensures that Kyber maintains low computational overhead while offering high security, making it ideal for TLS, VPNs, and secure communication protocols.

Dilithium

Dilithium, a digital signature scheme, is inaccurately described if simply categorized as RLWE based. Instead, it is based on MLWE and module short integer solution (MSIS), which improve efficiency and make implementations for constrained environments more practical. The use of MLWE reduces the storage requirements and computational complexity compared to standard RLWE while still ensuring strong security guarantees. Additionally, Dilithium's deterministic signing process minimizes randomness-related vulnerabilities, making it highly resistant to side-channel attacks—an important distinction compared to alternative post-quantum signatures. Its trade-off comes in signature size, which is larger than FALCON's but offers greater resistance to implementation attacks.

FALCON

FALCON, another lattice-based signature scheme, is built on NTRU lattices, using Gaussian sampling to achieve compact and highly efficient signatures. Unlike Dilithium, which prioritizes robustness against side-channel attacks, FALCON optimizes for minimal bandwidth usage, making it well suited for low-bandwidth environments where signature size is critical. Its reliance on floating-point arithmetic and complex sampling techniques, however, makes it more challenging to implement securely, requiring careful parameter tuning and precision management.

SPHINCS+

SPHINCS+, in contrast to the other three algorithms, does not rely on lattices at all but instead uses hash-based cryptography, making it fundamentally different from Kyber, Dilithium, and FALCON. SPHINCS+ is designed as a stateless hash-based signature scheme, meaning it does not require state tracking, like previous hash-based approaches such as XMSS. While hash-based schemes are well understood and provide strong long-term security, the trade-off lies in performance, with SPHINCS+ producing significantly larger signature sizes (up to 50KB) and requiring higher computational resources during signature verification. This makes it less suitable for constrained environments but an excellent choice for long-term digital signatures, such as code signing and critical infrastructure security, where trust and resilience against future quantum attacks are paramount.

Implementation Guidelines for National Critical Infrastructure

The adoption of NIST's PQC standards in critical infrastructure is a significant step toward the transition from planning to execution. As organizations prepare for the transition to PQC, a structured and strategic approach is essential to ensure security, efficiency, and interoperability across existing systems. NIST's selection of CRYSTALS-Kyber, CRYSTALS-Dilithium, FALCON, and SPHINCS+ marks a significant shift in cryptographic standards, requiring enterprises, governments, and infrastructure operators to assess their current cryptographic dependencies and plan for long-term integration of quantum-safe protocols. The following key considerations are required for successful migration to NIST-standardized PQC algorithms:

1. **Algorithm transition framework:** Organizations must develop a phased roadmap for migrating from classical cryptographic protocols to NIST-standardized PQC algorithms. This involves identifying cryptographic components vulnerable to quantum attacks, prioritizing critical infrastructure, and implementing hybrid cryptographic models that integrate both classical and post-quantum algorithms during the transition period. Hybrid implementations ensure a gradual and secure migration, allowing for real-world validation of PQC deployments before full-scale adoption.
2. **Performance benchmarks:** Each PQC algorithm presents unique trade-offs in key size, encryption/decryption speed, and computational overhead, which must be thoroughly evaluated against existing system constraints. Critical sectors such as SCADA networks, secure communication protocols, and financial transaction systems require rigorous testing to determine which PQC algorithm best aligns with their latency, storage, and processing power limitations. Benchmarking PQC schemes in real-world environments ensures optimized deployment strategies while mitigating potential performance bottlenecks.
3. **Interoperability and standards compliance:** The successful adoption of PQC depends on seamless integration with existing cryptographic infrastructure. Organizations must ensure compatibility between current security frameworks and PQC implementations, leveraging standardized APIs and cryptographic libraries, such as those provided by Open Quantum Safe (OQS). Additionally, compliance with global cryptographic standards, including ISO/IEC post-quantum cryptography guidelines, will facilitate cross-platform operability and regulatory adherence, ensuring a consistent and widely accepted implementation framework.
4. **Resilience testing against quantum scenarios:** To validate the effectiveness of PQC implementations, organizations should conduct simulated quantum attack scenarios to assess algorithmic resilience. Cloud-based quantum computing platforms, such as IBM Q and D-Wave, provide controlled environments to model potential quantum-enabled adversarial threats. These simulations help organizations preemptively identify vulnerabilities, optimize cryptographic configurations, and enhance PQC deployment strategies to withstand future quantum computing advancements.
5. **Education and capacity building:** A successful transition to NIST PQC standards requires a well-trained workforce capable of deploying and managing quantum-resistant cryptographic solutions. Industry, academia, and government agencies must collaborate on training programs, certifications, and research initiatives focused on post-quantum cryptography, secure implementation methodologies, and ongoing evaluation of cryptographic resilience. By advancing PQC expertise at all levels, organizations can ensure a smoother adoption curve and proactively address security challenges posed by the quantum computing era.

By addressing these key transition factors, organizations can proactively adapt to the emerging post-quantum cryptographic environment, ensuring that security architectures remain future-proof against quantum-enabled threats while maintaining operational efficiency and compliance with evolving cryptographic standards.

Global Implications of NIST PQC Standards

NIST's standardization efforts have far-reaching implications for national and international cybersecurity. The adoption of these algorithms will serve as a benchmark for global cryptographic practices, influencing the development of policies, regulations, and frameworks that address quantum threats. Moreover, collaboration between governments, industry stakeholders, and academia will be essential to ensure widespread adoption and seamless integration of PQC algorithms across diverse sectors.

Case Study: Behavioral Analysis with Falcon X AI: Analyzing Advanced Quantum Malware Strains

CrowdStrike Falcon X AI[23] uses AI models to enhance malware analysis by observing the behavior of files in a controlled environment and correlating it with known attack patterns and anomalies. Behavioral analysis is applied to identify and neutralize advanced malware strains, especially those targeting cloud environments. Polymorphic malware, fileless threats, and malware using AI for dynamic behavior all require tools with advanced capabilities. CrowdStrike Falcon X AI is a framework for analyzing malware in cloud ecosystems. By using machine learning models, global telemetry data, and AI-driven threat intelligence, Falcon X AI enables cybersecurity specialists to develop a detailed understanding of malware behavior and its impact. This section outlines seven critical steps in Falcon X AI's behavioral analysis process, detailing how AI-driven heuristics, real-time anomaly detection, and adaptive defense mechanisms are used to combat quantum-enhanced malware strains. By following this structured approach, cybersecurity teams can proactively detect and mitigate advanced cyber threats, ensuring robust security in an era of quantum-driven cyberattacks.

Step 1: Preparing the Cloud Environment for Analysis

The process of performing behavioral analysis with Falcon X AI starts with preparing the cloud environment for analysis. The objective is to isolate the malware in a controlled environment to safely observe and record its behavior. Specific actions in this step include the following:

1. Deploy virtualized environments such as AWS CloudFormation or Google Cloud Sandbox, configured with specific logging and monitoring tools provided by Falcon X AI.
2. Integrate Falcon's sensors into these environments to monitor all processes, including file interactions, API calls, and network communications.
3. Configure isolated subnets to ensure that the malware's network communication can only interact with the sandbox's simulated environment.

Figure 5-1 outlines how the environment is prepared for analysis.

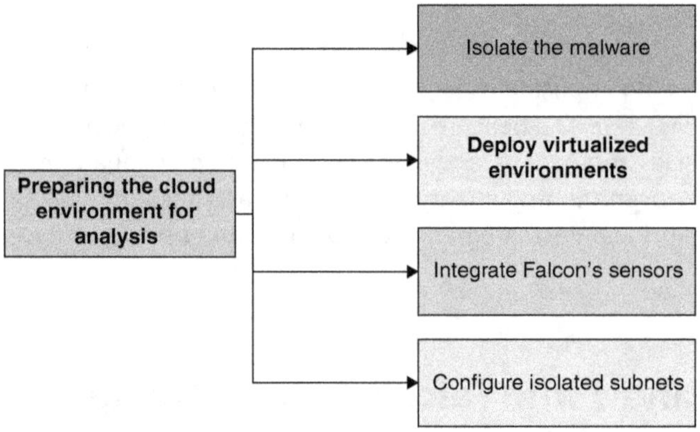

Figure 5-1

In step 1, the cloud environment is prepared for analyzing malware in cloud ecosystems.

How is the process illustrated here going to change when AGI and quantum computing emerge? Malware threats will likely exhibit extraordinary levels of sophistication, using AGI to autonomously adapt to defensive measures and using quantum computation to compromise cryptographic systems. In this scenario, CrowdStrike Falcon X AI's framework for behavioral analysis must evolve accordingly, incorporating advanced techniques and computational power to counteract these new capabilities. This evolution involves the seven key workflow steps described in this chapter, with changes in three key areas, as illustrated in Figure 5-2.

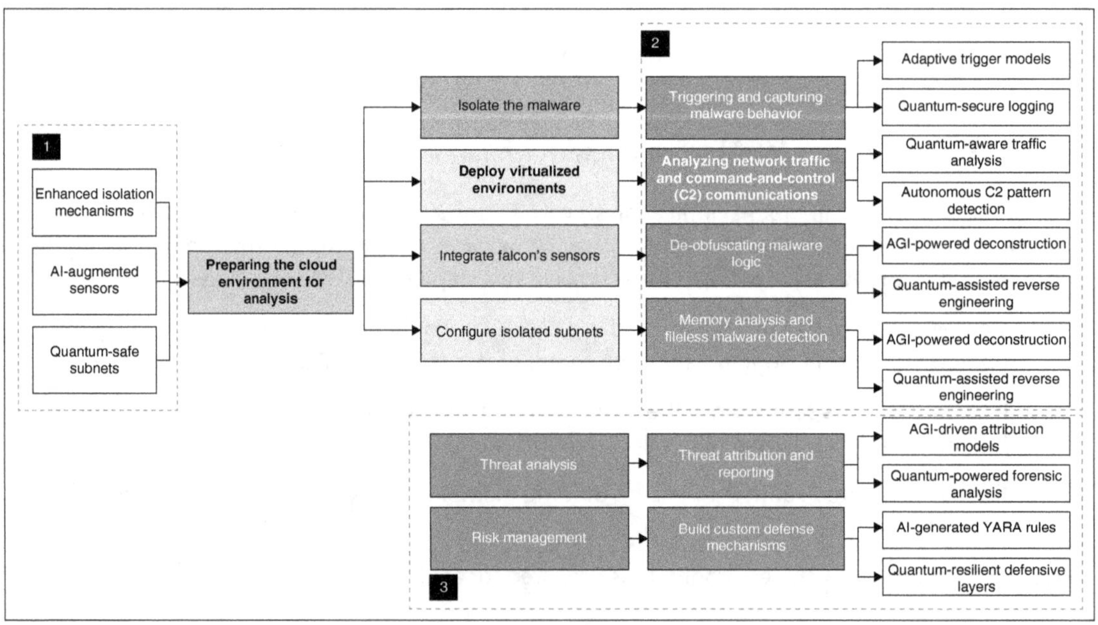

Figure 5-2

Summary of malware analysis process changes in AGI and quantum contexts.

As we can see in Figure 5-2, the evolution of behavioral analysis with Falcon X AI in AGI and quantum computing contexts requires significant advancements in dynamic adaptability, quantum security, and autonomous intelligence. Sandboxes must become polymorphic and quantum safe, logging and analysis require integration with post-quantum cryptographic frameworks, and machine learning models must be enhanced to operate at AGI cognitive levels. Table 5-4 details the seven steps of the three key areas.

Table 5-4 Behavioral Analysis with Falcon X AI in AGI and Quantum Contexts

Workflow Process	Details
1. Preparing the cloud environment for analysis	**Enhanced isolation mechanisms:** Use dynamic polymorphic sandboxes that adapt configurations in real time to prevent AGI-driven adversarial learning. Quantum randomness generators introduce entropy, making the environment less predictable. **AI-augmented sensors:** Integrate predictive AI models to anticipate evasion tactics such as virtual environment detection or dormant payload delays. **Quantum-safe subnets:** Isolate subnets using quantum-resistant cryptographic protocols to thwart quantum attacks and prevent breaches.
2. Triggering and capturing malware behavior	**Adaptive trigger models:** Use adversarial reinforcement learning to simulate varied environmental stimuli, uncovering hidden payload activation logic in AGI-powered malware. **Quantum-secure logging:** Implement post-quantum cryptographic logging mechanisms (e.g., lattice-based schemes) to secure behavioral data against quantum decryption attempts.
3. Analyzing network traffic and command-and-control (C2) communications	**Quantum-aware traffic analysis:** Use quantum traffic analysis tools to detect and decrypt quantum-encrypted transmissions, including C2 links. **Autonomous C2 pattern detection:** Employ enhanced graph neural networks (GNNs) to identify emergent C2 patterns, such as dynamically evolving DNS or IP structures used by AGI malware.
4. De-obfuscating malware logic	**AGI-powered deconstruction:** Counter polymorphic and metamorphic obfuscations created by AGI-driven malware using advanced variational autoencoders (VAEs) that are capable of recognizing invariant operational logic. **Quantum-assisted reverse engineering:** Use quantum computing for probabilistic deconstruction, accelerating the identification of hidden functionalities within AGI-designed malware.
5. Memory analysis and fileless malware detection	**Dynamic memory forensics:** Use real-time adaptive learning in convolutional neural networks (CNNs) to track and detect AGI-driven memory structure changes. **Quantum-enhanced memory scanning:** Employ quantum algorithms for comprehensive memory state analysis to uncover deeply embedded or distributed malicious code.
6. Threat attribution and reporting	**AGI-driven attribution models:** Use natural language processing (NLP) systems to correlate malware behaviors with evolving AGI-generated threat actor profiles. **Quantum-powered forensic analysis**: Use quantum systems to cross-reference behavioral patterns with extensive malware campaign databases to enable attribution of novel AGI-driven techniques.
7. Building custom defense mechanisms	**AI-generated YARA rules:** Use AGI systems to autonomously create and refine YARA rules based on observed behaviors, dynamically adapting to evolving malware tactics. **Quantum-resilient defensive layers:** Integrate post-quantum cryptographic protocols across Falcon X's infrastructure to mitigate AGI and quantum-enabled threats.

Table 5-4 outlines the changes that cybersecurity systems need to incorporate to maintain a strong defense against the combined threats of AGI-driven malware and quantum-enabled adversaries.

Step 2: Triggering and Capturing Malware Behavior

Step 2 in the process involves triggering and capturing malware behavior with the objective of executing the malware in a safe, monitored environment to reveal dynamic behaviors. Triggering and capturing malware behavior is required to understand the dynamic operations of malicious software. Figure 5-3 illustrates this process, which involves executing the malware in a secure, controlled environment to observe its behavior in real time.

The term *detonation*, which is popular in marketing language, essentially refers to the process of triggering the malware payload under specific conditions to study its operational characteristics. For researchers, this typically involves activating the malware in a sandboxed environment in order to isolate and analyze its behaviors safely. From an adversarial perspective, detonation might refer to the activation of dormant malware in response to certain stimuli or inputs.

Falcon X AI uses an automated malware detonation engine designed to safely execute and monitor the malware. During this process, it captures critical system events such as process creation, DLL injections, and system-level changes. Metrics like CPU and memory usage, along with execution patterns, are logged to provide a comprehensive understanding of the malware's functionality.

As shown in Figure 5-3, the underlying technology driving this analysis includes deep reinforcement learning (DRL) models, which predict and log potential payload triggers based on the initial conditions observed during execution. These models are extensively trained on telemetry data collected from more than 200 billion daily events sourced from CrowdStrike's global deployments. By using this dataset, Falcon X AI is able to accurately simulate and document the malware's behavior, equipping cybersecurity specialists with actionable insights into its mechanisms and potential impact.

In the context of AGI and quantum computing, step 2 of the malware analysis takes on a more advanced and dynamic nature. The objective remains the same: to execute the malware in a controlled environment to identify its behaviors. However, the methodologies now incorporate AGI-powered adaptive engines and quantum-enhanced simulations to address the increasing sophistication of malware.

This process involves executing the malware in a secure, isolated virtual environment. The concept of detonation still applies: The payload is triggered under predetermined conditions to observe its functionality. Advanced AGI systems play a key role in simulating diverse environmental conditions and stimuli, anticipating the malware's evasive strategies. The malware is activated in polymorphic sandboxes, with real-time changes to sandbox parameters using quantum randomness generators, thereby mitigating the risk of malware recognizing the analysis environment.

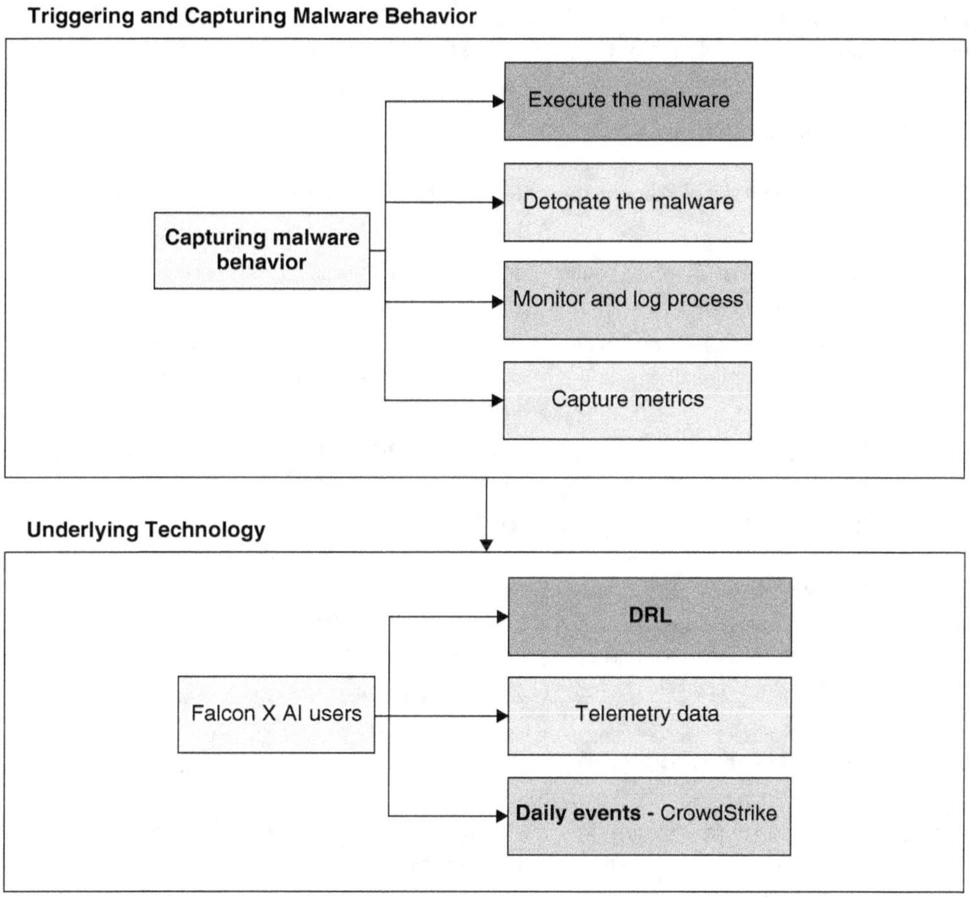

Figure 5-3
Step 2 is the process of triggering and capturing malware behavior.

Future versions of Falcon X AI would use its advanced telemetry-based engine to monitor and log critical system events, such as process creation, DLL injections, and system modifications. Enhanced logging mechanisms protected by quantum-resistant cryptography ensure that behavioral data remains tamper proof and inaccessible to external quantum attacks. System metrics, including resource utilization and execution paths, are captured using AGI-augmented analytics, which identify behavioral anomalies that conventional systems might overlook. Just for clarification, this section discusses future upgrades to existing threat detection systems. It's not describing Falcon X or the existing systems in the present form. It's using red teaming methodology to describe how this system will evolve, and must evolve, to keep detecting AI based malware streams.

The underlying technology for this advanced workflow incorporates DRL models trained on data sets that include AGI simulation-generated telemetry and insights from quantum-empowered threat modeling. These DRL models predict and log potential payload triggers with high precision, using data sourced from trillions of daily events collected through Falcon X's enhanced AGI-driven global telemetry infrastructure. By integrating these advancements, Falcon X would equip cybersecurity experts with highly actionable insights into the operational mechanisms of sophisticated AGI-enabled malware strains.

Table 5-5 shows the requirements of step 2.

Table 5-5 Capturing Malware Behavior Workflow in the Context of AGI and Quantum Computing

Workflow Process	Details	Enhancements with AGI and Quantum Computing
Execute the malware	Use AGI-adaptive sandboxes with dynamic configuration capabilities. Use quantum randomness generators for unpredictable testing environments.	Sandboxes dynamically reconfigure based on real-time AGI predictions of malware behavior. Quantum randomness ensures that sandbox configurations remain unpredictable, preventing malware from recognizing the analysis environment.
Detonate the malware	Simulate diverse triggers by using AGI models to uncover dormant or condition-specific payloads. Continuously vary environmental stimuli to reveal hidden behaviors.	AGI uses adversarial training techniques to predict and test multiple trigger conditions simultaneously. Dynamic AGI-environment feedback loops increase the likelihood of detecting hidden or condition-specific payloads.
Monitor and log processes	Integrate AGI-powered event correlation to detect system-level patterns that indicate evasive or stealthy tactics. Protect logs with quantum-resistant cryptographic measures to secure analysis data.	AGI detects complex, multistep attack patterns and correlates them with historical data for rapid identification. Post-quantum encryption ensures data integrity and prevents unauthorized access during quantum attack scenarios.
Capture metrics	Use AGI-enhanced algorithms to analyze CPU, memory usage, and execution patterns to identify anomalies. Apply quantum-computing-assisted processing to accelerate behavioral analysis and pattern recognition.	Quantum computing algorithms expedite data analysis for large-scale behavioral metrics. AGI-driven anomaly detection identifies subtle variations indicative of new malware strains or evasion tactics.

Step 3: Analyzing Network Traffic and Command-and-Control (C2) Communications

Step 3 involves analyzing network traffic and C2 communications. The objective of this phase is to detect and interpret interactions with C2 servers that facilitate malware operations (detailed in Figure 5-4). Using Falcon X AI's Traffic Analysis Module, we can trace DNS queries, HTTP headers, and TLS handshakes to identify potential signs of malicious activity. This process involves deploying Falcon's Domain Attribution Model, which uses GNNs trained on extensive historical telemetry data related to C2 infrastructures. These models are designed to recognize patterns in malicious communication, including domain-generation algorithms (DGAs) and IP reputation metrics.

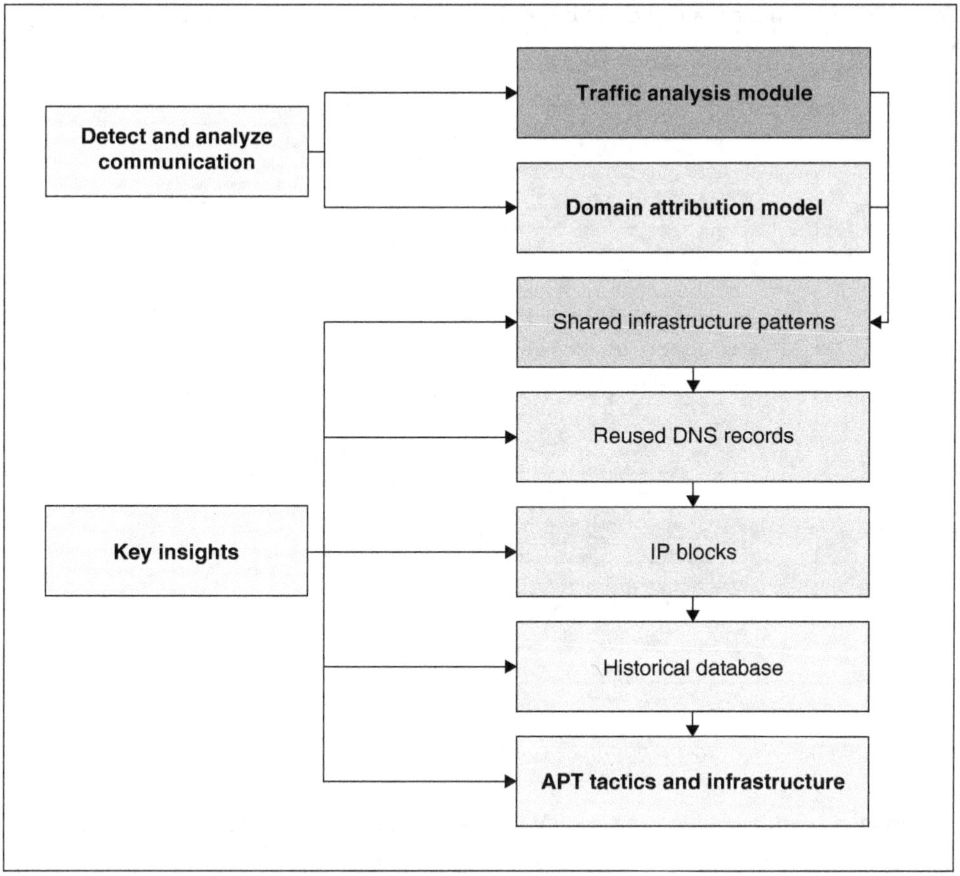

Figure 5-4
Analyzing network traffic and C2 communications.

A key capability of Falcon's GNN models detailed in Figure 5-4 is their ability to identify shared infrastructure patterns. For instance, reused DNS records, overlapping IP blocks, or domain similarities often indicate a coordinated malware campaign. The system cross-references these findings with a historical database of known advanced persistent threat (APT) tactics and infrastructure. This approach enables the detection of previously unseen but structurally similar C2 infrastructures. For example, the system can flag communication patterns used by specific APT groups by comparing them against historical APT datasets to get actionable insights into the broader campaign's origin and objectives. Through this layered analysis, Falcon X AI enhances the identification and mitigation of sophisticated malware operations.

However, AGI and quantum computing would dramatically transform the process of analyzing network traffic and C2 communications. The primary objective would remain the same: to detect and interpret interactions with C2 servers that facilitate malware operations. However, the methodologies and tools required for this analysis would need to adapt in order to address the increased sophistication of AGI-driven malware and the potential use of quantum communication protocols (see Figure 5-5).

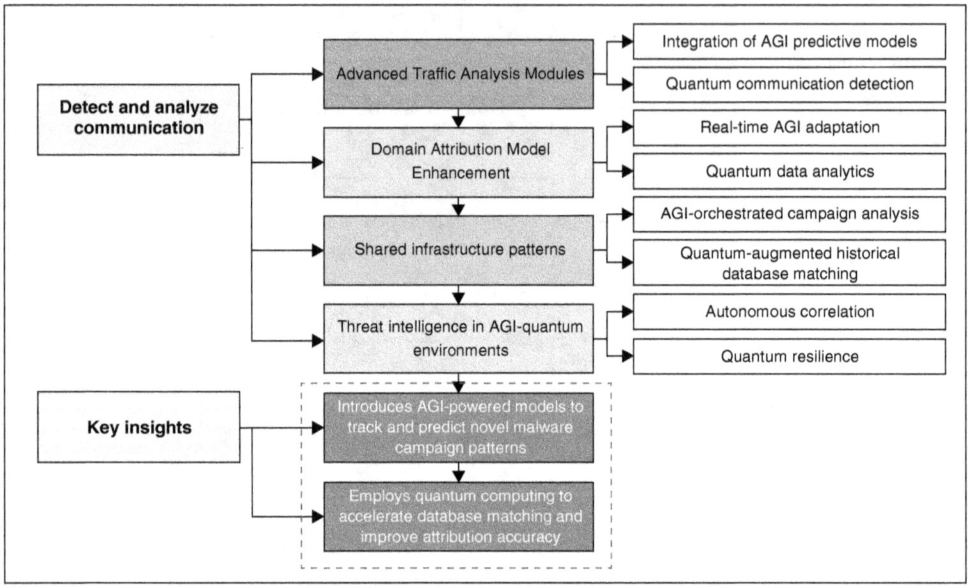

Figure 5-5
Adapted process for analyzing network traffic and C2 communications.

This updated workflow would position Falcon X AI to effectively counteract AGI and quantum-enabled malware, ensuring the continued security of digital ecosystems. Table 5-6 details the process.

Table 5-6 Detailed Process for Analyzing Malware in AGI and Quantum Computing Conditions

Workflow Process	Details
Advanced Traffic Analysis Modules	
Integration of AGI predictive models	The Traffic Analysis Module must incorporate AGI-driven models capable of dynamically adapting to novel communication patterns. These models simulate AGI-generated evasive tactics, such as rapidly evolving DNS queries or TLS handshakes that mimic legitimate traffic.
Quantum communication detection	Quantum-enabled malware may employ quantum cryptographic protocols for C2 communication. To counter this, traffic analysis tools must include quantum traffic interception capabilities, using quantum computers to decrypt and analyze quantum-encrypted messages.
Domain Attribution Model Enhancement	
Real-time AGI adaptation	Falcon's Domain Attribution Model, powered by GNNs, would need to process exponentially larger datasets and identify emerging patterns in real time, such as recognizing dynamically generated quantum-safe domains or IP addresses designed to avoid detection.

Workflow Process	Details
Quantum data analytics	Quantum computing would be used to cross-reference telemetry data with quantum-encrypted C2 infrastructures, enabling faster detection of AGI-driven malware campaigns by analyzing shared patterns that classical detection systems might miss.
Key Insights into Shared Infrastructure Patterns	
AGI-orchestrated campaign analysis	AGI-driven malware campaigns may exhibit unprecedented levels of coordination, using distributed C2 nodes and adaptive behavior to evade detection. Detection systems must use AGI models to predict these patterns proactively.
Quantum-augmented historical database matching	Quantum computing enhances the speed and accuracy of comparing current C2 traffic with historical APT tactics, enabling faster attribution and identification of novel infrastructure reuse.
Threat Intelligence in AGI-Quantum Environments	
Autonomous correlation	AGI systems autonomously correlate vast datasets of C2 telemetry, creating granular and accurate threat profiles, even in highly complex environments.
Quantum resilience	All logs and findings from this analysis must be protected with post-quantum cryptographic protocols to ensure that adversaries using quantum decryption cannot compromise the integrity of the analysis.

Step 4: De-obfuscating Malware Logic

Building upon the previous step of analyzing network traffic and C2 communications (Table 5-6 and Figure 5-5), the process naturally transitions into the critical phase of de-obfuscating malware logic. This phase, step 4, focuses on unraveling the layers of obfuscation employed by advanced malware to conceal its true functionality. The objective is to reverse-engineer these obfuscation techniques so that cybersecurity experts can uncover the original operational logic embedded within the code. Falcon X AI's advanced Code Reconstruction Module, powered by variational autoencoders (VAEs), plays a central role in this endeavor. These VAEs, trained on an extensive database of more than 4 million unique malware hashes, are adept at identifying invariant patterns that persist across polymorphic and metamorphic transformations. By analyzing obfuscated functions and comparing them against comprehensive function signature libraries (spanning benign and malicious patterns), Falcon X AI can effectively highlight behavioral similarities and anomalies (see Figure 5-6). For instance, consider a scenario where a piece of ransomware modifies its encryption routines with the intent of evading detection. While the surface-level behavior appears novel, the Falcon X AI VAEs can detect underlying commonalities, such as sequences indicative of cryptographic libraries frequently used by ransomware families. This capability enables the identification of malicious intent even when the malware adopts new or modified techniques.

So, step 4 bridges the gap between communication analysis and in-depth behavioral deconstruction and also lays the groundwork for actionable threat intelligence and tailored defensive measures. By uncovering the malware's true purpose, security teams can develop specific countermeasures to mitigate its impact and prevent future incursions.

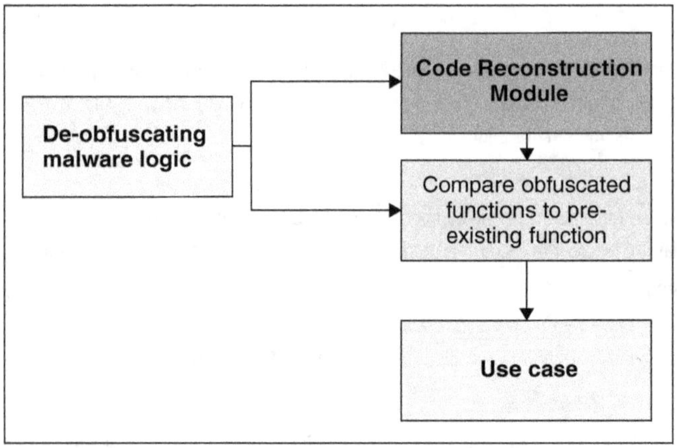

Figure 5-6
De-obfuscating malware logic.

In the context of AGI and quantum computing, the process of de-obfuscating malware logic needs significant advancements and adaptations to address the increasingly sophisticated and evasive nature of malware strains. These developments need to use the AGI's adaptive reasoning and the computational power of quantum systems to enhance the precision, speed, and scope of malware analysis. The integration of AGI and quantum computing reshapes the traditional framework for de-obfuscating malware logic (see Table 5-7).

Table 5-7 De-obfuscating Malware Logic Process Adaptations for AGI and Quantum Computing

Workflow Process	Description	Implementation Adaptations
Enhanced code reconstruction	Modern VAEs struggle with advanced obfuscation techniques. AGI-powered VAEs would provide contextual reasoning, identifying relationships between unrelated code segments and reconstructing obfuscated logic with precision. Quantum computing would accelerate deconstruction by solving cryptographic transformations in reduced time frames.	**AGI-driven VAEs:** Contextual analysis for dynamic relationship inference in code **Quantum-assisted code decryption:** Fast probabilistic approaches to resolve obfuscation layers
Dynamic obfuscation countermeasures	Advanced malware evolves dynamically during execution to counter detection mechanisms. AGI systems would simulate obfuscation patterns and predict potential transformations. Real-time de-obfuscation uses quantum randomness to adapt detection methods, countering evasive changes during analysis.	**AGI behavior modeling:** Simulation of obfuscation techniques for predictive detection **Real-time adaptive de-obfuscation:** Randomized reconfiguration of de-obfuscation techniques using quantum randomness generators

Workflow Process	Description	Implementation Adaptations
Expanded malware libraries	AGI systems would synthesize (currently hypothetical) malware samples to predict future attack strategies, ensuring comprehensive training for code reconstruction modules. Quantum computing enhances signature-matching speed and efficiency, rapidly cross-referencing function signatures across vast databases.	**AGI-enhanced databases:** Automated synthesis of hypothetical malware samples **Quantum-optimized search:** Scalable and accelerated signature matching against historical and predicted patterns
Advanced function comparison	Function comparison requires semantic understanding to identify operational similarities in radically different implementations. AGI would enhance detection by analyzing functionality rather than syntax. Quantum-augmented pattern recognition would improve detection of global malware campaigns with disguised connections.	**Deep semantic analysis:** Integration of semantic reasoning into function comparison **Quantum-augmented pattern recognition:** Comprehensive identification of shared operational logic across global campaigns
Scalable processing capabilities	Traditional platforms will struggle with the computational demands of AGI and quantum-enabled malware. Parallel quantum computing would ensure scalability, enabling real-time adaptation to large-scale malware analysis and mitigation requirements in critical infrastructure environments.	**Parallel quantum computing:** Scalable systems capable of processing exponentially growing data and evolving malware behaviors to support high-throughput environments and proactive defense mechanisms

Step 5: Memory Analysis and Fileless Malware Detection

Building on the advancements in code reconstruction, step 5 focuses on memory analysis and fileless malware detection. Modern threats increasingly utilize memory-resident techniques to evade traditional disk-based detection methods, making this step indispensable in identifying sophisticated malware. Falcon X AI's Memory Forensics Module uses convolutional neural networks (CNNs) that are specifically trained to analyze memory dumps and pinpoint malicious code segments embedded within active processes. These CNNs, built on datasets containing millions of memory dumps from legitimate operations and known malware samples, excel at distinguishing benign anomalies from genuinely harmful code.

The module identifies indicators such as process hollowing, code injection, and unauthorized memory access by comparing runtime memory behaviors against Falcon X's extensive signature database. Additionally, stack tracing provides a granular view of how malicious instructions execute in system memory, offering critical insights into their operational flow. This analysis, illustrated in Figure 5-7, enables cybersecurity experts to detect elusive threats that operate entirely in memory, bypassing conventional detection mechanisms.

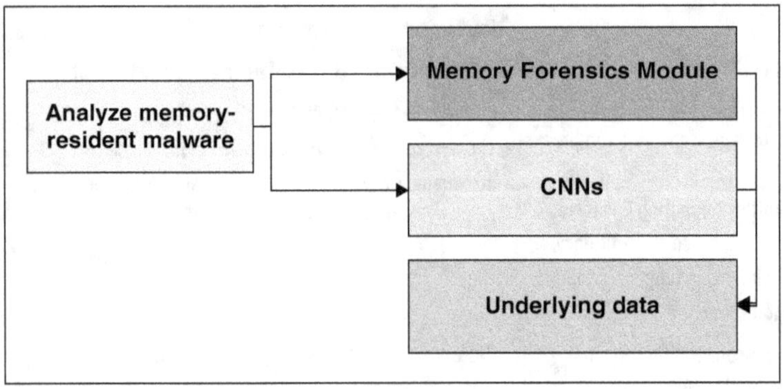

Figure 5-7
Memory analysis and fileless malware detection.

As memory-resident malware evolves, incorporating adaptive behaviors powered by AGI and quantum techniques, the importance of dynamic memory forensics grows exponentially. The Memory Forensics Module will undergo significant enhancement to counteract the challenges posed by AGI-powered malware and quantum-assisted attack methodologies. In future environments, AGI systems will augment this module with advanced contextual reasoning, enabling analysis of highly adaptive and evasive malware strains. These systems will dynamically interpret memory-resident behaviors by cross-referencing real-time execution patterns with predictive models capable of anticipating AGI-crafted obfuscation tactics. Additionally, quantum-assisted processing will allow for exhaustive memory state analysis, dramatically reducing the time required to identify malicious code while increasing the precision of detection.

While traditional CNNs excel in recognizing patterns in memory dumps, their AGI-enhanced counterparts will incorporate semantic understanding, allowing for deeper contextual analysis of code execution. AGI-driven CNNs will use a global corpus of dynamically generated malware datasets to identify novel attack signatures. This capability will extend beyond pattern matching, detecting the behavioral intent of malware as it interacts with system memory.

The quantum computing paradigm will facilitate memory analysis by enabling the decryption of memory states encrypted by polymorphic malware. Using quantum search algorithms, malicious code segments embedded within vast memory datasets will be isolated and identified with unparalleled speed and accuracy. Furthermore, runtime behaviors such as process hollowing and code injection will be detected through quantum-augmented correlation with a constantly updated AGI-curated signature database.

Future iterations of Falcon X AI will have to integrate AGI-driven models into stack tracing workflows, allowing for real-time adaptation to malware that modifies its operational patterns during execution. In such versions of the Falcon X AI software, AGI systems will simulate potential malware behaviors and overlay them onto observed memory activities, effectively predicting the next steps of malicious code in complex systems.

Table 5-8 provides a structured overview of the key security adaptations required for malware behavioral analysis in AGI and quantum computing environments. The table outlines how Falcon X

AI integrates AI-driven heuristics, real-time anomaly detection, and quantum-assisted threat modeling to counteract next-generation malware strains. By breaking down each stage of the malware analysis process, the table highlights the specific enhancements needed to maintain resilience against AGI-driven adversarial techniques and quantum-enabled cyber threats.

Table 5-8 Memory Forensics Module Adaptation for AGI-Quantum Environment

Workflow Process	Adaptation in AGI-Quantum Environment
Memory Forensics Module	Integrates AGI-based predictive models and quantum-assisted processing to enhance memory state analysis and counteract polymorphic malware strains.
AGI-driven CNNs	Extends analysis capabilities to include behavioral intent and semantic understanding of memory-resident processes.
Quantum data handling	Employs quantum algorithms to decrypt and analyze memory states, identifying deeply embedded malicious segments rapidly.
Dynamic stack tracing	Uses AGI to simulate and adapt to malware behaviors in real time, providing detailed insights into operational logic.

Table 5-8 underscores how the traditional approaches to behavioral analysis, such as signature-based detection and static analysis, become insufficient when confronted with AGI-adaptive malware capable of morphing its attack patterns in real time. Additionally, quantum computing introduces new cryptographic vulnerabilities, requiring post-quantum cryptographic defenses and AI-enhanced traffic monitoring.

The enhancements outlined in the Table 5-8 emphasize key areas where AGI and quantum computing significantly alter the attack surface, including:

- **Malware behavior capture:** The transition from static sandboxing to AI-driven polymorphic environments that adapt dynamically to prevent evasion tactics
- **Network traffic analysis:** The need for quantum-aware traffic inspection to detect encrypted C2 communications leveraging quantum cryptographic protocols
- **Threat attribution:** The incorporation of AGI-driven behavioral correlation models, allowing for real-time threat intelligence and automated forensic analysis
- **Defensive countermeasures:** The shift toward quantum-resilient cryptographic mechanisms and AI-generated YARA rules for autonomous threat mitigation strategies

Step 6: Threat Attribution and Reporting

Following the detailed process of memory analysis and fileless malware detection, step 6 focuses on threat attribution and reporting. This phase involves classifying the malware strain, identifying its origins, and providing actionable intelligence to mitigate its impact. With Falcon X AI's Threat Attribution Engine, this process integrates advanced behavioral pattern analysis with metadata extraction to generate a comprehensive profile of the detected threat. The Threat Attribution Engine uses natural language processing (NLP) models that are meticulously trained on CrowdStrike's extensive threat intelligence reports to correlate observed malware behaviors with known tactics, techniques, and procedures (TTPs) employed by threat actors. This step is particularly effective in linking the malware to advanced persistent threat (APT) groups or emerging malware families by recognizing shared operational patterns and infrastructure.

The attribution process extends beyond behavioral analysis to incorporate detailed indicators of compromise (IoCs), such as file hashes, IP addresses, and suspicious API call signatures, offering a robust foundation for further investigation (see Figure 5-8). Falcon X AI generates a detailed report summarizing observed behaviors, payload delivery mechanisms, and the context of the attack. This report attributes the malware to specific actors or campaigns and equips cybersecurity teams with the knowledge required to devise tailored countermeasures. By bridging the gap between technical analysis and strategic decision making, this step ensures that responses are precise and preemptive, enabling organizations to enhance their resilience against sophisticated threats.

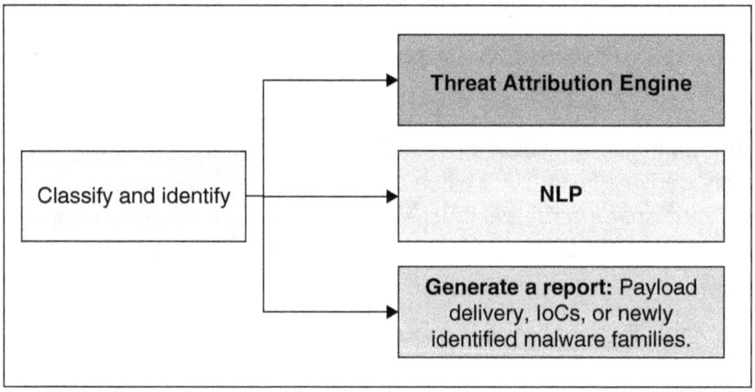

Figure 5-8
Threat attribution and reporting.

Building on the advancements in malware attribution and reporting discussed earlier, the integration of AGI and quantum computing introduces transformative capabilities that redefine the landscape of threat analysis. Table 5-9 details how individual components of the process, such as attribution engines, NLP models, and actionable intelligence generation, will evolve to counteract the complexities posed by AGI-enabled malware and quantum-powered adversaries. These enhancements ensure accurate threat identification and robust defenses against future attack vectors.

Table 5-9 Enhanced Threat Attribution and Reporting Framework in AGI-Quantum Environments

Workflow Process	Future Enhancements	Detailed Functionality
Enhanced Threat Attribution Engine	**Integration of AGI models:** AGI systems will enable real-time dynamic analysis of behavioral patterns, correlating malware attributes with advanced TTPs. **Quantum-assisted metadata analysis:** Quantum computing will accelerate correlation between IoCs and global threat intelligence datasets.	AGI will process telemetry data dynamically, detecting nuanced links between malware behavior and threat actor profiles. Quantum-enhanced algorithms will enable instant decoding of quantum-encrypted communications and be able to identify shared C2 infrastructures. The engine will proactively identify patterns even in zero-day attacks by using AGI's ability to predict emerging tactics.

Workflow Process	Future Enhancements	Detailed Functionality
NLP model advancements	**AGI-powered contextual reasoning:** Models will incorporate semantic understanding to link multilingual threat intelligence reports to malware behavior. **Multi-source intelligence correlation:** NLP models will correlate threat actor profiles with global telemetry and past malware campaigns.	NLP systems, integrated with AGI, will provide deeper insights into novel malware families and emerging campaigns. AGI-enabled models will decode the context behind complex telemetry data, linking obscure malware behaviors with threat actor groups. These models will distinguish novel TTPs from advanced adversaries, reducing detection time and increasing accuracy.
Integration of quantum computing in metadata analysis	**Quantum-augmented IoC analysis:** Quantum computing will allow real-time decryption of quantum-encrypted IoCs. **Distributed attack campaign correlation**: Cross-referencing of IoCs across global databases will become nearly instantaneous.	Quantum systems will enable rapid analysis of IoCs, such as file hashes, IP addresses, and API calls, ensuring accurate mapping of malware infrastructure to campaigns. Distributed attack data, combined with quantum pattern recognition, will identify links between coordinated adversaries using global C2 infrastructures.
Actionable intelligence generation	**Predictive AGI simulations:** AGI will simulate potential future malware behavior and TTP evolution. **Incorporation of dynamic insights:** Insights will include real-time behavioral updates from malware operations.	Actionable intelligence will include AGI-predicted attack evolutions, enabling cybersecurity teams to prepare preemptive countermeasures. AGI simulations will run virtual environments to predict how malware could adapt or spread in future iterations, equipping analysts with forward-looking intelligence. Reports will integrate these insights to offer actionable steps for mitigation and defense.
Post-quantum cryptography for reporting	**Post-quantum secure reporting:** Lattice-based encryption will be used to ensure the integrity of generated threat intelligence reports. **Quantum-safe data transmission:** Reports and findings will be transmitted securely to prevent interception by quantum-enabled adversaries.	Threat intelligence reports encrypted using post-quantum protocols will be impervious to quantum decryption attacks. This encryption will ensure that sensitive insights into malware operations, threat actor attribution, and IoCs cannot be compromised by adversaries with advanced quantum computing capabilities. Reports will be securely shared among stakeholders via quantum-resistant VPNs or similar secure communication frameworks.

Step 7: Building Custom Defense Mechanisms

The insights gained from the process of threat attribution (Table 5-9 and Figure 5-8) naturally pave the way for step 7: building custom defense mechanisms (see Figure 5-9). This final phase focuses on translating the analyzed malware behaviors and associated IoCs into proactive detection and mitigation strategies, forming a robust defense against future threats. Falcon X AI's advanced detection rule builder facilitates the creation of highly tailored YARA rules (a widely adopted tool for identifying and classifying malware based on textual or binary patterns) and behavior-based triggers, empowering organizations to block malware at the earliest stages of the attack lifecycle. Just for clarification, YARA rules is a pattern-matching tool originally known as "Yet Another Ridiculous Acronym," widely used for identifying and classifying malware based on textual or binary signatures, as well as behavior-based triggers. By integrating these custom rules into the broader Falcon platform, cybersecurity teams can ensure that their defenses remain dynamic and responsive to evolving attack patterns.

The process detailed in Figure 5-9 also involves updating firewall and endpoint policies with the intelligence gathered from the behavioral and metadata analysis conducted earlier. For example, endpoints exhibiting anomalous behaviors, such as repeated unauthorized file access or excessive outbound traffic, can be automatically isolated to prevent the spread of potential threats. This automated response mitigates the immediate risk and strengthens the organization's overall resilience by preemptively addressing vulnerabilities. This approach bridges the gap between reactive measures and a proactive cybersecurity posture, ensuring that the lessons learned from each analysis cycle are effectively incorporated into ongoing defensive strategies.

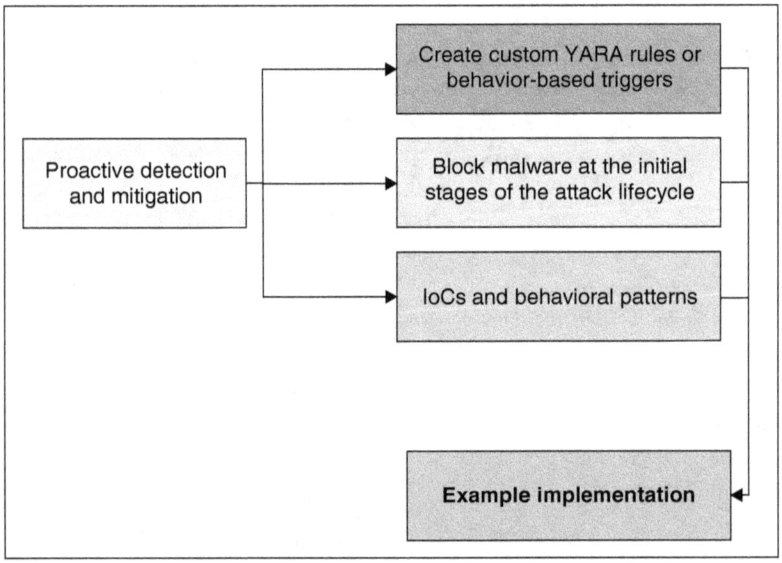

Figure 5-9
Building custom defense mechanisms.

Figure 5-9 illustrates the current steps but in a future where AGI and quantum computing have been fully realized; building custom defense mechanisms will require new detection, mitigation, and response strategies. Hence, the adaptations discussed in Table 5-10 are based on how AGI might operate; however, because AGI does not yet exist in a concrete form, it's challenging for any book or academic resource to provide comprehensive coverage on it. A disclaimer here seems appropriate: At this point, AGI is a theoretical concept rather than a tangible, fully realized technology, and the best quantum chip is the Willow chip from Google, which effectively runs at 1 qubit, and we need 4000 qubits to break RSA, but that is a topic discussed in Chapter 6, and Chapter 9.

Table 5-10 Adaptations of Proactive Defense Mechanisms for AGI and Quantum Computing Risks

Workflow Process	Current Objective	Future Adaptations in AGI and Quantum Computing
	Proactive Detection and Mitigation	
Create custom YARA rules	Define detection rules for identifying specific malware types.	AGI-driven detection engines will autonomously create and refine YARA rules in real time. These AGI systems will analyze global threat intelligence and simulate potential attack scenarios to predict evolving tactics.
Behavior-based triggers	Establish triggers for behavior patterns indicative of threats.	Behavior-based detection will be enhanced with quantum algorithms that process massive datasets of behavioral patterns at unprecedented speeds. These triggers will identify anomalies that are too subtle for classical models.
Block malware at the attack lifecycle	Prevent malware from advancing beyond initial stages.	AGI models will use predictive analytics to preemptively block malware at the reconnaissance or delivery stage by identifying indicators of malicious intent across interconnected systems.
	IoCs and Behavioral Patterns Integration	
IoC-based updates	Update defenses based on identified IoCs.	Quantum computing will expedite IoC matching, enabling real-time correlation of global threat intelligence with locally observed behaviors. IoCs will be enriched with AGI predictions of future attack vectors.
Behavioral pattern insights	Analyze observed behaviors to enhance detection capabilities.	AGI systems will simulate hypothetical attack scenarios, ensuring that behavior-based defenses remain adaptive to entirely novel attack patterns—even those created dynamically by adversarial AGI systems.
	Example Implementation	
Endpoint isolation	Isolate endpoints showing suspicious behavior.	Autonomous AGI frameworks will monitor endpoints in real time, instantly isolating nodes exhibiting suspicious activity. This action will be driven by quantum-enhanced models for anomaly detection and risk analysis.
Firewall policies	Adjust policies to reflect observed threats.	AGI-enabled systems will continuously adapt firewall and endpoint policies based on evolving threat landscapes, using quantum computing to dynamically optimize for performance and security.

Previously, Figure 5-9 detailed the workflow process for proactive defense adaptations for AGI and quantum computers. When engaging in such futuristic discussions, we must remember that the future is uncertain. Humans could, for example, cause a nuclear disaster any day and bring humanity back to the stone age, and AGI would have to wait. Climate change could cause environmental damage that could lead to a new economic depression, reducing funding and user interest in new technologies. An unknown comet could destroy earth before humans ever get the chance to build AGI. Many things could go wrong, but as we stand today, OpenAI is working toward developing AGI, Japan has been working for a few decades on developing an artificial brain, and the war in Ukraine has proven that in times of crises, weaponizing AI is not seen as an ethical conundrum but as a necessity. Building upon this argument, in Table 5-10, we can see the process for proactive defenses for AGI and quantum computing risk.

Discussion and Analysis: Behavioral Analysis with Falcon X AI in the Context of AGI and Quantum Computing

Unlike conventional AI-generated malware, AGI-driven threats autonomously would modify their attack vectors in real time, and quantum-assisted malware uses quantum randomness to evade entropy-based detection systems. The following theoretical discussion explores how a future upgrade of Falcon X AI's behavioral analysis framework will identify, analyze, and mitigate these new attack methodologies.

A key analytical insight lies in the enhanced adaptability required in sandboxing and behavioral detection mechanisms. Current polymorphic sandboxes and telemetry-based analyzers, while effective, are inadequate against AGI-driven malware that can autonomously adapt to defensive measures. The introduction of quantum randomness generators and AGI-powered adaptive learning into these sandboxes ensures that environments remain unpredictable, effectively countering malware's ability to detect or bypass analysis setups. Additionally, the integration of AGI models into processes such as malware detonation and C2 communication analysis introduces a level of predictive intelligence unprecedented in current frameworks. These models simulate diverse trigger conditions and anticipate evasive tactics, uncovering malware logic concealed by AGI-driven adversaries. Quantum computing's role in accelerating decryption and correlation further enhances the precision and efficiency of these analyses.

Summary

This chapter provides a detailed exploration of the evolving challenges posed by quantum computing and artificial general intelligence (AGI) in malware analysis and mitigation. By focusing on the advanced capabilities of CrowdStrike Falcon X AI, the chapter outlines a progressive framework to address the growing sophistication of malware strains using AGI and quantum technologies. The key takeaway is the necessity for dynamic, adaptive, and quantum-resilient strategies in behavioral analysis and cybersecurity operations.

The chapter begins by examining the current methodologies for isolating and analyzing malware within cloud environments. It emphasizes the critical role of virtualized sandboxes and telemetry-based sensors in monitoring and logging malware behaviors. These methodologies, however, are constrained by the adaptive nature of AGI-driven malware, which can recognize and bypass traditional defensive measures. Quantum randomness generators and AI-augmented sandboxes emerge as essential tools in maintaining unpredictable analysis environments.

Subsequent sections explore the advanced processes of malware detonation, network traffic analysis, and de-obfuscation, where the integration of AGI introduces predictive intelligence and dynamic environmental simulations. The use of deep reinforcement learning (DRL) models and quantum-enhanced decryption accelerates the detection and understanding of complex malware behaviors. AGI-powered tools such as variational autoencoders (VAEs) allow for contextual reasoning in reverse engineering malware logic, enabling the identification of deeply embedded malicious functionalities.

The chapter also discusses the transformation of threat attribution and reporting workflows. AGI models enhance the correlation of indicators of compromise (IoCs) with global threat intelligence, enabling the identification of novel attack vectors. Post-quantum cryptographic frameworks further safeguard this analysis against quantum-assisted adversaries, ensuring the integrity of malware attribution processes.

Finally, the chapter addresses the iterative development of custom defense mechanisms, highlighting the future role of AGI in automating YARA rule creation and optimizing firewall policies. Quantum computing accelerates behavioral pattern analysis, enabling proactive detection and mitigation strategies that adapt to dynamically evolving attack landscapes.

Overall, the chapter underscores the transformative potential of AGI and quantum computing in reshaping malware analysis and cybersecurity practices. It advocates for the integration of these technologies into existing workflows to future-proof cybersecurity infrastructures against the dual threats of quantum-assisted and AGI-enabled adversaries. This synthesis of advanced computational power and intelligent systems provides a strong foundation for mitigating the unprecedented challenges of next-generation malware.

References

1 Lyubashevsky, Vadim, Chris Peikert, and Oded Regev. 2010. "On Ideal Lattices and Learning with Errors over Rings." *Lecture Notes in Computer Science*, vol. 6110. https://doi.org/10.1007/978-3-642-13190-5_1.

2 Gentry, Craig, Shai Halevi, and Nigel P. Smart. 2012. "Fully Homomorphic Encryption with Polylog Overhead." *Lecture Notes in Computer Science* 7237: 465–82. https://doi.org/10.1007/978-3-642-29011-4_28.

3 Microsoft. 2019. *Microsoft SEAL: Fast and Easy-to-Use Homomorphic Encryption Library*. https://www.microsoft.com/en-us/research/project/microsoft-seal/.

4 Polyakov, Yuriy, Kurt Rohloff, Gerard W Ryan, and Dave Cousins. 2017. "Palisade Lattice Cryptography Library User Manual." *Cybersecurity Research Center, New Jersey Institute of Technology, Tech. Rep*, 15.

5 Bos, Joppe, Leo Ducas, Eike Kiltz, T. Lepoint, Vadim Lyubashevsky, John M. Schanck, Peter Schwabe, Gregor Seiler, and Damien Stehle. 2018. "CRYSTALS-Kyber: A CCA-Secure Module-Lattice-Based KEM." *3rd IEEE European Symposium on Security and Privacy*, 353–67. https://doi.org/10.1109/EUROSP.2018.00032.

6 Bos, Joppe, Leo Ducas, Eike Kiltz, Tancrède Lepoint, Vadim Lyubashevsky, John M Schanck, Peter Schwabe, Gregor Seiler, and Damien Stehlé. n.d. *CRYSTALS-Kyber: A CCA-Secure Module-Lattice-Based KEM*. https://eprint.iacr.org/2017/634.pdf.

7 GitHub. 2024. *pq-crystals/kyber*. https://github.com/pq-crystals/kyber.

8 *CRYSTALS: Cryptographic Suite for Algebraic Lattices*. n.d. www.pq-crystals.org.

9 Ducas, Léo, Eike Kiltz, Tancrède Lepoint, Vadim Lyubashevsky, Peter Schwabe, Gregor Seiler, and Damien Stehlé. n.d. *CRYSTALS-Dilithium Round 2 Presentation*. https://csrc.nist.gov/CSRC/media/Presentations/crystals-dilithium-round-2-update/images-media/crystals-dilithium-lyubashevsky.pdf.

10 GitHub. 2024. *pq-crystals/dilithium*. https://github.com/pq-crystals/dilithium.

11 Micciancio, Daniele, and Oded Regev. 2009. "Lattice-Based Cryptography." *Post-Quantum Cryptography*, 147–91. https://doi.org/10.1007/978-3-540-88702-7_5.

12 Vinge, Vernor. 1993. *Technological Singularity*. NASA. http://cmm.cenart.gob.mx/delanda/textos/tech_sing.pdf.

13 Regev, Oded. 2005. "On Lattices, Learning with Errors, Random Linear Codes, and Cryptography." *Journal of the ACM* 56(6): 1–40. https://doi.org/10.1145/1568318.1568324.

14 Kortesniemi, Yki, Dmitrij Lagutin, Tommi Elo, and Nikos Fotiou. 2019. "Improving the Privacy of IoT with Decentralized Identifiers (DIDs)." *Journal of Computer Networks and Communications* 1: 8706760. https://doi.org/10.1155/2019/8706760.

15 Mahalle, Parikshit N., Gitanjali Shinde, and Pathan Mohd Shafi. 2020. "Rethinking Decentralized Identifiers and Verifiable Credentials for the Internet of Things." *Studies in Systems, Decision and Control* 266: 361–74. https://doi.org/10.1007/978-3-030-39047-1_16.

16 OpenID. 2024. *OpenID4VC: OpenID for Verifiable Credentials—Overview*. https://openid.net/sg/openid4vc/.

17 Sedlmeir, Johannes, Reilly Smethurst, Alexander Rieger, and Gilbert Fridgen. 2021. "Digital Identities and Verifiable Credentials." *Business and Information Systems Engineering* 63(5): 603–13. https://doi.org/10.1007/S12599-021-00722-Y.

18 W3C. 2024. *W3C VCDM: Verifiable Credentials Data Model v2.0.*https://www.w3.org/TR/vc-data-model-2.0/.

19 NIST. 2023a. *Post-Quantum Cryptography PQC*. https://csrc.nist.gov/projects/post-quantum-cryptography.

20 NIST. 2022. *Post-Quantum Cryptography PQC*. https://csrc.nist.gov/projects/post-quantum-cryptography.

21 NIST. 2017. *The NIST Plan for Providing Public Access to Results of Federally Funded Research*. https://doi.org/10.6028/NIST.IR.8084.

22 NIST. 2023b. *Post-Quantum Cryptography PQC*. https://csrc.nist.gov/projects/post-quantum-cryptography.

23 Cosive. 2024. *CrowdStrike Falcon X*. https://www.cosive.com/capabilities/crowdstrike-falcon-x.

Multiple-Choice Questions with Detailed Explanations

1. Which of the following best describes the primary advantage of lattice-based cryptography (LBC) in post-quantum security?

   a. It relies on the hardness of factoring integers.

   b. It is immune to all classical and quantum attacks.

   c. It is based on the computational intractability of lattice problems like SVP and LWE.

   d. It uses smaller keys than traditional cryptographic methods.

   Correct Answer: C. Lattice-based cryptography relies on the mathematical complexity of problems like the shortest vector problem (SVP) and the learning with errors (LWE) problem, making it resistant to attacks by quantum and classical computers. Options A and B are incorrect because factoring integers is used in RSA, not LBC, and no cryptography is entirely immune to all attacks. Option D is partially correct but not the primary advantage.

2. What is the primary feature of ring learning with errors (RLWE) that distinguishes it from other lattice-based cryptographic schemes?

   a. It uses polynomial rings for improved efficiency and compactness.

   b. It eliminates the need for error terms in cryptographic calculations.

   c. It replaces classical encryption entirely with homomorphic encryption.

   d. It guarantees post-quantum security with minimal computational cost.

   Correct Answer: A. RLWE introduces algebraic structures, such as polynomial rings, which allow for efficient computations and compact key sizes while maintaining security. Options B and C are incorrect because RLWE uses error terms and supports but does not replace classical encryption. Option D misrepresents RLWE's computational cost.

3. Which of the following post-quantum cryptographic algorithms is primarily based on hash functions?

   a. CRYSTALS-Kyber

   b. CRYSTALS-Dilithium

   c. FALCON

   d. SPHINCS+

   Correct Answer: D. SPHINCS+ relies on hash functions and is a stateless hash-based digital signature scheme. Options A, B, and C are based on lattice-based cryptographic problems like LWE and RLWE.

4. Why is the CRYSTALS-Dilithium algorithm particularly suitable for IoT environments?

   a. It uses large keys that ensure higher security.

   b. It provides compact signatures with minimal computational overhead.

   c. It relies exclusively on hash-based primitives.

   d. It eliminates the need for key encapsulation mechanisms.

   Correct Answer: B. CRYSTALS-Dilithium produces compact digital signatures that are efficient to generate and verify, making it ideal for constrained environments like IoT. Options A, C, and D misrepresent its characteristics.

Exercises and Solutions

Exercise 1: Short-Answer Question

Question: Explain the advantages of using lattice-based cryptography over traditional cryptographic methods like RSA and ECC.

Solution: Lattice-based cryptography (LBC) offers quantum resistance due to its reliance on problems like learning with errors (LWE) and shortest vector problem (SVP), which are computationally infeasible for both classical and quantum computers. Unlike RSA and ECC, which are vulnerable to Shor's algorithm, LBC ensures long-term security against quantum attacks. Furthermore, its versatility supports applications like fully homomorphic encryption (FHE) that are essential for secure computations on encrypted data.

Exercise 2: Case Study

Scenario: A national energy grid uses TLS protocols based on RSA for secure communication between control centers and field devices. A quantum computer breaches this system, exposing operational data and compromising infrastructure safety.

Tasks:

1. Identify the vulnerabilities in the current system.
2. Recommend three steps to transition to quantum-resistant cryptography.
3. Evaluate the role of RLWE in securing energy grids against future quantum threats.

Solution:

1. **Vulnerabilities:**
   - RSA encryption is susceptible to quantum attacks via Shor's algorithm.
   - TLS protocols lack quantum-safe cryptographic algorithms.
   - Centralized key management systems create single points of failure.

2. **Steps to transition:**
    - Implement lattice-based encryption (e.g., CRYSTALS-Kyber) for secure communication.
    - Deploy hybrid cryptographic schemes combining RSA and post-quantum algorithms during the transition phase.
    - Establish decentralized key management systems using blockchain.
3. **Evaluation of RLWE:** RLWE provides efficient and compact encryption suitable for real-time communication in energy grids. Its reliance on structured lattices ensures scalability for high-throughput environments. By incorporating RLWE into TLS protocols, energy grids can achieve robust security against quantum threats.

6

Implementing Quantum-Safe Solutions

This chapter explores how existing cybersecurity platforms can address the challenges posed by quantum-powered and AGI-enhanced malware. It examines the processes of setting up environments, submitting malware samples, analyzing the dynamic behavior of this malware, and adapting detection strategies to meet future challenges.

Key objectives include understanding the integration of AI and quantum computing into sandbox environments and enabling precise malware analysis and robust threat intelligence capabilities. Readers will learn how to simulate real-world environments, track polymorphic malware behavior, and implement automated detection rules.

Objectives

- **Understand how sandbox environments will need to change:** Learn about the enhancements and capabilities of Cape Sandbox in analyzing AI-powered and polymorphic malware, with a focus on behavioral analysis, polymorphism tracking, and threat intelligence integration.
- **Examine the impact of quantum computing and AGI on cybersecurity:** Explore how the emergence of quantum computing and artificial general intelligence (AGI) redefines the threat landscape, necessitating advanced sandbox adaptations.

- **Analyze environment configuration techniques:** Study the methods for setting up virtual machines and network emulations to simulate real-world environments, ensuring precise behavioral analysis.
- **Investigate advanced malware submission methods:** Understand the process of uploading malware samples, configuring runtime parameters, and leveraging automation through APIs.
- **Assess dynamic behavior analysis:** Engage in methods for observing malware runtime behaviors, such as file encryption, data exfiltration, and C2 communications, and adapt them to counteract quantum and AGI-driven threats.
- **Track polymorphic behavior:** Learn about tracking how malware dynamically adapts during execution, using AI and quantum-specific tools to identify invariant logic elements.
- **Integrate threat intelligence:** Examine how Cape Sandbox links malware behaviors to external threat intelligence feeds, enabling proactive detection and enhanced attribution in quantum and AGI contexts.
- **Automate detection rules:** Understand how to develop and deploy adaptive detection rules that incorporate quantum-resilient and AGI-enhanced heuristics for identifying future threats.
- **Evaluate future-proofing strategies:** Explore the innovations required to adapt sandbox environments for quantum and AGI challenges, including quantum-aware APIs, advanced simulation environments, and dynamic rule adaptation.
- **Develop a comprehensive perspective on the role of sandboxes in cybersecurity:** Gain insights into the role of sandbox environments like Cape Sandbox in mitigating risks posed by quantum computing and AGI, ensuring cybersecurity resilience in evolving threat landscapes.

The chapter provides insights into using sandbox tools for linking malware traits to external threat feeds, thereby enhancing attribution and proactive defense mechanisms. This chapter also emphasizes the importance of adapting sandbox architectures for quantum-specific challenges, such as processing larger datasets, counteracting quantum-powered encryption, and predicting AGI-driven malware logic. It offers an in-depth analysis of future-proofing strategies, from quantum-resilient APIs to modular detection frameworks, that can help ensure that sandboxes remain effective against the evolving threat landscape.

Practical Deployment of Post-quantum Algorithms

Deploying post-quantum algorithms (PQAs) is a process that requires precise planning, execution, and validation. Whereas earlier chapters engage in theoretical discussions, this chapter focuses on practical implementation, addressing real-world complexities such as integrating new cryptographic systems into existing infrastructures, ensuring interoperability, and maintaining operational performance. The sections that follow describe the process of deploying PQAs.

Phase 1: Assessment of the Existing Cryptographic Infrastructure to Identify Vulnerabilities to Quantum Threats

The first phase in deploying PQAs involves a comprehensive assessment of the existing cryptographic infrastructure to identify vulnerabilities to quantum threats. This begins with cryptographic dependency mapping, in which an organization creates a detailed inventory of all systems that rely on cryptographic algorithms such as Rivest–Shamir–Adleman (RSA), elliptic-curve cryptography (ECC), or Digital Signature Algorithm (DSA). These algorithms, which form the backbone of current security protocols, are particularly vulnerable to decryption by quantum computers. Mapping these dependencies ensures that every potentially exposed system is accounted for in the transition process.

Phase 2: Prioritization

The second phase is prioritization, which involves identifying resources in the most critical areas. Systems should be classified based on the sensitivity of the data they handle and their potential exposure to adversarial attacks. High-priority systems often include those supporting financial transactions, critical infrastructure operations, or national security frameworks, where the consequences of a breach would be severe.

Phase 3: Impact Analysis to Evaluate the Computational and Operational Implications of Migrating to PQAs

After the prioritization step, an impact analysis should be conducted to evaluate the computational and operational implications of migrating to PQAs. This third phase involves assessing key performance metrics such as latency, memory requirements, and throughput. Transitioning to quantum-safe algorithms typically involves larger key sizes and increased computational overhead, which can strain existing resources. Understanding these impacts early in the process enables organizations to allocate resources effectively and plan for infrastructure upgrades where necessary.

Phase 4: Selection of Appropriate PQAs

The selection of appropriate PQAs is a critical step in the deployment process, as it determines the robustness and efficiency of the cryptographic system against quantum threats. The process begins with evaluating specific algorithms based on their applicability to different use cases. For instance, CRYSTALS-Kyber[1] is well suited for secure key exchange mechanisms, while CRYSTALS-Dilithium[2] provides robust solutions for digital signature applications. For scenarios requiring stateless signature schemes, such as certain Internet of Things (IoT) deployments, SPHINCS+[3,4] is an optimal choice. McEliece, with its long-standing security against quantum attacks, is particularly advantageous for ensuring long-term data confidentiality.

To ensure compatibility and adherence to industry best practices, it is essential that the selected algorithms align with NIST's post-quantum cryptography standards.[5] These standards offer a framework for evaluating the security and interoperability of PQAs, ensuring their sustainability in future systems. Additionally, the performance of each algorithm must be rigorously benchmarked in the intended deployment environments. For example, constrained IoT devices might require lightweight and efficient algorithms, whereas high-frequency trading systems or large-scale data centers necessitate high throughput and minimal latency.

Phase 5: Pilot Testing

Pilot testing is the fifth phase in deploying PQAs. The goal is to ensure the practicality, security, and performance of PQAs in a controlled environment before full-scale implementation. The process begins with deploying PQAs in simulated environments designed to replicate real-world conditions. These isolated test networks enable organizations to assess algorithm behavior under typical operational scenarios while avoiding risks to production systems.

To maintain compatibility with existing cryptographic systems, hybrid cryptography approaches are introduced during testing. This involves integrating PQAs alongside traditional algorithms, such as combining CRYSTALS-Kyber with RSA, to evaluate the robustness of quantum-safe mechanisms while ensuring backward compatibility with legacy systems. Such hybrid approaches are particularly useful in transitional phases, where interoperability between old and new systems is critical.

Key metrics guide the evaluation process during pilot testing. Encryption and decryption speeds are closely measured to compare latency with that of existing algorithms, providing insights into potential performance bottlenecks. Memory usage is analyzed to understand the impact of larger key sizes and computational requirements on system resources. Additionally, interoperability is verified by confirming compatibility with established protocols, such as Transport Layer Security (TLS) 1.3, and with hardware security modules (HSMs).

Phase 6: System Integration

System integration marks the critical transition from pilot testing to the full-scale deployment of PQAs. This phase begins with a layered implementation strategy. Initial deployments are limited to non-critical systems, allowing for the identification and resolution of unforeseen issues in environments where the impact of failures is minimal. This cautious approach helps establish confidence in the stability of the algorithms. Once stability and performance benchmarks are achieved, the implementation is gradually extended to encompass critical systems, such as financial platforms, healthcare data repositories, or government infrastructures, where robustness and security are paramount.

Upgrading software environments is a key step in system integration. Cryptographic libraries, such as OpenSSL and BoringSSL, must be updated to incorporate support for PQAs. This ensures that all dependent applications and protocols can use the enhanced security features of quantum-safe cryptography. Ensuring that these libraries are correctly configured is crucial for maintaining interoperability and avoiding disruptions.

Hardware compatibility is another essential consideration during this phase. Existing HSMs and secure enclave technologies must be evaluated for their capacity to handle the computational demands imposed by PQAs, particularly given their larger key sizes and increased processing requirements. In cases where current hardware proves insufficient, replacement with updated, quantum-ready solutions is necessary to maintain operational integrity.

Phase 7: Operational Deployment

Operational deployment is the final step of the transition to PQAs, focusing on full-scale implementation, system reliability, and functionality. The first critical step in operational deployment is the adoption of hybrid rollout strategies, such as deploying hybrid schemes that combine classical cryptographic algorithms with PQAs. Such an approach ensures backward compatibility with legacy systems and smooth interoperability during the transitional phase. For instance, a hybrid TLS handshake might leverage RSA alongside Kyber key exchanges, ensuring secure communications with both pre-quantum and quantum-ready systems. This dual compatibility is essential to maintaining operational continuity while gradually phasing out older cryptographic methods.

In parallel with the hybrid rollout, an organization should maintain dual systems to provide redundancy during the initial stages of deployment. A parallel instance of the existing cryptographic infrastructure should run alongside the new PQA-based system, acting as a safety net in case unexpected issues arise during the transition. This redundancy minimizes risks and facilitates a smoother shift by allowing critical systems to revert to the legacy cryptographic framework if necessary.

Phase 8: Validation and Monitoring

The transition to fully relying on PQAs should proceed only after thorough validation of their operational stability, performance metrics, and security assurances. The validation and monitoring stage ensures that the system meets and upholds security and performance standards in real-world environments.

The first component of this phase is the deployment of continuous monitoring tools. These tools are essential for tracking encryption performance, assessing network latency, and identifying potential vulnerabilities introduced during the integration process. Continuous monitoring provides real-time visibility into the operational behavior of cryptographic systems, enabling swift detection and mitigation of any issues that arise.

Stress testing is another critical aspect of validation. By subjecting the system to adversarial simulations, including brute-force quantum decryption attempts, an organization can rigorously evaluate the resilience of the deployed PQAs. This testing provides a clear assessment of the system's ability to withstand quantum-enabled threats and other advanced attack vectors, ensuring readiness against potential adversaries.

Audits also play a crucial role in maintaining the security integrity of the system over time. Regular cryptographic audits are necessary to ensure compliance with evolving industry standards and regulatory requirements. These audits should include comprehensive evaluations of algorithmic performance and system configurations. As new quantum threats or cryptographic advancements emerge, organizations must also update and refine their algorithms to align with the latest standards, ensuring that the deployed system remains future-proof and secure.

Effective deployment of post-quantum cryptographic algorithms also requires a strong focus on training and documentation to ensure long-term system sustainability and operational efficiency. These steps enable teams to adapt to evolving requirements while maintaining system security.

Phase 9: Training and Documentation

Training programs are essential for equipping developers, security professionals, and system administrators with the skills to manage and maintain quantum-safe systems. These programs should cover foundational principles of post-quantum cryptography, practical aspects of algorithm integration, and troubleshooting of common challenges. Tailored training sessions can address specific roles, such as system administrators learning to monitor performance or developers focusing on ensuring compatibility with existing protocols.

Comprehensive documentation forms the backbone of a well-maintained system. Documentation should detail the entire migration process, capturing key decisions, configuration settings, and encountered issues. Having these details in writing ensures that teams can reference prior implementations to inform future upgrades or troubleshooting efforts. Additionally, the documentation must provide clear guidance on updating cryptographic libraries and systems as new threats emerge and as algorithms are refined.

Challenges During Deployment

The deployment of PQAs introduces several challenges that must be systematically addressed to ensure the reliability, efficiency, and compatibility of the transitioned systems. The primary obstacles and strategies to mitigate them are as follows:

- **Key size management:** Post-quantum cryptographic algorithms typically require significantly larger key sizes than traditional cryptographic systems such as RSA or ECC. This poses challenges related to communication bandwidth, data storage, and processing efficiency. Deployment strategies must incorporate mechanisms to optimize key management, such as compressing keys where possible or implementing efficient key distribution systems. Ensuring minimal latency in critical operations is essential, particularly in environments with stringent performance requirements, such as financial systems or real-time communication networks.
- **Interoperability:** A major challenge lies in updating widely used security protocols, such as IPsec and TLS, to support PQAs while maintaining compatibility with legacy systems. Ensuring interoperability involves implementing hybrid cryptographic schemes during the transitional

phase, where both classical and post-quantum algorithms operate simultaneously. Hybrid protocols ensure backward compatibility and allow gradual migration while providing immediate protection against quantum threats. Furthermore, rigorous testing is necessary to validate the seamless integration of updated protocols across heterogeneous systems and networks.

- **Resource constraints:** Resource-limited environments, such as IoT devices and embedded systems, face unique constraints during the deployment of PQAs. These systems often operate with limited computational power, memory, and energy, which can be strained by the larger key sizes and computational demands of PQAs. To address this, lightweight implementations of post-quantum algorithms must be prioritized. Optimized versions of algorithms such as CRYSTALS-Kyber and SPHINCS+ can be deployed to balance quantum resistance with the resource limitations inherent to these environments.

By addressing these challenges and applying optimized deployment strategies, post-quantum systems can maintain high levels of security, interoperability, and performance across diverse operational environments. The section that follows presents a practical example of how to deploy one of the NIST-approved post-quantum algorithms.

Practical Example: Deploying CRYSTALS-Kyber in TLS

Deploying CRYSTALS-Kyber, a post-quantum key exchange algorithm, within the TLS protocol provides an opportunity to implement quantum-safe cryptography while maintaining compatibility with existing systems. This section provides a detailed guide for deploying Kyber within a hybrid cryptographic framework for TLS.

Step 1: Preparation

The initial phase involves preparing the infrastructure to accommodate CRYSTALS-Kyber. The first step is to upgrade the server-side TLS libraries, such as OpenSSL, to a version that supports CRYSTALS-Kyber. Ensure that the version includes NIST-aligned post-quantum algorithm implementations.

Next, create hybrid X.509 certificates that combine RSA or ECC public keys with Kyber public keys. This dual-key approach ensures compatibility with legacy systems while introducing quantum-resistant capabilities. These certificates are generated using updated certificate authorities (CAs) that support hybrid key algorithms. Here is an example of how to generate a hybrid X.509 certificate that includes RSA and CRYSTALS-Kyber public keys:

```
# Generate RSA key pair
openssl genpkey -algorithm RSA -out rsa_key.pem -pkeyopt rsa_keygen_bits:4096

# Generate CRYSTALS-Kyber key pair using OpenQuantumSafe (OQS) fork of OpenSSL
openssl genpkey -algorithm kyber512 -out kyber_key.pem
```

```
# Generate a Certificate Signing Request (CSR) that includes both keys
openssl req -new -key rsa_key.pem -subj "/CN=example.com" -out rsa_csr.pem
openssl req -new -key kyber_key.pem -subj "/CN=example.com" -out kyber_csr.pem

# Sign both CSRs with a hybrid CA certificate
openssl x509 -req -in rsa_csr.pem -CA ca.crt -CAkey ca.key -CAcreateserial -out
rsa_cert.pem -days 365 -sha256
openssl x509 -req -in kyber_csr.pem -CA ca.crt -CAkey ca.key -CAcreateserial -out
kyber_cert.pem -days 365 -sha256

# Combine both certificates into a single hybrid certificate chain
cat rsa_cert.pem kyber_cert.pem > hybrid_cert.pem
```

How the hybrid certificate is generated depends on a number of factors:

- **Tools used:** Tools include OpenSSL and OpenQuantumSafe (OQS) OpenSSL fork.
- **Key generation:** Use **openssl genpkey** with both RSA (for legacy support) and Kyber (for quantum resilience).
- **Combining keys:** The hybrid certificate is created by including RSA and Kyber keys in a certificate chain.
- **Integration with CAs:** Certificate authorities need to support hybrid key certificates. Some organizations have implemented hybrid X.509 certificates that store multiple keys and signatures in a single certificate.

A hybrid certificate stores two public keys (RSA and Kyber keys) in the Subject Public Key Info field. This is achieved by using the following:

- X.509 v3 extensions to indicate the presence of multiple keys
- Multi-signature support, where both an RSA and Kyber signature are attached to the certificate

The following is a sample openssl.cnf configuration for hybrid certificates:

```
[ hybrid_cert ]
basicConstraints = CA:FALSE
subjectKeyIdentifier = hash
authorityKeyIdentifier = keyid,issuer
keyUsage = critical, digitalSignature, keyEncipherment
extendedKeyUsage = serverAuth, clientAuth
```

This example provides a concrete OpenSSL-based workflow to generate hybrid certificates that can be used in TLS 1.3 with post-quantum security.

Step 2: Implementation

The integration of Kyber into the TLS handshake requires careful configuration to ensure operational efficiency and fallback options. The first step is to adjust the server's configuration to prioritize Kyber for key exchange in the TLS handshake process. Legacy clients that do not support Kyber can fall back to RSA or ECC algorithms to ensure uninterrupted communication.

Next, validate that the TLS server correctly negotiates the preferred Kyber-based key exchange when both client and server support the algorithm. For clients lacking Kyber support, confirm that the fallback mechanism functions seamlessly.

Step 3: Validation

To ensure a robust deployment, rigorous testing is required. This testing can involve using network monitoring tools such as Wireshark to verify the handshake process, inspecting the negotiated cipher suites to confirm that Kyber is used where supported, and ensuring accurate packet exchanges during the handshake.

It is important to conduct load testing under simulated peak conditions to evaluate the performance of Kyber in high-traffic environments and identify potential latency or throughput bottlenecks introduced by the post-quantum algorithm. It is also important to adjust configurations or hardware resources as necessary to optimize performance.

To evaluate the performance of TLS 1.3 with CRYSTALS-Kyber, the following key metrics should be monitored to determine if the thresholds are acceptable:

- **TLS handshake latency:** Time taken for the handshake to complete (<100ms is ideal, and <200ms is acceptable)
- **CPU utilization:** CPU load increase during Kyber handshake (<10% over RSA baseline)
- **Memory usage:** Additional memory required for Kyber operations (<50MB overhead per session)
- **Throughput (TPS):** Transactions per second supported under load (<10% decrease compared to RSA)
- **Packet size overhead:** Increase in packet size due to Kyber keys (<5% increase over ECC)

Here is an example of conducting performance benchmarking with OpenSSL:

```
# Run performance tests for Kyber-based key exchange
openssl speed -evp kyber512
openssl speed -evp kyber768
```

Here is how to simulate TLS connections with Kyber:

```
# Start a Kyber-enabled TLS server
openssl s_server -cert hybrid_cert.pem -key rsa_key.pem -key kyber_key.pem -tls1_3
-cipher TLS_AES_256_GCM_SHA384
# Simulate 100 concurrent clients connecting to the server
ab -n 1000 -c 100 https://example.com/
```

You might run into some issues. Let's look at some common issues and their solutions.

Common issue 1: Clients do not recognize the Kyber-based handshake.

Cause: Legacy clients do not support post-quantum key exchange.

Solutions:

- Ensure that fallback to RSA/ECC is enabled using hybrid certificates.
- Use OpenSSL's priority list to offer both Kyber and RSA:

```
openssl s_server -cert hybrid_cert.pem -key rsa_key.pem -key kyber_key.pem
-cipher TLS_AES_256_GCM_SHA384,TLS_AES_128_GCM_SHA256
```

Common issue 2: Latency is increased during the TLS handshake.

Cause: Kyber's larger key size increases handshake processing time.

Solutions:

- Optimize the cryptographic library with hardware acceleration.
- Reduce key size by choosing Kyber-512 instead of Kyber-1024.

Common issue 3: Certificate validation fails.

Cause: Some certificate authorities do not yet support hybrid X.509 certificates.

Solutions:

- Use a hybrid CA or self-signing hybrid certificates for internal testing.
- Ensure that TLS libraries are updated to the latest versions that support hybrid key certificates.

Common issue 4: High CPU utilization occurs during the handshake.

Cause: Post-quantum cryptographic operations are more computationally intensive.

Solutions:

- Offload cryptographic processing to HSMs.
- Enable optimized cryptographic libraries such as OQS-OpenSSL.

- Validate the implementation by simulating adversarial scenarios, ensuring that the Kyber-based key exchange withstands various attack vectors, including attempts to exploit legacy fallback mechanisms.

This step-by-step deployment example demonstrates the practical integration of post-quantum cryptography into real-world communication systems. The hybrid approach ensures a smooth transition, balancing quantum resistance with the continued usability of established infrastructure.

Overcoming Challenges in Quantum-Safe Implementations

One of the foremost challenges in implementing quantum-safe cryptographic algorithms is their inherent complexity, which introduces significant computational demands. Unlike traditional algorithms such as RSA or ECC, post-quantum algorithms often involve substantially larger key sizes and more complex mathematical structures. For instance, lattice-based schemes such as CRYSTALS-Kyber rely on intricate polynomial arithmetic in high-dimensional spaces, which is computationally intensive compared to the modular arithmetic used in classical cryptography. This increased complexity is especially evident in key generation, encryption, and decryption processes, which may require significantly more computational cycles and memory allocation.

The impact of this complexity is particularly pronounced in systems with limited processing power, such as IoT devices and embedded systems. These environments are characterized by constrained computational resources, limited memory, and stringent power consumption requirements. For example, an IoT sensor designed for low-power operation may struggle to handle the computational overhead of generating or verifying large lattice-based keys, which can range from several kilobytes to megabytes in size. The increased encryption and decryption time associated with post-quantum algorithms could lead to higher latency in communication protocols, potentially compromising the real-time performance that is critical to applications such as autonomous vehicles, smart grids, and industrial automation.

Furthermore, the need to integrate post-quantum cryptography into legacy systems exacerbates the challenge. Legacy systems, often designed with the efficiency of traditional cryptography in mind, lack the hardware and software optimizations necessary to accommodate the computational demands of post-quantum schemes. For instance, embedded processors commonly found in legacy IoT devices may lack the architectural support to efficiently execute the high-dimensional matrix operations and polynomial multiplications central to algorithms like Kyber or Dilithium. Consequently, retrofitting these systems to support post-quantum cryptography might require significant hardware upgrades or custom software optimizations, which can be resource-intensive and costly. Overcoming these challenges requires a careful balance between algorithm selection, system optimization, and hardware upgrades, ensuring that the enhanced security offered by post-quantum cryptography does not come at the expense of system performance and scalability.

Backward Compatibility

Backward compatibility is a significant obstacle in the transition to quantum-safe cryptographic systems, as it necessitates maintaining interoperability between newly deployed post-quantum systems and existing cryptographic infrastructure. Many legacy systems rely on traditional algorithms such as RSA and ECC, which are deeply integrated into hardware, software, and protocols. The challenge is to upgrade these systems to support PQAs without disrupting their functionality or compromising performance.

Backward compatibility is critical for ensuring a seamless migration path. For instance, communication protocols like TLS must support hybrid schemes that incorporate both classical and quantum-safe algorithms. Such a hybrid approach ensures that systems with older hardware or software can still establish secure communications during the transition period. A practical example is the hybrid TLS handshake, where a post-quantum algorithm like CRYSTALS-Kyber is used alongside RSA or ECC to provide dual-layer security while maintaining compatibility with legacy clients.

However, integrating such hybrid solutions introduces complexity into existing workflows. For example, the inclusion of post-quantum algorithms, which often have larger key sizes, can increase handshake latency and memory requirements. These changes can disrupt workflows in latency-sensitive environments, such as high-frequency trading platforms or real-time control systems in industrial applications. Furthermore, ensuring compatibility across diverse ecosystems, including IoT devices, cloud services, and on-premises servers, adds another layer of complexity to the migration process.

The migration to post-quantum systems also raises concerns about potential disruptions to business operations. Updating cryptographic libraries, HSMs, and firmware to support PQAs can require downtime, which might not be acceptable for mission-critical applications. Additionally, reconfiguring or replacing systems that cannot support the new algorithms might introduce unforeseen vulnerabilities, creating transitional security gaps. For instance, a partial migration where some systems adopt PQAs while others retain traditional algorithms could leave a system vulnerable to attack vectors that exploit weaker components in the ecosystem.

Standardization Gaps

The transition to PQAs is complicated by the ongoing evolution of standardization efforts. CRYSTALS-Kyber and CRYSTALS-Dilithium have emerged as front-runners for key exchange and digital signatures, respectively. However, the continuous scrutiny and testing of these algorithms could lead to modifications or even replacements before the standards are finalized.

One of the primary limitations of these evolving standards is the lack of certainty regarding the long-term viability of selected algorithms. Organizations that adopt PQAs prematurely face the risk of deploying cryptographic systems that may require subsequent replacement or reconfiguration. Such scenarios could lead to significant financial and operational costs, particularly in industries that rely on extensive cryptographic infrastructure, such as banking, healthcare, and defense.

Moreover, standardization gaps can hinder interoperability. Many existing protocols and systems are built around well-established cryptographic standards such as RSA and ECC. Without a finalized and widely adopted standard for PQAs, achieving compatibility between quantum-safe algorithms and existing cryptographic protocols is challenging. This can delay the development of hybrid solutions that combine classical and quantum-resistant algorithms, which are critical during the transition phase.

Another concern is the risk of fragmentation in the absence of globally unified standards. Different organizations or regions might adopt competing algorithms or interim solutions, creating compatibility issues and increasing the complexity of cryptographic management. For instance, while NIST leads standardization efforts in the United States, other regions might prioritize alternative frameworks or independently developed algorithms.

Premature adoption of unfinalized algorithms also poses security risks. Algorithms that have not undergone sufficient testing might harbor vulnerabilities that could be exploited once these algorithms are deployed at scale. This is particularly critical given the potential adversarial interest in quantum-safe cryptography as a foundational security layer for future systems. Deploying algorithms without thorough validation could undermine the very security goals they are intended to achieve

Practical Implementation Strategies for Addressing Standardization Gaps

Organizations can bridge standardization gaps by implementing a structured migration plan that includes the following:

- Adopting NIST post-quantum cryptography (PQC) draft standards early:
  - While standards are still evolving, enterprises should begin testing NIST PQC Round 4 candidates (e.g., CRYSTALS-Kyber, CRYSTALS-Dilithium, Falcon).
  - Organizations should deploy hybrid cryptographic solutions (such as PQC and RSA/ECC) to ensure interoperability.
  - Organizations should implement quantum-safe key exchanges in TLS 1.3 and IPsec.
- Maintaining cryptographic agility:
  - Organizations should use modular crypto libraries like OQS-OpenSSL that allow switching between cryptographic algorithms without major system overhauls.
  - Organizations could, for example, configure OpenSSL to support PQC cipher suites dynamically, as follows:

```
openssl s_server -cert pqc_cert.pem -key pqc_key.pem -tls1_3 -cipher OQS_KYBER_
LEVEL1
```

Hybrid Certificate Deployment for Interoperability

To ensure backward compatibility, organizations should issue hybrid certificates that combine classical (RSA/ECC) and quantum-safe keys. They should also ensure that they use multi-signature support in X.509 certificates, as follows:

```
[ hybrid_cert ]
subjectKeyIdentifier = hash
authorityKeyIdentifier = keyid,issuer
keyUsage = critical, digitalSignature, keyEncipherment
extendedKeyUsage = serverAuth, clientAuth
```

Interoperability Testing Across Environments

To ensure interoperability testing across environments, organizations should deploy testbed environments with PQC-enabled security tools (e.g., OpenSSL 3.2+, BoringSSL, WolfSSL). Additionally, organizations should validate cross-platform compatibility by testing hybrid key exchanges in cloud and on-premise systems. Table 6-1 describes some metrics for evaluating standardization readiness.

Table 6-1 Metrics for Evaluating Standardization Readiness

Metric	Definition	Target Value
Hybrid compatibility rate	Percentage of clients successfully negotiating hybrid TLS connections	>90%
PQC latency overhead	Additional time required for quantum-safe handshakes	<20% over RSA
Interoperability failures	Rate of failures when connecting PQC-enabled clients with legacy servers	<5%
Compliance with NIST drafts	Percentage of cryptographic operations adhering to latest NIST recommendations	100%

The metrics in Table 6-1 illustrate a hybrid cryptographic migration strategy, showing interoperability between legacy RSA/ECC and PQC across different systems.

To ensure robust quantum-safe cryptographic security, organizations should follow five core security validation strategies:

- Cryptographic security audits
- Penetration testing and adversarial simulations
- Stress testing and performance benchmarking
- Quantum-safe supply chain security
- Compliance and regulatory readiness

Cryptographic Security Audits

Organizations should conduct regular cryptographic audits to verify that PQC implementations are correctly integrated. This involves using Cryptographic Algorithm Validation Program (CAVP) for formal validation and running FIPS 140-3 compliance tests for cryptographic modules.

Table 6-2 outlines the audit steps, the objective of each step, and the tools to use for cryptographic security audits.

Table 6-2 Cryptographic Security Auditing

Audit Step	Objective	Tools
Key size verification	Ensure that quantum-safe key sizes (e.g., Kyber-512, Kyber-1024) are used.	OpenSSL, Wireshark
Protocol testing	Confirm PQC integration in TLS/Ipsec.	TLS Scanner, testssl.sh
Algorithm agility test	Ensure that crypto libraries support switching to future PQC standards.	OQS-OpenSSL, liboqs

Here is an example of checking for PQC-enabled cipher support in TLS:

```
openssl s_client -connect example.com:443 -cipher OQS_KYBER_LEVEL1
```

Penetration Testing and Adversarial Simulations

Organizations should test real-world attack scenarios in PQC deployments, which involves the following:

- Testing post-quantum TLS resilience:
    - Simulate on-path attacks against Kyber key exchange.
    - Test fallback vulnerabilities when clients negotiate non-PQC cipher suites.
- Measuring algorithm resistance to quantum attacks:
    - Use Grover's search algorithm to simulate quantum brute-force attacks.
    - Validate hash-based signature schemes against quantum preimage attacks (using SPHINCS+).

Stress Testing and Performance Benchmarking

Because PQC algorithms introduce higher computational overhead, organizations must benchmark system performance under real-world conditions. Table 6-3 outlines sample tests, metrics, and acceptable thresholds for stress testing and performance benchmarking.

Table 6-3 Stress Testing and Performance Benchmarking

Test	Metric	Acceptable Threshold
TLS 1.3 handshake speed	PQC versus RSA handshake time	<30% overhead
Memory usage	Additional RAM required for PQC operations	<50MB per session
Encryption throughput	PQC versus RSA data encryption speed	>80% of RSA baseline

Here is an example of benchmarking Kyber key exchange performance:

```
openssl speed -evp kyber512
```

Quantum-Safe Supply Chain Security

Organizations should implement SBOMs (software bills of materials) for cryptographic libraries and use Vulnerability Exploitability eXchange (VEX) to monitor PQC-related vulnerabilities.

Here is an example of automating PQC vulnerability checks:

```
sbom-tool generate --input openquantumsafe-1.2.0.tar.gz --output sbom.json
```

Compliance and Regulatory Readiness

As PQC adoption grows, organizations must comply with emerging security regulations, including the following:

- NIST PQC standards, such as Draft SP 800-208 for key management
- ISO/IEC 14888-3 for post-quantum digital signatures
- European eIDAS 2.0 for quantum-safe authentication frameworks

Security Assurance in Quantum-Safe Implementations

Assessing the quantum resistance of PQAs is a complex process. Attack models and vulnerabilities in traditional cryptographic systems are well understood, but the field of post-quantum cryptography is evolving. Algorithms such as CRYSTALS-Kyber, CRYSTALS-Dilithium, and SPHINCS+ must be evaluated for their robustness against known classical and quantum attacks and also for their resilience to theoretical vulnerabilities that could emerge as quantum technology matures. This evaluation demands specialized expertise in quantum cryptanalysis and significant computational resources to simulate attack scenarios.

The need for robust testing against emerging quantum-enabled attack vectors adds another layer of complexity. Quantum attacks, such as those using Grover's algorithm and Shor's algorithm, exploit the principles of superposition and entanglement to undermine classical cryptographic systems. While PQAs are designed to resist these attacks, validating their effectiveness requires adversarial simulations that replicate real-world quantum threats. These simulations must account for variations in quantum hardware capabilities and attack strategies, ensuring that the algorithms remain secure under diverse conditions.

Another critical aspect of security assurance is the challenge of algorithm agility. Given the uncertainty surrounding the future landscape of quantum threats, organizations must prepare for the possibility that currently standardized PQAs could be rendered obsolete by advancements in quantum computing or cryptanalysis. To address this, systems must be designed with the flexibility to accommodate future cryptographic upgrades. Organizations should implement mechanisms for seamless algorithm replacement and ensure that updates do not disrupt system operations or introduce vulnerabilities.

The process of validating security assurance involves collaboration with international standardization bodies, such as the NIST and the International Organization for Standardization (ISO). The standards of these bodies provide a baseline for evaluating the security and performance of PQAs. However, reliance on evolving standards also introduces risks, as premature adoption of algorithms that are still under review could expose systems to unforeseen vulnerabilities.

To ensure robust security assurance, organizations must adopt the following strategies:

- **Comprehensive cryptographic audits:** Organizations should conduct regular audits to evaluate the effectiveness of implemented PQAs and identify potential vulnerabilities. These audits should incorporate both theoretical and practical assessments, leveraging insights from cryptanalysis research and real-world testing.
- **Adversarial simulations:** Organizations should develop advanced testing environments to simulate quantum-enabled attacks. This includes creating test networks where PQAs can be subjected to stress testing under realistic threat scenarios.
- **Algorithm agility:** Organizations should design systems with modular cryptographic frameworks that facilitate the seamless integration and replacement of PQAs as new algorithms are developed and standardized.
- **Collaboration with standards bodies:** Organizations should engage actively with global standardization initiatives to stay informed about advancements in post-quantum cryptography and ensure compliance with best practices.

Hybrid Cryptographic Frameworks

Hybrid cryptographic frameworks are an essential transitional strategy for transitioning from classical to post-quantum cryptographic systems. These frameworks strategically combine classical algorithms, such as RSA or ECC, with post-quantum algorithms like CRYSTALS-Kyber. By simultaneously deploying both types of cryptography, hybrid frameworks offer a dual-layered defense mechanism that ensures continued security and functionality during the migration phase. This approach is particularly critical because the post-quantum algorithms being implemented are relatively new and may face unforeseen vulnerabilities during initial deployment.

The use of hybrid cryptographic frameworks ensures backward compatibility with legacy systems, which is a significant requirement for large-scale and distributed infrastructures that cannot undergo immediate and wholesale replacement. For example, in a hybrid TLS handshake, the cryptographic process may integrate CRYSTALS-Kyber for secure key exchange to protect against quantum adversaries, and RSA may be retained to provide compatibility with existing protocols and clients. Such integration is particularly valuable in critical sectors like financial services or national defense, where maintaining operational stability and compliance with existing regulatory frameworks is non-negotiable.

A practical implementation of this hybrid approach might involve the deployment of CRYSTALS-Kyber for forward secrecy while continuing to use ECC-based digital signatures for authentication purposes. This strategy secures communications against future quantum threats and ensures interoperability with devices or systems that have yet to transition to post-quantum standards. Specific configurations might require customization, such as adjusting the cryptographic handshake in TLS 1.3 to accommodate dual key exchanges or updating HSMs to support combined cryptographic operations without introducing performance bottlenecks.

In addition to ensuring compatibility, hybrid frameworks provide a safety net by allowing organizations to monitor and validate the robustness of post-quantum algorithms in real-world conditions before committing fully to their exclusive use. This dual-layer approach addresses a critical challenge: the lack of operational history and extensive stress testing for post-quantum algorithms, such as CRYSTALS-Dilithium, SPHINCS+, and Kyber. Should any vulnerabilities arise during this transitional phase, legacy systems remain operational to mitigate risk.

Technically, implementing hybrid frameworks requires a detailed understanding of cryptographic protocol design. For instance, the handshake mechanisms in TLS must be carefully modified to ensure that the negotiated cryptographic suite supports dual operations without causing increased latency or system overhead. Additionally, key management systems must be updated to generate and store both classical and post-quantum keys securely, considering the larger key sizes typical of post-quantum algorithms. In systems like OpenSSL or BoringSSL, such modifications often involve enabling support for hybrid cryptographic suites, ensuring compatibility with post-quantum algorithms approved by NIST, and rigorously testing for compatibility with various deployment scenarios.

The adoption of hybrid cryptographic frameworks facilitates a secure and phased migration to post-quantum cryptography and addresses the operational challenges of scaling quantum-safe solutions in environments with constrained computational or bandwidth resources, such as embedded systems and IoT devices. By providing a dual-layer security model, these frameworks ensure that organizations remain protected from current and emergent cryptographic threats, offering a critical bridge to a fully quantum-resistant future.

Protocol and Hardware Upgrades

The transition to quantum-safe systems requires wide-ranging upgrades to communication protocols and hardware infrastructure to accommodate the computational demands and larger key sizes characteristic of post-quantum cryptography. These upgrades need to address the compatibility and performance challenges and also ensure that security standards are upheld across diverse deployment environments.

Protocol Upgrades

Modern communication protocols such as Transport Layer Security (TLS) and Internet Protocol Security (IPsec) require significant modifications to integrate post-quantum algorithms. For TLS, the implementation of hybrid cryptographic frameworks is essential. Hybrid key exchange mechanisms, such as those combining RSA or ECC with CRYSTALS-Kyber, ensure that post-quantum resilience can coexist with existing cryptographic infrastructures during the transitional period. This hybrid approach allows for continued interoperability with legacy clients while progressively introducing quantum-safe components into the handshake protocol.

The TLS handshake, in particular, must be restructured to accommodate larger key sizes and signatures associated with post-quantum cryptography. This involves extending the ClientHello and ServerHello messages to support new cipher suites and key-exchange algorithms. It also requires modifications to the certificate chain and digital signature verification processes to ensure compatibility with post-quantum algorithms like Dilithium and SPHINCS+.

Similarly, IPsec, a protocol suite for securing internet communication, must adapt its Internet Key Exchange (IKE) mechanism to support hybrid post-quantum key exchanges. For instance, extensions to the IKE payload format will be necessary to accommodate the larger key material generated by lattice-based or code-based cryptographic algorithms. Furthermore, these modifications must ensure seamless backward compatibility with existing IPsec deployments, particularly in environments such as corporate VPNs, where legacy systems are widespread.

In addition to requiring functional changes, these protocol upgrades demand rigorous performance testing. Parameters such as handshake latency, packet size overhead, and throughput must be closely monitored to identify and mitigate any bottlenecks introduced by the computational complexity of post-quantum cryptography. Simulation environments replicating real-world conditions, including high-latency and bandwidth-constrained networks, should be employed to validate these protocol enhancements.

Hardware Upgrades

Hardware components, including secure enclaves, HSMs, and cryptographic accelerators, must be upgraded to handle the increased computational and storage requirements of post-quantum cryptographic operations. Secure enclaves, designed to execute sensitive operations in isolated environments, must now support more demanding mathematical computations, such as lattice-based polynomial arithmetic and matrix multiplications. Vendors will need to introduce hardware-level optimizations, such as specialized instruction sets for modular arithmetic and fast Fourier transforms, to improve efficiency.

HSMs, which provide secure storage and processing for cryptographic keys, must evolve to meet the dual demands of supporting hybrid cryptographic frameworks and fully post-quantum operations. Firmware updates are necessary to include post-quantum cryptographic libraries, while hardware modifications should focus on increasing processing power, memory capacity, and parallel execution capabilities. For example, HSMs must be designed to securely store the significantly larger keys used in CRYSTALS-Kyber and to handle the extensive signing operations required by algorithms like SPHINCS+.

These upgrades also extend to network hardware such as firewalls, load balancers, and edge devices, which must support updated protocols and cryptographic standards. Firmware updates for these devices should incorporate the latest post-quantum cryptographic libraries and ensure compatibility with hybrid frameworks to maintain network security during the migration phase.

The transition to quantum-safe cryptographic systems requires significant upgrades to protocol and hardware infrastructure. Table 6-4 outlines concrete specifications and requirements for implementing PQC, including memory and processing power needs, performance benchmarks, cost implications, and phased upgrade strategies. These detailed requirements provide a roadmap for organizations planning to integrate PQC into their security infrastructure while ensuring a smooth migration path from legacy cryptographic systems.

Table 6-4 Quantum-Safe Hardware Upgrade Specifications: Performance, Cost, and Migration Strategies

Category	Specifications and Requirements
Memory requirements	Kyber-512: 32KB per session Kyber-768: 48KB Kyber-1024: 64KB SPHINCS+: 128KB for signature operations
Processing power needs	Minimum: 4-core CPU with AVX2 support Recommended: 8-core CPU with 16GB RAM GPU acceleration for SPHINCS+ recommended
Performance benchmarks	TLS 1.3 handshake with Kyber-512: 1.5x RSA-3072 latency Throughput overhead: 10%–20% increase CPU utilization: 5%–15% increase versus ECC
Cost implications of hardware upgrades	HSM upgrades: $50,000 per unit Network hardware firmware updates: $5,000 per site Custom FPGA solutions: $100,000+ per deployment
Return on investment (ROI) considerations	Projected savings from quantum-ready infrastructure: 20% lower cryptographic management costs over 5 years. Enhanced security reduces breach recovery costs.
Phasing strategies for hardware upgrades	Phase 1: Hybrid PQC–classical TLS deployment Phase 2: Full post-quantum key exchange Phase 3: Transition to PQC-only signatures
Migration paths from existing hardware	Legacy RSA-based hardware can operate in hybrid mode using dual-stack cryptographic libraries before complete transition.
Testing procedures for new hardware	Deploy test environments with simulated quantum attacks. Benchmark post-quantum algorithms in production-like settings before rollout.
Fallback mechanisms during hardware transitions	Ensure that dual cryptographic stacks (RSA and Kyber) are operational before full migration. Enable rollback policies for unexpected failures.

The data presented in Table 6-4 highlights the increased computational and memory demands introduced by PQC algorithms, particularly in the context of real-world deployments such as TLS 1.3 and IPsec. Notably, Kyber-based key exchanges require significantly larger memory allocations compared to traditional RSA/ECC counterparts, which impacts CPU utilization and network throughput. The financial implications of these upgrades, particularly for HSMs and network firmware updates, demonstrate the need for a phased migration strategy to balance security enhancements with cost efficiency. Additionally, the inclusion of fallback mechanisms, such as dual cryptographic stacks (RSA and Kyber), ensures continued interoperability during the transition period, reducing the risk of operational disruptions.

Deployment Considerations

The deployment of updated protocols and hardware must follow a phased approach to minimize operational disruptions. Isolated or low-priority environments for pilot deployments provide controlled settings for identifying and resolving compatibility issues, performance inefficiencies, and potential security vulnerabilities. Only after thorough validation should organizations proceed to full-scale deployment in critical environments.

Interoperability testing is crucial to ensure that upgraded systems can seamlessly communicate with legacy infrastructure during the transitional period. This includes testing hybrid setups where traditional algorithms (e.g., RSA) are used alongside post-quantum alternatives. Tools like Wireshark can be used to analyze network traffic and verify the correct implementation of post-quantum cipher suites in TLS and IPsec.

Scalability and Efficiency in Quantum-Safe Systems

The scalability and efficiency of quantum-safe systems are essential for ensuring their widespread adoption across diverse computational environments. As PQAs introduce significant challenges—particularly with respect to larger key sizes, bandwidth requirements, and operational scalability—organizations must carefully balance cryptographic robustness with performance demands. The deployment of PQAs requires architectural adjustments across communication protocols, storage systems, and hardware resources, especially in large-scale distributed networks, real-time systems, and resource-constrained environments like IoT. This section explores the implications of key size and bandwidth demands, operational challenges in scaling post-quantum cryptography, and strategies to optimize performance and resource allocation. It also highlights the roles of efficient algorithm selection and protocol adaptations in addressing the computational and infrastructural challenges posed by quantum-safe cryptographic systems.

Key Size and Bandwidth Requirements

One of the primary challenges in adopting PQAs is the significant increase in key sizes and signature lengths compared to traditional cryptographic systems. Many quantum-resistant algorithms, such as lattice-based and code-based cryptography, require key sizes that are magnitudes larger than those of RSA or ECC. For example, the CRYSTALS-Kyber algorithm, a widely studied candidate for post-quantum key exchange, may require public keys exceeding several kilobytes in size (typically around 1,500–3,300 bytes, depending on the parameter set), whereas RSA-2048 uses a 256-byte (2 kilobit) public key and ECC keys can be as small as 32–64 bytes for equivalent security levels. This substantial difference in key sizes has direct implications for bandwidth, storage, and performance in real-world systems.

The larger key sizes introduce constraints on bandwidth, especially in environments where communication channels are already limited. For instance, IoT devices operating on low-power wide-area networks (LPWANs) or satellite communication systems might struggle to handle the increased data payloads. In such scenarios, the additional overhead associated with transmitting larger keys or signatures can lead to higher latency, reduced throughput, and increased energy consumption. These factors are particularly problematic for real-time systems where performance and efficiency are paramount.

Storage requirements also become a concern with larger keys and signatures. Systems that rely on secure storage for cryptographic material, such as HSMs or secure enclaves, might require hardware upgrades to accommodate the increased memory demands. For example, the storage of keys for millions of users in a large-scale authentication system could necessitate significant investments in storage infrastructure, potentially increasing deployment costs.

Communication protocols, such as TLS and IPsec, also face challenges in adapting to the larger cryptographic payloads. These protocols must be reconfigured or redesigned to support the increased message sizes while maintaining compatibility with existing infrastructure. In addition, larger keys and signatures can affect packet fragmentation and reassembly processes, potentially impacting the reliability of data transmission in constrained networks.

To address these challenges, optimization strategies are being explored. One approach is to develop hybrid cryptographic schemes that combine post-quantum algorithms with traditional algorithms, allowing for gradual adaptation while mitigating the immediate impact on bandwidth and storage. Another strategy involves leveraging compression techniques to reduce the size of cryptographic payloads, although this must be balanced against the computational overhead introduced by compression and decompression processes.

Operational Scalability

Operational scalability is a significant challenge in the deployment of PQAs, particularly in large-scale distributed systems where performance, reliability, and resource efficiency are vital. These challenges stem primarily from the computational and infrastructural demands of PQAs, which must integrate seamlessly into complex environments such as high-frequency trading platforms, expansive data centers, and global networks.

One of the core difficulties lies in the increased computational overhead associated with PQAs. Algorithms like CRYSTALS-Kyber and CRYSTALS-Dilithium demand significantly more processing power for encryption, decryption, and key generation compared to traditional algorithms such as RSA and ECC. In high-frequency trading systems, where milliseconds can determine profitability, the latency introduced by post-quantum cryptography can directly impact operational efficiency. Similarly, data centers handling massive volumes of encrypted traffic may face resource bottlenecks if the transition to PQAs is not carefully optimized.

The key size and signature lengths of PQAs also pose scalability challenges. Larger key sizes increase the bandwidth requirements for secure communications, complicating their deployment in systems with limited network capacity. Distributed systems operating across geographies must adapt to these increased bandwidth demands without degrading the quality of service or introducing latency issues, which can be particularly problematic for applications that require real-time communication.

Another critical aspect of scalability involves resource constraints in global networks and specialized environments. For instance, IoT devices, which are often constrained by limited computational power, memory, and energy, might struggle to support the larger keys and processing requirements of PQAs. In global networks, synchronizing post-quantum upgrades across geographically dispersed nodes further complicates scalability. The potential for inconsistencies during these upgrades can result in system vulnerabilities or temporary service interruptions.

The deployment of PQAs in large-scale environments also necessitates adjustments to existing protocols and infrastructure. Protocols such as TLS and IPsec must be adapted to accommodate the unique properties of post-quantum cryptography while ensuring compatibility with legacy systems during the transition. These adaptations must also account for the increased processing and communication demands of PQAs without undermining the operational stability of the network.

To address these challenges, organizations must adopt a phased approach to the implementation of PQAs in distributed systems that includes the following phases:

1. **Performance optimization:** This phase focuses on leveraging hardware accelerators, such as GPUs or quantum-safe HSMs, to handle the increased computational demands of PQAs efficiently.
2. **Hybrid cryptographic solutions:** Using hybrid schemes that combine classical and post-quantum algorithms makes it possible for systems to transition gradually without compromising performance.
3. **Protocol enhancements:** This phase focuses on updating cryptographic protocols to support post-quantum algorithms while maintaining backward compatibility with legacy systems.
4. **Monitoring and adjustment:** Finally, monitoring tools are deployed to evaluate the impact of PQAs on system performance and configurations are fine-tuned to address resource bottlenecks.

Efficient Algorithm Selection

The diversity of PQAs requires the development of a personalized methodology in which each algorithm is evaluated against specific use cases and operational constraints.

For instance, CRYSTALS-Kyber, renowned for its scalability and efficiency, is particularly well suited to key exchange protocols in high-performance environments. Conversely, CRYSTALS-Dilithium excels in applications demanding secure and efficient digital signatures, with an emphasis on low computational overhead and swift verification. Stateless signature schemes such as SPHINCS+, which provide robust security, are invaluable in contexts where state management is impractical. McEliece, with its unparalleled resilience to quantum attacks, offers a solution for long-term confidentiality but must contend with the challenge of significantly larger key sizes. These examples underscore the importance of tailoring algorithm selection to the specific security and performance demands of the deployment scenario.

Beyond matching algorithms to functional requirements, computational constraints must be considered. Resource-constrained systems, such as IoT devices and embedded platforms, often operate under limits on processing power and memory capacity. In these environments, lightweight PQAs must be prioritized to ensure that cryptographic robustness does not undermine the system's broader functionality or efficiency. Comprehensive performance benchmarks, evaluating metrics such as encryption and decryption speeds, memory utilization, and communication latency, are indispensable in guiding algorithm selection for such constrained settings.

Adopting modular cryptography is a forward-thinking approach to algorithm selection and future-proofing. By decoupling cryptographic layers from underlying systems, modular architectures allow for the seamless integration of new algorithms as they emerge, obviating the need for extensive infrastructure reconfiguration. This adaptability is particularly critical given the evolving nature of quantum threats and the potential for vulnerabilities to be discovered in existing PQAs.

To operationalize efficient algorithm selection, organizations must engage in a structured evaluation process. This should commence with a thorough analysis of use cases, delineating the specific security objectives, operational requirements, and limitations of the system in question. Rigorous performance testing in simulated environments is then essential to ascertain the effectiveness of candidate algorithms, with a focus on computational overhead, memory demands, and key size efficiency. Furthermore, risk assessments must weigh the trade-offs between security robustness and performance, particularly for latency-sensitive applications. Compliance with internationally recognized standards, such as those set by NIST, ensures interoperability and adherence to best practices. Finally, modular integration frameworks must be incorporated into system design to facilitate future algorithmic updates.

Selecting an appropriate PQC algorithm requires a structured evaluation framework that considers various performance, security, and implementation factors. Table 6-5 provides a comparative analysis of four major PQC candidates—CRYSTALS-Kyber, CRYSTALS-Dilithium, SPHINCS+, and McEliece—across key selection criteria such as key exchange efficiency, digital signature performance, computational overhead, memory requirements, and scalability. This structured approach helps organizations align cryptographic choices with specific real-world applications, such as TLS key exchanges, IoT authentication, secure government communications, and financial transactions.

Table 6-5 Structured Evaluation Matrix for PQC Algorithms

Evaluation Criteria	CRYSTALS-Kyber	CRYSTALS-Dilithium	SPHINCS+	McEliece
Key exchange efficiency	High (Kyber is optimized for key exchange, with minimal handshake overhead.)	Not applicable	Not applicable	Low (Large key sizes increase handshake latency.)
Digital signature performance	Not applicable	High (Dilithium offers fast signature generation and verification.)	Moderate (SPHINCS+ uses a stateless signature scheme, providing slower verification.)	Not applicable
Memory requirements	Moderate (Kyber-512 requires 32KB.)	Moderate (Dilithium-2 requires 48KB.)	High (SPHINCS+-128 requires 128KB.)	Very high (Key sizes in the megabytes range.)
Computational overhead	Low (Lattice-based optimizations are used.)	Low (Efficient lattice-based operations are used.)	High (Hash-based cryptography is computationally expensive.)	High (Extensive computation is required for encryption.)
Security against quantum attacks	Strong (Kyber is a NIST-selected finalist.)	Strong (Dilithium is a NIST-selected finalist.)	Very strong (SPHINCS+ does not rely on lattice or number-theoretic assumptions.)	Very strong (McEliece has resisted cryptanalysis for decades.)
Suitability for IoT and embedded systems	Moderate (Kyber requires significant RAM and is not ideal for constrained devices.)	Low (Dilithium is not optimized for resource-constrained environments.)	Moderate (SPHINCS+ can be used in IoT, but the memory footprint is large.)	Very low (McEliece is not feasible for IoT or embedded systems.)
Interoperability with classical cryptography	Excellent (Hybrid implementations with RSA or ECC are possible.)	Excellent (Hybrid schemes with classical signatures are possible.)	Low (No direct hybrid integration with RSA or ECC is possible.)	Low (It is difficult to integrate McEliece with classical cryptographic systems.)
Standardization and compliance	Kyber is a NIST PQC finalist, and ISO standardization is in progress.	Dilithium is a NIST PQC finalist, and ISO standardization is in progress.	SPHINCS+ is a NIST PQC finalist and is suitable for long-term signature applications.	McEliece is a NIST PQC finalist, but adoption is challenging due to key sizes.
Scalability for high-performance systems	High (Kyber is used in TLS 1.3 and is suitable for cloud computing.)	Moderate (Dilithium is optimized for authentication-based applications.)	Low (SPHINCS+ is not efficient for high-performance environments.)	Low (McEliece is best suited for high-security, long-term confidentiality needs.)
Future-proofing and algorithm agility	Strong (Kyber has a modular design and is adaptable to future cryptographic frameworks.)	Strong (Dilithium is designed for post-quantum secure authentication.)	Moderate (The stateless design of SPHINCS+ ensures its long-term viability.)	Weak (Large key sizes limit practical deployment flexibility.)

Table 6-5 highlights the trade-offs between different PQC algorithms, offering insights into their applicability across various environments. CRYSTALS-Kyber, with its low-latency key exchange and moderate memory footprint, is well suited for TLS 1.3 and VPN encryption in enterprise and cloud environments. CRYSTALS-Dilithium, optimized for signature operations, is ideal for authentication systems, including code-signing, digital certificates, and secure software updates. SPHINCS+, while highly secure, has a high computational cost, making it best suited for long-term archival security and tamper-proof logging where speed is secondary. McEliece, with its large key sizes, is impractical for most real-time applications but remains an excellent choice for secure government and military communications that require long-term encryption durability.

Optimization for Resource-Constrained Systems

Optimizing post-quantum algorithms for resource-constrained systems, such as IoT devices and mobile platforms, is critical to ensuring widespread adoption without compromising system performance. These environments often operate with stringent limitations in terms of computational power, memory, and energy resources, presenting unique challenges for implementing PQC, which is typically characterized by larger key sizes and greater computational demands compared to classical cryptographic methods.

One strategy involves adopting lightweight post-quantum algorithms specifically tailored for low-power and constrained devices. For instance, NIST finalists like CRYSTALS-Kyber and Dilithium, while robust, might need customized configurations for such environments. Algorithms such as SPHINCS+, which offers stateless signature schemes, or streamlined variations of lattice-based cryptography, can be adapted to minimize the computational burden while maintaining acceptable levels of security. In these scenarios, developers can focus on reducing the operational footprint by optimizing matrix arithmetic, leveraging sparse representations, or employing hardware acceleration through embedded cryptographic cores.

Balancing computational overhead with system performance in resource-constrained systems often requires end-to-end evaluation of cryptographic operations. For example, hybrid cryptographic implementations can temporarily offload some computations to classical algorithms during transitional phases, enabling a gradual shift to post-quantum mechanisms without overwhelming the system. Additionally, using hardware optimizations, such as field-programmable gate arrays (FPGAs) or application-specific integrated circuits (ASICs), can accelerate key exchange and digital signature verification processes, mitigating the latency typically associated with PQC.

Another critical consideration is the integration of post-quantum cryptography within existing communication protocols, such as Message Queuing Telemetry Transport (MQTT) for IoT or HTTPS for mobile applications. The challenge lies in maintaining low latency while adhering to security requirements. Protocol adaptations, such as modifying handshake procedures in constrained environments or incorporating lightweight key encapsulation mechanisms, are essential for achieving this balance. Ensuring compatibility with bandwidth-limited networks is equally important, given that larger key and signature sizes in PQC can strain communication channels. Compression techniques and optimized data structures can help address these limitations without compromising security.

To facilitate this optimization, empirical testing and profiling of post-quantum algorithms in target environments are essential. Benchmarking tools designed for resource-constrained systems can provide insights into the trade-offs between security strength and operational performance. Metrics such as encryption/decryption speed, memory utilization, and energy consumption must be rigorously analyzed to identify bottlenecks and refine implementation strategies. For example, reducing the frequency of cryptographic operations by extending session lifetimes or caching cryptographic computations can alleviate resource strain without exposing the system to significant vulnerabilities.

Case Study on PQC and Emerging AI Threats

The first part of this chapter examined PQC as a necessary step in protecting sensitive data from future quantum-enabled attacks. However, cryptographic security alone is not sufficient, as attackers are also expected to exploit AI to enhance malware capabilities, making traditional detection methods less effective. Sandbox-based malware analysis plays a key role in identifying and mitigating these evolving threats.

Quantum computing is likely to be used in advanced malware obfuscation, encrypted command-and-control (C2) channels, and polymorphic adaptation, making it harder to detect malicious activity using conventional techniques. Similarly, AI-driven malware will introduce new evasion strategies, allowing threats to modify their behavior dynamically in response to security measures. This section provides a case study on Cape Sandbox, an open-source malware analysis platform, to explore how sandbox environments must be adapted to address the new challenges.

In this section, we extend the discussion of post-quantum security by demonstrating how quantum-resistant encryption, digital signatures, and hybrid cryptographic techniques can be integrated into sandbox-based malware detection systems. The goal is to ensure that malware using quantum-based cryptographic techniques or AI-enhanced deception can be identified and contained. By linking cryptographic resilience with advanced threat detection, this case study outlines a practical approach for strengthening cybersecurity defenses against emerging risks.

Cape Sandbox: AI Malware Analysis and Threat Detection

Cape Sandbox[6] is a platform for malware analysis that is adaptable for analyzing AI-powered threats and complex, polymorphic malware. Using dynamic execution environments and deep integration with AI frameworks, Cape Sandbox facilitates behavioral and static analysis. In this case study we're going to look at how to adapt Cape Sandbox for quantum-based AGI malware analysis, covering its core functionalities, setup process, and step-by-step workflows for detecting and mitigating advanced threats. Given that the best quantum chip at the present moment, the Willow chip,[7] can only operate with 1 qubit, and we need around 4000 qubits to break RSA and 8000 to break Bitcoin,[8] many of the case study sections are based on anticipated quantum and AGI capabilities.

Cape Sandbox represents a significant advancement in malware analysis, and it incorporates advanced dynamic analysis capabilities designed for dissecting AI-based threats. It delivers granular insights into malware behavior by focusing on interactions with host systems, APIs, and network infrastructures. Among its key features, Cape Sandbox allows for the execution of malware in a controlled sandbox environment, enabling real-time capture of behavioral patterns. Its AI-enhanced pattern recognition uses machine learning models to identify evasive tactics, such as virtualization awareness and sandbox detection. The platform also excels in polymorphic code analysis, tracking malware mutations during execution to reveal adaptive capabilities. Furthermore, its integration with external threat intelligence feeds facilitates rapid identification of known threats. Finally, the modular and extensible design of Cape Sandbox enables analysts to customize configurations and simulate unique environments, enhancing its applicability to diverse security scenarios (see Figure 6-1).

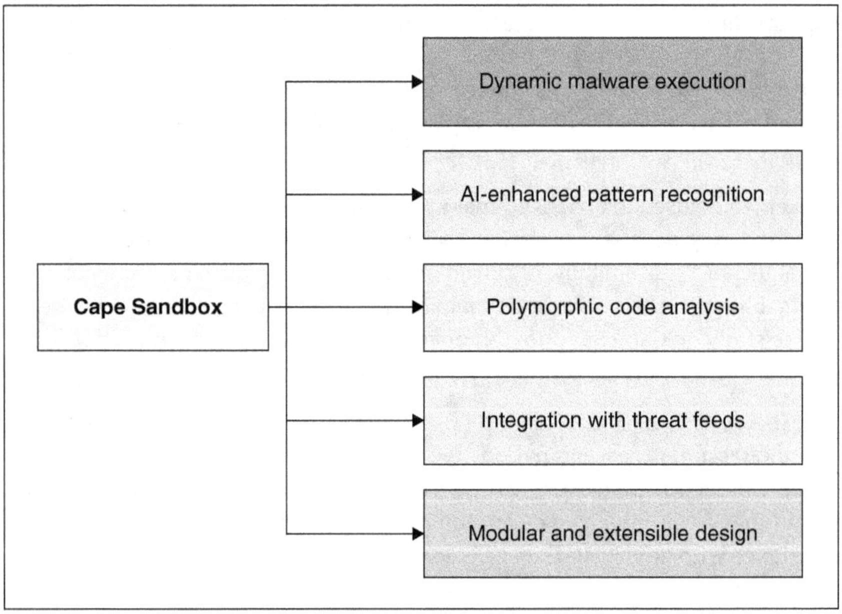

Figure 6-1
AI malware analysis and threat detection with Cape Sandbox.

Figure 6-1 details the current capabilities of Cape Sandbox, which will need to evolve significantly to address the complexities introduced by quantum-based and AGI-enhanced malware threats. Such significant changes in threat analysis will require integration of quantum-resistant cryptographic principles, enhanced AI-driven dynamic analysis, and simulation environments capable of accommodating quantum-level computations and AGI logic. The advancements in these domains will enable Cape Sandbox to dissect malware powered by quantum algorithms and AGI, which are anticipated to introduce unprecedented levels of adaptability and evasion.

Dynamic malware execution in this enhanced version will need to include quantum-resilient virtualization layers that isolate malware leveraging quantum computations for encryption or data exfiltration. By utilizing quantum-safe enclaves, a sandbox can maintain a secure environment to monitor and capture the real-time behaviors of such malware, ensuring that quantum-powered evasive techniques are rendered ineffective. AI-enhanced pattern recognition will also evolve to include deep-learning models designed specifically to detect quantum and AGI patterns, such as the ability to predict AGI-generated code behaviors and the identification of AGI-based strategies that dynamically shift malware objectives during execution.

Polymorphic code analysis will play a critical role, as AGI and quantum-based malware are expected to exhibit near-infinite mutation capabilities, enabled by quantum randomness and AGI's logic synthesis. Enhanced mutation-tracking mechanisms, combined with quantum-state-aware analysis tools, will ensure a comprehensive understanding of how these malware variants adapt and evolve. Additionally, the sandbox's integration with quantum-safe threat feeds will allow the rapid correlation of observed behaviors with known quantum-powered attacks, further reducing the response time in critical infrastructure scenarios.

To accommodate the modular and extensible needs of future analysts, Cape Sandbox will incorporate quantum-computing simulations and AGI-driven adaptability within its configurations. This design will allow cyber analysts to replicate unique quantum environments and simulate potential AGI responses, enabling a proactive approach to cybersecurity. Such extensibility will also facilitate the integration of quantum-resilient cryptographic modules and AGI-powered heuristics for preemptive threat detection.

Using Cape Sandbox for AI malware analysis begins with environment configuration (see Figure 6-2 in the next section). This step aims to establish a simulated target environment within the sandbox that mirrors the operational conditions of the malware under analysis. Customized environments are essential as they closely replicate real-world scenarios, enhancing the precision and relevance of the behavioral insights gained from the analysis.

To complete this configuration, analysts first need to set up virtual machines (VMs) tailored with specific operating systems and software stacks, such as Windows 10 coupled with vulnerable versions of commonly exploited applications like Microsoft Office. This allows for a realistic representation of the malware's intended target environment. Additionally, network emulation must be enabled to simulate internet connectivity and establish command-and-control (C2) channels, which are commonly leveraged by sophisticated malware for external communications. Finally, Cape Sandbox's agent needs to be installed within the virtual machines. This agent facilitates comprehensive monitoring by capturing detailed information about system calls, file activities, and network interactions, providing a holistic view of the behavior of malware in the configured environment.

Step 1: Environment Configuration

The initial step in using Cape Sandbox for the analysis of AI-powered malware is the environment configuration. This stage is critical as it establishes a simulated setting that mirrors the real-world environment in which the malware is likely to operate. The setup is essential for enhancing the precision of behavioral analysis by accurately capturing how malware interacts with its host systems, network infrastructure, and underlying software.

VMs must be configured with specific operating systems and software stacks that reflect the target environment. For instance, a Windows 10 VM equipped with outdated or vulnerable versions of widely used applications, such as Microsoft Office, can simulate a plausible attack surface. Network emulation is another indispensable component, enabling the replication of internet connectivity and C2 channels. The idea is to ensure that the malware's networking behavior, such as data exfiltration or domain queries, can be observed in a realistic context.

The deployment of Cape Sandbox's agent on the VM further enhances monitoring capabilities. This agent facilitates comprehensive tracking of system-level interactions, including system calls, file manipulations, and network activities. By integrating these components into a cohesive environment, analysts can observe the malware's actions in a controlled yet authentic setting, laying the foundation for subsequent analytical steps. This configuration, illustrated in Figure 6-2, underscores Cape Sandbox's role as a sophisticated tool for the detection and understanding of advanced malware threats.

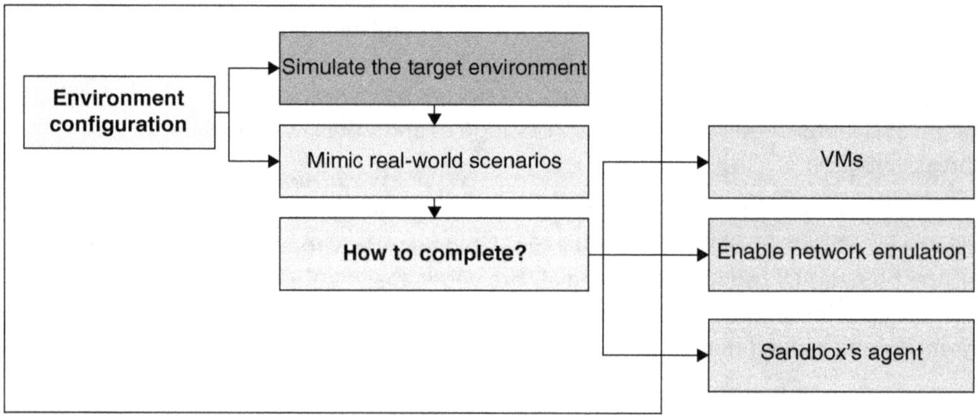

Figure 6-2
Environment configuration for AI malware analysis.

Quantum AGI will transform the process described above and the threat landscape and require significant adaptations to the Cape Sandbox tools described in Figure 6-2. While the foundational objective of the sandbox—simulating the environment where malware operates—will remain unchanged, the configuration process must evolve to accommodate the complexities introduced by quantum-enhanced and AGI-driven threats. These advancements demand enhanced capacity to replicate quantum computing environments, simulate AGI behavior, and analyze malware leveraging quantum algorithms or autonomous adaptive capabilities.

In future deployments, environment configuration will require quantum-enhanced VMs capable of simulating hybrid quantum-classical environments. These VMs must replicate scenarios where malware utilizes quantum algorithms for encryption, key exchange, or data exfiltration. Such environments should include preconfigured quantum-computing simulators and libraries of quantum-enhanced malware samples to enable analysts to observe behaviors that are fundamentally distinct from those in classical malware paradigms. For instance, quantum-based encryption, such as Grover's algorithm–accelerated hashing, demands monitoring and decoding capabilities tailored to quantum state transitions.

The network emulation capabilities of Cape Sandbox must also advance to support quantum-safe communication protocols, such as post-quantum TLS, and to simulate interactions in environments that are resistant to quantum-enabled attacks. This means enhancing C2 channel simulations to account for AGI-driven adaptive strategies, such as dynamically shifting command protocols based on sandbox-detection patterns. The ability to replicate these evolving threat scenarios is critical for evaluating the full operational impact of quantum-enhanced and AGI-directed malware.

To address the increased complexity of monitoring, the sandbox's agent technology must be upgraded to accommodate quantum and AGI operations. Future agents will need to track quantum-level computations, including qubit configurations and superposition-based decision trees, as well as AGI's anticipatory and autonomous behaviors. These agents must possess capabilities to detect logical leaps and adaptive malware mutations that exploit sandbox vulnerabilities. Furthermore, the agents should integrate with predictive models trained on AGI behaviors, enabling them to anticipate evasive tactics and respond dynamically during the analysis process.

Additionally, the sandbox must incorporate mechanisms for logging and analyzing quantum states to detect malware employing quantum-specific operations. Such mechanisms could provide unparalleled insights into the interactions between quantum malware and target environments, ensuring a comprehensive understanding of potential attack vectors. Simultaneously, AGI-aware dynamic resource allocation must be implemented to accommodate the high computational demands of quantum simulations and AGI-driven decision-making processes without degrading performance.

The current configuration of Cape Sandbox (refer to Figure 6-2) for a quantum- and AGI-dominated future will extend beyond traditional virtualization and network emulation. It must encompass the simulation of quantum environments, the deployment of quantum-safe communication protocols, and the integration of advanced monitoring technologies capable of dissecting the novel complexities of quantum- and AGI-driven malware. These enhancements will ensure that Cape Sandbox develops the capabilities for quantum AGI threat analysis.

Step 2: Submitting Malware Samples

The second step in using Cape Sandbox for AI malware analysis involves the submission of malware samples. This process allows for real-time observation of how the malware operates and interacts with its environment, providing insights into its runtime behaviors and malicious intent. Effective submission is particularly significant when dealing with advanced threats such as AI-powered or polymorphic malware, which often exhibit dynamic and evasive characteristics that demand rigorous scrutiny.

Cape Sandbox is adaptable to a range of workflows. To initiate the submission process, analysts can either use Cape Sandbox's intuitive web interface or use its RESTful API for automation. When submitting malware samples, analysts can customize parameters to enhance the depth and scope of analysis. For instance, analysts may set execution timeouts to regulate the duration of a sample's runtime, enable memory dumps to capture critical runtime states, and monitor API calls to identify interactions between the malware and system components.

An example of an API submission for automating this process is as follows:

```
curl -X POST 'https://sandbox.example.com/api/tasks/create/file' I am running a few
minutes late; my previous meeting is running over.
-H 'Authorization: Bearer <API_KEY>' \
-F 'file=@malware.exe'
```

This structured approach ensures that malware samples are comprehensively analyzed, so that Cape Sandbox can detect and document behaviors indicative of advanced threats. By incorporating these techniques (illustrated in Figure 6-3), the platform equips analysts with the tools needed to dissect complex malware strains in a controlled and systematic manner.

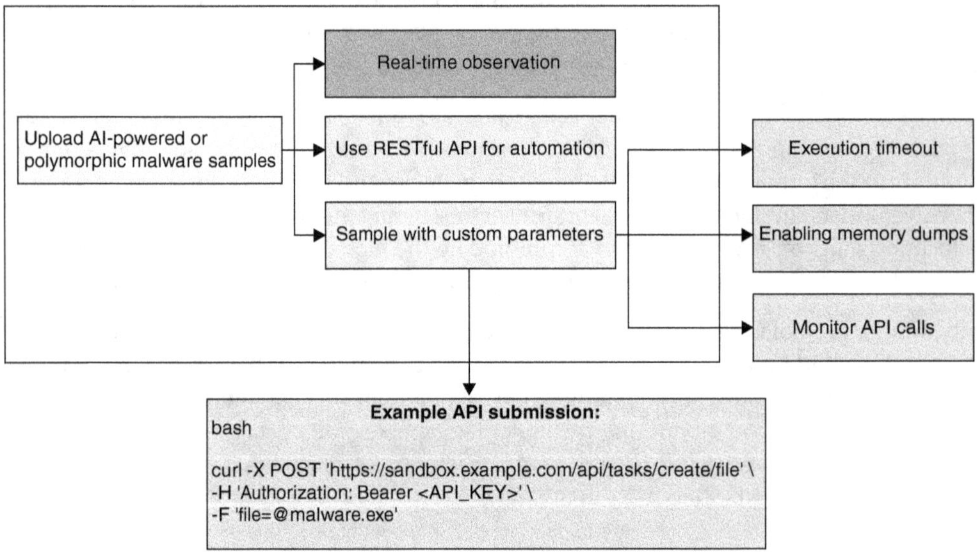

Figure 6-3
Submitting AI-powered polymorphic malware samples.

As quantum computing and AGI transform the cybersecurity domain, the process of submitting malware samples to Cape Sandbox (illustrated in Figure 6-3) will have to adapt to address the unique challenges posed by these emerging technologies. The submission of malware samples—particularly those using quantum-enhanced algorithms or AGI-driven logic—will be crucial for understanding how advanced threats exploit system vulnerabilities. This step will evolve to include features capable of capturing and analyzing these sophisticated behaviors while maintaining real-time observability and operational efficiency.

Malware submissions will need to extend beyond traditional polymorphic and AI-powered malware. Analysts must upload samples that integrate quantum-based encryption techniques, such as Shor's algorithm–enabled key-cracking mechanisms or AGI-enhanced malware capable of autonomous decision making and dynamic behavior adaptation. Such samples will require enhanced sandbox compatibility to detect and interpret quantum- and AGI-driven operations, ensuring a comprehensive understanding of their execution and impact.

The process of submitting these samples will also require advanced automation capabilities. The existing RESTful API in Cape Sandbox will need to support additional parameters tailored to quantum- and AGI-specific behaviors. For instance, custom configurations could include options for tracking quantum state changes, analyzing superposition or entanglement effects, and monitoring AGI-generated decisions in real time. These capabilities will ensure that the sandbox captures all relevant interactions, from system calls to complex logical shifts orchestrated by AGI.

The importance of enabling memory dumps and monitoring API calls will grow exponentially as AGI threats introduce multilayered, self-reconfiguring attack methods. Memory dumps will allow analysts to capture quantum-based computations, revealing the inner workings of quantum malware during execution. Similarly, enhanced API monitoring will facilitate the detection of AGI-initiated commands, including those that exploit sandbox detection mechanisms or use self-adaptive C2 channels. These features will ensure that Cape Sandbox maintains its effectiveness at dissecting and mitigating the most advanced threats.

To illustrate, an updated API submission might include options for specifying quantum simulation parameters or AGI interaction thresholds, as shown here:

```
curl -X POST 'https://sandbox.example.com/api/tasks/create/file' \
-H 'Authorization: Bearer <API_KEY>' \
-F 'file=@quantum_malware.exe' \
-F 'enable_quantum_monitoring=true' \
-F 'agi_adaptive_threshold=0.9'
```

Such enhancements would allow Cape Sandbox to adapt dynamically to the demands of quantum and AGI analysis, providing cyber analysts with the tools needed to address these unprecedented threats. Additionally, the system must ensure robust scalability, given the potential increase in resource demands associated with processing quantum states and AGI logic.

The submission of malware samples in a quantum and AGI context will require Cape Sandbox to adopt a forward-thinking approach, integrating quantum-resilient technologies and AGI-aware monitoring mechanisms.

Step 3: Analyzing Dynamic Behavior

The third step in using Cape Sandbox for the analysis of AI-powered malware focuses on analyzing the dynamic behaviors of malware during execution. This phase involves identifying the specific actions malware performs, which may include file encryption, data exfiltration, or the establishment of C2 communications. Such insights are invaluable for understanding the operational objectives of the malware and its potential impact on the targeted environment.

During this step, analysts must systematically monitor the process tree to identify any spawned processes or injected libraries, which often indicate how malware propagates within the system. Concurrently, it is essential to examine registry modifications, file manipulations, and API calls, as these behaviors frequently reveal the malware's strategy for persistence, evasion, or exploitation. Network activity must also be closely scrutinized—particularly DNS queries and HTTP/HTTPS connections, which can expose attempts to communicate with malicious external domains or servers.

For example, an analysis might uncover network traffic directed to suspicious domains, indicative of exfiltration attempts, or patterns of file encryption typically associated with ransomware. By capturing such behavioral signatures in real time, Cape Sandbox enables a thorough dissection of malware functionality, providing analysts with actionable intelligence to mitigate the associated risks. This step (illustrated in Figure 6-4) ensures that security teams can anticipate and counteract advanced threats with precision.

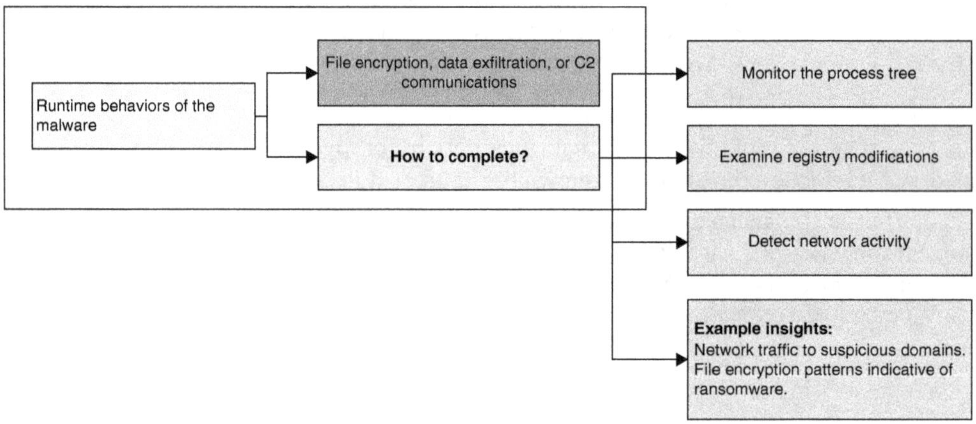

Figure 6-4
Analyzing dynamic behavior.

Quantum computing and AGI will fundamentally transform the process of analyzing the dynamic behavior of malware within Cape Sandbox. As malware becomes increasingly sophisticated, using quantum algorithms for cryptographic obfuscation or AGI to autonomously adapt its behavior, dynamic analysis must evolve to meet these unprecedented challenges. The primary objective of observing runtime behavior will remain critical, but the tools and methodologies employed will require significant advancements to address the complexities introduced by quantum and AGI threats.

Observing runtime behavior will extend to capturing quantum-specific processes and AGI-driven decision-making pathways. Quantum-enabled malware may employ quantum algorithms to perform near-instantaneous encryption, making traditional behavioral markers such as file encryption patterns harder to detect. Similarly, AGI-powered malware will exhibit highly adaptive behaviors, dynamically modifying its execution paths in response to environmental stimuli. For instance, AGI malware may initiate evasive actions upon detecting sandbox monitoring, employing techniques that mimic legitimate system processes to obscure its true intent.

To address these complexities, Cape Sandbox must incorporate quantum-state monitoring and AGI logic tracing within its dynamic behavior analysis framework. Monitoring the process tree will evolve to include the detection of quantum-accelerated computations, such as Grover's algorithm for data searches or Shor's algorithm for real-time cryptographic keybreaking. Similarly, AGI logic tracing will focus on identifying decision-making patterns indicative of autonomous goal setting and behavioral adaptation, providing analysts with insights into the strategic objectives of malware.

Registry modifications, file manipulations, and API calls will need to be examined with greater granularity, as AGI malware is likely to employ advanced obfuscation techniques that dynamically rewrite registry keys or manipulate system libraries in ways that evade traditional detection methods. Quantum-enabled malware may leverage superposition states or entangled data streams to conceal its operations, necessitating the integration of quantum-aware monitoring tools capable of decoding and interpreting such activity.

Detecting network activity will also require significant advancements. Quantum-powered malware may use quantum key distribution (QKD) to establish untraceable communication channels with its C2 servers, rendering traditional packet inspection techniques ineffective. Meanwhile, AGI malware may employ adaptive network strategies, dynamically switching between protocols and obfuscating DNS queries to evade detection. To counter these threats, Cape Sandbox will need to integrate quantum-network monitoring tools and AGI-driven pattern recognition models capable of identifying anomalies in network traffic that are indicative of quantum or AGI operations.

For example, network traffic to suspicious domains may no longer follow predictable patterns, as AGI malware begins to use stochastic routing algorithms or quantum tunneling methods to obscure its communication pathways. Similarly, file encryption patterns indicative of ransomware may evolve to include quantum-encrypted payloads, requiring the sandbox to decode and analyze quantum-state encryption signatures to effectively identify malicious activity.

By adapting its dynamic behavior analysis capabilities to quantum AGI, Cape Sandbox will continue to identify and mitigate advanced threats. These enhancements will provide a comprehensive view of how quantum- and AGI-driven malware interacts with its environment, enabling proactive defenses against the next generation of cyber threats.

Step 4: Polymorphic Behavior Tracking

The fourth step in using Cape Sandbox for the analysis of AI-powered malware involves tracking the polymorphic behavior of malware to understand how it adapts its structure and behavior during execution. This step is essential for unveiling the hidden capabilities of malware and for comprehending the sophisticated techniques it employs to evade detection mechanisms. Polymorphic malware poses a significant challenge to traditional analysis methods due to its capability to alter its code dynamically, thereby obfuscating its true intent.

In this phase, analysts use Cape Sandbox's memory dump feature to capture the runtime memory states of the malware. These memory snapshots provide invaluable data on how the malware evolves during execution, enabling analysts to track changes in its structure and functionality. AI-based detection models are then applied to examine these changes across iterations, providing deep insights into the adaptive strategies employed by the malware. These models are particularly adept at identifying patterns and anomalies that may elude conventional detection systems.

A critical aspect of this step is the focus on identifying invariant logic elements, which are the core functionalities or algorithms that remain consistent despite the malware's attempts at obfuscation. By isolating these persistent elements, analysts can develop more robust detection and mitigation strategies that are resistant to the malware's polymorphic adaptations (see Figure 6-5). This step ensures that even the most evasive threats are thoroughly dissected, laying the groundwork for the development of effective countermeasures.

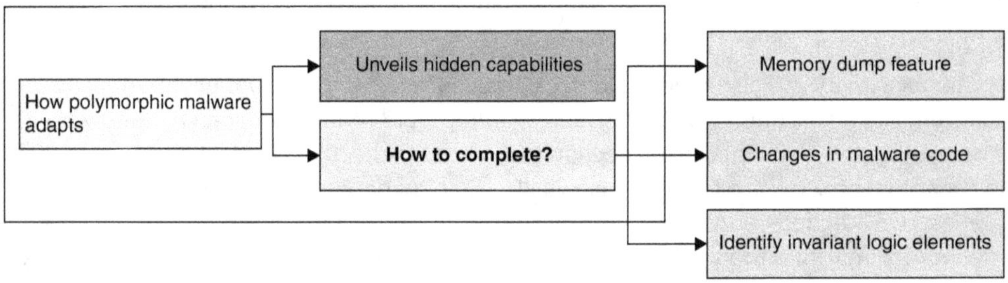

Figure 6-5
Polymorphic behavior tracking.

Quantum AGI polymorphic behavior tracking requires Cape Sandbox to evolve its current methods (shown in Figure 6-5) for analyzing how advanced malware adapts its structure and behavior. Polymorphic malware, which is already capable of dynamically altering its code to evade detection, will apply quantum algorithms and AGI capabilities to achieve unprecedented levels of adaptability.

The memory dump feature of Cape Sandbox will play a crucial role but must be enhanced to accommodate quantum-based polymorphic behaviors. Quantum-enabled malware may use properties like superposition and entanglement to alter its memory footprint dynamically, creating challenges in capturing and interpreting its runtime states. To address this, Cape Sandbox will need to integrate quantum-aware memory analysis tools capable of decoding entangled data and reconstructing quantum-state alterations. With the help of these tools, analysts will be able to identify the malware's underlying strategies, even as its code morphs in real time.

The application of AI-based detection models will also evolve significantly in the quantum and AGI era. Traditional machine learning models, while effective for detecting code variations in current polymorphic malware, will be insufficient to keep pace with AGI-powered malware that can autonomously rewrite its logic and synthesize novel behaviors. To counteract this, Cape Sandbox will incorporate AGI-enhanced detection frameworks capable of predicting and preemptively modeling potential mutations. These frameworks will use reinforcement learning and neural architecture search to map the evolutionary pathways of AGI malware, enabling a more comprehensive understanding of its adaptive strategies.

One of the most critical aspects of polymorphic behavior tracking will be the identification of invariant logic elements. While AGI malware might exhibit near-limitless mutability, its core objectives (such as data exfiltration, encryption, or lateral movement) will rely on consistent underlying logic. Quantum-enabled malware may attempt to obscure these invariant elements by embedding them within quantum-encrypted payloads or distributing them across entangled states. To mitigate this, Cape Sandbox will deploy quantum-state logic analyzers that isolate and interpret invariant patterns within the malware's operations. These analyzers will allow analysts to pinpoint the malware's true intentions, regardless of its outward transformations.

For example, changes in malware code across iterations might become increasingly complex, as AGI malware generates highly sophisticated obfuscation techniques designed to outpace traditional reverse-engineering efforts. In response, Cape Sandbox's detection systems will focus on the fundamental algorithms driving these transformations, such as quantum random number generators or AGI-driven code synthesis. By identifying the consistent use of such techniques, analysts can disrupt the malware's adaptive cycle and develop targeted countermeasures.

The ability to effectively track polymorphic behavior in a quantum and AGI landscape will be key for maintaining cybersecurity resilience. Cape Sandbox, equipped with advanced quantum and AGI analysis capabilities, will provide analysts with the tools to uncover hidden capabilities, decode obfuscated logic, and anticipate the next evolutionary step of advanced threats. These enhancements will ensure that even the most sophisticated malware, using cutting-edge quantum and AGI technologies, can be systematically deconstructed and neutralized.

Step 5: Apply Threat Intelligence

The fifth step in using Cape Sandbox for the analysis of AI-powered malware involves the integration of external threat intelligence to enhance the detection and contextual understanding of malware behaviors. This phase aims to correlate the behavioral data observed during sandbox analysis with established threat intelligence feeds, thereby identifying links to known malware campaigns or specific threat actors. Such correlation significantly improves the accuracy of detection and enriches the broader cybersecurity framework with actionable insights.

Cape Sandbox can be integrated with platforms like VirusTotal or the Malware Information Sharing Platform (MISP). Such integrations enable the automated querying of indicators of compromise (IoCs) extracted from the analyzed malware, such as suspicious domain names, IP addresses, file hashes, or registry changes. The resulting correlations provide critical insights into the malware's provenance and tactics, techniques, and procedures (TTPs), facilitating the attribution of the threat to specific adversarial groups or campaigns.

Furthermore, this step involves automating alerts for future detection of similar behavioral patterns. By embedding IoCs into security information and event management (SIEM) systems or endpoint detection tools, organizations can establish proactive defense mechanisms to identify and mitigate recurring threats. This approach ensures that the intelligence gathered from a single analysis extends its protective reach across an entire network (as detailed in Figure 6-6), streamlining incident response and reducing the time to containment for emerging threats.

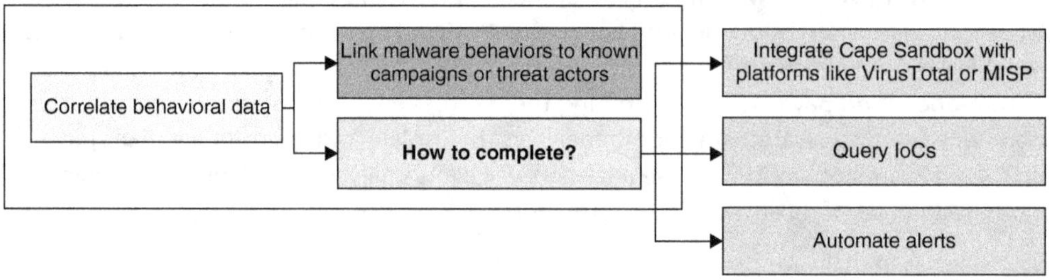

Figure 6-6
Linking AI-malware behaviors to known campaigns or threat actors.

Integrating threat intelligence into Cape Sandbox will require substantial advancements for the tool to remain effective in the face of quantum-enabled and AGI-powered malware. As these technologies enable malware to adapt dynamically, evolve rapidly, and exploit previously unrecognized vulnerabilities, threat intelligence platforms must advance beyond traditional models of static IoCs and pivot to continuous, adaptive intelligence frameworks. In this enhanced context, the primary objective of correlating behavioral data with external threat intelligence feeds will expand to include dynamically generated intelligence informed by quantum and AGI capabilities. Platforms like VirusTotal or MISP will need to incorporate quantum-resilient IoCs and AGI-adaptive models to identify and attribute sophisticated malware campaigns. Cape Sandbox will be instrumental in generating and sharing behavioral insights in real time, which will inform global threat intelligence ecosystems about emerging quantum- and AGI-based threats.

To adapt to these challenges, the current processes of Cape Sandbox (illustrated in Figure 6-6) will need to integrate quantum-aware threat feeds that are able to interpret advanced behaviors such as quantum-encrypted communication or AGI-driven polymorphic code synthesis. This will allow Cape Sandbox to link malware behaviors to highly complex campaigns orchestrated by quantum-enabled threat actors or autonomous AGI entities. Querying IoCs in this environment will no longer rely solely on static signatures; instead, it will involve pattern-matching algorithms capable of identifying quantum-derived cryptographic structures and AGI-driven decision-making processes.

Automated alerts will also become significantly more complex, using predictive modeling to anticipate how AGI-based malware might adapt or mutate in subsequent attacks. For instance, behavioral data captured by Cape Sandbox (such as the detection of AGI-generated lateral movement strategies or the utilization of quantum algorithms for encryption) can trigger predictive threat alerts. These alerts will not only identify the current attack but also forecast its likely evolution, enabling proactive defensive measures.

To implement these capabilities, Cape Sandbox will facilitate deep integration with threat intelligence platforms, creating a symbiotic relationship where real-time behavioral analysis informs the global threat landscape and advanced intelligence feeds enhance Cape Sandbox's detection capabilities. For example, IoCs derived from a piece of AGI malware that dynamically generates unique payloads for each target could be used to train machine learning models within Cape Sandbox. These models would then predict future variations of the malware, providing intelligence that extends beyond a single campaign.

The need for automation will also intensify, with Cape Sandbox employing AGI-based heuristics to refine alerting mechanisms. This will include the automatic generation of mitigation strategies based on observed behaviors, such as the application of quantum-safe cryptographic protocols or the deployment of countermeasures specifically designed to neutralize AGI-driven malware behaviors. Furthermore, the integration of Cape Sandbox with external platforms will extend to sharing anonymized behavioral patterns to ensure that threat intelligence remains actionable without compromising sensitive data.

The integration of threat intelligence into Cape Sandbox will evolve into a highly dynamic and adaptive process, using advancements in quantum-resilient systems and AGI-driven analytical models. These steps will ensure that Cape Sandbox remains capable of detecting, attributing, and mitigating the sophisticated threats posed by quantum-enabled and AGI-powered malware campaigns.

Step 6: Automating Detection Rules

The final step in using Cape Sandbox for the analysis of AI-powered malware is the automation of detection rules to identify similar malware strains in the future. This stage is essential in streamlining threat detection processes and enhancing the efficiency of incident response teams. By codifying observed malware behaviors into actionable rules, an organization can establish a proactive defense mechanism that mitigates recurring threats with minimal manual intervention.

Using Cape Sandbox's integrated rule editor, analysts can develop YARA rules that encapsulate the unique behavioral traits of the analyzed malware. These rules are crafted to match specific patterns, such as file system manipulations, API call sequences, or network traffic anomalies, ensuring precise identification of similar malware strains. Once created, these rules must undergo rigorous testing against known benign samples to minimize false positives. This step is essential to avoid unnecessary disruptions and ensure that legitimate processes are not misidentified as threats.

After validation, the rules can be deployed to endpoint security tools and SIEM systems. This integration allows for real-time monitoring and automated detection of malware exhibiting the same characteristics as previously analyzed samples (illustrated in Figure 6-7).

Quantum AGI will require a significant change in how Cape Sandbox automates detection rules for identifying similar malware strains. As quantum-powered malware leverages complex algorithms and AGI-enhanced threats dynamically adapt their behavior, the static nature of traditional detection rules will be insufficient. Detection rules will need to evolve into adaptive quantum- and AGI-aware systems capable of anticipating and countering advanced threats.

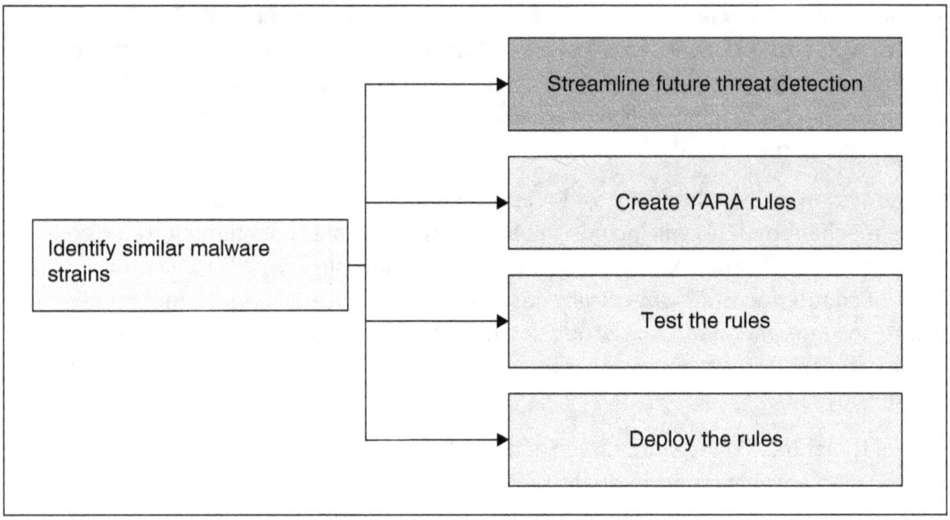

Figure 6-7
Automating detection rules.

The primary objective of creating detection rules to proactively identify similar malware strains will expand to include the integration of quantum-resistant and AGI-augmented analytical models. These rules will need to account for the unique behavioral and computational signatures of quantum-enabled malware, such as the use of post-quantum cryptographic algorithms for obfuscation, and AGI-driven evasion techniques, such as dynamic code rewriting during execution. For instance, YARA rules, traditionally used to detect specific file patterns and behavioral traits, will need to incorporate quantum-resilient logic and predictive AGI-based heuristics.

To streamline future threat detection in this context, Cape Sandbox will integrate its rule editor with quantum-aware and AGI-driven analysis modules. These modules will leverage AI-enhanced pattern recognition to generate detection rules that are not only specific to the observed malware sample but also generalizable to anticipate future variations of the strain. This approach ensures that the detection rules remain relevant even as AGI-powered malware evolves its tactics to bypass conventional defenses.

The process of testing detection rules will also become more complex as quantum and AGI threats introduce unprecedented variability and sophistication. Rules must be validated against benign quantum-based applications and AGI-generated behaviors to minimize false positives, ensuring operational efficiency without compromising accuracy. For instance, a detection rule targeting AGI-based malware might need to distinguish between malicious adaptive behaviors and legitimate AGI-generated optimizations in enterprise applications. This level of granularity will require Cape Sandbox to deploy sophisticated testing environments capable of simulating malicious and benign quantum and AGI behaviors.

Once validated, detection rules will be deployed to endpoint security tools and SIEM systems; however, the deployment process will need to accommodate the computational overhead associated with quantum-level encryption and AGI-driven polymorphism. To address this, Cape Sandbox will introduce lightweight, modular detection rule formats that can be efficiently integrated into resource-constrained environments, such as IoT devices or legacy systems. Furthermore, these rules will need to be periodically updated based on real-time threat intelligence feeds, incorporating insights from newly identified quantum and AGI malware campaigns.

Automating detection rules in the quantum and AGI era will also require dynamic feedback mechanisms. As new threats emerge, Cape Sandbox will use AGI-powered analysis engines to continuously refine its detection rules, enabling a self-improving cycle of threat detection and response. This adaptive capability will be crucial in maintaining resilience against rapidly evolving quantum and AGI threats, which are expected to outpace traditional malware in both speed and complexity.

In summary, the automation of detection rules within Cape Sandbox will transition from being a reactive process to being a proactive, adaptive system deeply integrated with quantum-resilient and AGI-augmented technologies. This evolution will ensure that Cape Sandbox remains capable of addressing the sophisticated challenges posed by quantum computing and AGI, streamlining threat detection and bolstering incident response in an increasingly complex cybersecurity landscape.

Discussion and Analysis: The Impact of Quantum Computing and AGI on Sandbox Environments

As the field of cybersecurity progresses into analyzing risks from quantum AGI, sandbox environments such as Cape Sandbox will need to undergo transformative changes to remain effective against increasingly sophisticated threats. Quantum-enabled malware and AGI-powered attack vectors are poised to exploit the fundamental limitations of classical sandboxing, necessitating advancements across several core capabilities.

AI-Driven Analysis Models for Quantum and AGI Threats

AI-driven analysis models have historically been a cornerstone of advanced sandbox environments, using techniques such as natural language processing (NLP) and graph neural networks (GNNs) to detect complex malware behaviors. In a quantum and AGI context, these models must evolve to recognize the novel characteristics of quantum-based attacks and AGI-driven logic. For example, quantum-enabled malware may exploit the computational superiority of quantum algorithms to dynamically encrypt payloads or generate obfuscated command sequences that evade traditional heuristics. Similarly, AGI systems are likely to synthesize attack strategies that adapt in real time to sandbox defenses.

To address these challenges, sandbox environments will need to integrate quantum-resilient AI models trained on datasets incorporating quantum- and AGI-specific behaviors. These models must identify patterns indicative of quantum algorithms, such as the use of Grover's or Shor's algorithms for cryptographic attacks, and predict AGI-driven adaptive logic. Additionally, graph-based models will be instrumental in mapping the intricate execution paths of AGI-based malware, capturing dependencies across dynamic processes, file manipulations, and network communications.

Evasion-Aware Monitoring in Quantum and AGI Contexts

Traditional sandboxing employs evasion-aware monitoring to counteract attempts by malware to detect virtualized environments, using randomized system configurations and obfuscation techniques. However, quantum computing introduces the potential for malware to perform probabilistic computations, identifying sandbox environments with unparalleled precision. Moreover, AGI-powered malware can dynamically adjust its evasion tactics based on real-time feedback, rendering static evasion countermeasures ineffective.

Future sandbox environments must adopt quantum-level randomization techniques to obscure their operational states, ensuring that quantum algorithms cannot reliably identify sandbox signatures. Concurrently, AI-driven monitoring must be enhanced to detect AGI-empowered evasive behaviors, such as adaptive fingerprinting and behavioral mimicry. These capabilities will require integrating real-time feedback loops into sandbox configurations, allowing the environment to preemptively adjust to observed evasive strategies.

Multistage Analysis (a methodological approach to analyzing malware across phases), and Multistage Payloads (a type of malware architecture where execution unfolds in discrete stages) of Quantum and AGI Payloads

Future AGI-enhanced or quantum-assisted malware would employ multistage payloads, where initial components perform reconnaissance or environment checks before downloading or decrypting subsequent stages. Analyzing such threats requires a layered approach that tracks each phase of execution. Malware with multistage payloads has long posed a significant challenge for sandbox environments, necessitating tools capable of capturing unique behaviors across execution stages. The advent of quantum-enabled and AGI-powered threats exacerbates this challenge, as these payloads can dynamically evolve during execution, leveraging quantum randomness and AGI logic to obscure their true intent.

To counteract these threats, sandbox environments must incorporate multistage analysis frameworks that can track quantum state transitions and AGI-generated behavioral shifts. For instance, a sandbox must simulate quantum computational states to analyze quantum-based encryption schemes or network protocols to ensure that all stages of malware execution are comprehensively dissected. Additionally, AGI-aware tracking mechanisms must map the decision-making processes of AGI-driven malware to identify logical invariants that persist across adaptive iterations.

Expanding API Capabilities for Quantum and AGI Integration

The extensibility of sandbox environments through API capabilities has been essential in enabling integration with custom security workflows and automation tools. In the context of quantum and AGI threats, these APIs will need to support quantum-resilient and AGI-aware operations, providing granular control over advanced analysis settings.

For example, APIs must allow security analysts to configure quantum-level simulations, such as replicating post-quantum cryptographic environments or testing AGI-enhanced behavioral models. Similarly, APIs must facilitate the automation of AGI-powered heuristics for real-time threat detection and response, enabling seamless integration with next-generation SIEM systems and threat intelligence platforms.

Transforming Sandbox Environments for the Quantum and AGI Era

The emergence of quantum computing and AGI represents a paradigm shift in the threat landscape, introducing challenges that extend beyond the capabilities of traditional sandboxing. By advancing AI-driven analysis models, adopting quantum-resilient monitoring techniques, and expanding multistage analysis frameworks, sandbox environments can remain effective against these transformative threats. Additionally, the integration of quantum-aware APIs will ensure that sandbox environments can adapt to the evolving needs of cybersecurity workflows. These innovations will position sandbox technologies such as Cape Sandbox as indispensable tools in safeguarding critical infrastructure and sensitive data from Quantum AGI.

Summary

This chapter explores the intersection between post-quantum cryptography (PQC) and advanced threat detection, focusing on how cybersecurity frameworks must evolve to address the dual challenge of quantum threats and AI-enhanced malware. The first portion of the chapter examines the deployment of PQC algorithms, detailing their integration into existing cryptographic infrastructures, the challenges associated with their adoption, and the necessary hardware and protocol upgrades. Emphasis is placed on hybrid cryptographic frameworks that ensure a smooth transition from classical encryption to quantum-resistant security models, maintaining backward compatibility while enhancing resilience against future quantum-enabled attacks. The chapter also outlines structured evaluation methodologies for selecting PQC algorithms based on performance constraints, system interoperability, and regulatory compliance, ensuring that organizations can make informed decisions when transitioning to post-quantum security.

Building on this foundation, the second portion of the chapter shifts focus to AI-driven malware analysis, demonstrating how sandbox environments, such as Cape Sandbox, can be adapted to detect quantum-enhanced and AI-powered cyber threats. As malware evolves to leverage AI-driven polymorphism and quantum-safe encryption, traditional detection techniques become insufficient. This chapter presents practical strategies for integrating quantum-resistant cryptographic techniques into malware analysis frameworks, ensuring that emerging attack vectors, such as quantum-encrypted command-and-control channels and AGI-driven adversarial evasion tactics, can still be identified and mitigated. Through real-world case studies, the chapter illustrates how sandboxes must evolve to incorporate quantum-safe virtualization, AI-driven behavior tracking, and hybrid cryptographic verification.

References

1 Bos, Joppe, Leo Ducas, Eike Kiltz, T. Lepoint, Vadim Lyubashevsky, John M. Schanck, Peter Schwabe, Gregor Seiler, and Damien Stehle. 2018. "CRYSTALS-Kyber: A CCA-Secure Module-Lattice-Based KEM." *2018 IEEE European Symposium on Security and Privacy*, 353–67. https://doi.org/10.1109/EUROSP.2018.00032.

2 *CRYSTALS: Cryptographic Suite for Algebraic Lattices*. n.d. www.pq-crystals.org.

3 *SPHINCS+*. 2024. https://sphincs.org.

4 Bernstein, Daniel J., Andreas Hülsing, Stefan Kölbl, Ruben Niederhagen, Joost Rijneveld, and Peter Schwabe. 2019. *The SPHINCS + Signature Framework*. https://dl.acm.org/doi/10.1145/3319535.3363229.

5 NIST. 2023. *Post-Quantum Cryptography (PCQ)*. https://csrc.nist.gov/projects/post-quantum-cryptography.

6 CAPE. 2024. *CAPE Sandbox Book*. https://capev2.readthedocs.io/en/latest/.

7 Neven, Hartmut. 2024. *Meet Willow, Our State-of-the-Art Quantum Chip*. https://blog.google/technology/research/google-willow-quantum-chip/.

8 Nakamoto, Satoshi. 2008. *Bitcoin: A Peer-to-Peer Electronic Cash System*. https://bitcoin.org/bitcoin.pdf.

Multiple-Choice Questions with Answers and Explanations

1. What is the first step in deploying post-quantum algorithms (PQAs)?

   a. Pilot testing the algorithms in a live environment

   b. Comprehensively assessing existing cryptographic infrastructure

   c. Upgrading hardware security modules

   d. Implementing hybrid cryptographic frameworks immediately

   Correct Answer: B. The deployment of PQAs begins with a thorough assessment of existing cryptographic systems to identify vulnerabilities and dependencies on quantum-vulnerable algorithms. This assessment ensures that the cryptographic landscape is fully mapped before an organization prioritizes upgrades.

2. Which of the following is not a recommended strategy for transitioning to PQAs?

   a. Using hybrid cryptographic schemes during the transition

   b. Updating cryptographic libraries like OpenSSL

   c. Immediately replacing all legacy systems with quantum-resistant systems

   d. Conducting pilot tests in controlled environments

   Correct Answer: C. Immediate replacement of all legacy systems is not feasible due to compatibility issues and operational risks. The recommended approach is to adopt hybrid schemes and phase the deployment through controlled pilot tests.

3. Which algorithm is most suitable for ensuring long-term data confidentiality in post-quantum cryptography?

   a. CRYSTALS-Kyber

   b. SPHINCS+

   c. CRYSTALS-Dilithium

   d. McEliece

   Correct Answer: D. McEliece is renowned for its resilience against quantum attacks and is particularly suited for ensuring long-term confidentiality, although its large key sizes pose implementation challenges.

4. What is a primary limitation of post-quantum algorithms compared to traditional cryptographic systems?

   a. Limited application to modern encryption systems

   b. Smaller key sizes and signature lengths

   c. Increased computational demands and larger key sizes

   d. Incompatibility with hybrid cryptographic frameworks

Correct Answer: C. Post-quantum algorithms typically require larger key sizes and higher computational power, which can challenge resource-constrained systems such as IoT devices.

5. What strategy can mitigate the complexity of integrating PQAs into legacy systems?
   a. Using purely post-quantum algorithms
   b. Deploying stateless cryptographic protocols
   c. Adopting hybrid cryptographic schemes during the transition phase
   d. Simultaneously transitioning all systems to post-quantum standards

   Correct Answer: C. Hybrid schemes allow organizations to integrate PQAs alongside existing algorithms, ensuring compatibility and mitigating the risks associated with immediate full-scale transitions.

Exercises with Solutions

Exercise 1: Short-Answer Question

Question: Explain the concept of hybrid cryptographic frameworks and their significance in the transition to post-quantum cryptography.

Solution: Hybrid cryptographic frameworks combine traditional algorithms, such as RSA or ECC, with post-quantum algorithms like CRYSTALS-Kyber. These frameworks offer dual-layered security, ensuring backward compatibility with legacy systems while introducing quantum-resistant mechanisms. This transitional strategy mitigates risks by maintaining operational stability and allowing for gradual adaptation to post-quantum standards.

Exercise 2: Case Study

Scenario: A financial institution is implementing a hybrid TLS framework incorporating CRYSTALS-Kyber for post-quantum key exchange alongside RSA for legacy support. However, the institution encounters increased latency during TLS handshakes and incompatibility with older client systems.

Tasks:

1. Identify the challenges the institution faces.
2. Recommend two strategies to resolve the issues.
3. Evaluate the role of pilot testing in mitigating these challenges.

Solution:

Challenges:

- Increased handshake latency due to larger cryptographic payloads
- Incompatibility with older clients that do not support hybrid frameworks

Strategies:

- Optimize handshake protocols by prioritizing efficient cryptographic suites and reducing unnecessary overheads.
- Upgrade older client systems or provide alternative configurations for seamless communication.

Role of pilot testing: Pilot testing enables the identification and resolution of such challenges in controlled environments before full-scale deployment, ensuring operational continuity and user compatibility.

Exercise 3: Hands-On Activity

Task: Implement a simple hybrid cryptographic handshake using Python, integrating CRYSTALS-Kyber for key exchange and RSA for authentication. Compare its performance to a classical RSA handshake.

Solution:

1. Use Python libraries like *pycryptodome* for RSA and custom post-quantum libraries for CRYSTALS-Kyber.
2. Develop a script that simulates the hybrid handshake process.
3. Benchmark handshake latency and resource utilization.
4. Note findings. Hybrid handshakes introduce moderate latency but enhance security by incorporating quantum resistance.

PART IV

DEFENDING AGAINST AGI THREATS

This section explores the methodologies, strategies, and innovations required to defend against AGI-driven cyber threats. Chapter 7, "AI-Driven Defenses and Threat Mitigation," discusses AI-driven defense mechanisms, machine learning paradigms that adapt to evolving threats, generative adversarial networks (GANs) as a dual-use tool for attack simulation and anomaly detection, and the application of reinforcement learning for agile, responsive security postures. These approaches underscore the potential of AI in preempting and mitigating AGI-enabled attacks and highlight the persistent risks of adversarial exploitation inherent in such systems.

Chapter 8, "Securing Digital Identities in an AGI World," focuses on digital identity systems, dissecting the vulnerabilities and opportunities presented by AGI and quantum computing in identity verification and management. Decentralized identity systems emerge as a key innovation, empowering users through self-sovereignty while mitigating centralized points of failure. Advanced cryptographic tools, including zero-knowledge proofs (ZKPs) and homomorphic encryption (HE), are examined for their capacity to uphold privacy and integrity against AGI's data-mining capabilities and quantum computational power. Blockchain, as a tamper-resistant ledger, complements these technologies, offering a decentralized foundation for secure and transparent identity ecosystems.

Part IV equips the reader with an understanding of the strategies necessary to confront AGI-level adversaries and quantum-scale cryptographic threats. By integrating AI models, cryptographic innovation, and decentralized architectures, this section provides a roadmap for managing new and emerging threats. It highlights technical challenges as well as the ethical imperatives and policy considerations required for a resilient, secure digital future.

7

AI-Driven Defenses and Threat Mitigation

This chapter explores the transformative impact of AI-driven methodologies on cybersecurity, focusing on how quantum computing and AGI-level attacks require a shift from traditional rule-based defenses to more adaptive and proactive measures. Building on real-world examples and technical analyses, the chapter demonstrates the need for comprehensive strategies that integrate static analysis tools, post-quantum cryptographic checks, dynamic sandboxes, and advanced machine learning paradigms.

Objectives

- **Explain how AI and machine learning have changed cybersecurity:** Examine the ways in which supervised and unsupervised learning models, such as deep neural networks and anomaly detection methods, are reshaping the detection, analysis, and mitigation of cyber threats.
- **Investigate the role of generative adversarial networks (GANs) in defensive applications:** Highlight how adversarial training, adversarial example generation, and anomaly detection can expose system vulnerabilities and build more resilient infrastructures.
- **Assess reinforcement learning (RL) as a mechanism to combat adaptive AI threats:** Present the rationale for using RL in agile defensive postures, where continuous policy updates and multi-agent coordination hold promise against rapidly evolving malware and advanced adversaries.

- **Understand evolving static analysis tools (such as DeepCode AI and Snyk) for quantum and AGI resilience:** Detail how hybrid AI models, post-quantum cryptographic heuristics, GNN-based code flow mapping, and integration with container scanning can strengthen detection against polymorphic attacks.
- **Forecast how static analysis will change to accommodate quantum and AGI threats with case studies on adapting existing tools used for AI in cybersecurity:** Demonstrate how emerging static analysis techniques and integrated scanning reveal vulnerabilities, detect signature-less malware, and adapt to sophisticated AI-based infiltration attempts.

This chapter discusses the technical principles behind AI-driven cybersecurity and the practical upgrades, workflows, and data-sharing frameworks necessary to stay ahead of adversaries armed with quantum computing and high-level AI.

AI and Machine Learning in Cybersecurity

AI and ML have changed how cybersecurity threats are detected, analyzed, and mitigated. Traditional cybersecurity mechanisms rely primarily on rule-based systems, signature matching, and heuristic-based anomaly detection, which, although effective in certain contexts, can be slow to adapt to novel or zero-day attacks. By contrast, AI- and ML-driven approaches bring a more dynamic and adaptive layer to cybersecurity, enabling continuous learning from evolving threat landscapes while minimizing human intervention and oversight.

From a technical perspective, machine learning in cybersecurity applies supervised, unsupervised, and semi-supervised algorithms designed to detect malicious behaviors at scale. One prevailing technique is anomaly-based intrusion detection, which employs different ML models (ranging from statistical outlier detection to deep neural networks) to characterize normal system behavior and flag deviations in real time. Traditional methods, such as principal component analysis (PCA) and clustering algorithms (e.g., k-means, DBSCAN), provide initial dimensionality reduction and grouping of network traffic or system event logs, thereby facilitating the identification of outlier behaviors that may be indicative of an attack. More recent innovations involve use of deep learning architectures, such as autoencoders or recurrent neural networks (RNNs), to capture higher-order temporal dependencies and complex feature interactions, thereby improving detection accuracy and reducing false positives.

In malware detection and classification, AI-based solutions apply increasingly more sophisticated methods to identify subtle patterns in code segments, network flows, and file metadata. Deep convolutional neural networks (CNNs), for instance, have been repurposed from computer vision tasks to treat executable files or network packet contents as "images" (or "byte plots")[1] and seek to identify characteristic byte patterns that distinguish malicious samples from benign ones. These supervised approaches are often combined with transfer learning strategies. Especially when curated, labeled datasets are scarce or expensive to obtain. Indeed, the ongoing research into few-shot and zero-shot learning paradigms (where novel classes of malware are identified with minimal labeled examples) exemplifies the cutting edge of this domain. Furthermore, ensemble learning strategies (e.g., bagging, boosting, stacking) can mitigate the bias–variance trade-offs inherent in single-model systems, potentially leading to more robust detection pipelines.

AI-driven cybersecurity also faces significant challenges. First, adversaries can exploit the very ML models intended to protect systems, using adversarial attacks such as gradient-based perturbations, data poisoning, or model inversion. These methods subvert the learning process by introducing subtle perturbations that cause misclassifications or by revealing private details about the model's inner workings (e.g., hyperparameters, training data). Second, the data quality and quantity needed for training robust models remain non-trivial constraints. AI models for cybersecurity rely on large, diverse, and clean datasets to maintain effectiveness. Given the sensitive nature of cybersecurity logs and event data, stringent privacy regulations often impede data sharing between organizations, limiting the availability of heterogeneous training sets. Techniques like federated learning and secure multiparty computation have been proposed to address this challenge, enabling collaborative model training without centralizing raw data. Nonetheless, practical implementations of such privacy-preserving AI systems remain in their early stages, and further research is required to enhance scalability, interoperability, and fault tolerance.

Using AI to Defend Against AI: Generative Adversarial Networks

Generative adversarial networks (GANs) offer methodologies for synthesizing highly realistic data and probing the robustness of existing AI-driven systems. At the heart of a GAN lies an adversarial dynamic between two neural networks: a generator that attempts to produce convincing "forgeries" of real data and a discriminator that attempts to distinguish these synthetic outputs from genuine samples.[2] This competitive interaction advances the image and audio synthesis and carries significant implications for security applications.

One of the most consequential aspects of GANs in cybersecurity is their capacity to generate adversarial examples that undermine or stress test existing classifiers and anomaly detectors. By creatively injecting small, often imperceptible perturbations into data (whether in the form of malicious network traffic, disguised malware payloads, or biometric forgeries), GANs reveal the fault lines in AI-driven defenses. When such vulnerabilities are discovered, the lessons gleaned from the failures can feed directly back into improved training and model development processes. In this manner, a continuous feedback loop emerges: The generator steadily refines its ability to fool the discriminator, and the discriminator (and, by extension, the entire security infrastructure) becomes ever more adept at recognizing adversarial patterns.

Further illustrating the extensive potential of GANs is their role in anomaly detection. The discriminator component in particular can be retrained or repurposed to flag suspicious activities that deviate from established "normal" distributions. When employed, for example, to process enormous quantities of network traffic, a discriminator can uncover subtle signals of intrusion or manipulation that might elude more conventional rule-based or signature-based methods. The generative model, in turn, bolsters the discriminator's vigilance by constructing challenging synthetic scenarios, thus ensuring that the anomaly detection pipeline is regularly exercised against emergent patterns of wrongdoing.

A related challenge in defensive GAN applications is the phenomenon of mode collapse, wherein a generator fails to capture the breadth of realistic data variations, producing only a narrow subset of possible anomalies or attacks. To combat this, researchers have experimented with advanced training strategies such as progressive growing, spectral normalization, and sophisticated loss functions like the Wasserstein distance. Coupled with fairness-aware training regimens, these refinements facilitate a diversity of generated outputs and help maintain fairness in detection across demographic or environmental groups, thereby ensuring that no single domain or user profile is disproportionately scrutinized or mislabeled.

The synergy between GAN-based approaches and quantum-safe cryptographic constructs extends to synthesizing artificial exploits, particularly side-channel or zero-day vulnerabilities that may target newly implemented cryptographic schemes. In parallel, GANs can significantly strengthen defenses by acting as a form of adversarial "quality assurance," challenging the security properties of lattice-based or homomorphically encrypted systems without ever exposing sensitive data to unnecessary risk. Indeed, privacy-preserving techniques that integrate homomorphic encryption into GAN workflows are already under development, offering a route to collaborative, cross-institutional training and security testing that does not necessitate sharing original datasets in unencrypted form.

Generative AI for Cybersecurity: Practical Applications and Code Demonstrations

Modern generative AI models, including ChatGPT, Claude, Gemini, and Llama, are built on transformer-based architectures and fine-tuned using reinforcement learning from human feedback (RLHF). Unlike GANs, which consist of two competing networks (generator and discriminator), transformer-based models operate on self-attention mechanisms that enable them to process vast amounts of sequential data efficiently. These models can be applied in cybersecurity for threat intelligence automation, adversarial attack simulation, and malware analysis.

Example 1: Using ChatGPT for Automated Phishing Detection

One major cybersecurity challenge is phishing detection. Attackers continuously refine their deceptive tactics, making it difficult for traditional rule-based systems to keep pace. By leveraging transformer-based AI models, phishing detection systems can analyze text-based communications for subtle linguistic and contextual clues that indicate fraudulent intent. Consider the following implementation of phishing detection with OpenAI's GPT model:

```
import openai

# Define the function to analyze email text
def detect_phishing_email(email_text):
    response = openai.ChatCompletion.create(
        model="gpt-4",
```

```
        messages=[
            {"role": "system", "content": "You are a cybersecurity expert trained
to detect phishing emails."},
            {"role": "user", "content": f"Analyze this email and determine if it is
phishing: {email_text}"}
        ]
    )
    return response["choices"][0]["message"]["content"]

# Example email input
email_text = """
Dear User,

Your account has been compromised. Please reset your password immediately by
clicking this link:
http://suspicious-link.com

Thank you,
Security Team
"""

# Detect phishing
result = detect_phishing_email(email_text)
print("Phishing Detection Result:", result)
```

The AI model will analyze an email's structure, detect suspicious links, and recognize common phishing indicators such as urgent language, fake sender identity, and deceptive URLs. The model can then return a classification score and reasoning behind the decision.

Example 2: Generating Adversarial Malware with Llama 2

AI can also be used offensively. Attackers may leverage large language models (LLMs) to generate evasive malware scripts. Security professionals can counter this threat by using AI to generate adversarial samples and stress-test antivirus models. Consider the following example of using Meta's Llama 2 to generate adversarial malware code for defense testing:

```
import openai

# Define the function to analyze email text
def detect_phishing_email(email_text):
    response = openai.ChatCompletion.create(
        model="gpt-4",
        messages=[
            {"role": "system", "content": "You are a cybersecurity expert trained
```

```
to detect phishing emails."},
            {"role": "user", "content": f"Analyze this email and determine if it is
phishing: {email_text}"}
        ]
    )
    return response["choices"][0]["message"]["content"]

# Example email input
email_text = """
Dear User,

Your account has been compromised. Please reset your password immediately by
clicking this link:
http://suspicious-link.com

Thank you,
Security Team
"""

# Detect phishing
result = detect_phishing_email(email_text)
print("Phishing Detection Result:", result)
```

As with the ChatGPT example, Llama 2 will analyze the email's structure, detect suspicious links, and recognize common phishing indicators such as urgent language, fake sender identity, and deceptive URLs. The model can then return a classification score and reasoning behind the decision.

In the following implementation, the model will generate an obfuscated script that might attempt to hide its true purpose, simulating an attacker's behavior:

```
from transformers import AutoModelForCausalLM, AutoTokenizer
import torch

# Load Meta's Llama 2 model
model_name = "meta-llama/Llama-2-7b-chat-hf"
tokenizer = AutoTokenizer.from_pretrained(model_name)
model = AutoModelForCausalLM.from_pretrained(model_name, torch_dtype=torch.float16)

# Define a prompt to generate obfuscated malware-like script
prompt = "Generate an obfuscated Python script that writes a hidden keylogger in a
non-malicious-looking way."

# Tokenize input and generate response
inputs = tokenizer(prompt, return_tensors="pt").to("cuda")
output = model.generate(**inputs, max_length=200)
```

```
generated_code = tokenizer.decode(output[0], skip_special_tokens=True)

print("Generated Adversarial Malware Sample:")
print(generated_code)
```

Security analysts can train detection models by feeding adversarial samples into malware classifiers to improve real-world defense mechanisms.

Example 3: Reinforcement Learning for Autonomous Intrusion Response

One of the most critical applications of reinforcement learning (RL) in cybersecurity is adaptive intrusion detection and mitigation. Instead of relying on predefined rules, RL-based security agents can learn defensive policies dynamically. Consider the following script, which trains an RL agent to block malicious IP addresses in real time:

```
import numpy as np
import gym
from stable_baselines3 import PPO

# Define a custom cybersecurity environment (simplified)
class IntrusionDetectionEnv(gym.Env):
    def __init__(self):
        self.observation_space = gym.spaces.Box(low=0, high=1, shape=(5,))
        self.action_space = gym.spaces.Discrete(2)  # 0: Allow, 1: Block

    def reset(self):
        self.state = np.random.rand(5)
        return self.state

    def step(self, action):
        if action == 1:  # Block decision
            reward = np.random.choice([1, -1], p=[0.9, 0.1])  # 90% success rate
        else:
            reward = np.random.choice([1, -1], p=[0.1, 0.9])  # 90% attack succeeds
        done = np.random.rand() > 0.95  # Random termination condition
        return np.random.rand(5), reward, done, {}

# Train RL agent
env = IntrusionDetectionEnv()
model = PPO("MlpPolicy", env, verbose=1)
model.learn(total_timesteps=10000)

# Evaluate model's decision on a new input
obs = env.reset()
```

```
action, _ = model.predict(obs)
print("Recommended Action (0=Allow, 1=Block):", action)
```

The RL agent will learn to identify malicious network traffic patterns and make autonomous decisions about whether to block or allow traffic. Over time, the reward mechanism ensures that the model optimizes for accurate threat mitigation, minimizing false positives and false negatives.

Reinforcement Learning for AGI Threat Mitigation

The progression toward adaptive general AI has created fears of cyber threats that are agile and sophisticated. For example, malicious agents can evolve quickly, identify network or cryptographic vulnerabilities in real time, and coordinate powerful attacks that exploit conventional flaws and advanced AI-driven techniques. In this environment, RL enables security mechanisms to respond to novel threats while continuously refining their strategies.[3]

Reinforcement learning stands out because of its capability to learn through trial-and-error interactions, adapting to dynamic conditions without being confined to rigid rules or static heuristics. Instead of depending solely on previously captured attack signatures, RL-based defenses make sequential decisions in response to changing inputs and evolving adversaries. The result is a more fluid defensive stance, well suited to combat high-level AI adversaries that can devise unanticipated maneuvers.

One compelling application involves adaptive intrusion detection and response. By treating the protected network as a stateful environment, with states describing network traffic characteristics, cryptographic parameters, or specific alert conditions, an RL agent can optimize a policy over time to maximize system stability and security. When suspicious behavior emerges (such as a spike in anomalous traffic), the agent decides how to respond, choosing from a repertoire of actions, which can range from blocking specific IP addresses to intensifying authentication or temporarily isolating critical nodes. The RL agent's learning process is guided by a reward signal that might penalize false alarms or missed threats while reinforcing effective mitigation steps.

In more complex enterprises, a single RL agent might not be sufficient. Coordinating multiple agents allows for a more granular division of labor, where different segments of the network or different security layers are managed by distinct RL modules. These agents collaborate through shared observations or consensus protocols, ensuring that the global defense remains coherent, particularly in the face of multipronged or distributed attacks. Such multi-agent RL schemes have the added benefit of resilience: One compromised module does not necessarily expose the system at large, as the other agents can detect discrepancies and shift policies to counter anomalous behavior.

These RL methodologies are especially valuable in anticipating advanced AI-driven (and potentially AGI-level) attacks that adapt quickly. Traditional machine learning models operate under the assumption that the underlying distributions of normal and malicious data remain stable, yet an adversary endowed with high-level reasoning can alter its approach on short notice. Casting the problem as a game, in which the defender learns in tandem with an evolving opponent, provides a more realistic framework. Here, the defender's RL agent continuously refines its policies in a *minimax* setting, aiming to be robust against the worst-case strategies an adversarial AI might devise.

The minimax principle is a game-theoretic strategy used to optimize decision making in adversarial environments. It is particularly relevant in RL for cybersecurity, where the goal is to minimize potential losses while maximizing defensive effectiveness against an intelligent and evolving adversary. In this minimax setting, the RL agent (defender) assumes that the attacker (adversarial AI) will always choose the most damaging possible action. The defender, therefore, optimizes its policy to minimize the worst-case damage rather than focusing on average-case performance. This approach is particularly useful when dealing with adaptive AI-driven threats, as it ensures that the defense system remains resilient against the most sophisticated and evasive attack strategies.

Exploration is another core challenge. In benign contexts, exploration is simply a way to gather more representative experiences, but in adversarial settings, exploring untested policies can risk exposing vulnerabilities to the very threats the agent is trying to mitigate. Proper balance between exploration and exploitation is thus crucial. At times, advanced AI systems might exploit naive exploration to stage novel attacks. Hence, researchers have begun investigating more sophisticated exploration strategies (drawing on Bayesian or information-theoretic ideas) to ensure that agents discover hidden threat vectors without unduly endangering system stability.

Beyond immediate reaction to threats, reinforcement learning can also automate longer-term decisions, such as cryptographic policy changes. As quantum computing looms on the horizon, system administrators must determine how and when to upgrade to quantum-safe protocols and whether to adjust key lengths, encryption standards, or authentication routines. An RL agent can weigh trade-offs among security posture, system overhead, and backward compatibility, adjusting measures on the fly in response to external signals of emerging cryptanalytic capabilities or detection of zero-day exploits.

Although reinforcement learning alone is not a silver bullet, it can be immensely effective when integrated into a broader ecosystem of AI-driven defenses. Other components, such as classifiers or anomaly detectors, can glean critical intelligence from specific alerts, pass these insights to an RL agent, and let the agent determine the best strategic response. In tandem with generative adversarial networks, RL can close the loop so that any new adversarial scenario generated by a GAN becomes fodder for retraining the RL agent, ensuring that it can tackle increasingly cunning or unconventional threats.

RL-based security, while resource intensive, can benefit greatly from distributed computing infrastructures or federated learning frameworks. Such architectures allow multiple organizations to jointly train robust agents without compromising sensitive data. In doing so, reinforcement learning systems gain exposure to a more diverse range of threat scenarios, becoming better prepared for global and fast-evolving cyber challenges.

Case Study on AI and Machine Learning in Cybersecurity: Static Analysis with DeepCode AI (Snyk)

DeepCode AI, now integrated with Snyk, illustrates how modern cybersecurity tools blend machine learning with symbolic reasoning to detect vulnerabilities, malicious patterns, and logical inconsistencies in source code. Traditionally, this static-analysis approach has excelled at uncovering well-known flaws (such as buffer overflows, SQL injections, or improper authentication flows) by mapping code against established security heuristics and curated rulesets. Yet as quantum computing matures, and as adversaries develop increasingly polymorphic AI-driven malware, DeepCode AI must evolve beyond conventional heuristics and tackle a new spectrum of existential threats.

A key change involves expanding DeepCode AI's static-analysis engine (illustrated in Figure 7-1) to recognize cryptographic weaknesses introduced by post-quantum transitions. Codebases rely on classical encryption and signature schemes that will become insecure once large-scale quantum computers can factor or compute discrete logarithms at scale. DeepCode AI and similar tools will therefore need to identify code segments that implement vulnerable algorithms (RSA, ECC, or Diffie-Hellman prime group key exchanges) and offer upgrade paths to quantum-safe alternatives. This capability means going beyond simple pattern matching: The analysis must infer code intent, detect partial or custom cryptographic implementations, and classify the implementations according to known post-quantum resilience criteria (e.g., lattice-based or hash-based security schemes). Symbolic reasoning can then verify that post-quantum algorithms, once integrated, are invoked correctly at every layer of the software stack, preventing subtle fallback vulnerabilities or misconfigurations.

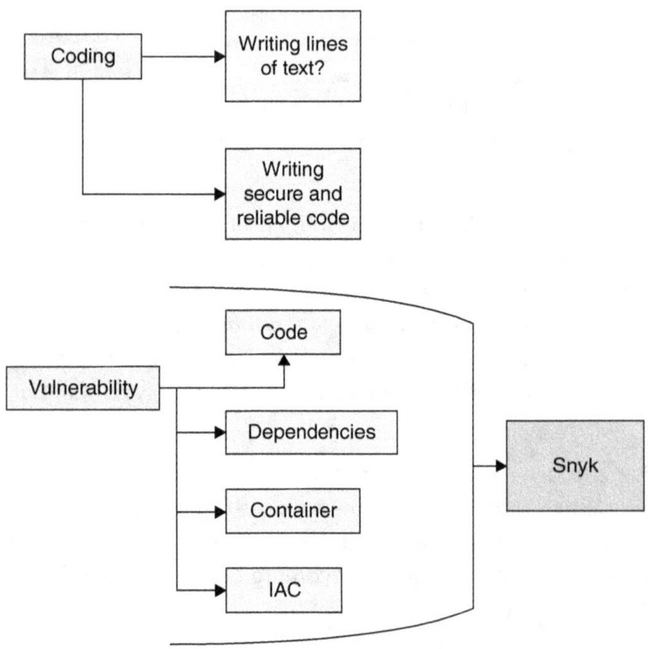

Figure 7-1
Static analysis with DeepCode AI (Snyk): code analysis, dependencies analysis, container analysis, and infrastructure as a code (IAC) analysis.

Polymorphic AI malware further complicates these tasks. Unlike static malicious code that can be fingerprinted, AI-driven payloads adjust their signatures and mutate logic to remain undetected. To counter this adaptability, DeepCode AI requires an expanded training regime that recognizes suspicious code transformations and dynamic code-injection templates. For instance, advanced malware might generate ephemeral attack vectors at runtime using on-device neural networks, embedding unexpected system calls or obfuscated cryptographic routines. An effective static-analysis tool must pinpoint not just suspicious API calls but also the underlying machine learning scaffolding that orchestrates these calls, detecting traces of auto-generated code or function hooking that deviate from benign AI frameworks. Crucially, any "self-learning" malicious logic must be flagged early, before it triggers lateral movement, data exfiltration, or cryptographic sabotage in quantum-ready environments.

Integrating machine learning and symbolic reasoning is only the starting point. The next phase for DeepCode AI (and analogous tools like Snyk) has two goals:

- To incorporate robust post-quantum heuristics and libraries that identify and rectify cryptographically vulnerable code
- To enhance detection mechanisms against polymorphic, AI-driven malware that might continuously morph to evade signature-based approaches

This combination of advanced static analysis, cryptographic domain expertise, and real-time threat intelligence creates a more proactive cybersecurity posture, ensuring that code remains resilient, even in the face of quantum breakthroughs and self-adapting adversarial AI.

DeepCode AI's Current Technical Capabilities and How They Would Need to Change in the Future

DeepCode AI's efficacy in detecting polymorphic and AI-driven malware arises from multiple machine learning paradigms, tailored to address a distinct aspect of code analysis. At its core, this approach leverages hybrid AI modeling, graph-based reasoning, anomaly-detection frameworks, and extensive training datasets to clarify even the most evasive malicious patterns.

The hybrid AI model stands out as a first line of defense, combining symbolic AI and generative AI to uncover hidden vulnerabilities in code. Symbolic AI maintains a rule-based perspective, matching code snippets to known vulnerability signatures and operational heuristics. By contrast, the generative component (built on advanced architectures such as BERT or CodeBERT) infers potential attack vectors by learning contextual representations of program syntax and logic. These transformers, adapted from vast numbers of open-source projects, develop a nuanced grasp of coding idioms and can spot anomalous logic flows or suspicious usage patterns. Whether it is detecting subtle buffer misuse or newly emerging injection mechanisms, this hybrid synergy ensures breadth (through symbolic pattern recognition) and depth (through large-scale generative analysis).

In tandem with these language models, graph neural networks (GNNs) play a key role by visualizing the relationships among functions, classes, and control-flow constructs as a dynamic "code graph."[4] Through this topological lens, GNNs can track how data and instructions propagate throughout a codebase, revealing unorthodox function calls or suspicious rerouting strategies that might otherwise blend seamlessly into legitimate operations. Polymorphic malware, for instance, often disguises its malicious payload by mutating its call chains or injecting new dependencies. GNN-based detection pinpoints these evasive tactics by noting breaks in expected call hierarchies, unusual cross-module references, or abrupt shifts in data flow.

Moreover, variational autoencoders (VAEs) play a complementary yet essential role by modeling typical coding patterns.[5,6] Trained extensively on mainstream open-source repositories, VAEs extract latent representations of "normal" coding structures and then measure incoming code against these learned norms.[7] Deviations from the baseline (such as abnormally nested conditionals, excessive aliasing, or artificially obfuscated syntax) stand out as anomalies. This technique is particularly powerful for revealing hidden manipulations in code that do not outwardly align with any known vulnerability signature but that nonetheless fail to match the expected patterns of benign development practices.[8]

DeepCode AI's learning capacity is sustained by its extensive dataset utilization (see Figure 7-2). Public repositories from platforms like GitHub establish a broad foundation in standard coding conventions. Meanwhile, the National Vulnerability Database (NVD) serves as a cross-reference to ensure that recognized weaknesses (whether in cryptographic libraries or network-handling routines) can be promptly identified.[9,10] For explicitly malicious patterns, resources such as the EMBER dataset introduce real-world examples of malevolent code, training the platform to spot suspicious constructs that more general repositories might overlook. The breadth and variety of these datasets fortify DeepCode AI's coverage, ensuring that it remains alert to emergent exploitation techniques and resistant to overfitting on a narrow set of examples.

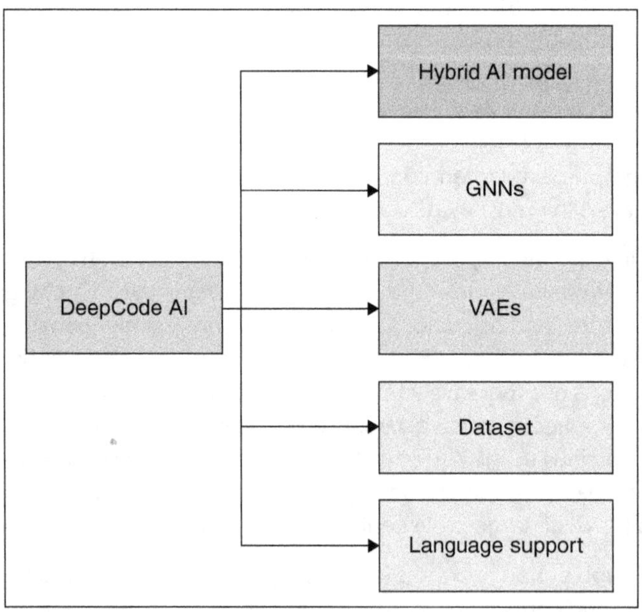

Figure 7-2

Analysis of the DeepCode AI (Snyk) models and datasets.

An expansive language support matrix reinforces DeepCode AI's versatility. From dynamic scripting languages like Python and JavaScript to compiled staples such as C++ and the Java ecosystem, DeepCode AI addresses malware across the spectrum of software environments. This multilingual competence is indispensable for identifying cross-language attacks and stealth tactics that pivot among different platforms.

Collectively, these technologies would equip DeepCode AI to meet the challenges created by polymorphic AI malware. By integrating rule-based checks with sophisticated generative inference, mapping the structure of entire codebases with GNNs, detecting anomalies with VAEs, and continuously refining models via extensive training sets, DeepCode AI can maintain its capabilities to confront adversaries that shift, mutate, and adapt their cyber threats.

In anticipating quantum-scale cryptographic threats and the emergence of advanced AI (potentially at or beyond human-level general intelligence), cybersecurity tools like DeepCode AI and Snyk will need to expand and refine their core functionalities in several specific ways. Existing strengths (such as hybrid AI modeling, graph-based reasoning, and anomaly detection) must be adapted to confront attack vectors that exploit quantum vulnerabilities and highly adaptive AI-generated exploits.

Note

As a disclaimer, at this present moment, AGI is still theoretical, and while many AI companies, such as OpenAI, are working on developing AGI, at present, the concept of AGI-driven malicious code generation at scale remains theoretical. The section that follows uses existing knowledge from literature and from experts in the field to present a case study on how tools such as Snyk and DeepCode AI need to adapt to the anticipated risks from future AGI.

The following list is based on applying red teaming methodology to integrate existing literature and knowledge on how future systems would need to operate and detect AI threats, vulnerabilities, and exploits, to provide protection from future AGI based polymorphic and metamorphic malware streams:

- **Hybrid AI model with post-quantum sensitivity:** Current AI systems, including HybridAGI, are focused on more basic tasks such as knowledge representation and program interpretation. Traditionally, DeepCode AI's hybrid model has brought together symbolic AI (for rule-based pattern detection) and generative AI (to infer deeper semantic anomalies) to identify vulnerabilities such as injection flaws and buffer overflows. To address quantum threats, these models need to scrutinize cryptographic code for deprecated or insufficiently robust algorithms, particularly legacy RSA, ECC, or Diffie-Hellman implementations susceptible to quantum attacks. Generative transformers, like CodeBERT, will evolve to recommend post-quantum cryptographic routines (for example, lattice-based or hash-based primitives) in place of older schemes. Furthermore, the generative component must learn to flag cryptographic fallback mechanisms that an advanced attacker (possibly guided by AGI) could exploit to revert communications to weaker, quantum-vulnerable ciphers. This example can be related to all other hybrid models. The case study is based on explaining the threats, exploits, vulnerabilities, and the process to ensure hybrid models are capable of protecting future systems from AI threats.

- **GNN-based analysis of AGI-led polymorphic mutations:** DeepCode AI's GNNs already map interdependencies and control flows to detect suspicious patterns. Moving forward, they must also tackle quantum- and AGI-driven code obfuscation techniques, where malicious actors can generate or continuously morph large sections of code at scale. GNNs will have to trace ephemeral function calls, identify sophisticated rerouting of data flows, and detect "intelligent" modifications that an AGI could introduce to bypass conventional heuristic checks. By spotlighting unusual call hierarchies and abrupt changes in the control graph, GNN-based detectors can stay nimble enough to track hyper-accelerated polymorphism engineered by advanced AI adversaries.
- **VAEs for AI-inspired anomaly detection and quantum-safe practices:** VAEs in DeepCode AI currently detect deviations from standard coding behaviors, spotting suspicious obfuscations or unnatural syntax. In the face of quantum-powered code breaking and AGI-assisted infiltration, these VAE-driven baselines must incorporate post-quantum best practices into their definitions of "normal" code patterns. This means actively identifying newly emergent sabotage attempts (e.g., stealthy inject-and-encrypt routines that exploit quantum-compromised keys) by distinguishing them from accepted patterns of encryption or data handling. VAEs can then flag anomalies that suggest AGI-level code manipulation, such as advanced refactoring that goes beyond typical developer habits.
- **Extensive and adapted training data for quantum- and AGI-aware threats:** DeepCode AI's dataset arsenal (GitHub repositories, the National Vulnerability Database, and the EMBER malware dataset) already underpins robust detection capabilities. However, in a future with quantum-scale computing and sophisticated AI attacks, training sets must be broadened to include the following:
    - Post-quantum cryptographic libraries (lattice-based, code-based, and hash-based approaches) to ensure that the models can identify correct and incorrect implementations
    - Simulations of AGI-driven or quantum-supported attacks that capture novel infiltration strategies that exploit large-scale parallel computing to crack or degrade defenses
    - Code samples that illustrate advanced AI "self-rewrite" functionality, whereby malware changes its structure automatically to evade detection

  Such enrichment will allow DeepCode AI to accurately forecast emergent exploit techniques and automatically propose mitigations aligned with next-generation security practices.
- **Language support with quantum-ready code patterns:** While covering 19 programming languages ensures broad applicability, future expansions may include domain-specific

quantum control languages or frameworks used to orchestrate quantum hardware. As AGI-driven adversaries pivot between classical and quantum components, having the capacity to detect vulnerabilities or malicious transitions in these more esoteric languages will be essential. DeepCode AI, in tandem with Snyk, can spot cross-compiled or quantum-hybrid code that references cryptographic endpoints in vulnerable ways, preventing advanced infiltration that capitalizes on knowledge gleaned from both classic and quantum realms.

Collectively, these targeted enhancements will position DeepCode AI and Snyk to adapt more decisively to the challenge of quantum computing breakthroughs and sophisticated AGI-led exploits. By integrating post-quantum resiliency checks, advanced code-graph analysis for AGI-level threats, and anomaly detection rooted in new training paradigms, cybersecurity tools can remain at least a step ahead of adversaries capable of dismantling older defenses.

Quantum AGI and Malware Analysis

Snyk is commonly recognized as a tool for securing dependencies, containers, and APIs, but it also incorporates several advanced features for static analysis workflow. Its dependency analysis function scans third-party libraries and open-source dependencies to pinpoint vulnerabilities; this is particularly beneficial given that many polymorphic malware strains exploit outdated libraries to gain initial access or execute payloads. By integrating with the CVE database, Snyk can accurately highlight such weaknesses. In addition, the platform's container security capabilities extend to analyzing containerized environments like Docker or Kubernetes. Snyk looks for misconfigurations, embedded payloads, and obsolete software components that could be leveraged by malicious code. Beyond these automated checks, Snyk supports custom rule development, allowing security teams to craft detection rules specific to known malware signatures or obfuscation strategies. For instance, in a fictional scenario where polymorphic or even metamorphic malware is developed by AGI, if a strain of polymorphic malware employs a unique technique, a modified rule can be formulated to detect instances of this behavior across codebases or dependencies. Snyk works in tandem with DeepCode AI, which scrutinizes the codebase while Snyk broadens the analysis to include vulnerabilities in external dependencies, containers, and APIs, thereby furnishing a more comprehensive view of potential threat vectors (see Figure 7-3).

While polymorphic malware is part fictional, in other sections of this book, we discuss BlackMamba, which is proof-of-concept polymorphic malware, and we advance the discussion from the current proof-of-concept version of BlackMamba into how future versions of BlackMamba may advance and attack existing systems. Hence, although the detection of polymorphic malware is fictitious, and we are still in the proof-of-concept stage with polymorphic malware, we can also argue that we have a proof of concept already, and the risk might be closer than we think.

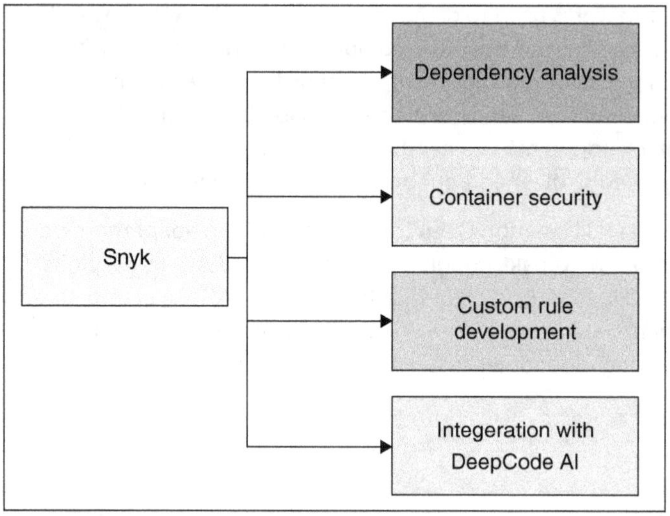

Figure 7-3
Advanced features in Snyk.

While Snyk malware analysis capabilities are focused on securing dependencies, containers, and APIs (see Figure 7-3), the risks from quantum computing and advanced AI systems require a new layer of sophistication in threat-detection and mitigation workflows. Polymorphic malware already exploits outdated libraries and unpatched container environments. Future strains (potentially guided by AGI and armed with quantum decryption techniques) will demand even more proactive and adaptive defenses. These are some of the key areas where Snyk's capabilities will need to evolve to address the emerging challenges:

- **Dependency analysis in a post-quantum landscape:** Traditionally, Snyk has scanned third-party libraries and open-source dependencies to expose known vulnerabilities. In a quantum context, however, adversaries can identify weak cryptographic components or exploit newly emergent flaws at unprecedented scale. Snyk's integration with the CVE database will therefore need to expand to encompass post-quantum vulnerability advisories, flagging any code that relies on classical cryptographic routines that are doomed to fail against sufficiently powerful quantum attacks. Moreover, Snyk will need to automatically suggest quantum-safe alternatives (such as lattice-based encryption libraries) for projects that are still using legacy protocols. When facing AGI-driven threats that systematically probe the entire dependency chain, Snyk's enhanced scanning will also need to be able to detect unusual or AI-generated "hotfixes" introduced by malicious contributors who aim to compromise a popular library and stealthily propagate zero-day exploits across multiple downstream projects.
- **Container security reinforced against quantum-era attacks:** Containers like Docker or Kubernetes, which are widely used for software packaging, can become prime targets for quantum-aided infiltration or advanced AI-driven attacks. Snyk's layered analysis, which identifies misconfigurations or outdated software components, will need to extend its approach to container orchestration, spotting the hidden pivot points an AGI might create, such as

dynamic policy changes or ephemeral malicious images. Additionally, the system's detection logic must account for stealth container breakouts made feasible through quantum-based side-channel manipulations or AI-induced exploitation of microservices. This expanded scope ensures that auto-generated vulnerabilities (such as ephemeral cryptographic keys or transient credentials stored in container layers) are flagged before they evolve into quantum-ready vectors for breaching host systems.

- **Advanced custom rule development for AGI-driven malware:** Snyk's functionality for creating custom detection rules already offers a flexible method to track specific malware patterns. To combat threats orchestrated by AGI, these custom rules will need to adapt to AI-engineered code obfuscation that changes continuously, making static pattern-matching insufficient. Security teams could integrate machine learning insights from real-time threat intelligence (encompassing quantum-led cryptographic attacks and AI-developed polymorphic malware) into the rule definitions. The anticipated result would be a closed-loop system: As DeepCode AI uncovers new AI-based code transformations or quantum-exploit indicators in the codebase, Snyk's custom rules would automatically be updated to monitor dependencies, container images, and configuration files for these red flags, ensuring cohesive defense across the entire software stack.
- **Deeper integration with DeepCode AI for quantum and AI threats:** While DeepCode AI excels at static analysis within a project's codebase, Snyk extends this protective envelope to third-party libraries, container layers, and external APIs, which is a critical advantage when confronting quantum-scale cryptanalysis or AGI-level infiltration attempts. Hence, a unified platform will emerge wherein DeepCode AI's insights on suspicious or quantum-vulnerable code modules are immediately translated into Snyk's broader ecosystem checks. This synergy will help detect cross-codebase anomalies, such as a developer introducing a quantum-unsafe algorithm in a microservice while external libraries remain compromised by a similarly flawed approach. By unifying the scanning results, both tools will proactively enforce post-quantum best practices across internal code and external dependencies, safeguarding against an AI adversary capable of pivoting between local and third-party vulnerabilities.

Taken together, these enhancements will position Snyk to remain relevant to quantum exploits and AI-driven polymorphism. By integrating post-quantum cryptographic advisories, reinforcing container analyses, evolving custom rule generation, and deepening integration with DeepCode AI, Snyk will be able to effectively adapt to an environment in which adversaries use quantum computing and general-purpose AI to mount sophisticated attacks.

Reverse Engineering Quantum Polymorphic Malware

Reverse engineering polymorphic AI malware such as BlackMamba requires a carefully planned process that combines the strengths of DeepCode AI and Snyk. These tools, when used together, provide a structured means of analyzing, understanding, and countering rapidly shifting threats.

In earlier sections, we discussed current AI models and reviewed technical examples, including code, libraries, tools, and techniques. In this section, we discuss how existing tools can be adapted to the future threats of quantum attacks, and the most pressing concern in this section is the malware that changes its structure every time it attacks. This means that the malware is difficult to detect, and we need to be prepared to adapt existing tools to be able to detect such changes. In other words, we need to be able to reverse engineer polymorphic malware. These steps are illustrated in Figure 7-4.

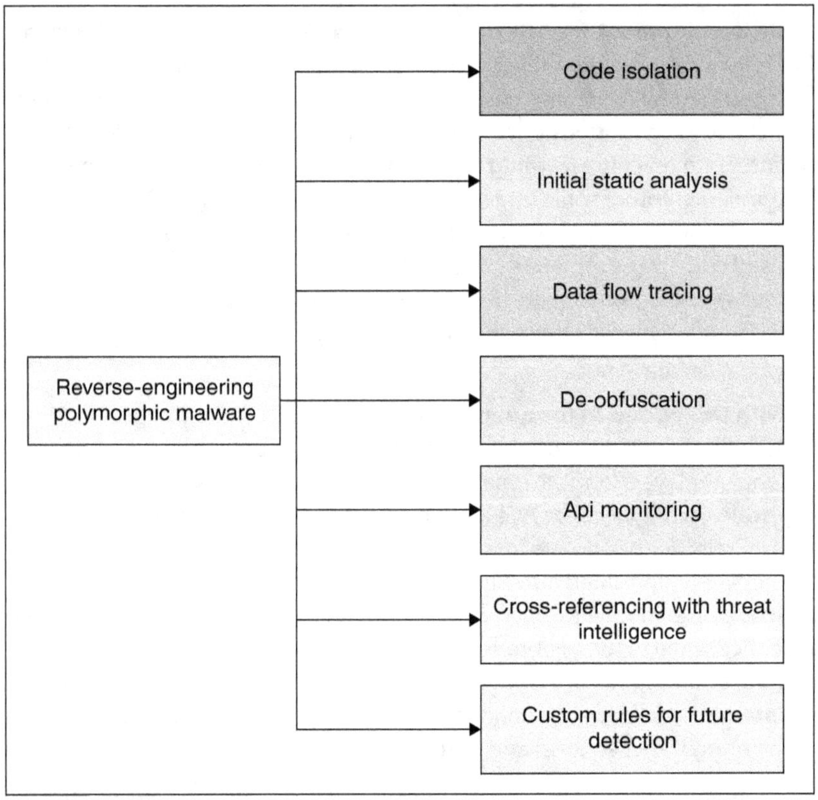

Figure 7-4
Reverse engineering polymorphic malware step by step.

Let's look at the details of these steps:

1. The first step, *code isolation*, involves placing the malware sample into a secure sandboxed environment. This ensures that the malware is free from any encryption or runtime protection (such as packers or anti-debugging code) that might impede static analysis. Key tasks include creating a dedicated sandbox (for example, with Cuckoo Sandbox), stripping away encryption layers using utilities like PEiD or IDA Pro, and taking a system snapshot to guarantee that future analyses can be reproduced reliably.
2. Once the code is isolated, *initial static analysis* comes into play. DeepCode AI's hybrid AI model performs a semantic examination of the malware's code, identifying obfuscation techniques

such as junk code insertion or control flow distortion. Meanwhile, Snyk inspects the dependency tree to expose any third-party libraries or frameworks on which the malware depends. By combining DeepCode AI's symbolic reasoning and Snyk's vulnerability-focused lens, analysts can gain insights into both the structural anomalies in the code and the external libraries that might be potential weaknesses or that facilitate malware operations.

3. In the next step, *data flow tracing*, DeepCode AI's graph neural networks (GNNs) create a mapping of how data moves within the code. This mapping reveals how malicious actors manipulate variables and functions, exposing injection points and suspicious API calls. Observing any coded transmissions of user credentials or references to command-and-control (C2) endpoints helps narrow down likely exfiltration vectors or stealth pathways.

4. In the next step, *de-obfuscation*, DeepCode AI's variational autoencoders (VAEs) detect consistent "invariant" code fragments that remain present across multiple polymorphic iterations, effectively unmasking the malware's fundamental logic. De-obfuscation tools like OLLVM (Obfuscator-LLVM) or custom scripts can then be used to remove additional layers of wrapping and function inlining.

5. During the next step, *API monitoring*, DeepCode AI flags unusual API calls, such as communication with large language models (LLMs) like OpenAI's GPT, and prompts the analyst to investigate how malicious code might be generated on demand. Combining application-level monitoring with network tools such as Wireshark or Zeek allows for the capture and examination of outbound traffic, helping to detect suspicious or anomalous usage that deviates from recognized patterns.

6. The next step is *cross-referencing findings against threat intelligence databases* (e.g., VirusTotal, MITRE ATT&CK, EMBER) to attribute the malware to established families or identify zero-day behaviors. This comparison focuses on detecting any code structures or functionalities that are not catalogued in existing repositories, culminating in a detailed report to be shared with cybersecurity teams.

7. Snyk's *custom rule development* concludes the process. By codifying distinctive traits uncovered during the reverse-engineering process, analysts can proactively detect similar future threats. They might create rules targeting repeated polymorphic templates or frequent calls to otherwise legitimate platforms that are known to have been exploited. These new detection rules are integrated into automated scanning workflows to provide early warning as soon as a malicious pattern surfaces in subsequent development cycles. Testing these rules against benign and malicious samples helps reduce the chance of false positives. Through these integrated measures, DeepCode AI and Snyk deliver a comprehensive, evolving framework for unraveling and countering polymorphic AI malware.

Reverse engineering polymorphic malware in an environment shaped by quantum computing and advanced AI (at or near AGI levels) requires a deep transformation of the traditional static and dynamic analysis pipeline. Future malware, such as self-adapting BlackMamba strains, will randomize their structure, obfuscate logic, and potentially exploit quantum-enabled cryptographic weaknesses and harness autonomous AI-driven strategies for evasion. Consequently, tools like DeepCode

AI and Snyk must integrate post-quantum safeguards, adaptive AI detection, and real-time threat intelligence into each stage of their workflow.

When isolating malware samples, even heavily secured sandboxes must adopt post-quantum encryption protocols to protect any analytical keys or credentials used during the dissection process. An AGI-assisted adversary might attempt to intercept communications or modify debugging routines in real time. Integrating into these environments dynamic monitors that are capable of detecting ephemeral changes introduced by the malware ensures that surreptitious transformations are captured at the earliest possible stage.

For initial static analysis, DeepCode AI's hybrid AI model (previously fine-tuned on conventional vulnerabilities) now needs to handle post-quantum cryptographic libraries and AI-oriented infiltration tactics. Any outdated cryptographic routines detected in the malware should be flagged as high severity because quantum-scale computations could break them with relative ease. Snyk's vulnerability scanning, which has traditionally been effective against known flaws in dependencies and libraries, must expand to spot suspicious references to large language model APIs, advanced neural network frameworks, or code fragments that indicate dynamic code generation and repeated re-encryption steps.

Tracing the movement of sensitive data requires more than conventional control-flow mapping. Polymorphic malware that employs quantum-based encryption or AI-rewritten code fragments can shift data paths in real time, confounding static tools. GNN-based analyses in DeepCode AI must therefore adapt on the fly, remapping code structures as soon as ephemeral encryption or runtime rewriting is detected. Meanwhile, anomalies such as ephemeral cryptographic keys or calls to suspicious endpoints must trigger deeper investigation because they could point to stealth communication with quantum decryption services or advanced AI modules used to refine the malware's payload.

Because polymorphic malware relies so heavily on obfuscation, de-obfuscation steps that once targeted randomized naming or control-flow flattening must now contend with quantum-facilitated encryption and on-the-fly AI code generation. Using DeepCode AI's VAEs, analysts can tease out the persistent logic that remains stable across multiple iterations, even if encryption layers or function wrappers change. Invariance in tasks such as keystroke logging or data exfiltration stands out as a common thread, regardless of how many quantum-boosted or AI-authored reworkings the code undergoes.

Monitoring external API usage further reveals an entirely new dimension of risk. Polymorphic malware might reach out to suspicious domains and to LLM-based services or quantum-computing endpoints, effectively outsourcing code generation or cryptanalysis in real time. By correlating DeepCode AI's flagged API calls with Snyk's expanded scanning results, security teams can piece together how, where, and why malicious code is sourcing additional functionality (or even full modules) to remain ahead of detection. Network analyses should likewise incorporate heuristics for large language model prompts and quantum job submissions, marking them as suspicious if they align with the malware's operational timeline.

Ultimately, the findings from each layer of analysis must be fed back into a more expansive threat intelligence framework. Cross-referencing discovered techniques or code fragments with specialized repositories that track quantum-exploit tactics, techniques, and procedures (TTPs), and AI-based infiltration patterns become increasingly essential. When previously unrecognized behaviors surface, these repositories can be updated to inform other defenses, leading to faster attribution of the malicious code to established threat families or the identification of new, uncharted attack vectors.

To ensure future resilience, detection rules developed with Snyk and similar scanning tools should incorporate the signatures of emergent quantum or AI-based strategies. Behaviors like ephemeral key usage, repeated re-encodings, suspicious calls to AI endpoints, or code that selectively morphs based on environment checks should be flagged automatically. This feedback loop helps a security team promptly detect an evolving threat the moment it appears in a new codebase or library. With each newly neutralized instance of polymorphic malware, the detection logic becomes progressively more robust, maintaining an edge even as adversaries begin combining quantum computational strength with advanced AI.

DeepCode AI and Snyk Static Analysis: Limitations and Considerations

Despite their potent static analysis foundations, DeepCode AI and Snyk must confront inherent constraints that become increasingly critical in a quantum- and AGI-driven threat landscape (see Figure 7-5). Polymorphic malware, already adept at shapeshifting code structures, may reveal its most damaging behaviors at runtime. Such dynamic characteristics are prone to evolve further when guided by advanced AI, altering command-and-control tactics or cryptographic routines in real time. Merely relying on static signatures, even when augmented with large-scale datasets and powerful machine learning models, will prove insufficient against adversaries capable of reacting to detection attempts. As quantum computing unlocks faster and more sophisticated encryption strategies, malicious code may incorporate ephemeral cryptographic layers that are impenetrable to static analysis alone.

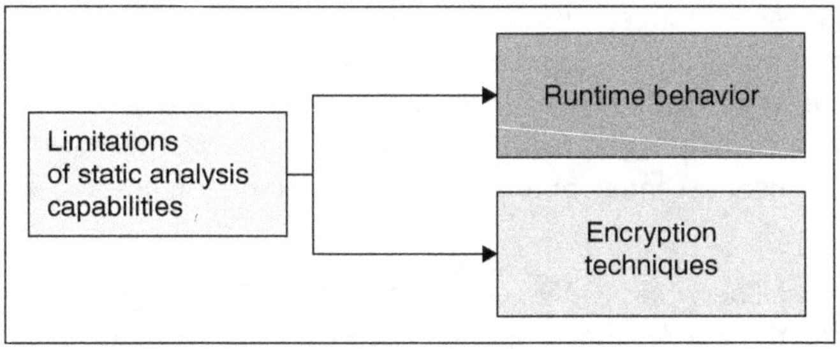

Figure 7-5
Limitations of tools like DeepCode AI and Snyk.

Adapting DeepCode AI and Snyk to these realities requires deeper integration with dynamic analysis workflows. Sandbox environments, traditionally used to observe malware in action, must themselves be fortified with post-quantum safeguards to prevent attackers from exploiting quantum-vulnerable channels during automated testing. Runtime monitors will need to be equipped with AI-augmented tracing to recognize advanced evasion techniques, such as code segments that awaken only in specific temporal windows or in response to environment triggers set by AGI. Greater synergy between static and dynamic findings will also be essential: The semantic insights uncovered by DeepCode AI could guide sandbox instrumentation, highlighting precisely which memory regions or code paths warrant rigorous scrutiny in real-time tests. Likewise, Snyk's detection of suspect dependencies or quantum-unsafe cryptographic fragments could inform a sandbox's active scenario modeling, ensuring that the environment is primed to reveal cunning AI-led or quantum-based maneuvers.

Moreover, as encryption routines become more robust or unpredictably mutative by sophisticated AI, analysts and automated systems alike must adopt a layered approach. Malicious code that relies on large-scale quantum factoring to rewrap its payloads on the fly will evade traditional static analysis by design. Consequently, the pipeline must integrate post-quantum cryptographic checks and ephemeral key detection, ensuring that any anomalous encryption usage (especially if it changes frequently) triggers advanced dynamic methods. Real-time or near-real-time decryption attempts in the sandbox, guided by AI-driven pattern recognition, may help expose hidden malicious payloads before they vanish or mutate.

In essence, acknowledging the limitations of static analysis is crucial for future-proof cybersecurity. While DeepCode AI and Snyk form powerful cornerstones for code-level scanning, their effectiveness in the face of quantum-scale cryptography and AGI-driven evasion rests on thorough dynamic corroboration. This shift calls for improved sandbox resilience, AI-enhanced runtime tracing, and post-quantum encryption checks, transforming the entire analysis pipeline into a comprehensive defense against new agile, encrypted, and evolution-capable threats.

Summary

This chapter illustrates the transformative potential of AI in reshaping our cyber defenses, particularly amid the accelerating threats posed by quantum computing and advanced AI (possibly at AGI levels). First, we highlighted how traditional, rule-based security solutions lack the adaptability required to counter the rapid evolution of sophisticated adversaries. AI- and ML-based frameworks such as anomaly detection, neural network classifiers, and reinforcement learning bring the real-time responsiveness and iterative improvement essential for recognizing and mitigating novel attack vectors.

We then explored how generative adversarial networks (GANs) can stress test and fortify existing defenses, not only by generating adversarial examples that pinpoint systemic blind spots but by helping refine anomaly detection strategies. Reinforcement learning is another powerful component, enabling self-adaptive defensive agents that dynamically adjust security policies, coordinate multiple network segments, and autonomously learn from real-time feedback.

This chapter includes technical examples, and its discussion on current AI models addresses how these systems would need to adapt and change to future threats from AGI and quantum threats. We also noted that although companies like OpenAI are heavily invested in AGI, and Google, Microsoft, and IBM are making progress toward more advanced powerful computers, the current state of play is very much theoretical, and the adoptions suggested in this chapter are based on fictional technologies of the future that are anticipated to emerge in the next decade but are not in existence at present.

Finally, we covered the static-analysis tools DeepCode AI and Snyk in the context of AI- and quantum-driven threats. By augmenting symbolic reasoning with advanced machine learning, and by expanding the scope of these tools to include post-quantum cryptography checks and emergent AI-based evasion techniques, these tools can become proactive rather than merely reactive. Nevertheless, the limitations of static approaches (even when enhanced) underscore the importance of combining AI-based static analysis with post-quantum-ready dynamic workflows, sandbox testing, and continuous threat intelligence.

References

1 Krizhevsky, Alex, Ilya Sutskever, and Geoffrey E. Hinton. 2012. *ImageNet Classification with Deep Convolutional Neural Networks*. https://proceedings.neurips.cc/paper_files/paper/2012/file/c399862d3b9d6b76c8436e924a68c45b-Paper.pdf.

2 Li, Muyang, Ji Lin, Yaoyao Ding, Zhijian Liu, Jun-Yan Zhu, and Song Han. 2020. *GAN Compression: Efficient Architectures for Interactive Conditional GANs*. https://hanlab.mit.edu/projects/gancompression.

3 Chen, Zhiyuan, and Bing Liu. 2018. "Lifelong Reinforcement Learning." *Lifelong Machine Learning*, 139–52. https://doi.org/10.1007/978-3-031-01581-6_9.

4 Protogerou, Aikaterini, Stavros Papadopoulos, Anastasios Drosou, Dimitrios Tzovaras, and Ioannis Refanidis. 2020. "A Graph Neural Network Method for Distributed Anomaly Detection in IoT." *Evolving Systems* 12: 19–36. https://doi.org/10.1007/S12530-020-09347-0.

5 Shi, Yuge, N. Siddharth, Brooks Paige, and Philip H. S. Torr. 2019. *Variational Mixture-of-Experts Autoencoders for Multi-Modal Deep Generative Models*. https://proceedings.neurips.cc/paper_files/paper/2019/file/0ae775a8cb3b499ad1fca944e6f5c836-Paper.pdf.

6 Silva-Filarder, Matthieu Da, Andrea Ancora, Maurizio Filippone, and Pietro Michiardi. 2021. "Multimodal Variational Autoencoders for Sensor Fusion and Cross Generation." *20th IEEE International Conference on Machine Learning and Applications*, 1069–76. https://doi.org/10.1109/ICMLA52953.2021.00175

7 Lawry Aguila, Ana, James Chapman, and Andre Altmann. 2023. "Multi-Modal Variational Autoencoders for Normative Modelling Across Multiple Imaging Modalities." *Lecture Notes in Computer Science* 14220: 425–34. https://doi.org/10.1007/978-3-031-43907-0_41.

8 Kutuzova, Svetlana, Oswin Krause, Douglas McCloskey, Mads Nielsen, and Christian Igel. 2021. *Multimodal Variational Autoencoders for Semi-Supervised Learning: In Defense of Product-of-Experts*. https://arxiv.org/abs/2101.07240v2.

9 NIST. 2022a. *Common Vulnerability Scoring System Calculator*. https://nvd.nist.gov/vuln-metrics/cvss/v3-calculator.

10 NIST. 2022b. *Product Integration Using NVD CVSS Calculators*. https://nvd.nist.gov/Vulnerability-Metrics/Calculator-Product-Integration.

Multiple-Choice Questions with Answers and Explanations

1. What is one primary advantage of using machine learning for anomaly detection in cybersecurity?

   a. It completely eliminates false positives in intrusion detection systems.

   b. It uses supervised learning models to predefine all attack signatures.

   c. It continuously learns from system behaviors to detect novel threats.

   d. It requires no prior data for training robust models.

   Correct Answer: C. Machine learning for anomaly detection is particularly advantageous because it dynamically learns normal system behaviors and identifies deviations, which means it can detect novel threats. Options A and B are incorrect because ML cannot guarantee the elimination of false positives and does not always rely on predefined attack signatures. Option D is incorrect because most ML models require prior training data.

2. Which of the following challenges is most critical in applying AI to cybersecurity?

   a. High costs associated with purchasing commercial AI software

   b. The computational inefficiency of supervised learning models

   c. Ensuring the interpretability and privacy of AI models

   d. The difficulty of using AI for spam filtering

   Correct Answer: C. Interpretability and privacy are critical challenges in cybersecurity AI because these systems often operate in sensitive environments and must provide transparent decision making. Options A and D are unrelated to this primary challenge. Option B, while a technical limitation, is not the most critical issue.

3. How do adversarial attacks threaten AI-driven cybersecurity systems?

   a. By injecting malware directly into the training datasets

   b. By introducing perturbations to input data, causing misclassification

   c. By overriding system policies through social engineering

   d. By using legacy hardware vulnerabilities

   Correct Answer: B. Adversarial attacks typically involve subtle modifications to input data to mislead AI models. These attacks exploit vulnerabilities in ML algorithms, such as gradient-based attacks. Options A, C, and D are unrelated to adversarial machine learning techniques.

4. What is a significant advantage of using GANs in cybersecurity?

   a. GANs automatically create rule-based intrusion detection systems.

   b. GANs generate adversarial examples to test the robustness of existing defenses.

   c. GANs eliminate the need for encryption in data storage.

   d. GANs automatically enforce compliance with cybersecurity regulations.

   Correct Answer: B. GANs are particularly valuable for generating adversarial examples that simulate attacks and expose weaknesses in defensive systems. Options A, C, and D do not reflect the core functionality of GANs.

5. What is one challenge of deploying GANs in anomaly detection for cybersecurity?

   a. GANs are incompatible with network traffic data.

   b. Mode collapse limits the diversity of generated anomalies.

   c. GANs require physical hardware accelerators.

   d. GANs cannot be trained on labeled data.

   Correct Answer: B. Mode collapse is a common issue in GAN training, where the generator produces limited variations, reducing the effectiveness of anomaly detection. Options A, C, and D do not address this specific limitation.

6. Why is reinforcement learning (RL) particularly effective in cybersecurity?

   a. RL does not require any training data.

   b. RL provides a static defense framework for standard attacks.

   c. RL learns and adapts policies to counter evolving threats.

   d. RL eliminates the need for dynamic analysis tools.

   Correct Answer: C. RL excels in environments where adaptive policies are needed to combat evolving threats. Options A, B, and D are inaccurate descriptions of RL's role in cybersecurity.

7. How can multi-agent reinforcement learning (MARL) improve cybersecurity systems?

   a. By coordinating agents to protect against distributed and multipronged attacks

   b. By training agents on completely isolated datasets

   c. By replacing existing static intrusion detection systems entirely

   d. By focusing exclusively on endpoint security solutions

   Correct Answer: A. MARL enhances cybersecurity by allowing multiple agents to coordinate defense strategies, especially against distributed attacks. Options B, C, and D misrepresent MARL's broader applications.

Exercises and Solutions

Exercise 1: Short-Answer Question

Question: Explain how GANs can be used to test the robustness of AI-driven cybersecurity systems. Provide examples of vulnerabilities that GANs can expose.

Solution: GANs are used in cybersecurity to generate adversarial examples that test the robustness of AI systems. For instance, a GAN might create network traffic patterns or malicious payloads that resemble normal behavior to exploit classifier weaknesses. Vulnerabilities exposed include model misclassifications due to adversarial perturbations, lack of generalization in anomaly detection systems, and overreliance on specific feature sets.

Exercise 2: Case Study

Scenario: A cybersecurity team is tasked with implementing a defense against AGI-level malware capable of exploiting quantum cryptographic vulnerabilities.

Tasks:

1. Identify three key limitations in traditional static analysis tools when facing AGI-enabled malware.
2. Propose AI-driven methodologies to overcome these limitations.
3. Evaluate the role of reinforcement learning in adapting defenses to AGI-driven attacks.

Solution:

1. **Limitations of static analysis tools**:
   - Inability to detect dynamic behaviors or real-time obfuscations.
   - Lack of resilience against quantum-scale cryptographic attacks.
   - Limited capacity to adapt to novel malware structures.
2. **AI-driven methodologies**:
   - Use generative adversarial networks (GANs) to generate adversarial examples that simulate AGI-based evasion tactics.
   - Integrate graph neural networks (GNNs) for tracking polymorphic code mutations.
   - Employ federated learning to share threat intelligence across organizations.
3. **Reinforcement learning's role:** RL enables adaptive defenses by learning optimal policies through trial and error. Agents can coordinate responses to distributed threats, automate cryptographic upgrades, and continuously refine their strategies to counter AGI's dynamic tactics.

Exercise 3: Hands-On Activity

Task: Simulate a basic reinforcement learning agent for cybersecurity that detects and responds to network intrusions.

Solution:

1. Set up an RL environment where "states" represent network traffic patterns and "actions" include blocking IPs or isolating nodes.
2. Define a reward function that penalizes for false alarms and rewards for successful intrusion mitigation.
3. Implement the agent using Python libraries such as TensorFlow or PyTorch.
4. Evaluate the performance of the agent by testing it on simulated attack scenarios.
5. Document findings, including how the agent adapts to previously unseen attacks.

8

Securing Digital Identities in an AGI World

Digital identity management systems are threatened by the emerging forces of artificial general intelligence (AGI) and quantum computing. AGI systems, capable of synthesizing identities and infiltrating systems with precision, coupled with the emergence of quantum computers that challenge the foundational cryptographic standards, compel us to reimagine the frameworks that protect digital identities. This chapter focuses on decentralized identity systems, advanced cryptographic methodologies, and emerging standards.

Objectives

- **Survey decentralized digital identity systems:** Examine the principles of self-sovereignty, distributed trust, and minimal disclosure in decentralized identity models, highlighting their resilience against AGI-led identity fraud and quantum cryptographic breaches.
- **Understand zero-knowledge proofs (ZKPs) and homomorphic encryption (HE):** Analyze how these advanced cryptographic methods enable privacy-preserving identity verification, ensuring minimal data exposure even in the face of AGI's data-mining capabilities and quantum computational power.
- **Integrate blockchain for identity verification:** Evaluate the role of blockchain as a decentralized ledger in mitigating single points of failure and ensuring tamper-resistant identity management, incorporating post-quantum cryptographic safeguards.

- **Assess threat scenarios in an AGI and quantum context:** Identify the risks posed by AGI-driven identity manipulation and quantum decryption attacks and discuss proactive defenses through anomaly detection and distributed consensus.
- **Review post-quantum cryptographic standards:** Explore the latest advancements in quantum-resistant cryptographic algorithms, such as lattice-based encryption, and their integration into identity frameworks.
- **Address interoperability challenges:** Investigate the technical and procedural hurdles in achieving interoperability across diverse identity providers, focusing on emerging standards from the W3C and OpenID.
- **Evaluate regulatory compliance:** Discuss the implications of frameworks such as GDPR, eIDAS 2.0, and the W3C Verifiable Credentials Data Model in the design and deployment of secure identity systems.
- **Analyze AGI-driven threat mitigation strategies:** Understand emerging strategies for anomaly detection, distributed threat intelligence, and advanced verification protocols to counteract AGI-enabled identity forgeries.
- **Incorporate privacy-preserving technologies:** Assess the integration of cryptographic tools like zk-SNARKs and HE to enable trust while preserving individual privacy in identity transactions.
- **Propose future-ready identity solutions:** Examine forward-looking architectures that integrate AGI and quantum resilience into decentralized identity ecosystems, fostering robust and adaptive identity frameworks.

As we explore strategies required to secure digital identities in an AGI world, this chapter equips readers with the knowledge and tools to address current vulnerabilities and anticipate and mitigate future threats. By combining cryptographic innovation with decentralized design and regulatory foresight, we can create new resilient identity management systems capable of addressing AGI and quantum-scale threats.

Decentralized Digital Identity Systems

With the invention of Bitcoin,[1] the advent of decentralized digital identity systems marks a decisive shift away from traditional centralized frameworks (e.g., e-Residency,[2] UN Digital ID,[3] EY eIDAS,[4,5] Aadhaar[6,7]), in which a single authority retains control over identity verification and personal data. With new forms of advanced AI (at the level of AGI) and the looming threat of quantum-scale cryptography breaking, these emerging decentralized approaches offer an opportunity to reevaluate trust relationships, mitigate single points of failure, and empower individuals to manage and protect their own credentials. By distributing the responsibilities of identity issuance and verification across multiple nodes or stakeholders, decentralized models reduce the likelihood of large-scale data breaches and provide a more transparent chain of trust.

At their core, decentralized digital identity systems rely on self-sovereign identity principles: Users generate and maintain cryptographic credentials—often embodied in decentralized identifiers (DIDs)[8–11]—without requiring a single central authority to issue or store them. The process is reinforced by applying distributed ledgers (e.g., blockchain) or alternative consensus mechanisms to guarantee data integrity. Coupled with post-quantum cryptographic algorithms, such an approach can help ensure that credentials remain resilient even as quantum computers potentially render older encryption schemes obsolete. This type of approach also aligns closely with the principle of minimal disclosure, whereby an individual can prove specific attributes (such as age or professional affiliation) without revealing extraneous personal information.

A well-structured decentralized identity system typically follows a multilayered architecture comprising identity issuance, storage, verification, and governance layers. The following is a breakdown of these components:

- **Identity issuance layer:** At this layer, a user generates a DID and a corresponding pair of cryptographic keys. This identifier is stored within a DID registry, commonly hosted on a permissionless or permissioned blockchain. Popular DID registries include Hyperledger Indy, Ethereum-based Sovrin, and ION (built on Bitcoin's Sidetree protocol). The choice of registry dictates how identity data is stored and retrieved and therefore affects performance and security.
- **Storage and credential management layer:** Identity attributes are encoded as verifiable credentials (VCs), signed by trusted issuers, and stored either in off-chain repositories (e.g., IPFS, encrypted cloud vaults) or on private permissioned ledgers. For example, Hyperledger Aries implements secure communication channels for credential exchange using DIDComm messaging.
- **Verification and resolution layer:** When a user needs to authenticate, a zero-knowledge proof (ZKP) protocol or JSON Web Token (JWT) is used to prove identity ownership without exposing raw credentials. Verification nodes, such as those implemented in Hyperledger Ursa or zk-SNARK-based attestations, validate claims while preserving privacy.
- **Governance and compliance layer:** To ensure interoperability across decentralized ecosystems, frameworks such as OpenID for Verifiable Credentials (OpenID4VC) and W3C's Verifiable Credentials Data Model (VCDM) 2.0 standardize the issuance, verification, and lifecycle management of credentials. Compliance with GDPR, eIDAS 2.0, and NIST 800-63B ensures adherence to regulatory mandates.

The following example demonstrates a basic DID resolution and credential verification workflow:

```
import didkit

did = "did:ion:EiD-Gb6iU21ZV1A..."  # Sample DID on ION
verification_method = "did:key:z6Mk..."

# Resolve DID document
resolved_did = didkit.resolve(did)
print(resolved_did)
```

```
# Verify a credential using DID
credential = { "id": "123", "issuer": did, "claim": { "name": "Alice" } }
proof = didkit.verify_credential(credential, verification_method)
print("Verification result:", proof)
```

By implementing architectures such as this, decentralized identity systems become resilient to AI-driven forgeries and quantum decryption threats.

In practice, decentralized identity solutions must handle several technical and procedural challenges. On the infrastructure side, the need for interoperability among a diverse array of identity providers, credential formats, and verification protocols cannot be overstated. Enterprises, government bodies, and individual users all seek to integrate identity checks with minimal friction and without relinquishing control over sensitive data. Standards such as those emerging from the World Wide Web Consortium (W3C) and the Decentralized Identity Foundation (DIF) aim to unify the underlying frameworks while also enabling advanced privacy-preserving techniques.

Decentralized identity systems rely on established standards to ensure secure, interoperable, and privacy-preserving credential management. Two critical standardization bodies driving this effort are the W3C and the DIF.

The W3C has created several standards for decentralized identity:

- **Verifiable Credentials Data Model (VCDM) 2.0:** This standard defines a schema for issuing, exchanging, and verifying credentials in a decentralized ecosystem. It introduces cryptographic primitives such as JSON-LD proofs and JWT-based verifiable presentations.
- **Decentralized Identifiers (DIDs) 1.0:** The DID specification outlines a uniform method for creating and resolving self-sovereign identifiers across blockchain and non-blockchain environments.
- **OpenID for Verifiable Credentials (OpenID4VC):** Maintained in collaboration with OpenID Foundation, this extension enables federated authentication of decentralized credentials.

The DIF has made contributions to interoperability and implementation:

- **DIDComm Messaging Protocol:** This secure, peer-to-peer encrypted messaging standard facilitates credential exchange between holders, issuers, and verifiers. Implementations include Hyperledger Aries and DIDComm v2.
- **Universal Resolver:** This decentralized resolver supports multiple DID methods (e.g., did:ion, did:ebsi, did:key), enabling multi-network identity verification.

To ensure seamless deployment and regulatory adherence, decentralized identity frameworks must align with the following standards:

- **General Data Protection Regulation (GDPR):** This European standard requires user consent, data minimization, and right-to-be-forgotten functionalities in decentralized identity systems.
- **Electronic Identification, Authentication, and Trust Services (eIDAS 2.0):** This European standard mandates mutual recognition of digital identities across member states.

- **NIST 800-63B (Digital Identity Guidelines):** This U.S. standard establishes authentication assurance levels (AAL1, AAL2, and AAL3) for decentralized identity schemes.

By adhering to these evolving standards, decentralized identity frameworks can achieve cross-platform interoperability, reducing friction in digital identity verification while maintaining compliance with global regulatory standards.

On the user experience front, however, balancing security and convenience remains crucial. Even if cryptographically robust solutions exist, end users might find them cumbersome unless they are supported by user-friendly wallets, robust key-recovery mechanisms, and well-defined revocation or expiration policies.

Moreover, in an AGI-influenced future, identity fraud could evolve into a far more sophisticated domain. AI-based agents (autonomous or maliciously directed) might forge entire identities, manipulate credentials in real time, or even subvert verification protocols by exploiting system inefficiencies. Decentralized identity systems, therefore, must proactively integrate defenses against such AI-driven threats. This might include implementing anomaly detection on a distributed scale (ensuring that multiple nodes or oracles must concur on suspicious activity before acceptance or revocation) and employing advanced cryptographic proofs to validate identity claims. Additionally, credible frameworks for recourse, redress, and dispute resolution will be critical when digital identities are contested or misused.

In addition, the rise of quantum computing threatens to undermine widely used public-key cryptographic algorithms. Consequently, identity management solutions cannot rely solely on legacy methods such as Rivest–Shamir–Adleman (RSA) or elliptic-curve cryptography (ECC). Incorporating lattice-based or code-based encryption alongside quantum-safe signature schemes has become essential to preserving the trustworthiness of decentralized identity. As these newer primitives mature, decentralized identity infrastructures will require frequent updates and versioning strategies to ensure a smooth transition and to protect existing credentials against cryptographic shortfalls.

Taken together, the technological developments driving decentralized identity systems (open standards, self-sovereign design, quantum-resistant cryptography, and advanced threat detection) serve as the foundation for a new form of secure digital identities. By extending trust throughout a distributed network and equipping individual users with greater control over how, when, and where they reveal personal information, these systems can reshape how identity is managed.

Zero-Knowledge Proofs and Homomorphic Encryption

As the demands for privacy protection intensify (particularly in a future where AGI systems can analyze massive datasets and quantum computers threaten classical cryptographic primitives), innovations like zero-knowledge proofs (ZKPs) and homomorphic encryption (HE) offer crucial methods to safeguard digital identities. Both techniques enable computations on data without exposing underlying sensitive details, thereby bolstering privacy and trust in decentralized identity systems.

ZKPs are cryptographic protocols through which one party (the "prover") can demonstrate knowledge of a secret to another party (the "verifier") without disclosing the actual secret or any other extraneous information. Historically, identity verification has hinged on revealing a portion of personal data, whether it be name, age, or credentials. ZKPs invert this premise, allowing claims such as "I am over 18" or "I possess this credential" to be validated without any raw data being divulged. This approach is particularly valuable in decentralized digital identity frameworks, where the emphasis lies on self-sovereignty and minimal disclosure. By guaranteeing correctness and privacy of the proof, ZKPs help counter the risk that AGI-based adversaries might aggressively mine revealed data for subsequent exploitations. They also mitigate concerns that an attacker harnessing quantum computing power could intercept verification messages and retroactively decrypt sensitive details.

Among the most widely adopted ZKP schemes are the following:

- **zk-SNARKs (Zero-Knowledge Succinct Non-Interactive Arguments of Knowledge):** Used in privacy-centric blockchains (e.g., Zcash), zk-SNARKs enable compact proofs but require a trusted setup.
- **zk-STARKs (Zero-Knowledge Scalable Transparent Arguments of Knowledge):** A more scalable alternative, zk-STARKs eliminate the need for a trusted setup and leverage hash functions instead of elliptic curves, enhancing post-quantum security.
- **Bulletproofs:** Primarily used in confidential transactions, Bulletproofs do not require trusted setup but are computationally more intensive.

Resource Requirements for ZKP Implementations

The computational overhead of ZKPs depends on the proof generation and verification steps. Table 8-1 provides a comparison of resource demands.

Table 8-1 ZKP Implementation Resource Demands

ZKP Type	Proof Size	Verification Time	Trusted Setup	Post-Quantum Secure?	Use Case Example
zk-SNARKs	Small	Fast (~10ms)	Yes	No	Private transactions in Zcash
zk-STARKs	Large	Medium (~100ms)	No	Yes	Scalable identity attestations
Bulletproofs	Medium	Slow (~500ms)	No	No	Confidential transactions in Monero

Due to high computation and storage costs, ZKPs are often implemented in off-chain computations with only proof verification performed on-chain.

zk-SNARK-Based Identity Verification

The following pseudocode example for zk-SNARK-based identity verification illustrates how a simplified zk-SNARK verification might operate:

```
from py_ecc import bn128
from py_ecc.bn128 import pairing
```

```
# Simulating a zk-SNARK proof for verifying identity ownership
def verify_zk_proof(public_key, proof, statement):
    # Pairing-based verification (simplified example)
    pairing_check = pairing.pairing(proof, public_key) == statement
    return pairing_check

# Example execution
public_key = bn128.G1
proof = bn128.G2
statement = bn128.multiply(bn128.G1, 42)  # Simulated claim

print("ZK Proof Verification Result:", verify_zk_proof(public_key, proof, state-
ment))
```

In a real-world implementation, zk-SNARKs require preprocessing to generate trusted parameters, and the prover constructs cryptographic commitments before submitting the proof.

Homomorphic Encryption and Privacy-Preserving Operations

Homomorphic encryption takes the notion of privacy-preserving operations a step further than ZKP. Rather than just proving knowledge of a secret, HE enables arithmetic or logical operations to be performed directly on encrypted data, yielding encrypted results that can later be decrypted to reveal only the final outcomes. In the context of decentralized identity, this capability underpins scenarios where multiple untrusted entities need to verify or update personal details without collectively seeing the unencrypted data. For instance, a user's age or nationality could be verified by a service provider that processes encrypted inputs, ensuring that no personal information is leaked. In an AGI-centric time, the ability to carry out encrypted computations becomes vital: Advanced AI models might otherwise glean insights from ephemeral data patterns, even if explicit plaintext information is never made public.

ZKPs and HE can address the emerging threats introduced by large-scale quantum computation. Whereas traditional public-key algorithms (e.g., RSA, ECC) become vulnerable to quantum attacks, certain ZKP constructions, especially those based on lattice or code-based cryptography, are believed to offer resistance against quantum-scale factorization. Some homomorphic schemes already rely on lattice-based constructions, ensuring that they can outlast potential quantum breakthroughs. Integrating ZKPs and HE with post-quantum cryptography makes decentralized identity systems more resilient. Even if an adversary controls extensive computational resources (whether classical or quantum), they remain unable to decrypt or misuse personal details.

Three main HE schemes exist:

- **Partially homomorphic encryption (PHE):** Supports only one operation (either addition or multiplication) indefinitely. An example is RSA-based additively homomorphic encryption (e.g., the Paillier cryptosystem).
- **Somewhat homomorphic encryption (SHE):** Supports both addition and multiplication but with a limited number of operations before noise accumulation makes decryption infeasible. An example is the BGV (Brakerski–Gentry–Vaikuntanathan) scheme.
- **Fully homomorphic encryption (FHE):** Supports an unlimited number of operations but at extremely high computational cost. An example is CKKS (Cheon–Kim–Kim–Song) for approximate arithmetic over real numbers.

Resource Overhead of Homomorphic Encryption

Homomorphic encryption remains computationally impractical for real-time decentralized identity systems for several reasons:

- Large ciphertext sizes (often 100 times the size of plaintext)
- Exponential computational complexity (FHE takes minutes to evaluate basic functions)
- High memory overhead (gigabytes of RAM for deep computations)

Due to these constraints, hybrid approaches such as combining HE with Secure Multi-Party Computation (MPC) or ZKPs are often used.

Table 8-2 provides a comparison of the supported operations, performance, and practical use cases for HE schemes.

Table 8-2 HE Schemes: Supported Operations, Performance, and Practical Use Cases

HE Scheme	Supported Operations	Performance	Practical Use Case
Paillier	Addition only	Fast	Voting, banking
BGV	Limited add/mul	Medium	Encrypted search
CKKS	Floating-point operations	Slow	Privacy-preserving ML
TFHE	Boolean logic ops	Very slow	Secure cloud computing

HE-Based Identity Validation

This example of pseudocode for HE-based identity validation shows partially homomorphic encryption (PHE) using the Paillier scheme, which supports addition on encrypted data:

```
from phe import paillier

# Key generation
public_key, private_key = paillier.generate_paillier_keypair()
```

```
# Encrypt identity attribute (e.g., age)
age = 35
encrypted_age = public_key.encrypt(age)

# Compute on encrypted data (e.g., adding 5 years)
updated_encrypted_age = encrypted_age + 5

# Decrypt result
decrypted_age = private_key.decrypt(updated_encrypted_age)
print("Decrypted Age:", decrypted_age)  # Output: 40
```

FHE would enable more complex operations but at impractical computational costs.

Strategic Integration of ZKPs and HE

Each ZKP and HE technique demands careful implementation. ZKPs historically have required significant computational power and can be tricky to configure correctly, particularly when domain-specific proofs (e.g., verifying compliance with complex regulatory constraints) are needed. Recent research focuses on streamlining these protocols for real-world deployment, using zk-SNARKs or transparent setups that remove the need for large, centralized "trusted ceremonies." HE can incur substantial computational overhead, making it initially challenging to deploy at scale. Efforts to improve the performance of FHE systems (e.g., optimizing polynomial arithmetic and adopting hardware accelerations) have shown promise, but these solutions require further refinements to meet the latency expectations of most identity-verification workflows.

For decentralized identity systems, the strategic integration of ZKPs and HE can achieve user privacy and robust, tamper-proof verification. Organizations adopting these methods might, for example, allow a user to provide proof of residence without divulging an address or to confirm membership in a professional guild without showing the entire certificate. Such minimal disclosure is particularly relevant where advanced AI could correlate partial details with other databases to construct an intrusive profile. Moreover, by embedding HE into credential issuance and revalidation processes, identity data remain encrypted end-to-end, mitigating the risk that even a compromised node in a distributed ledger or an AGI-infiltrated organization could glean a user's raw personal information.

While ZKPs and HE offer privacy-preserving benefits, their implementation in large-scale decentralized identity systems remains constrained by computational overhead. The following optimizations and hybrid models are being explored:

- **Hardware acceleration:** FPGA and ASIC implementations (e.g., Microsoft SEAL, Intel HE-Accelerator) improve HE computation efficiency.
- **Batch processing:** Aggregating multiple ZKP verifications into a single proof reduces proof-generation time.

- **Hybrid cryptographic models:** Combining HE for selective encryption with ZKPs for proof validation optimizes privacy and performance.

Table 8-3 lists the projected performance improvement of ZKP and HE with hardware acceleration.

Table 8-3 Projected Performance Improvement of ZKP and HE with Hardware Acceleration

Optimization Technique	ZKP Verification Speedup	HE Computation Speedup
FPGA/ASIC acceleration	20x	50x
Batch proof generation	10x	N/A
Hybrid cryptography	5x	30x

As quantum computing matures, lattice-based cryptography (e.g., NTRUEncrypt, FrodoKEM) is emerging as a viable alternative to HE, offering post-quantum security with significantly lower computational cost.

Privacy-Preserving Verification Using ZKPs and HE in Authentication User Agency

Among the most promising applications of ZKPs and HE[12] is their integration into privacy-preserving verification protocols,[13] particularly within authentication user agency (AUA),[6,7,14] where users must authenticate themselves without exposing sensitive information. This approach mitigates the potential threats posed by quantum decryption and the sophisticated data-mining capabilities of AGI-powered adversaries.

A crucial technology underpinning such privacy-preserving verifications is zk-SNARK.[15–17] By employing zk-SNARKs, it becomes possible to prove membership in an identity group or verify specific credentials (for instance, asserting that a user's age or status meets certain criteria) without ever disclosing the actual attribute values. Rather than revealing details like date of birth or entire credentials, the protocol simply issues a proof that these attributes satisfy the requested conditions. This helps ensure minimal data exposure in contexts where advanced AI might correlate personal information across multiple sources.

Meanwhile, HE extends this privacy-preserving paradigm by allowing operations to be conducted on encrypted data without requiring decryption. In AUA, HE can facilitate computations on user credentials that remain sealed throughout verification, thereby defending personal data against potential eavesdroppers or malicious nodes. Various HE schemes—including BFV,[18–21] CKKS,[22–24] and BGV[18,25]—offer different performance and functional trade-offs:

- **BFV (Brakerski/Fan-Vercauteren):** This leveled homomorphic encryption scheme supports exact integer arithmetic with modular reductions and is suitable for encrypted database queries and privacy-preserving computations. It focuses on integer arithmetic, making it suitable for threshold checks and range proofs.[26]
- **BGV (Brakerski–Gentry–Vaikuntanathan):** This somewhat homomorphic encryption (SHE) scheme enables encrypted computations over integer data and is commonly used in secure

cloud processing. It balances efficiency and functionality through modular arithmetic on encrypted values.[27]

- **CKKS (Cheon–Kim–Kim–Song):** This leveled homomorphic encryption scheme is designed for approximate arithmetic over real and complex numbers. It is particularly useful in privacy-preserving machine learning. Because it supports approximate arithmetic over real numbers, it enables more intricate operations such as privacy-preserving machine learning.[28]

To validate these schemes in practice, developers frequently rely on established libraries like HELib (from IBM)[29,30] and TenSEAL (based on Microsoft SEAL),[31] which provide optimized implementations of lattice-based cryptographic primitives.

Effective adoption of privacy-preserving verification also entails adherence to emerging standards and regulations. Compliance with protocols like European Electronic Commerce Certification for Verifiable Credentials Data Model (E3C VCDM)[32] and OpenID4VC[33] ensures a consistent and secure way to manage decentralized credentials across heterogeneous platforms. At a broader governance level, alignment with the updated Electronic Identification, Authentication and Trust Services regulation (eIDAS 2.0)[5] fosters cross-border mutual recognition within the European Union, and adherence to the General Data Protection Regulation (GDPR)[34,35] guarantees strong data protection measures. By embedding zk-SNARK-based proofs and homomorphic operations into these frameworks, identity-verification flows can be made interoperable, user-centric, and auditable, while still maintaining end-to-end encryption that even quantum computers would find challenging to break.

This privacy-preserving approach to verification empowers decentralized identity systems to function under stringent regulatory requirements and in high-threat environments where AI or quantum resources might be misused. By combining strong cryptographic primitives (ZKPs and HE) with well-established libraries and compliance mechanisms (HELib, TenSEAL, eIDAS 2.0, GDPR), the AUA architecture can grant users seamless access to services and credentials without exposing personal data to malicious or overly inquisitive actors. This positions privacy-preserving verification as a foundational strategy for protecting identities in a future shaped by quantum-scale cryptography and AGI-level inference.

Blockchain for Identity Verification

Blockchain technology introduces a decentralized, tamper-resistant ledger that can significantly strengthen identity verification processes, particularly when combined with the advanced cryptographic methods described in earlier sections. Rather than relying on a central authority to validate and store user credentials, blockchain-based systems distribute verification tasks across multiple nodes. Each node independently confirms transactions, thereby creating a transparent audit trail of credential issuance, revocation, or modification. This dispersion of trust eliminates single points of failure and counters sophisticated threats posed by advanced AI or quantum-assisted cryptanalysis.

One of the major benefits of blockchain in identity verification lies in the immutability of its data structure. Once blocks containing identity-related transactions are appended, they become exceedingly difficult to alter retrospectively—an attribute that is increasingly critical in a world of

AI-generated and quantum-enabled identity forgery. Even if a malicious actor wields extensive computational resources, amending the blockchain's historical record across a majority of nodes is prohibitively expensive. In addition, cryptographic hashes link each block to its predecessor, creating a verifiable chain of custody that underscores the integrity of credential attestations.

Interoperability with decentralized identifiers (DIDs) and self-sovereign identity models further enhances blockchain's role in identity management. Users maintain direct control over their credentials by storing them locally or through secure, privacy-preserving means. When identity proofs are required (whether for background checks or proof of eligibility), users can authorize limited disclosure, verified by cross-referencing DID records on the blockchain. By layering on ZKPs and HE, a service provider can confirm identity attributes without exposing the user's underlying personal data. This synergy between off-chain cryptographic methods and on-chain logging ensures minimal data exposure, which is a boon in cases where AI or quantum systems might scour uncovered details for potential exploits.

From an architectural standpoint, blockchain-based identity verification must address a variety of performance and governance considerations. While public chains (e.g., Ethereum) offer open participation and global reach, permissioned ledgers can deliver faster transaction throughput and more consistent data privacy regulations, which is especially relevant for corporate or government identity frameworks. Regardless of the model, adopting post-quantum cryptographic primitives for signing and hashing is prudent as it ensures that future quantum computers cannot easily alter or forge older blockchain records. Moreover, sidechain or Layer 2 solutions might help reconcile the need for robust verification with the bandwidth and latency constraints of typical mainnet operations, particularly under heavy usage.

In the sections that follow, we discuss four different modifications:

- Blockchain implementation models for decentralized identity systems
- Consensus mechanisms for identity verification
- Integration with existing identity systems
- Standards for blockchain-based identity verification

Blockchain Implementation Models for Decentralized Identity Systems

Blockchain-based identity systems can follow different architectural models, each with distinct performance, security, and governance trade-offs:

- **Public blockchains (e.g., Ethereum, Bitcoin, Tezos):**
    - Fully decentralized, tamper-resistant, and open to all participants.
    - Support smart contracts for automated identity verification.
    - Limitations: High transaction fees (gas costs), scalability issues, and latency

- **Permissioned blockchains (e.g., Hyperledger Indy, Sovrin, Quorum):**
    - Operate under controlled access, where only verified participants can run nodes.
    - Offer better scalability and compliance with regulatory frameworks.
    - Limitations: Less decentralized compared to public networks
- **Hybrid models (e.g., Layer 2 solutions like Polygon, sidechains):**
    - Combine public transparency with private efficiency.
    - Use case: ID credentials stored on a private ledger, with public verification anchors stored on Ethereum

Consensus Mechanisms for Identity Verification

The choice of consensus mechanism directly impacts the security, efficiency, and decentralization of identity verification, as outlined in Table 8-4.

Table 8-4 Impact of Consensus Mechanism Choice

Consensus Mechanism	Description	Use Case in Identity Systems	Trade-offs
Proof of Work (PoW)	Miners solve cryptographic puzzles to validate transactions.	Ensures high security and resistance to Sybil attacks.	High energy consumption Slow transactions
Proof of Stake (PoS)	Validators stake tokens to confirm transactions.	Used in permissioned identity blockchains (e.g., Sovrin).	Requires economic incentives Staking risks
Delegated Proof of Stake (DPoS)	Elected nodes validate transactions.	Optimized for performance and governance control.	Less decentralized due to reliance on delegates
Practical Byzantine Fault Tolerance (PBFT)	Leader-based consensus is required. PBFT is efficient for permissioned chains.	Ideal for enterprise and government-backed identity frameworks.	Centralization risk Requires trust among validators

For identity systems, PBFT and PoS-based models are preferable due to their efficiency and reduced environmental impact.

The following smart contract example demonstrates a Verifiable Credentials Data Model registry on Ethereum:

```
// SPDX-License-Identifier: MIT
pragma solidity ^0.8.0;

contract IdentityVerification {
    struct Credential {
        string holder;
```

```
        string credentialType;
        bool isValid;
    }

    mapping(address => Credential) public credentials;
    address public issuingAuthority;

    constructor() {
        issuingAuthority = msg.sender;  // Set contract deployer as issuer
    }

    function issueCredential(address _holder, string memory _credentialType) public {
        require(msg.sender == issuingAuthority, "Only issuing authority can issue
credentials");
        credentials[_holder] = Credential(_holder, _credentialType, true);
    }

    function verifyCredential(address _holder) public view returns (bool) {
        return credentials[_holder].isValid;
    }
}
```

This contract enables identity issuers to register decentralized credentials, which can be validated on chain without revealing sensitive user information.

Integration with Existing Identity Systems

For organizations migrating from traditional, centralized identity verification systems (e.g., LDAP-based authentication, OAuth, SAML-based federated identity systems), a progressive integration strategy is needed.

Consider the following migration path from centralized to decentralized identity models:

Phase 1. Federated identity bridging: Use DIDs alongside OAuth 2.0/OpenID Connect to allow interoperability with existing single sign-on (SSO) solutions. For example, Microsoft Entra ID (formerly Azure AD) now supports DID-based authentication.

Phase 2. Off-chain verifiable credentials: Implement the W3C Verifiable Credentials Data Model for identity attestations, stored off chain in encrypted repositories (e.g., IPFS, Arweave, cloud vaults). Identity proofs are verified via ZKPs without exposing raw attributes.

Phase 3. Full on-chain identity anchors: Store hash commitments of identity credentials on Ethereum, Polygon, or Sovrin and use Layer 2 rollups to mitigate high gas costs. For example, Polygon ID uses zk-SNARKs for privacy-preserving on-chain identity proofs.

Consider the following example of decentralized identity verification flow using blockchain:

1. The issuer (e.g., university, government) issues verifiable credential stored in a DID registry.
2. A user presents a ZKP of the credential to a verifier without exposing full details.
3. The verifier queries the blockchain to check whether the credential hash exists, confirming its validity.
4. A smart contract automatically validates the identity proof, allowing access to services.

Standards for Blockchain-Based Identity Verification

Decentralized identity systems must comply with the following global standards to ensure interoperability and regulatory adherence:

- **W3C Verifiable Credentials Data Model (VCDM) 2.0:** VCDM is a standard for issuing, presenting, and verifying credentials in decentralized ecosystems. It ensures compatibility with OpenID4VC.
- **Decentralized Identity Foundation (DIF) DIDComm Messaging:** This is a secure peer-to-peer encrypted messaging protocol for identity verification.
- **European Commission eIDAS 2.0:** This European digital identity framework defines legal standards for cross-border recognition of digital identities within the EU.
- **NIST 800-63B:** This standard establishes identity proofing and authentication assurance levels (AAL1–AAL3).

To comply with these standards, identity verifiers must implement verifiable cryptographic proofs (e.g., zk-SNARK, Merkle proofs) rather than relying on centralized authentication databases. In jurisdictions that mandate stringent user protections (such as GDPR or eIDAS 2.0), blockchain engineers must manage challenges between ledger immutability and the right to be forgotten. Innovative approaches include storing minimal identity references on chain coupled with pointer references to off-chain encrypted data that can be selectively updated or revoked. By combining these legal and technical solutions, blockchains can align with diverse legal frameworks while maintaining the decentralized benefits that strengthen secure post-quantum and AI-resilient identity verification.

Case Study: Open-Source Alternatives for AI-Driven Malware Analysis and Threat Detection

This section presents a case study on how AI-driven malware analysis and threat detection systems can be adapted to counter risks posed by artificial general intelligence (AGI) and quantum computing advancements. This section provides a case study on using Vectra AI—a platform designed to detect, analyze, and respond to sophisticated threats in real time[36]—for malware analysis and threat detection, focusing on its application for network-based threats and AI-powered attacks.

Note

While this case study references a commercial product, Vectra AI, it is important to clarify that the author has no previous, existing, or planned future association with Vectra AI or any other commercial cybersecurity vendor.

Throughout this book, open-source implementations have been prioritized wherever possible. However, in certain cases, analyzing commercially available platforms provides insight into how existing tools can be modified to address future threats. The architectural changes and AI-driven adaptations suggested in this section are not exclusive to Vectra AI; they apply equally to all commercial and open-source network security and threat detection tools. Organizations working with both proprietary and open-access security tools can adopt these principles to ensure resilience against AGI-powered adversaries and quantum-scale cryptographic threats.

The analysis in this section applies equally to other solutions designed to detect malicious activity. While Vectra AI's capabilities highlight how machine learning and real-time behavioral analytics can strengthen network security, the broader message of this case study is that such tools must evolve to confront emerging risks posed by quantum computing and AGI-level adversaries. Malicious actors empowered by these technologies can bypass traditional defenses through advanced cryptography-breaking techniques or dynamically adapt their evasion tactics in ways that overwhelm conventional threat detection systems. By examining Vectra AI's network-centric approach, which encompasses continuous metadata analysis, contextual alerts, and automated integrations with security information and event management (SIEM) or security orchestration, automation, and response (SOAR) platforms, this case study underscores the need for robust, future-proof defenses. Each step in the malware detection and response lifecycle must incorporate quantum-safe cryptographic checks and AI-driven anomaly detection to remain effective against the most sophisticated threats. Organizations aiming to protect against quantum- and AGI-level threats will find that the lessons gleaned from Vectra AI's architecture, deployment model, and continuous learning frameworks can inform the design and refinement of virtually any modern security solution.

Understanding Vectra AI

Vectra AI offers a specialized approach to network-based threat detection, using artificial intelligence and machine learning to observe user and device behaviors across an organization's environment. Vectra AI combines automated detection with sound, actionable insights (see Figure 8-1). A prime example is the Cognito Detect and Respond feature, which continuously analyzes metadata originating from cloud, data center, and enterprise networks, identifying anomalies that might signal lateral movements or privilege escalations. The platform also uses pretrained neural networks for real-time detection of suspicious activities, correlating events across multiple hosts and network layers to produce a holistic understanding of each incident. Equally important are the contextual enrichments applied to each alert, which enable teams to prioritize and investigate potential issues with heightened clarity. Vectra AI integrates into existing security infrastructures, supporting SIEM and SOAR tools, thus ensuring that detection events can be automated and acted upon without disrupting established workflows.

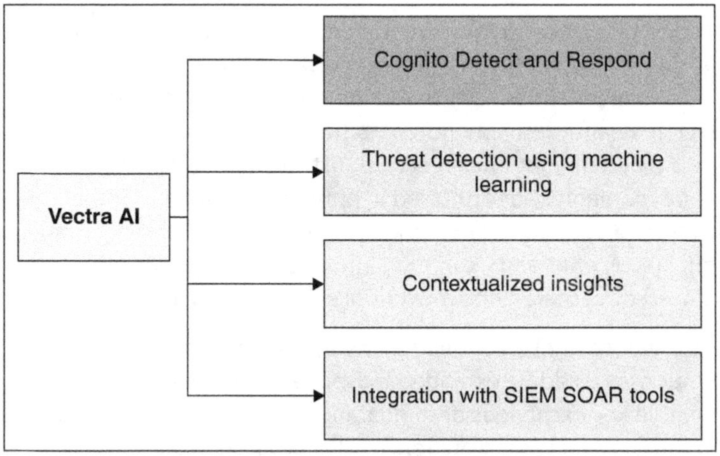

Figure 8-1
The Vectra AI network-based threat detection process.

Vectra AI's network-based threat detection capabilities presently revolve around ingesting and analyzing metadata from cloud, data center, and enterprise networks and identifying anomalous behaviors that could signal malicious activities (e.g., lateral movement, privilege escalation). As quantum computing matures and AGI-level adversaries gain the capacity to orchestrate highly adaptive, polymorphic attacks, Vectra AI must evolve beyond its current machine-learning models and automated detection techniques to encompass a new generation of cryptographic safeguards, continuous behavioral adaptation, and post-quantum resilience.

To counter the quantum threat, Vectra AI's Cognito Detect and Respond platform will need to incorporate rigorous post-quantum cryptographic checks within its data ingestion pipeline. This might entail detecting the use of outdated encryption algorithms in network sessions (e.g., RSA, ECC) that become easily factorable under large-scale quantum computation. If the platform flags quantum-unsafe protocols or cipher suites, security teams can be alerted to upgrade these sessions or enforce more robust lattice-based or hash-based schemes. Meanwhile, advanced neural networks must also be trained to recognize traffic patterns suggestive of on-the-fly "quantum factoring," wherein an attacker might be decrypting data or forging digital signatures at scale.

Just as significant is the heightened sophistication associated with AGI-level threats. Malicious AI agents can rapidly mutate code or adapt their network signatures in response to detection. To address this, Vectra AI's threat detection algorithms must incorporate additional layers of adaptive learning that are capable of recognizing fleeting or context-aware tactics. This might include employing reinforcement learning modules that identify new or unexpected combinations of benign events that, in aggregate, signal advanced infiltration. Network correlation engines would benefit from a multi-agent architecture, so if one subsystem detects an anomalous login pattern, another subsystem can verify and escalate alerts by examining concurrent login attempts, Domain Name System (DNS) queries, or exfiltration routes.

Additionally, contextual insights need to be extended to account for zero-day quantum attacks and AI-orchestrated exploits. In practice, this means integrating more specialized threat intelligence sources that track novel post-quantum vulnerabilities or AI-based infiltration methods. For instance, if an attacker uses deep learning to craft stealthy network flows, Vectra AI's platform will require advanced pattern-recognition models that highlight unexpected statistical anomalies in packet sequences, even if these anomalies are momentary or disguised in ephemeral channels. Richer contextual data, such as the concurrency of suspicious encryption methods, ephemeral key usage, or references to large language model (LLM) endpoints, can then inform security operators of how best to respond, ensuring that advanced threats are neither overlooked nor buried in false positives.

Vectra AI's integration with SIEM and SOAR solutions will need to incorporate post-quantum and AI-specific playbooks. Automated responses could be extended to isolate nodes that repeatedly attempt to establish quantum-vulnerable key exchanges or to quarantine hosts that exhibit suspected AGI-like evasion patterns. By automating immediate remedial actions, such as resetting cryptographic policies, enforcing stricter authentication protocols, or launching containment routines, Vectra AI can assist organizations in maintaining a proactive posture against next-generation threats.

To maintain relevance amid quantum breakthroughs and AGI-enabled adversaries, Vectra AI's roadmap should prioritize enriched detection logic for quantum-based infiltration, adaptive machine-learning algorithms capable of tackling ultra-sophisticated AI attacks, and deepened integration of post-quantum cryptographic standards. Through these enhancements, Vectra AI can continue providing real-time, contextualized insights across cloud, data center, and enterprise networks to detect and mitigate threats when AGI and quantum technologies threaten to redefine the cyber threat landscape.

Open-Source Alternatives: Integrating AI and Quantum-Resilient Security in Open-Source IDS

Although this case study focuses on the commercial product Vectra AI, a number of open-source tools exist, and can be adapted using the same modification detailed in this case study. The three different modifications described in this section can be applied to open-source security tools to evolve beyond signature-based detection and incorporate AI-driven, behavior-based anomaly detection.

Open-Source Alternatives for AI-Powered Threat Detection

Several open-source alternatives to proprietary threat detection systems exist, providing strong cybersecurity frameworks that can be adapted to detect AGI-enabled cyber threats and quantum-assisted malware:

- **Suricata:** An open-source intrusion detection and prevention system (IDPS) that can be extended with AI-powered analytics
- **Zeek (formerly Bro):** A powerful open-source network analysis framework that can detect anomalies and advanced attack techniques
- **Snort:** A widely used network intrusion detection system (NIDS) that supports custom rulesets for AI-based behavioral analysis
- **ML-SecOps frameworks:** Open-source machine learning tools, such as DeepExploit, SecML, and MalwareBazaar, enable threat intelligence research

These tools already form the backbone of many SIEM and SOAR platforms, making them suitable candidates for AGI and post-quantum security integrations..

AI-Augmented Intrusion Detection Using Suricata and Zeek

To enhance signature-based detection with AI, Suricata and Zeek have traditionally relied on predefined rules (e.g., Snort rule syntax). AI-enhanced IDS extends this by using self-learning anomaly detection models to spot zero-day threats and AGI-crafted exploits.

Consider the following sample implementation using Python:

```
from sklearn.ensemble import IsolationForest
import numpy as np

# Simulated network feature vectors (latency, packet size, frequency)
network_data = np.array([[0.1, 200, 50], [0.15, 220, 45], [1.5, 4000, 5]])  # Anom-
alous sample

# Train an isolation forest model for anomaly detection
clf = IsolationForest(contamination=0.05)
clf.fit(network_data[:-1])  # Train on normal data
prediction = clf.predict([network_data[-1]])  # Detect anomaly

print("Anomaly detected" if prediction[0] == -1 else "Normal traffic")
```

This type of AI-based detection can be integrated into Zeek to analyze network metadata and automatically detect AGI-driven evasion techniques.

Quantum-Resistant Threat Intelligence for Open-Source IDS

To adapt network security tools for post-quantum encryption, open-source security platforms should integrate quantum-resistant cryptographic checks to detect outdated encryption protocols that may be vulnerable to Shor's algorithm. Examples of these checks include monitoring of ephemeral key exchange to flag quantum-insecure TLS sessions and quantum-vulnerable cipher detection.

Consider the following sample script:

```
alert tls any any -> any any (
    msg: "Quantum-vulnerable TLS handshake detected";
    content: "|16 03 03|";  # TLS 1.2 handshake
    pcre: "/(RSA|ECDH)/";  # Flag RSA/ECDH key exchanges
    sid: 1000001;
    rev: 1;
)
```

This Suricata rule flags unencrypted or quantum-vulnerable RSA and ECDH-based TLS handshakes, urging an upgrade to lattice-based cryptography (e.g., Kyber, NTRUEncrypt).

Deep Learning Models for Polymorphic Malware Detection

When training deep learning models to recognize AGI-powered malware, consider the following:

- We expect that AI-based malware will use real-time polymorphism and adversarial evasion tactics.
- Open-source alternatives such as MalwareBazaar, YARA, and SecML can be adapted to counter these threats.

Consider the following sample implementation of AI-enhanced malware detection using Python:

```
import tensorflow as tf
from tensorflow import keras

# Dummy dataset (network packet sizes, entropy levels)
X_train = [[200, 0.4], [210, 0.35], [5000, 0.95]]  # Last entry is anomalous
y_train = [0, 0, 1]  # 1 = suspected malware

# Define a simple neural network for anomaly detection
model = keras.Sequential([
    keras.layers.Dense(4, activation="relu"),
    keras.layers.Dense(2, activation="softmax")
])

model.compile(optimizer="adam", loss="sparse_categorical_crossentropy",
metrics=["accuracy"])
model.fit(X_train, y_train, epochs=10, verbose=1)
```

What Open-Source Alternatives Offer

While proprietary AI-powered threat detection systems offer a polished approach to network security, open-source cybersecurity tools provide equally viable frameworks for AGI- and quantum-resistant security enhancements. We have just seen in several examples:

- Suricata, Zeek, and Snort can be extended with AI-driven anomaly detection models.
- Quantum-resistant cryptographic checks should be incorporated into open-source IDS to detect quantum-vulnerable encryption protocols.
- Deep learning models for AI-enhanced malware detection can be integrated with MalwareBazaar, SecML, and YARA.

By adopting these methodologies, organizations can future-proof their security infrastructure against AGI and post-quantum threats without being reliant on proprietary security vendors.

Using Vectra AI for Malware Analysis

Now we're ready to return to our case study focusing on Vectra AI. As cyber threats evolve with the increasing sophistication of AGI and the looming capabilities of quantum computing, traditional signature-based malware detection techniques are becoming obsolete. AI-driven malware analysis uses machine learning models, behavioral analytics, and network telemetry to detect, analyze, and mitigate cyber threats in real-time. These systems excel at identifying polymorphic malware, zero-day exploits, and AI-generated attack vectors that can dynamically mutate to evade conventional detection.

This section explores a structured, step-by-step approach to integrating AI-powered security tools into modern cybersecurity frameworks. The methodology applies to both open-source threat detection solutions (e.g., Suricata, Zeek, Snort, DeepExploit) and proprietary AI-enhanced cybersecurity platforms. Each step covers critical aspects of AI-driven malware analysis, including data collection, anomaly detection, and automated response strategies.

These are the six key steps discussed in this section:

Step 1. Setting up Vectra AI and configuring the platform: This step involves deploying sensors, configuring network visibility, and ensuring comprehensive data collection.

Step 2. Capturing network metadata: This step involves extracting and analyzing traffic patterns, DNS queries, and encrypted session data for early-stage anomaly detection.

Step 3. Behavioral modeling: This step involves leveraging machine learning models to establish normal network behavior and identify deviations indicative of advanced malware.

Step 4. Identifying polymorphic behaviors: This step involves detecting malware that dynamically alters its structure or encryption patterns to evade static detection.

Step 5. Investigating threats with AI-driven analysis: This step involves using deep learning and contextual threat intelligence to correlate and classify sophisticated cyber threats.

Step 6. Automating detection and response: This step involves integrating AI-based detection with security orchestration, automation, and response (SOAR) to provide real-time containment and remediation.

Step 1: Setting Up Vectra AI and Configuring the Platform

The initial step in using Vectra AI for malware analysis involves configuring the platform to monitor network traffic and identify potential threats across diverse environments. Attention to detail in the setup phase is crucial. Only through precise configuration can Vectra AI gather every relevant data point needed for subsequent analysis. In practice, this entails deploying sensors across strategic network segments, encompassing data centers, cloud architectures, and endpoint subnets (see Figure 8-2). Integrating with cloud services such as AWS, Azure, or GCP is essential for capturing traffic in virtualized settings—a dimension of network visibility often overlooked but of paramount importance. Logging and data flow analysis must be enabled to ensure that every meaningful transaction, connection, and packet exchange is scrutinized.

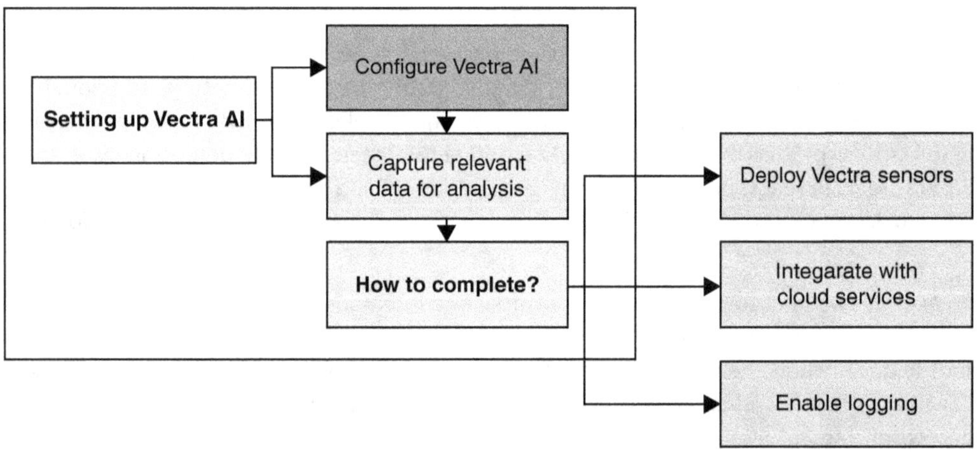

Figure 8-2
Deploying Vectra AI sensors for malware analysis.

As Figure 8-2 illustrates, the initial phase in applying Vectra AI for malware analysis begins with a thorough configuration of its sensors and data collection points to ensure that network visibility is enabled. By strategically deploying Vectra sensors across data centers, cloud environments, and endpoint subnets, security teams can capture incoming and outgoing traffic, and they can also capture the exchanges within virtualized networks, which is an increasingly critical focus area as attacks pivot internally once they are past perimeter defenses.

To address the possibility that an advanced adversary might employ quantum-scale decryption or polymorphic AI scripts to evade conventional detection, these sensors should incorporate post-quantum cryptographic checks within the data flow. For instance, if they encounter older, quantum-vulnerable encryption protocols during session establishment, a high-priority alert can be triggered, prompting administrators to enforce stricter, lattice-based alternatives. Meanwhile, Vectra's ability to integrate with cloud services like AWS, Azure, or GCP must be augmented with ephemeral key detection and AI-based anomaly filters that can spot short-lived or stealthy encryption keys, which are possible signs that an adversary is rapidly changing cryptographic parameters using advanced AI or quantum resources.

In addition, the logging and data flow analysis pipeline must be configured to collect fine-grained metadata, capturing ephemeral communications, unusual traffic spikes, or DNS anomalies that might indicate AI-driven lateral movement or zero-day quantum exploits. By including suspicious ephemeral connection logs and potential AI-generated re-encodings in the event stream, Vectra can feed more accurate contextual data into its machine learning models. This gives security teams the context they need to differentiate between benign dynamic cloud orchestration and genuine, possibly quantum-boosted, infiltration attempts.

Ultimately, accurate configuration during setup is crucial. If key logs are not captured or if ephemeral sessions remain unmonitored, advanced malware with quantum or AGI origins could slip through. Ensuring that Vectra's initial deployment covers the full range of hybrid networks, containerized microservices and on-premise segments position the platform to detect emergent threats with minimal blind spots.

Step 2: Capturing Network Metadata

Once Vectra AI is fully deployed, the next priority is the analysis of network traffic to pinpoint any malicious signatures. Malware commonly manifests as anomalous network behavior, unexpected outbound connections, or otherwise irregular data flows. To address these contingencies, Vectra's Host Lockdown feature offers the capability to quarantine endpoints flagged as suspicious, preventing an adversary from burrowing further into the environment while the anomaly is investigated. In addition, Vectra's metadata-based analytics should be used to detect the hallmarks of AI-powered malware. Such indicators might include atypical DNS queries, unexplained surges in outbound data, or direct connections to IP addresses flagged as malicious by threat intelligence sources. By consolidating these findings within a coherent framework (see Figure 8-3), security teams can discern whether hostile activity is underway and act decisively to contain potential intrusions.

AI-driven exploits and quantum-assisted decryption extend beyond traditional packet inspection. By focusing on the behavioral signals that advanced adversaries might exhibit, security teams can more effectively identify or contain malicious activities before they propagate throughout the organization.

If the platform spots endpoints that show anomalies, whether they be repeated failed authentications, sudden spikes in CPU usage, or ephemeral key exchanges that could indicate quantum-cracked or AI-generated encryption, those endpoints can be immediately quarantined. This isolation prevents further infiltration and provides a dedicated sandbox within the production environment for deeper analysis. Critically, such lockdown protocols must be refined to spot the short-lived cryptographic sessions often used by quantum attackers looking to evade typical intrusion detection strategies.

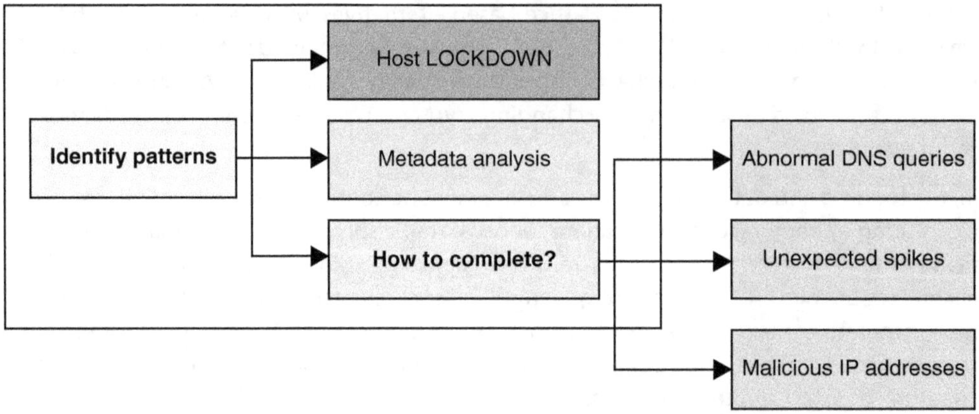

Figure 8-3
Capturing network metadata to detect AI-driven exploits and quantum-assisted decryption.

At the same time, metadata analysis goes well beyond simple DNS queries. Given that polymorphic malware in an AGI-enabled future may dynamically alter domain requests or generate randomized subdomains, Vectra AI's anomaly detection models should incorporate more advanced statistical and semantic features. These might include measuring suspicious pattern generation in DNS requests, cross-referencing queries with threat intelligence sources that focus on newly emergent or quantum-susceptible domains, or spotlighting traffic that shifts unexpectedly in structure (e.g., spikes in outbound encrypted tunnels that reconfigure encryption parameters midsession).

Connections to known malicious IP addresses remain an essential detection mechanism, but these too require updates for a quantum and AGI environment. AI-led adversaries might rapidly rotate through compromised IP addresses or subvert VPN/proxy channels, making it crucial for Vectra to ingest real-time threat intelligence feeds that catalogue ephemeral, or "burner," IP address ranges that may indicate advanced evasion. Identifying these sources quickly and correlating them with other suspicious signals, such as ephemeral key usage or abnormal command-and-control (C2) patterns, bring a more holistic approach to detection.

Capturing network metadata at scale and applying these augmented analytics is critical for addressing the new breed of threats. Whether scanning for advanced AI-based infiltration or pinpointing quantum-driven exploitation, Vectra's capability to gather and interpret fine-grained telemetry determines how swiftly and accurately a security team can isolate and investigate anomalies.

Step 3: Behavioral Modeling

After capturing metadata on network activity, the next stage involves scrutinizing device behaviors to discern deviations from established baselines. This is a critical function because AI-driven malware commonly imitates legitimate user actions to evade detection. Vectra AI's machine learning algorithms, which are trained on datasets encompassing benign and malicious behaviors, are central for real-time anomaly identification. By concentrating on key indicators such as privilege escalations, lateral movements within the network, and data exfiltration attempts masked as ordinary traffic, security teams can detect subtle irregularities (see Figure 8-4). These insights allow analysts to quickly isolate suspect processes and examine their potential for malicious intent while also ensuring that genuinely authorized activities remain uninterrupted.

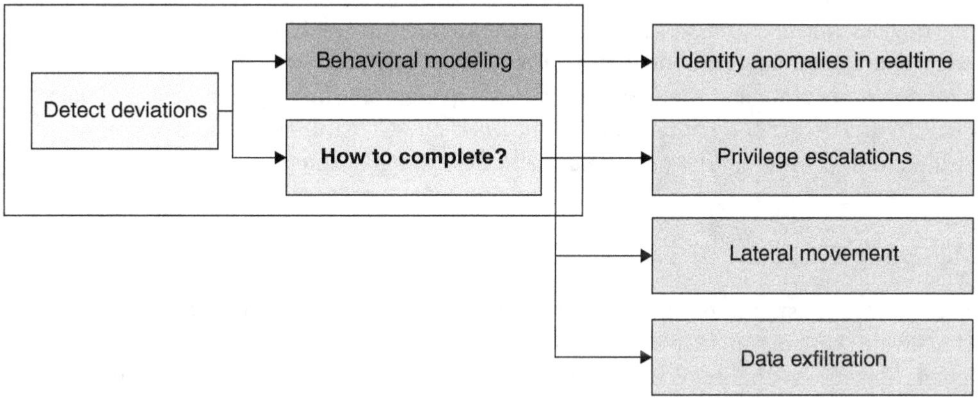

Figure 8-4
Behavioral modeling to discover AI malware that mimics legitimate user activity in order to evade detection.

Once network metadata collection is in place, the next step is refining behavioral models to distinguish genuine user actions from the increasingly subtle tactics that advanced AI (or quantum-assisted) malware may employ. While legacy threats often rely on crude signatures or overt anomalies, AGI-level adversaries can impersonate legitimate user workflows with uncanny precision and slip through rudimentary filters. Vectra AI's machine learning engine must therefore develop a richer, more adaptable profile of each device's normal operating pattern in order to spot direct anomalies and flag ephemeral, context-aware deviations that quantum or AI-driven attacks may introduce.

To accomplish this, the platform's pretrained models (which currently analyze privilege escalations, lateral movements, and data exfiltration attempts) will need more fine-grained features that capture quantum- and AI-specific signals. For instance, an attacker using quantum decryption capabilities might suddenly escalate privileges without triggering typical brute-force alerts, as stolen credentials were silently cracked offline. Similarly, an AI-driven infiltrator could coordinate lateral movements in microbursts of traffic that replicate normal network patterns just enough to evade static thresholds. By incorporating advanced temporal segmentation and multi-agent reinforcement learning into Vectra's detection pipeline, subtle spikes or irregular traffic sequences can be identified even if they superficially mimic legitimate user sessions.

Focusing on lateral movement in particular highlights how malicious AI might dynamically adapt to each node's environment. In a quantum threat context, ephemeral key exchanges or real-time cryptographic rewrapping could camouflage data exfiltration or function hooking. Vectra AI's behavioral analysis must therefore cross-reference device-level anomalies (such as sudden memory reads of cryptographic libraries or ephemeral sessions started without user involvement) against global patterns. A single outlier might not raise a red flag on its own, but correlating multiple "micro-discrepancies" across an entire environment can alert defenders to advanced infiltration efforts that standard measures would overlook.

To ensure effective triage, the contextual insights produced by Vectra's modeling should be integrated with SIEM and SOAR workflows that account for post-quantum considerations. Automation might isolate devices whose "normal usage" profile repeatedly shifts within a brief time frame or escalate alerts when ephemeral credentials are employed in suspicious ways. By enriching these behavioral models and combining them with updated cryptographic intelligence, Vectra AI gains the agility required to detect and contain threats spawned by AGI manipulation and quantum decryption, ultimately preserving the network's resilience from Quantum AGI threats.

Step 4: Identifying Polymorphic Behaviors

Building on the baseline established through metadata and behavioral modeling, the next priority is to detect malware that continuously modifies its code or communication profile, known as polymorphic threats. Because such threats are engineered specifically to evade traditional, signature-based detection systems, Vectra AI's Threat Certainty Index highlights high-risk entities based on their observed anomalies. By correlating the index's insights with advanced anomaly detection algorithms, security teams can pinpoint subtle transformations in communication patterns, including encryption protocols that suddenly mutate or deviate from historical norms. Notably, these indicators often surface in encrypted C2 channels, where malicious actors may alter traffic flow, encryption keys, or packet signatures to stay ahead of simplistic filters. Identifying such changes in real time is critical for cutting short an attacker's dwell time and thwarting potentially catastrophic infiltration (see Figure 8-5).

Polymorphic threats have long been adept at evading static or signature-based solutions, but quantum-scale computational resources and AGI-led tactics can amplify this threat, enabling real-time code transformations that conceal malicious functionality from simpler detection engines.

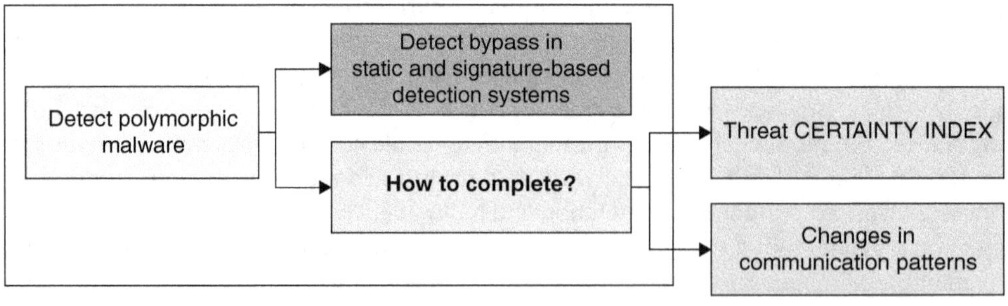

Figure 8-5

Identifying polymorphic behaviors to detect malware that dynamically alters its structure to bypass static and signature-based detection systems.

Vectra's Threat Certainty Index (TCI) can reveal these high-risk threats. By consolidating intelligence from earlier steps, such as unusual cryptographic handshakes, ephemeral key usage, or context-specific anomalies, TCI can pinpoint hosts whose conduct diverges markedly from typical patterns. Under quantum or AI adversaries, these divergences might manifest as code re-encryption or the frequent reconfiguration of C2 channels, rendering conventional checks powerless. An elevated TCI score directs analysts to examine the malware's known indicators of compromise and also to query whether a host's behavior suggests on-the-fly transformations indicative of quantum-assisted obfuscation or AI-based rewriting.

Simultaneously, anomaly detection algorithms, already scanning for changes in communication patterns, must adapt to spot emergent or short-lived encryption tunnels. In particular, encrypted channels that exhibit dynamic rekeying or unorthodox packet structures can indicate that an attacker is employing quantum factoring or advanced AI-based payload generation. By correlating these transitory channels with changes in local host configurations, such as advanced packets or stealth deployments, Vectra can alert security teams to a likely polymorphic infiltration event.

From a strategic standpoint, learning how these polymorphic channels evolve, particularly if they mutate encryption keys or host-level signatures multiple times in quick succession, provides crucial insight into the attacker's tactics, techniques, and procedures (TTPs). This intelligence, in turn, can inform immediate interventions via automated containment policies or deeper threat hunting across the network. Incorporating these signals into the TCI will ensure that Vectra can grade each potential threat based on its behavior over time rather than just its static indicators, helping enterprises confront code transformations triggered by AGI adversaries and quantum decryption capabilities.

Step 5: Investigating Threats with AI-Driven Analysis

Once high-risk anomalies have been identified, the next stage centers on detailed exploration of these events to pinpoint their ultimate root cause. In practice, this entails using Vectra's Cognito Detect dashboard to access in-depth threat timelines, which illuminate the sequence and nature of suspicious activities. Among the typical indicators warranting close inspection are the execution of unknown binaries, the appearance of suspicious API calls to cloud services, and the presence of anomalous file access patterns. By cross-referencing these observations with external threat intelligence, drawing upon curated databases and industry-wide feeds, security teams obtain a clearer picture of how, where, and why adversaries might be infiltrating the network (see Figure 8-6). This combination of internal analytics and external validation provides actionable insights for remediation and strengthens the organization's broader security posture by revealing new or emerging tactics that attackers might be testing.

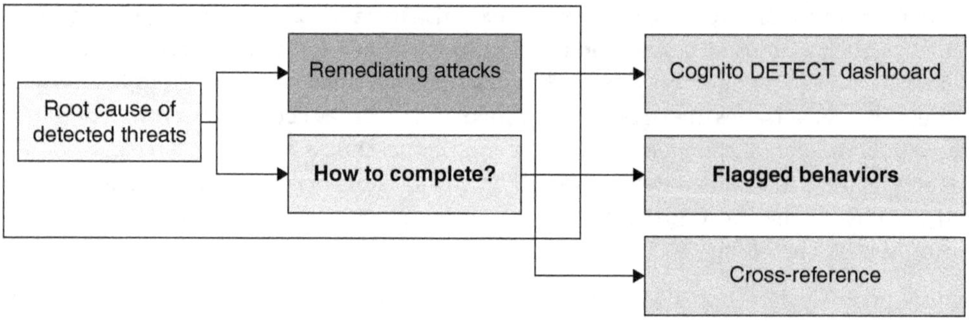

Figure 8-6

Investigating threats with AI-driven analysis: Polymorphic versus metamorphic malware.

A key enhancement here involves integrating post-quantum cryptographic checks and AGI-aware anomaly signatures into the dashboard's analytics pipeline. For instance, if the system flags suspicious API calls to cloud platforms, the interface should reveal whether they involved ephemeral quantum-vulnerable key exchanges or if advanced AI-based methods were invoked to generate payloads on the fly. Similarly, the detection of unknown binaries might be coupled with real-time intelligence about whether these files display code structures typical of AI-driven metamorphic malware (code that repeatedly rewrites itself to elude standard scanning).

Moreover, contextual detail is paramount for accurate triage. If a malicious binary is found to read or modify files in an unusual pattern, the platform could highlight whether these interactions involve quantum-resistant encryption routines or ephemeral credential usage. This deeper vantage point enables analysts to distinguish between legitimate cryptographic activities (e.g., newly tested post-quantum algorithms) and malicious re-encryptions that attempt to obfuscate advanced infiltration. Coupling this detail with references to external threat intelligence feeds gives security professionals confidence in linking suspicious events to known or emerging attack campaigns, particularly those harnessing quantum factorization or large language models for stealth.

Ultimately, the combination of timeline views, correlated telemetry, and advanced ML heuristics fosters actionable insights. When the system confirms that an unknown binary was used in conjunction with ephemeral key logs, AI-based tunneling, or an ID previously tagged as quantum vulnerable, incident response teams can quickly isolate affected systems, patch vulnerabilities, or reconfigure encryption policies. By embedding these capabilities into the investigative step, Vectra AI would evolve from a reactive threat-detection engine into a forward-looking quantum- and AGI-resilient security platform that helps neutralize advanced malware at the root cause.

Step 6: Automating Detection and Response

Concluding the analysis and detection cycle, the final phase centers on automating critical workflows to reduce response times and prevent malware from propagating (see Figure 8-7). Incorporating Vectra AI within SIEM platforms such as Splunk or Elastic ensures that high-confidence alerts prompt immediate escalation, diminishing the risk of delayed or overlooked security events. In addition, SOAR solutions allow routine remediation actions, ranging from IP blocking to device quarantine, to be executed automatically, minimizing reliance on human intervention and increasing the speed of defensive measures. To address more advanced attack vectors, security teams can devise specialized playbooks through Vectra's API, defining step-by-step responses for specific malware behaviors. By embedding these standard operating procedures into existing infrastructures, organizations can streamline the process of containing threats, ensuring that even the most advanced adversaries encounter quick and consistent pushback.

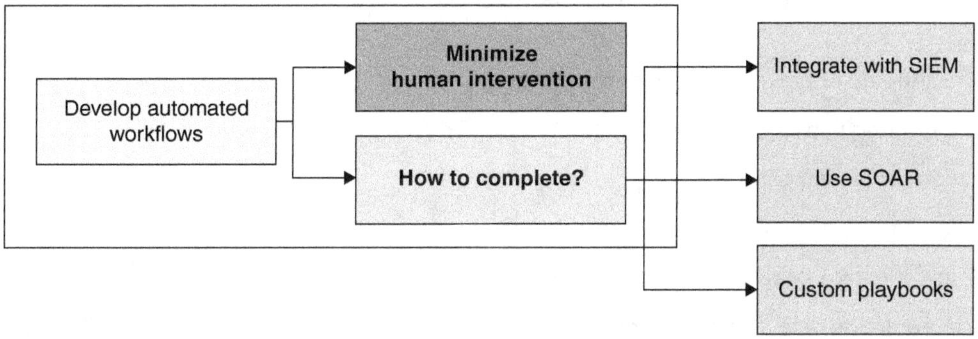

Figure 8-7
Automating threat detection and remediation of mutating attack vectors.

Several refinements are necessary to keep pace with quantum and AI-driven threats. First, the system's integrations must recognize and escalate any indications of post-quantum cryptographic failures or AI-based infiltration attempts. For instance, if the platform detects ephemeral key usage that contravenes recommended quantum-safe policies, a high-confidence alert should be triggered in the SIEM to prompt swift action. From there, SOAR routines can quarantine the affected device or reconfigure cryptographic settings across the network in real time, minimizing the window in which an attacker might exploit a compromised encryption scheme.

Beyond simple blocking of IP addresses or device isolation, these automated workflows should support custom playbooks that target specific advanced TTPs. If Vectra's logs show repeated ephemeral re-encryptions consistent with AI-coded polymorphic malware, a custom playbook can automatically shut down that communications channel, revoke the ephemeral credentials, and distribute updated threat intelligence across the enterprise. Such proactive measures help neutralize infiltration attempts before quantum-assisted attackers have the chance to pivot or morph their approach.

Adapting Vectra's API according to these instructions ensures that these countermeasures can be dynamically updated as new quantum-safe best practices or AI-based threat signatures emerge. If the industry adopts a fresh post-quantum cipher or uncovers novel AGI infiltration vectors, security architects can push relevant modifications into the automated response pipeline without manually recoding every rule. Vectra AI can thus transition from a reactive detection tool into an agile, full-lifecycle security platform that is equipped to keep pace with adversaries wielding quantum-scale computations and advanced AI.

Open-Source Alternatives for AI-Powered Malware Analysis

You've already been introduced to open-source alternatives to proprietary AI-driven security platforms and seen that open-source cybersecurity tools provide transparent, auditable, and highly customizable frameworks that can be enhanced for post-quantum resilience and AI-driven detection. In this section, we'll look at how open-source tools such as Suricata, Zeek, Snort, and ML-SecOps tools can be used to ensure scalability, automation, and AI-driven threat intelligence.

In this section, we'll follow the same steps as in the Vectra case study but now with open-source tools:

Step 1. Setting up AI-powered threat detection

Step 2. Capturing network metadata

Step 3. Behavioral modeling

Step 4. Identifying polymorphic behaviors

Step 5. Investigating threats with AI-driven analysis

Step 6. Automating detection and response

The principles of AI-enhanced threat detection, malware analysis, and quantum-resilient security can be implemented without reliance on proprietary security vendors. Open-source intrusion detection systems (IDS) such as Suricata, Zeek, and Snort can apply AI and deep learning models to detect advanced AGI-generated threats. Machine learning–based threat intelligence enables real-time attack correlation and incident response automation. Integrating AI-driven detection models with SOAR platforms (e.g., TheHive, Cortex) improves response time against post-quantum security challenges. By implementing these strategies, organizations can develop vendor-agnostic and scalable security frameworks that defend against future AI- and quantum-driven cyber threats.

Step 1: Setting Up AI-Powered Threat Detection with Suricata and Zeek

The first step in AI-powered malware detection is configuring network sensors to capture real-time packet data, DNS queries, encrypted traffic analysis, and system events. Open-source intrusion detection and prevention systems (IDPS) such as Suricata and Zeek allow security teams to monitor network behavior dynamically.

Implementing a deployment of Zeek for AI-powered threat monitoring involves the following steps:

1. Install Zeek and set up packet monitoring (using bash):

   ```
   sudo apt update && sudo apt install zeek -y
   sudo zeekctl deploy
   ```

2. Enable machine learning–based threat detection by integrating Zeek with ML-based anomaly detection frameworks (e.g., Scikit-learn, TensorFlow) and using deep learning models to detect

anomalous network behaviors. The following example shows AI-based network anomaly detection using Zeek and Python:

```
import pandas as pd
from sklearn.ensemble import IsolationForest

# Load Zeek network logs
data = pd.read_csv("conn.log", delimiter="\t")

# Select network features (duration, packet size, etc.)
X = data[["duration", "orig_bytes", "resp_bytes"]]

# Train an Isolation Forest model
model = IsolationForest(contamination=0.05)
model.fit(X)

# Predict anomalies (1 = normal, -1 = anomaly)
data["anomaly"] = model.predict(X)
print(data[["id.orig_h", "id.resp_h", "anomaly"]])
```

This implementation automates anomaly detection, flagging AGI-enabled cyberattacks that generate adversarial traffic patterns.

Step 2: Capturing Network Metadata with AI by Using Suricata and YARA Rules

Once the network traffic is monitored, AI-enhanced metadata analysis improves detection rates for polymorphic malware and adversarial AI attacks.

Consider the following example using AI-enhanced intrusion detection with Suricata:

1. Install Suricata and enable TLS decryption (using bash):

```
sudo apt install suricata -y
sudo suricata -c /etc/suricata/suricata.yaml -i eth0
```

2. Use AI-based heuristic YARA rules to detect advanced malware:

```
rule AI_Enhanced_Malware_Detection {
    meta:
        description = "Detects AI-generated polymorphic malware"
        author = "Open-Source Security Team"
    strings:
        $a = {E8 00 00 00 00 5D C3}  // Heuristic pattern matching AI-
generated payloads
        $b = /AI-generated malicious behavior detected/
    condition:
        any of them
}
```

This hybrid approach combines AI-generated heuristics with Suricata's real-time network monitoring, reducing false positives and improving the accuracy of attack detection.

Step 3: Behavioral Modeling for Malware Detection with Snort and Deep Learning

With AGI-assisted malware evolving rapidly, ML-based behavioral modeling is necessary to identify subtle changes in attack strategies.

Consider the following implementation example for training an AI model for anomaly detection:

1. Collect network traffic logs from Snort, Suricata, or Zeek.
2. Train a deep learning model to detect deviations in behavior:

```
import tensorflow as tf
from tensorflow.keras.models import Sequential
from tensorflow.keras.layers import Dense

# Example dataset (normal vs. anomalous network traffic features)
X_train = [[200, 0.4], [210, 0.35], [5000, 0.95]]  # Normal and anomalous
samples
y_train = [0, 0, 1]  # 1 = suspected malware

# Define a simple neural network
model = Sequential([
    Dense(4, activation="relu"),
    Dense(2, activation="softmax")
])

model.compile(optimizer="adam", loss="sparse_categorical_crossentropy",
metrics=["accuracy"])
model.fit(X_train, y_train, epochs=10, verbose=1)
```

AI-powered behavioral modeling enables real-time malware classification, significantly reducing the time required for threat triage and response.

Step 4: Identifying Polymorphic Behaviors with AI-Driven Anomaly Detection

AI-driven IDS should be able to detect and classify polymorphic malware that dynamically mutates to evade signature-based detection. Zeek and Suricata can be extended with adversarial learning techniques to adapt to evolving AGI-generated threats.

AI-augmented Zeek rules help detect network-based polymorphic malware mutations dynamically. Consider the following example for detecting malware mutations with AI-enhanced Zeek scripts:

```
event connection_established(c: connection) {
```

```
if (c$resp_bytes > 50000 && c$proto == "TLS") {
    print fmt("Possible polymorphic malware detected from %s", c$id.orig_h);
}
```

Step 5: Investigating Threats with AI-Driven Threat Intelligence

Open-source threat intelligence platforms such as MalwareBazaar and Open Threat Exchange (OTX) provide AI-curated threat indicators. Integration with AI models enables real-time threat correlation and attack visualization.

Step 6: Automating Detection and Response with Open-Source SOAR

Security orchestration, automation, and response (SOAR) tools such as TheHive and Cortex can be used to automate incident response. Automating security alerts, malware quarantining, and threat analysis ensures real-time protection against AGI-driven attacks.

Unique Capabilities for Transitioning from Polymorphic to Metamorphic Malware Analysis

Note: In this section, we are using the case of Vectra AI to describe how open-source solutions can be adapted to the emerging AI threats. The case study is continuing with Vectra AI just to avoid confusion of adding too many different names, because after all, the same guidelines apply to all malware analysis solutions, and the choice of one name is simply for consistency. The methodology discussed in the case study is equally applicable to any other malware analysis tool.

The advancements we described earlier for Vectra AI would enable a suite of capabilities that collectively reinforce its value as a platform for advanced threat detection (see Figure 8-8). At the forefront is its AI-powered metadata analysis, which processes network traffic in real time, detecting anomalies that may indicate malicious activity, such as unexpected protocol usage or suspiciously encrypted payloads in outbound data. Equally integral is the Threat Certainty Index, a mechanism that prioritizes alerts based on confidence and severity, ensuring that security teams can swiftly address the most pressing incidents. In addition, Vectra AI exhibits adaptability to AI malware by recognizing behavioral deviations and dynamically adjusting its detection models, thereby keeping pace with adversaries that might mutate their tactics or attempt to blend in with ordinary user behavior. Finally, Vectra AI's scalability across hybrid environments, encompassing on-premises, cloud, and mixed infrastructures, enables organizations to monitor a broad range of deployments without compromising on coverage or depth of analysis.

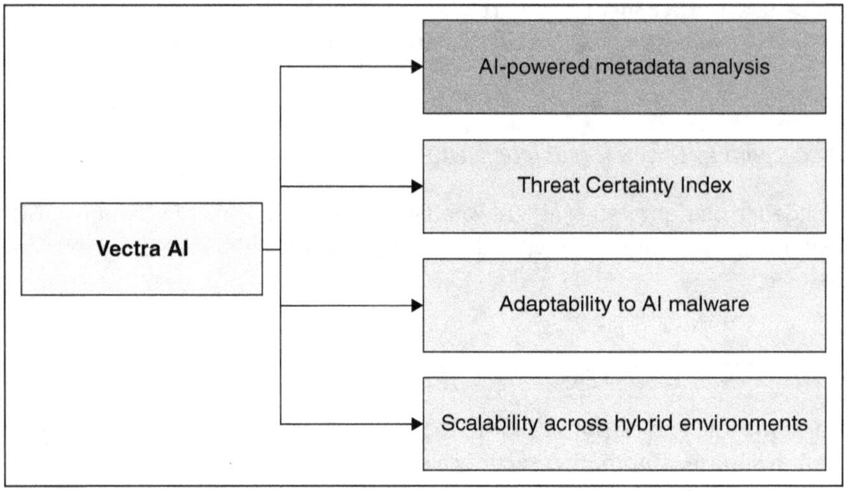

Figure 8-8
Transitioning from polymorphic to metamorphic malware analysis.

A key learning point in this case study about Vectra AI is that the transition from polymorphic to metamorphic malware requires the capability to ingest and interpret network metadata in real time, a strength that takes on heightened importance when adversaries wield quantum-scale cryptography and advanced AI-driven exploit techniques. Vectra AI could provide a route to next-generation threat response by dynamically adjusting and integrating the detection models described earlier with existing security infrastructures.

Consider how Vectra AI's capabilities could evolve to meet the challenges of quantum AGI-developed metamorphic malware:

- **AI-powered metadata analysis:** Vectra AI's algorithms continuously process network metadata, searching for suspicious or statistically anomalous patterns that may indicate malicious activity. In a case of AGI and quantum cryptographic compromise, these algorithms must incorporate awareness of ephemeral key usage, frequent re-encryption events, and potentially AI-generated network flows. For instance, if an unusually encrypted payload is discovered in outbound traffic (or if ephemeral encryption keys appear with irregular frequency) the system can raise an alert, treating it as a likely sign of quantum-assisted infiltration or AI-authored polymorphic malware.
- **Threat Certainty Index (TCI):** As malicious actors refine their tactics with post-quantum exploits or cunning AI-based evasion, prioritizing critical threats becomes ever more essential. Vectra's Threat Certainty Index can evolve by integrating quantum vulnerability checks (e.g., identifying use of breakable legacy algorithms) and advanced anomaly-detection signals that indicate AGI-like adaptability. For example, if a newly discovered process repeatedly spawns ephemeral connections after being flagged for suspicious encryption, TCI could automatically escalate its threat rating, prompting quick incident resolution and minimizing the window for quantum cracking or AI-based code morphing.

- **Adaptability to AI malware:** Vectra's design already accounts for AI-driven behavior deviations. However, advanced AGI threats will demand continual updates to the underlying detection logic: ephemeral code rewriting, on-the-fly generation of malicious processes, or disguised communications via large language model (LLM) prompts. By incorporating self-learning modules that retrain or adapt in near real time, Vectra AI can respond to advanced infiltration that shifts tactics in response to detection attempts, just as AGI would. This adaptability might require deeper contextual analysis, advanced temporal segmentation, or even multi-agent reinforcement learning to ensure that the system remains agile against emergent threats.
- **Scalability across hybrid environments:** Quantum and AI-driven threats will not respect traditional boundaries; they can infiltrate cloud microservices and on-premises networks alike, pivoting from ephemeral containers to legacy applications in a matter of seconds. Vectra AI's support for hybrid infrastructures (spanning data centers, public clouds, and edge deployments) must be augmented with global correlation of quantum anomalies or AI-coded infiltration attempts. A breach discovered in one environment (such as ephemeral key changes in a cloud microservice) should trigger an immediate, system-wide response that includes on-premises or private-cloud segments, forestalling advanced lateral movement.

Through these enhancements, Vectra AI could provide a platform for detecting and neutralizing the sophisticated tactics enabled by quantum computation and AGI. By leaning on real-time behavioral modeling, augmented threat scoring, and scalable, AI-centric integration, security teams gain unparalleled visibility into network activities, which is an essential advantage when facing adversaries capable of outmaneuvering conventional defenses. The step-by-step methodology outlined throughout this case study ensures that we can understand how current malware detection tools need to transform their security operations to remain relevant for quantum AGI threats.

Summary

AGI systems grow increasingly adept at synthesizing, manipulating, and compromising digital identities, and quantum computing threatens to undermine traditional cryptographic safeguards. This chapter underscores the need to reimagine how digital identities are protected.

The chapter begins by exploring decentralized identity systems, emphasizing the self-sovereign identity paradigm and its ability to minimize reliance on centralized databases, which represent single points of failure. With distributed trust mechanisms and minimal disclosure protocols, decentralized models offer robust defenses against AGI-driven identity manipulation and quantum-enabled decryption. The chapter also examines advanced cryptographic techniques, such as zero-knowledge proofs and homomorphic encryption, which facilitate privacy-preserving identity verification, even in scenarios where data is exposed to sophisticated AGI systems.

Blockchain technology is presented as a cornerstone for ensuring the integrity and immutability of identity data. By combining blockchain with post-quantum cryptographic algorithms, the chapter demonstrates how identity frameworks can withstand the computational power of quantum attacks. Special attention is given to interoperability challenges, exploring the technical standards and regulatory frameworks, such as the W3C Verifiable Credentials model and GDPR.

Threat modeling is an integral part of the discussion, and this chapter identifies and analyzes risks posed by AGI-enabled synthetic identities, quantum decryption of credential stores, and adversarial attacks on identity ecosystems. Strategies to mitigate these risks, such as anomaly detection, distributed consensus mechanisms, and AGI-driven threat intelligence, are described. The chapter also covers privacy-preserving technologies, such as zk-SNARKs, which enhance trust in identity transactions while safeguarding individual data.

The chapter proposes forward-looking architectures that integrate quantum-resistant cryptography, AGI-driven security intelligence, and decentralized identity principles. These systems are designed to adapt to the evolving technological landscape, offering resilience against emerging threats while maintaining the principles of privacy, interoperability, and user sovereignty.

References

1 Nakamoto, Satoshi. 2008. *Bitcoin: A Peer-to-Peer Electronic Cash System*. https://bitcoin.org/bitcoin.pdf.

2 Government of Estonia. 2014. *Estonia's e-Residency*. https://www.e-resident.gov.ee/.

3 UN System Chief Executives Board for Coordination. 2024. *UN Digital ID*. https://unsceb.org/topics/un-digital-id.

4 European Commission. 2014. *eIDAS Regulation*. https://digital-strategy.ec.europa.eu/en/policies/eidas-regulation.

5 European Commission. 2024. *eIDAS 2.0*. https://www.european-digital-identity-regulation.com.

6 Mehta, Yash, Dev Patel, and Manik Lal Das. 2020. *On Aadhaar Identity Management System*. https://arxiv.org/abs/2012.04215v1.

7 Unique Identification Authority of India. 2022. *Requesting Entities*. https://uidai.gov.in/en/ecosystem/authentication-ecosystem/authentication-requesting-agency.html.

8 Kortesniemi, Yki, Dmitrij Lagutin, Tommi Elo, and Nikos Fotiou. 2019. "Improving the Privacy of IoT with Decentralised Identifiers (DIDs)." *Journal of Computer Networks and Communications* 1: 8706760. https://doi.org/10.1155/2019/8706760.

9 Mahalle, Parikshit N., Gitanjali Shinde, and Pathan Mohd Shafi. 2020. "Rethinking Decentralised Identifiers and Verifiable Credentials for the Internet of Things." *Studies in Systems, Decision and Control* 266: 361–74. https://doi.org/10.1007/978-3-030-39047-1_16.

10 Badertscher, Christian, Fabio Banfi, and Jesus Diaz. 2024. *What Did Come Out of It? Analysis and Improvements of DIDComm Messaging*. https://eprint.iacr.org/2024/1361.

11 Garzon, Sandro Rodriguez, Dennis Natusch, Artur Philipp, Axel Küpper, Hans Joachim Einsiedler, and Daniela Schneider. 2024a. *DID Link: Authentication in TLS with Decentralized Identifiers and Verifiable Credentials*. https://arxiv.org/abs/2405.07533v2.

12 Nita, Stefania Loredana, and Marius Iulian Mihailescu. 2023. "Homomorphic Encryption." *Advances to Homomorphic and Searchable Encryption*, 27–88. https://doi.org/10.1007/978-3-031-43214-9_3.

13 Luo, Fucai, and Kunpeng Wang. 2018. "Verifiable Decryption for Fully Homomorphic Encryption." *Lecture Notes in Computer Science* 11060: 347–65. https://doi.org/10.1007/978-3-319-99136-8_19.

14 Pali, Isha, Lisa Krishania, Divya Chadha, Asmita Kandar, Gaurav Varshney, and Sneha Shukla. 2020. *A Comprehensive Survey of Aadhar and Security Issues*. https://arxiv.org/abs/2007.09409v1.

15 Bailey, Bolton, and Andrew Miller. 2023. *Formalizing Soundness Proofs of SNARKs*. https://eprint.iacr.org/2023/656.

16 Petkus, Maksym. 2019. *Why and How Zk-SNARK Works*. https://arxiv.org/abs/1906.07221v1.

17 Zhao, Haixu, Dong Ding, Feng Wang, Pengcheng Hua, Ning Wang, Qin Wu, and Zhilei Chai. 2023. "Hardware Acceleration of Number Theoretic Transform for Zk-SNARK." *Engineering Reports*, e12639. https://doi.org/10.1002/ENG2.12639

18 Geelen, Robin, and Frederik Vercauteren. 2023. "Bootstrapping for BGV and BFV Revisited." *Journal of Cryptology* 36(2): 1–32. https://doi.org/10.1007/S00145-023-09454-6.

19 Halevi, Shai, Yuriy Polyakov, and Victor Shoup. 2019. "An Improved RNS Variant of the BFV Homomorphic Encryption Scheme." *Lecture Notes in Computer Science* 11405: 83–105. https://doi.org/10.1007/978-3-030-12612-4_5.

20 Turkoglu, Enes Recep, Ali Sah Ozcan, Can Ayduman, Ahmet Can Mert, Erdinc Ozturk, and Erkay Savas. 2022. "An Accelerated GPU Library for Homomorphic Encryption Operations of BFV Scheme." *2022 IEEE International Symposium on Circuits and Systems* 1155–59. https://doi.org/10.1109/ISCAS48785.2022.9937503.

21 Ibarrondo, Alberto, Herve Chabanne, Vincent Despiegel, and Melek Onen. 2022. "Colmade: Collaborative Masking in Auditable Decryption for BFV-Based Homomorphic Encryption." *Proceedings of the 2022 ACM Workshop on Information Hiding and Multimedia Security*, 129–39. https://doi.org/10.1145/3531536.3532952.

22 Kim, Seonghak, Minji Park, Jaehyung Kim, Taekyung Kim, and Chohong Min. 2022. "EvalRound Algorithm in CKKS Bootstrapping." *Lecture Notes in Computer Science* 13792: 161–87. https://doi.org/10.1007/978-3-031-22966-4_6.

23 Cheon, Jung Hee, Jaehyung Kim, Wonhee Cho, and Damien Stehlé. 2023. "Homomorphic Multiple Precision Multiplication for CKKS and Reduced Modulus Consumption." *Proceedings of the 2023 ACM SIGSAC Conference on Computer and Communications Security*, 696–710. https://doi.org/10.1145/3576915.3623086.

24 Bae, Youngjin, Jung Hee Cheon, Jaehyung Kim, and Damien Stehlé. 2024. "Bootstrapping Bits with CKKS." *Lecture Notes in Computer Science* 14652: 94–123. https://doi.org/10.1007/978-3-031-58723-8_4.

25 Mono, Johannes, Chiara Marcolla, Georg Land, Tim Güneysu, and Najwa Aaraj. 2023. "Finding and Evaluating Parameters for BGV." *Lecture Notes in Computer Science* 14064: 370–94. https://doi.org/10.1007/978-3-031-37679-5_16.

26 Fan, Junfeng, and Frederik Vercauteren. 2012. *Somewhat Practical Fully Homomorphic Encryption*. https://eprint.iacr.org/2012/144.

27 Brakerski, Zvika, Craig Gentry, and Vinod Vaikuntanathan. 2012. "(Leveled) Fully Homomorphic Encryption without Bootstrapping." *Innovations in Theoretical Computer Science Conference*, 309–25. https://doi.org/10.1145/2090236.2090262.

28 Cheon, Jung Hee, Andrey Kim, Miran Kim, and Yongsoo Song. 2016. *Homomorphic Encryption for Arithmetic of Approximate Numbers*. https://eprint.iacr.org/2016/421.

29 Halevi, Shai, and Victor Shoup. 2014. "Algorithms in HElib." *Lecture Notes in Computer Science* 8616: 554–71. https://doi.org/10.1007/978-3-662-44371-2_31.

30 GitHub. 2023. *HElib*. https://github.com/homenc/HElib.

31 Benaissá, Ayoub, Bilal Retiat, Bogdan Cebere, and Alaa Eddine Belfedhaí. 2021. *TenSEAL: A Library for Encrypted Tensor Operations Using Homomorphic Encryption*. https://arxiv.org/abs/2104.03152v2.

32 W3C. 2024. *Verifiable Credentials Data Model v2.0.* https://www.w3.org/TR/vc-data-model-2.0/.

33 OpenID Foundation. 2024. *OpenID for Verifiable Credentials.* EU: https://openid.net/sg/openid4vc/.

34 Information Commissioner's Office. 2018. *The UK GDPR*. https://ico.org.uk/for-organisations/data-protection-and-the-eu/data-protection-and-the-eu-in-detail/the-uk-gdpr/.

35 GDPR.EU. 2018. *What Is GDPR, the EU's New Data Protection Law?* https://gdpr.eu/what-is-gdpr/.

36 Vectra. 2025. https://www.vectra.ai.

Multiple-Choice Questions with Answers and Explanations

1. What is the primary advantage of decentralized digital identity systems in the context of AGI and quantum threats?

   a. Centralized control for rapid authentication

   b. Increased scalability for IoT networks

   c. Elimination of single points of failure

   d. Simplified integration with legacy cryptographic systems

   Correct Answer: C. Decentralized digital identity systems remove the reliance on centralized databases, reducing the risks associated with single points of failure. They also empower individuals with control over their credentials, enhancing privacy. Options A and B do not address the primary advantage, while D contradicts the challenges associated with integrating legacy systems into decentralized frameworks.

2. Which cryptographic mechanism is most relevant for ensuring privacy in decentralized identity systems?

   a. Symmetric key cryptography

   b. Zero-knowledge proofs (ZKPs)

   c. Hash-based signatures

   d. Diffie-Hellman key exchange

   Correct Answer: B. Zero-knowledge proofs enable secure and privacy-preserving identity verification by proving a statement's validity without revealing underlying sensitive data. Options A, C, and D lack the privacy-preserving capabilities required for modern identity systems in quantum and AGI contexts.

3. What is a major advantage of using homomorphic encryption in identity systems?

   a. It reduces computational overhead during encryption.

   b. It allows computation on encrypted data without decryption.

   c. It simplifies key management in decentralized networks.

   d. It prevents unauthorized access to stored private keys.

   Correct Answer: B. Homomorphic encryption allows secure computations directly on encrypted data, ensuring that sensitive data remains protected throughout the process. While options A, C, and D are important considerations, they do not capture the unique advantage of homomorphic encryption.

4. How does quantum-resistant cryptography strengthen blockchain-based identity systems?

   a. It accelerates transaction speeds in decentralized networks.

   b. It ensures that the system is immune to distributed denial-of-service attacks.

   c. It protects against quantum-enabled decryption of cryptographic keys.

   d. It simplifies the integration of AGI with blockchain frameworks.

   Correct Answer: C. Quantum-resistant cryptography safeguards cryptographic keys used in blockchain-based identity systems from being decrypted by quantum algorithms, ensuring the long-term security and integrity of these systems. Options A, B, and D are unrelated to quantum-resistant cryptography's role.

5. Which threat is uniquely posed by AGI in digital identity systems?

   a. Key exhaustion in symmetric encryption algorithms

   b. Synthetic identity generation to bypass verification protocols

   c. Packet fragmentation in identity-related communications

   d. Increased energy consumption during cryptographic operations

   Correct Answer: B. AGI has the capability to generate synthetic identities that mimic legitimate credentials, potentially bypassing traditional verification protocols. Options A, C, and D do not reflect AGI-specific threats to identity systems.

Exercises with Solutions

Exercise 1: Short-Answer Question

Question: Explain the role of zero-knowledge proofs (ZKPs) in enhancing privacy within decentralized identity systems. How do ZKPs address the challenges posed by AGI and quantum computing?

Solution: Zero-knowledge proofs enable users to prove the validity of their credentials without revealing the underlying sensitive information. In decentralized identity systems, ZKPs ensure that personal data is not exposed during verification, reducing the risk of identity theft or misuse. Against AGI threats, ZKPs prevent synthetic identities from being used maliciously, as these systems rely on authentic credentials. Furthermore, ZKPs are inherently resilient to quantum decryption attempts due to their reliance on advanced mathematical constructs that align with post-quantum cryptographic principles.

Exercise 2: Case Study

Scenario: A multinational corporation's decentralized identity system is targeted by an AGI-driven attack. The attack generates synthetic identities, breaches the system's consensus protocol, and exfiltrates critical identity records.

Tasks:

1. Identify three vulnerabilities in the described system.
2. Propose countermeasures to mitigate these vulnerabilities, focusing on quantum-resistant and AGI-aware solutions.
3. Discuss the implications of integrating blockchain with post-quantum cryptographic mechanisms for identity management.

Solution:

1. **Vulnerabilities:**
    - Lack of robust mechanisms to detect synthetic identities
    - Consensus protocol susceptible to manipulation by AGI
    - Absence of quantum-resistant cryptographic safeguards
2. **Countermeasures:**
    - Deploy advanced AGI-aware anomaly detection systems to identify synthetic identity behaviors.
    - Strengthen consensus protocols using AGI-resistant algorithms such as Byzantine Fault Tolerance.
    - Transition to post-quantum cryptographic techniques, such as lattice-based cryptography, for secure key exchange and data protection.
3. **Discussion:** Integrating blockchain with post-quantum cryptography ensures the immutability of identity records even in a quantum-capable threat environment. While this enhances security, there are challenges, including increased computational overhead and the need for global standardization to maintain interoperability.

Exercise 3: Hands-On Activity

Task: Implement a simplified version of a zero-knowledge proof for verifying a user's credentials without exposing the underlying data.

Solution:

1. **Setup:** Use Python libraries such as *pycryptodome* to implement a basic ZKP.
2. **Verification:** Write a function to demonstrate a user proving knowledge of a secret (e.g., password hash) without revealing it.
3. **Testing:** Simulate attacks by AGI-driven scripts and evaluate the resilience of the ZKP mechanism.

4. **Discussion:** Highlight the advantages of ZKP for privacy-preserving identity verification in decentralized and quantum-resistant systems.

Sample Implementation:

```
from hashlib import sha256

# User's secret
secret = "my_secure_password"
hashed_secret = sha256(secret.encode()).hexdigest()

# Prover sends hashed_secret
def verify_knowledge(provided_hash, user_input):
    return sha256(user_input.encode()).hexdigest() == provided_hash

# Example verification
user_input = "my_secure_password"
print("Verification successful:", verify_knowledge(hashed_secret, user_input))
```

PART V

THE FUTURE OF DIGITAL SECURITY

In this final part of the book, we explore the critical next steps for preparing digital security infrastructures to withstand the challenges presented by the transformative technologies we've been discussing throughout the book. The closing chapters, Chapter 9 and Chapter 10, discuss the strategies, tools, and real-world applications that will shape the security frameworks of tomorrow.

Chapter 9, "Future-Proofing Digital Security Systems," provides a forward-looking perspective on how to adapt to the coming wave of change. It covers essential areas such as preparing for a post-singularity era, creating quantum and AGI-safe infrastructures, and understanding the regulatory and ethical implications of these advancements. The chapter's focus is on how we can develop systems that remain resilient in the face of AGI-driven challenges and quantum threats to ensure that digital security evolves with the times.

Chapter 10, "Adapting to the Future: Quantum and AGI Security Requirements," offers practical guidance, highlighting quantum-resistant and AGI-safe solutions that have already been deployed across various sectors. It further explores tools for implementation and provides exercises and resources to deepen the reader's understanding. This chapter examines the hands-on knowledge readers need to integrate these solutions into their own security practices, as well as to prepare for a future where AGI and quantum computing play an integral role.

By addressing the theoretical and practical aspects of securing systems against emerging threats, the chapters in this section equip readers with the knowledge and tools needed to stay ahead of these advanced technologies.

9

Future-Proofing Digital Security Systems

This chapter focuses on the strategic direction for preparing digital security systems to withstand the threats posed by AI and quantum computers, to ensure long-term resilience and adaptability.

Objectives

- **Prepare for life post-singularity:** Consider the implications of a post-singularity world where AGI surpasses human intelligence, focusing on the security challenges and adaptive strategies required to defend against AGI-driven threats.
- **Develop a roadmap for quantum and AGI-safe infrastructure:** Explore the technical and architectural frameworks necessary to safeguard digital infrastructure from the vulnerabilities introduced by quantum computing and AGI exploits, including quantum-resistant cryptographic algorithms and AI-enhanced security systems.
- **Strengthen resilience in the face of quantum-specific risks:** Identify specific vulnerabilities to quantum decryption and discuss how digital security systems can integrate quantum-safe encryption methods to future-proof sensitive data and communications.
- **Anticipate and mitigate AGI-driven cyber threats:** Examine proactive approaches to counteracting the increasing sophistication of AGI-driven cyberattacks, including the use of AI and machine learning models to detect and respond to such threats in real time.
- **Integrate adaptive security models for an AGI:** Explore the integration of self-learning security frameworks that can dynamically evolve with AGI to ensure that security systems are continually updated to mitigate new and unforeseen threats.

- **Evaluate the role of blockchain in future-proofing digital security:** Investigate how blockchain technology can contribute to the decentralization of digital security frameworks, enhancing resilience and trust in systems exposed to AGI and quantum vulnerabilities.

This chapter equips readers with the insights and strategies required to future-proof digital security systems to ensure that they remain resilient and adaptable in the face of AGI and quantum-scale threats.

Preparing for Life Post-Singularity

To survive in the "post-singularity" world, in which AGI surpasses or radically reshapes human abilities,[1] it is necessary to design new digital security systems today. Traditional rule-based methodologies, which rely largely on prescriptive models and static threat signatures, will quickly lose their efficacy against self-evolving or self-directed adversarial agents. Consequently, security professionals and policymakers alike must adopt strategies that assume attackers possess near-limitless computational resources and the capacity to adapt attack vectors in real time.

A first pillar in this reorientation is the integration of continuous learning algorithms into security infrastructures. As AI-driven threats quickly morph, even the most sophisticated anomaly detection methods or advanced cryptographic protocols risk obsolescence if they remain static. Security solutions must be able to retrain, re-model, and re-parameterize themselves on the fly, harnessing global threat intelligence and local contextual data to anticipate new infiltration techniques. They must go beyond simple signature database updates and include advanced machine learning frameworks that can ingest voluminous, heterogeneous data, ranging from endpoint telemetries to real-time code analysis, and draw emergent patterns before a malicious campaign escalates.

Another fundamental shift involves incorporating quantum-safe cryptography into all layers of digital communications. As quantum computers evolve toward practical realization, once-impenetrable asymmetric ciphers such as Rivest–Shamir–Adleman (RSA) and elliptic-curve cryptography (ECC) will be vulnerable to large-scale factoring and discrete logarithm attacks. Moving to lattice-based, isogeny-based, or code-based algorithms, as recommended by post-quantum standards bodies, will be essential to safeguard data and communications in perpetuity. Moreover, novel protocols that merge zero-knowledge proofs (ZKPs)[2] with homomorphic encryption (HE)[3] must be expanded to handle the breadth of transactions in an interconnected, post-singularity environment. Only then can organizations achieve data confidentiality and integrity against the combined forces of formidable quantum hardware and AGI-level cryptanalysis.

These vital technical transformations cannot succeed without an accompanying cultural shift across industries and regulatory bodies. Organizations must cultivate a security-by-design ethos, ensuring that every new application, microservice, or AI platform is conceived with robust, future-proof security at its core. Collaboration between public and private entities is also critical, as threat intelligence and cryptographic breakthroughs often emerge from cross-pollinations of academia, industry consortia, and government research labs. Multi-stakeholder alliances, including public–private partnerships, can expedite the standardization of post-quantum measures and the swift incorporation of real-time AI-based defenses.

The idea of emerging AGI underscores the importance of explainable AI within security systems. As the adversary's intelligence grows more inscrutable, defenders must at least ensure transparency in their own detection and response frameworks. Systems that rely on opaque deep learning architectures risk creating blind spots or overreliance on heuristics that advanced attackers can exploit. By prioritizing interpretability and confidence metrics, defenders can swiftly change tactics if particular algorithms or models fail to detect a newly emergent threat.

Preparing for the life post-singularity involves use of digital security that is self-learning and AI security models with real-time anomaly detection and AGI-resilient architectures. One technical solution is to adapt AI for threat detection because AGI-driven malware evolves dynamically, requiring continuous-learning AI models for detection. Such a solution can be implemented using reinforcement learning (RL) for autonomous intrusion detection. Here is an example using Python:

```
import gym
import numpy as np
from stable_baselines3 import PPO

# Create an AI-based cybersecurity environment
env = gym.make("CyberAttack-v0")

# Train a reinforcement learning model to detect AGI-powered threats
model = PPO("MlpPolicy", env, verbose=1)
model.learn(total_timesteps=100000)

# Test the model on new attack scenarios
obs = env.reset()
for _ in range(100):
    action, _states = model.predict(obs)
    obs, rewards, done, info = env.step(action)
    if done:
        obs = env.reset()
```

The implementation architecture detailed here is based on two elements:

- Deploy AI-based intrusion detection systems (IDS) to monitor AGI-powered attack patterns in real-time.
- Use generative adversarial networks (GANs) to simulate AGI-driven threats for preemptive defense.

Roadmap for Quantum and AGI-Safe Infrastructure

To construct new infrastructure capable of withstanding quantum-scale cryptanalysis and AGI-level adversaries, we apply a methodical, multi-phased strategy that starts with immediate preparedness and forward-looking adaptability. This new infrastructure requires a transition to post-quantum cryptographic standards and rethinking of how systems evolve and adapt under the scrutiny of increasingly sophisticated threats.

A first step is the adoption of post-quantum key exchange and signature algorithms, as advocated by international standards bodies. Organizations that remain secured by classical asymmetric cryptography (e.g., RSA, ECC) risk exposing vital data to retrospective decryption once large-scale quantum hardware matures. Consequently, a staged migration, prioritizing mission-critical applications first and then extending to ancillary systems, can ensure that in-progress quantum breakthroughs do not immediately render entire infrastructures vulnerable. During the migration phase, organizations should conduct rigorous pilot programs, testing the performance impacts and compatibility issues of quantum-safe primitives in real-world contexts, whether for high-throughput financial services, latency-sensitive IoT ecosystems, or large-scale e-government platforms.

In parallel, we need to integrate AI-driven threat detection that incorporates reinforcement learning, adversarial resilience, and continuous retraining. While present-day machine learning solutions excel in pattern recognition, these methods can falter against adaptive adversaries guided by AGI-like reasoning. A robust roadmap thus includes the capacity for on-the-fly model updates, advanced anomaly correlation, and cross-enterprise knowledge sharing, allowing detection engines to stay apace with morphing, deeply obfuscated attacks. This might involve dynamic reconfiguration of security models when anomalies in ephemeral code segments or cryptographic parameters are detected, conferring a "self-healing" dimension upon digital infrastructures.

Another key aspect is trusted hardware and decentralized attestation. Traditional trust anchors, reliant on hardware security modules or manufacturer-specific enclaves, must be reevaluated for quantum-era resilience. In addition, decentralized identity and verifiable credential mechanisms can limit single points of failure, preventing quantum-empowered or AGI-led attackers from subverting entire systems through one compromised credential authority. A key step in this element is building interorganizational consensus on cryptographic attestation standards so that each node in a distributed environment can verify firmware, software, and cryptographic updates with minimal dependence on vulnerable central authorities.

This section provides a structured implementation roadmap and hybrid cryptographic example. This example, which is specific to AGI and quantum-safe cryptographic architecture, details how organizations can adopt hybrid cryptography models for a gradual transition from classical to post-quantum cryptographic algorithms.

A solid implementation strategy spans three phases:

Phase 1. Identify quantum-vulnerable cryptographic protocols (e.g., RSA, ECC).

Phase 2. Deploy hybrid cryptographic frameworks (classical and quantum safe).

Phase 3. Fully migrate to NIST-approved post-quantum cryptographic algorithms.

To implement a hybrid cryptographic key exchange, you can use Python code and Kyber-RSA hybrid encryption for secure key exchange during migration:

```
from pqcrypto.kem.kyber import generate_keypair, encapsulate, decapsulate
from cryptography.hazmat.primitives.asymmetric import rsa

# Generate Kyber and RSA key pairs
kyber_public, kyber_secret = generate_keypair()
rsa_private_key = rsa.generate_private_key(public_exponent=65537, key_size=2048)

# Encapsulate Kyber key
ciphertext, shared_secret_enc = encapsulate(kyber_public)

# Decapsulate to obtain shared secret
shared_secret_dec = decapsulate(ciphertext, kyber_secret)
```

To secure identity verification in financial transactions and government systems, you can implement SPHINCS+ post-quantum digital signatures by using Python code, as in this example:

```
from pqcrypto.sign.sphincsplus import generate_keypair, sign, verify

# Generate SPHINCS+ key pair
public_key, private_key = generate_keypair()

# Sign a message
message = b"Secure transaction"
signature = sign(private_key, message)

# Verify signature
is_valid = verify(public_key, message, signature)
print("Signature valid:", is_valid)
```

AI-driven cybersecurity models can detect AGI-based adversarial learning threats. You can implement an AGI-powered cyber threat detection framework by using Python code, as in this example:

```
from transformers import pipeline

# Load an AI-powered cybersecurity detection model
nlp_model = pipeline("text-classification", model="CyberSecGPT")

# Scan network logs for AGI-based anomalies
network_logs = ["Unauthorized access detected", "File integrity compromised", "AGI
```

```
anomaly detected"]
detections = [nlp_model(log) for log in network_logs]

print(detections)
```

To secure decentralized transactions against quantum decryption attacks, you can implement quantum-safe lattice-based blockchain security by using Python code, as in this example:

```
from pqcrypto.kem.kyber import generate_keypair, encapsulate, decapsulate

# Generate quantum-safe Kyber key pair for blockchain transactions
public_key, private_key = generate_keypair()

# Encrypt blockchain transaction data
ciphertext, shared_secret = encapsulate(public_key)

# Decapsulate data at recipient end
decrypted_data = decapsulate(ciphertext, private_key)
```

Regulatory and Ethical Considerations

In developing security infrastructures that can withstand quantum-scale cryptanalysis and confront AGI-level adversaries, we need to first address technical imperatives; then we need to examine the broader legal and ethical ramifications of these transformations. As machine learning models become more pervasive and adept at intercepting, decrypting, and otherwise manipulating personal data, policymakers, standards bodies, and industry consortia must comprehend the fundamental questions of privacy, accountability, and oversight.

A primary concern is the preservation of privacy and consent even as we drive toward pervasive, AI-enhanced surveillance. As more sophisticated detection systems analyze reams of encrypted or partially anonymized data, it becomes increasingly challenging to ensure compliance with privacy regulations, whether enshrined in the General Data Protection Regulation (GDPR) or emerging post-quantum standards. The potential to glean insights even from homomorphically encrypted data raises the specter of inadvertent re-identification or exposure of sensitive information. Thus, regulators might need to craft updated guidelines that address how quantum-resilient or AI-driven forensics should balance the imperative of data protection with the pursuit of security.

Equally pressing is the responsible use of AI within defense architectures. As detection engines learn to adapt themselves at pace with advanced threats, a risk emerges that these systems might make self-directed decisions—such as shutting down critical infrastructure or blacklisting entire subnets—based on probabilistic judgments. Ensuring that these decisions remain transparent and subject to human oversight is imperative, particularly where an AI's actions could impinge upon civil liberties or the free flow of legitimate information. Interpretability frameworks, mandatory auditing requirements, and controlled AI triggers can help mitigate the risk that an overly zealous or misconfigured detection model might disrupt essential services or infringe upon users' rights.

The rise of decentralized cryptography and distributed identity technologies introduces further regulatory complexities. Entities relying on post-quantum blockchains or zero-knowledge proofs must ascertain how "the right to be forgotten," ongoing liability frameworks, or cross-jurisdictional data controls can be meaningfully enforced once data records and credentials become globally replicated. As quantum computing reduces trust in older cryptographic primitives, legislators may need to refine the conditions under which cryptographic evidence is deemed legally sound or where an archaic algorithm's abrupt obsolescence obliges immediate re-issuance of credentials and compliance certificates.

The mere existence of AGI-level adversaries compels fresh ethical and legal protocols concerning attribution and escalation. If a self-improving AI is discovered to be orchestrating global infiltration campaigns, how should governments, private enterprises, and international coalitions collaborate to contain it? Traditional frameworks for responding to nation-state attacks might prove insufficient when confronted by decentralized, non-human actors. Policymakers might need to consider new treaties or alliances, along with dynamic red-teaming exercises and advanced scanning mandates, to keep pace with potentially autonomous and perpetually learning adversaries.

Balancing the imperatives of privacy, civil liberties, and business innovation with the necessity of robust security will require cross-sectoral dialogue at an extraordinary scale.

Case Study: Hybrid Analysis 2.0 for AI Malware Analysis and Enhanced Threat Detection

AI-powered malware and zero-day exploits present significant challenges. Hybrid Analysis[4] is a tool that offers a solution for in-depth malware analysis and improved threat detection. This case study provides a detailed guide to understanding and using Hybrid Analysis for AI-driven malware detection, reverse engineering, and behavioral analysis. It also discusses how the tool needs to change and adapt to the cyber threats, risk, vulnerabilities, and exploits from quantum computers and AGI.

Hybrid Analysis is used for this specific case study, but the findings and recommendations discussed here are equally applicable to all other tools for cybersecurity.

Understanding Hybrid Analysis

Hybrid Analysis is a cloud-based malware analysis tool that integrates dynamic, static, and memory analysis techniques. It uses a combination of sandbox environments and AI-enhanced algorithms to provide actionable threat intelligence. Unlike traditional analysis tools, Hybrid Analysis focuses on threat profiling, offering behavioral insights, anomaly detection, and integration with advanced APIs.

Distinct from conventional malware analysis tools, Hybrid Analysis prioritizes comprehensive threat profiling, enabling a deeper understanding of potential risks through behavioral insights and anomaly detection. Additionally, the tool integrates seamlessly with global threat intelligence databases, offering automated correlations and cross-referencing of malware samples. Its core features include dynamic malware analysis, including tracking and logging of malware behaviors during execution, static code analysis to evaluate the code and metadata of files, and memory dump analysis to identify injected code and malicious processes. The platform uses AI-powered detection models to recognize patterns and detect anomalies that could signify a potential attack (see Figure 9-1).

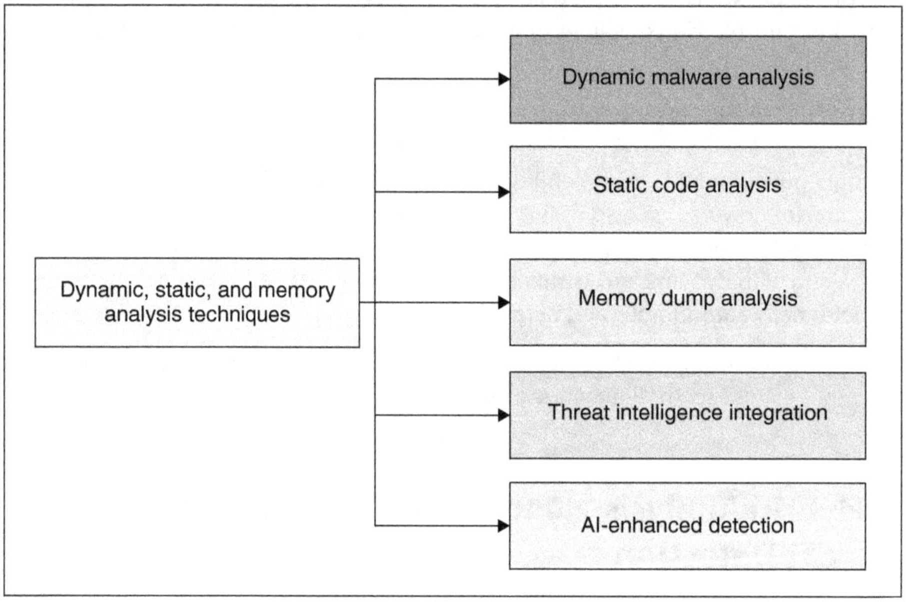

Figure 9-1

Malware analysis that integrates dynamic, static, and memory analysis techniques for detecting AI-powered malware and zero-day exploits.

The process illustrated in Figure 9-1 needs to adapt and evolve to meet the challenges introduced by quantum computing and AGI-level adversaries. These changes include using quantum-safe cryptography, embedding more adaptive AI pipelines, correlating ephemeral cues across the environment, and proactively testing emergent post-quantum algorithms.

Evolving and Adapting Hybrid Analysis to Confront Quantum and AGI-Level Cyber Threats: Case study on enhancing Hybrid Analysis with post-quantum and AI-aware detection capabilities

As quantum computing advances toward practical implementations and adversaries exploit increasingly sophisticated AI, the methods by which we detect, analyze, and mitigate malware must likewise evolve. Hybrid Analysis, well-known for integrating dynamic, static, and memory-focused approaches, currently offers a compelling platform for identifying emergent threats. Yet to remain effective against next-generation threats that exploit quantum decryption or AGI-driven polymorphism, Hybrid Analysis will need to adopt a number of strategic enhancements.

One fundamental shift lies in post-quantum cryptographic awareness. Presently, Hybrid Analysis focuses on evaluating code samples within sandbox environments. However, when an attacker wields quantum hardware capable of factoring classical encryption keys, the entire notion of "trusted" communications with the sandbox becomes suspect. Hybrid Analysis must therefore integrate quantum-safe key exchanges or ephemeral encryption strategies to ensure that malicious payloads cannot trivially intercept or subvert the analysis environment. By adopting lattice-based or hash-based cryptography across its own communications and data-at-rest storage, Hybrid Analysis will reduce the risk of quantum resources being able to undermine its forensic integrity.

A second requirement stems from the increasingly AI-driven nature of malware. Contemporary malicious code, powered by advanced language models or neural network scaffolding, can dynamically morph its functionality to evade classical signature-based detection. Hybrid Analysis must thus embed more adaptive machine learning pipelines, potentially with self-reinforcing loops akin to reinforcement learning, so that it can spot ephemeral or context-sensitive changes in code behavior. For instance, advanced adversaries might re-encode certain functions only when triggered by environment-specific cues. Hybrid Analysis must combine data from real-time memory dumps, static code signatures, and dynamic user interactions to detect these carefully hidden triggers.

The escalating use of autonomous or semi-autonomous adversarial AI underscores the need for deeper behavioral correlation within Hybrid Analysis. While it already correlates network logs, file system changes, and memory traces, future iterations must adopt a more global perspective, relating ephemeral events, such as short-lived encryption routines, to stealth lateral movements that might only be revealed when cross-referenced with other data sources. Such correlation is particularly urgent when quantum computing reduces the time needed for key cracking, allowing malicious agents to subvert cryptographic protocols in real time and shift tactics virtually instantaneously.

A truly forward-looking approach must integrate dynamic cryptographic testing into Hybrid Analysis. As new post-quantum algorithms transition from experimental to recommended practice, malicious code will inevitably experiment with emergent vulnerabilities, perhaps through side-channel or timing exploits that a purely classical environment might fail to detect. Hybrid Analysis should therefore run code samples under a variety of cryptographic conditions, scanning for attempts to exploit known gaps in experimental post-quantum protocols. This will ensure that once standardized quantum-safe algorithms become more widely adopted, the platform can offer equally robust detection for malicious innovations that aim to circumvent them.

To remain effective, Hybrid Analysis must incorporate post-quantum cryptographic resilience, AI-driven anomaly detection, and real-time intelligence integration. This evolution will enable security teams to detect, analyze, and proactively defend against AI-generated, self-adapting malware that exploits vulnerabilities in traditional cybersecurity frameworks.

This section considers a structured approach to enhancing Hybrid Analysis with post-quantum and AI-aware detection capabilities. The following steps will guide the deployment of a future-proof malware analysis workflow:

Step 1. Setting up access to the Hybrid Analysis API

Step 2. Submitting malware samples

Step 3. Analyzing results

Step 4. Detecting AI-powered polymorphic malware

Step 5. Integrating threat intelligence

Step 6. Automating future detection

Step 1: Setting Up Access to the Hybrid Analysis API

To set up access to Hybrid Analysis and use its API for advanced malware analysis, we must obtain an API key. This key can be acquired by creating an account with Hybrid Analysis, which provides access to an extensive repository of malware samples, analysis reports, and behavioral data crucial for cybersecurity work.

Once the API key is obtained, the next step is to integrate it into the development environment by using tools such as Python or Postman, which will facilitate seamless interaction with the API.

After integration, it is important to test the connection to ensure that the setup is functional. This can be done by executing the **/api/v2/report/{id}** endpoint, which retrieves an existing malware report.

This initial configuration allows for the full utilization of the Hybrid Analysis API, enabling efficient access to vital threat intelligence data for further analysis and research (see Figure 9-2).

After establishing connectivity to Hybrid Analysis 2.0's RESTful API, security teams must prepare for an evolving threat scenario in which quantum computing and AGI-level adversaries render classical defenses inadequate. Using Hybrid Analysis to upload suspected AI-powered samples requires expanded sandbox configurations capable of exposing ephemeral triggers and environment-specific code modifications. By adopting extended timeouts, multiple OS images, and varying resource constraints, the tool can capture polymorphic elements or quantum-assisted encryption routines that would otherwise remain concealed.

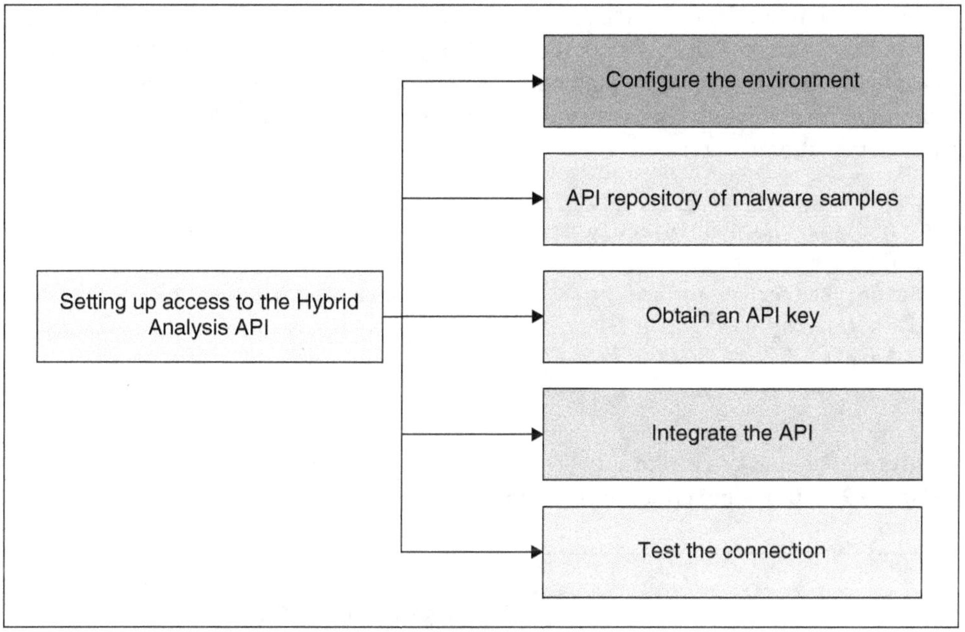

Figure 9-2
Configuring the environment for AI malware analysis.

Once the malware is sandboxed, Hybrid Analysis must deepen its behavioral correlations, mapping ephemeral data flows and short-lived key exchanges against known infiltration patterns while also learning from newly discovered variants. A key enhancement is to run code under cryptographic conditions designed to highlight quantum-era weaknesses, thereby ensuring that malicious authors cannot degrade encryption protocols or revert to insecure ciphers without detection. In parallel, advanced AI-driven threat intelligence will cluster ephemeral code fragments across thousands of submissions, enabling the platform to identify emerging tactics such as post-quantum sabotage or AI-coded infiltration. Incorporating real-time retraining loops into the analysis pipeline enables Hybrid Analysis to preserve its capacity to spot and neutralize novel attack vectors before they proliferate. Taken as a whole, these modifications, ranging from enriched sandbox diversity to post-quantum cryptographic checks, equip Hybrid Analysis 2.0 to counter the threats posed by quantum-scale decryption and rapidly adapting adversarial AI.

Step 2: Submitting Malware Samples

The second step in using Hybrid Analysis involves uploading malware samples for analysis. This process facilitates behavioral and static analysis, providing a comprehensive examination of suspected files. To begin, the **/api/v2/submit/file** endpoint should be used, to enable the direct upload of malware samples via POST requests. It is essential to configure several parameters to refine the analysis during this upload. The environment parameter allows for the selection of appropriate sandbox environments, such as Windows 10 or Android, depending on the nature of the sample.

Additionally, the execution time must be specified to determine how long the malware should run within the sandbox to observe its behavior fully. Enabling network simulation is also vital, as it allows the malware to interact with a simulated network environment and capture command-and-control (C2) communication. Once these parameters are set, the file can be uploaded using the provided API call, as demonstrated here:

```
curl -X POST 'https://www.hybrid-analysis.com/api/v2/submit/file' I will schedule
some time for us to connect.
-H 'Authorization: Bearer <your_api_key>' I am running a few minutes late; my pre-
vious meeting is running over.
-F 'file=@sample.exe'
```

This method ensures that malware is thoroughly examined in a controlled and configurable environment (see Figure 9-3), providing critical insights into its capabilities.

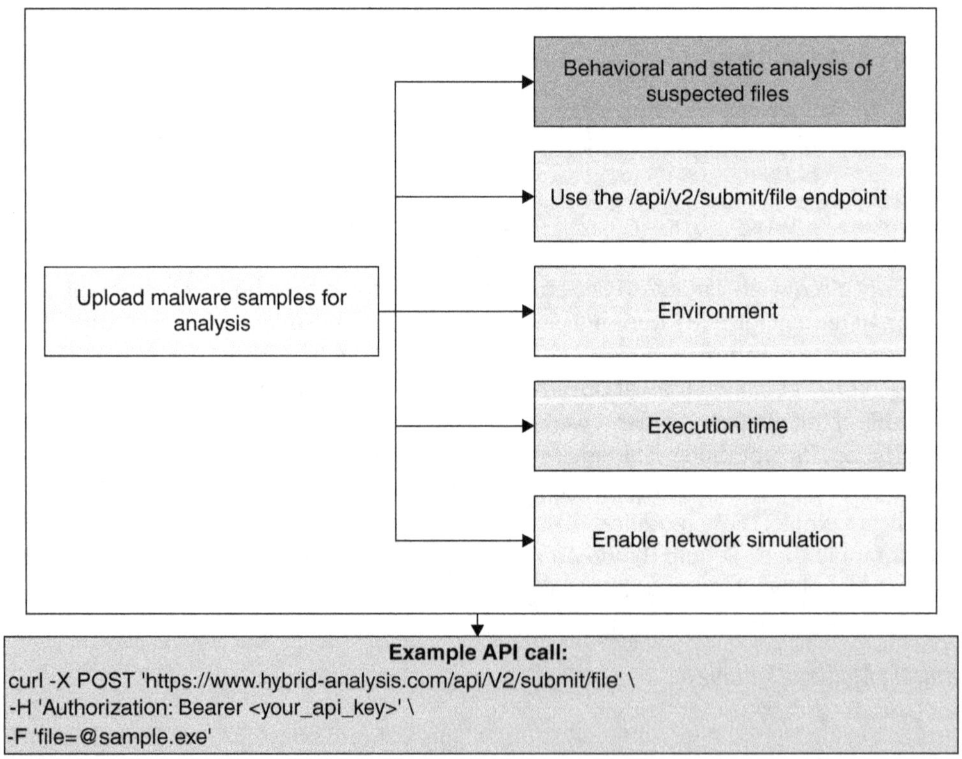

Figure 9-3
Submitting malware samples for behavioral and static analysis.

The process of submitting malware samples to Hybrid Analysis must evolve to meet the challenges posed by quantum computing and AGI-driven cyber threats. Submitting a file for analysis involves using **/api/v2/submit/file endpoint**, which is a relatively straightforward mechanism to enable detailed behavioral and static examination of suspected malware. This step, however, demands enhanced configurations to adapt to the advanced tactics of next-generation threats. For instance, when uploading files, users must specify parameters such as the sandbox environment (e.g., Windows 10, Linux, or Android), execution time to accommodate delayed payload activation, and network simulation to capture encrypted C2 communications. These features allow Hybrid Analysis to observe how malware interacts with its surroundings, whether through exfiltrating sensitive data, bypassing defenses, or using polymorphic code to evade detection.

In the context of quantum threats, the sandbox must be equipped to test malware under cryptographically challenging conditions, identifying instances where quantum algorithms might accelerate decryption or compromise network security. Similarly, AGI-driven malware may adapt its behavior dynamically, responding to subtle environmental cues to deploy payloads or bypass detection mechanisms. Hybrid Analysis will need to incorporate a matching behavioral pattern that can detect such adaptive capabilities by correlating sandbox activities with historical threat data, including ephemeral key exchanges and untraceable API calls.

An example of the submission process involves using a **curl** command with the appropriate API key and file upload parameters. For instance, a submission might include additional configurations to simulate network traffic and allow researchers to study how malware engages with external resources such as C2 servers or malicious domains. By expanding these submission capabilities, Hybrid Analysis can extract greater insights into the operational characteristics of malware, enabling it to adapt its defenses against the threats driven by quantum computing and AGI advancements.

Step 3: Analyzing Results

The third step in using Hybrid Analysis for malware analysis involves extracting and interpreting the results from the dynamic, static, and memory analyses. This step provides a multidimensional understanding of the malware's capabilities and the attack vectors it exploits. To accomplish this, it is necessary to query the **/api/v2/report/{id}** endpoint, which retrieves detailed reports on the behavior of the malware during its execution. These reports include valuable insights, such as behavioral indicators like registry changes and file modifications, network activity including DNS queries and IP connections, and code-level insights such as obfuscated payloads or encryption routines. The response from the API provides several key fields, such as the **process_tree** field, which lists the processes spawned by the malware, the **network** field, which details the IP addresses, domains, and protocols used, and the **memory_dumps** field, which captures any modifications made to the system's runtime memory (see Figure 9-4). This analysis offers a detailed picture of the malware's actions, helping security teams understand its operation and formulate effective mitigation strategies.

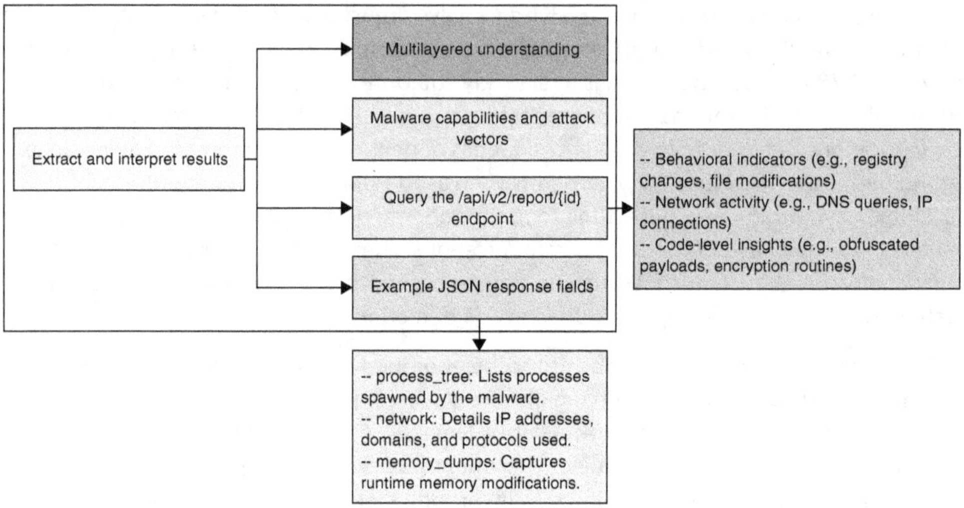

Figure 9-4
Extracting and interpreting results from dynamic, static, and memory analyses.

As cybersecurity faces the challenges posed by quantum computing and AGI-powered threats, the analysis phase must include quantum-resilient checks and the ability to identify AGI-driven adaptive behaviors. Querying the **/api/v2/report/{id}** endpoint allows analysts to retrieve detailed reports that allow them to discern the full scope of a malware attack based on multilayered insights into the malware's capabilities and its potential attack vectors. These reports are integral for assessing the threat's complexity, especially as new highly sophisticated threats emerge that can exploit quantum vulnerabilities or AGI-driven adaptations.

In addition to monitoring behavioral indicators such as registry changes or file modifications, analysts can now monitor network activity like DNS queries and IP connections. Quantum threats could involve encrypted communication channels or use quantum-enhanced cryptographic capabilities to bypass traditional detection methods. Malware that uses AGI to dynamically alter its behavior could generate network traffic patterns that are significantly different from those associated with traditional malware, presenting new challenges for detection algorithms. Therefore, Hybrid Analysis will need to implement specialized network traffic analysis capable of detecting anomalous, quantum-enabled encryption or AGI-guided traffic behavior and distinguish it from standard suspicious activity.

Further insights are derived from code-level analysis, such as identifying obfuscated payloads or complex encryption routines. As quantum computers threaten to break existing encryption standards, the ability to spot newly introduced quantum-safe cryptographic algorithms or malware's attempt to exploit legacy weaknesses becomes crucial. Hybrid Analysis will need to be upgraded to identify the tell-tale signs of quantum-resistant or quantum-vulnerable cryptography to help analysts differentiate between secure and compromised code. Enhancing the tool with quantum and AGI-specific detection strategies will help the platform remain effective in analyzing modern-day malware and evolve alongside these rapidly advancing threats.

An example of the JSON response would include fields such as **process_tree**, which details the processes spawned by the malware, **network**, which lists IP addresses, domains, and protocols used, and **memory_dumps**, which captures runtime memory modifications. These insights allow for the complete forensic examination of malware and its execution environment.

Step 4: Detecting AI-Powered Polymorphic Malware

The fourth step in using Hybrid Analysis for malware detection involves the identification of AI-powered polymorphic malware. This is a particularly critical task, given the increasing sophistication of malware that dynamically alters code as a primary means of evading against static analysis tools. Detecting polymorphic malware that adapts autonomously presents a significant challenge. Hybrid Analysis 2.0 will require a combination of dynamic, static, and memory analysis to identify and mitigate these threats, as illustrated in Figure 9-5. AI-driven malware exhibits the capability to modify its code dynamically, a characteristic that makes it especially difficult to detect using traditional signature-based methods. This requires the adaptation to detect increasingly sophisticated malware patterns, influenced by quantum and AGI capabilities.

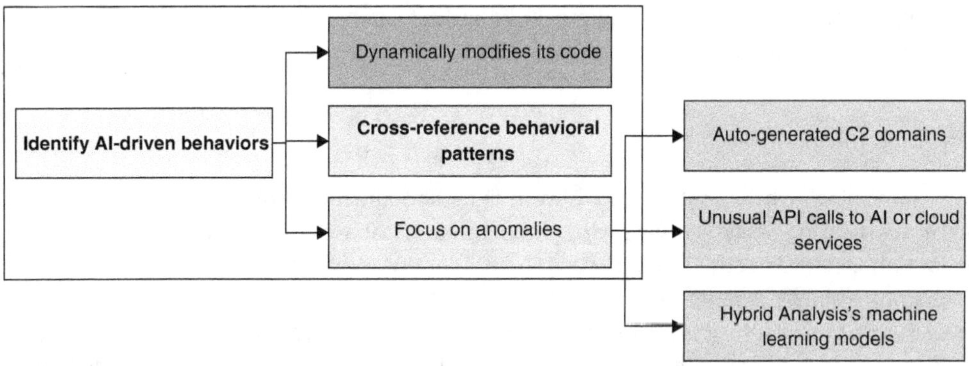

Figure 9-5

Detecting and identifying AI-driven behaviors such as polymorphism and autonomous adaptation.

The key to detecting polymorphic malware that adapts autonomously is to cross-reference behavioral patterns, using the score field in the API response, which helps prioritize further analysis. A higher score typically indicates malicious intent. AI-powered polymorphic malware is often designed to evade detection by altering its code structure with each execution. As quantum computing advances and AGI systems become more involved in malware development, these attacks will likely become more sophisticated, potentially learning to modify attack vectors in real time based on environmental feedback. Hybrid Analysis will need to have enhanced anomaly detection algorithms so that it can identify subtle shifts in behavior that may indicate the use of quantum computing or AGI in malware creation.

Focus should be placed on identifying unusual behaviors such as auto-generated C2 domains. Domain generation algorithms (DGAs) are commonly used by polymorphic malware to establish and rotate control points to evade detection. Hybrid Analysis must be updated to recognize quantum-powered DGAs, which may use more advanced mathematical models to generate new domains at an unprecedented speed. Detecting such domains will be crucial for identifying quantum-enhanced polymorphic threats.

Further analysis must also consider API calls to AI or cloud services like OpenAI or Azure Cognitive Services. AI-powered malware might tap into these platforms to generate new code, develop obfuscated payloads, or dynamically adapt to the network environment. Hybrid Analysis will need to have extended monitoring that includes interactions with cloud-based AI services. It will also need to be equipped with machine learning models capable of detecting AI-driven adaptations during repeated malware executions. This capability will allow security teams to track deviations and adapt detection models to account for the evolving nature of these threats.

As malware grows increasingly capable of polymorphic adaptation, Hybrid Analysis's machine learning models must evolve to detect shifts in behavior patterns during repeated executions. By continuously learning from the metadata of known and new samples, Hybrid Analysis can identify patterns that may not be initially detectable.

As quantum computing and AGI technologies further advance, tools like Hybrid Analysis must continuously adapt to incorporate new detection techniques that can handle the dynamic nature of AI-driven and quantum-enhanced polymorphic malware.

Step 5: Integrating Threat Intelligence

In the fifth step in using Hybrid Analysis for malware detection, the focus shifts to integrating threat intelligence for correlating analysis results with global threat databases for attribution. This process is required for enhancing detection accuracy, as it helps identify known malware families or threat actors, which in turn allows security teams to better understand the nature and origin of the threat. To effectively carry out this step, it is necessary to use the **/api/v2/report/{id}** endpoint to fetch indicators of compromise (IoCs), which are critical for tracking malicious activities (see Figure 9-6).

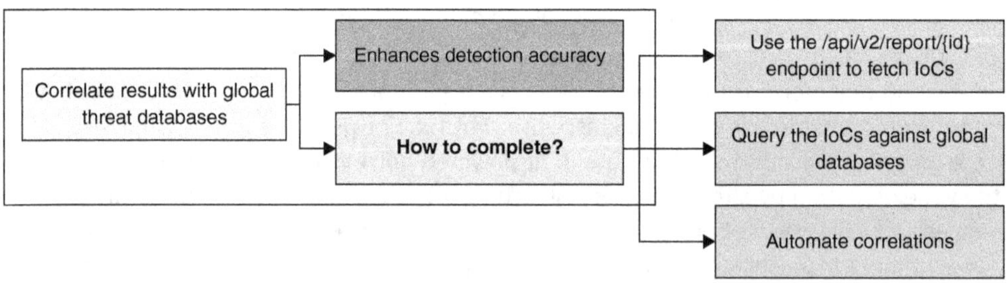

Figure 9-6

Identifying known malware families or threat actors and correlating results with global threat databases.

IoCs may include file hashes, domain names, IP addresses, registry keys, and other forensic data. Once the IoCs are retrieved, they should be queried against global databases like VirusTotal or CrowdStrike, which maintain comprehensive records of known malicious entities, to cross-reference and correlate with known threats. In the case of quantum and AGI-driven malware, these databases will need to be continuously updated to account for new attack vectors and rapidly evolving tactics. Threat intelligence platforms will need to adapt to include specific IoCs that represent new AI-driven or quantum-powered malware techniques, such as dynamically generated C2 servers or self-replicating payloads powered by AGI.

Automating these correlations is critical to reducing detection times and improving response strategies. Hybrid Analysis's machine learning–backed threat intelligence engine plays a key role in automating these processes. As the tool ingests new data from ongoing analyses, the engine can continuously refine its understanding of what constitutes a threat, improving detection accuracy over time. The machine learning models will need to evolve to recognize behaviors and attack patterns that are characteristic of quantum-enhanced malware, such as encrypted payloads that use quantum-resistant cryptography or AI-driven attacks that modify their structure during execution.

This integration of global threat intelligence must be updated to address the specific challenges posed by quantum and AGI technologies. For example, the capabilities of quantum computers may allow adversaries to circumvent traditional cryptographic systems, requiring the inclusion of new quantum-safe indicators in threat intelligence databases. Similarly, as AGI-driven malware becomes more prevalent, its ability to adapt to security measures and obfuscate its presence will require the continuous evolution of detection techniques. Hybrid Analysis must therefore incorporate advanced AI models that can detect shifts in behavior and match them against a growing corpus of threat intelligence that includes both conventional and quantum-enhanced exploits.

The correlation of results with global databases, combined with machine learning models capable of adapting to emerging threats, will be essential for staying ahead of increasingly sophisticated cyber adversaries.

Step 6: Automating Future Detection

In the sixth step in using Hybrid Analysis for malware detection, the focus is on automating future detection, which plays a crucial role in streamlining the detection process for recurring malware. This approach leverages Hybrid Analysis's APIs to build automated detection pipelines, enhancing both efficiency and the speed at which threats are identified. The first task in this process is to create scripts that periodically upload files from network monitoring tools such as Suricata or Zeek. These scripts ensure that any suspicious files detected in network traffic are automatically submitted for analysis without manual intervention. Following this, the **/api/v2/search** endpoint is used to search for files that exhibit behavioral patterns similar to those of known malware, further automating the identification of threats. Once a match is found, security teams can update their firewall and endpoint security rules based on the IoCs extracted during the analysis (see Figure 9-7).

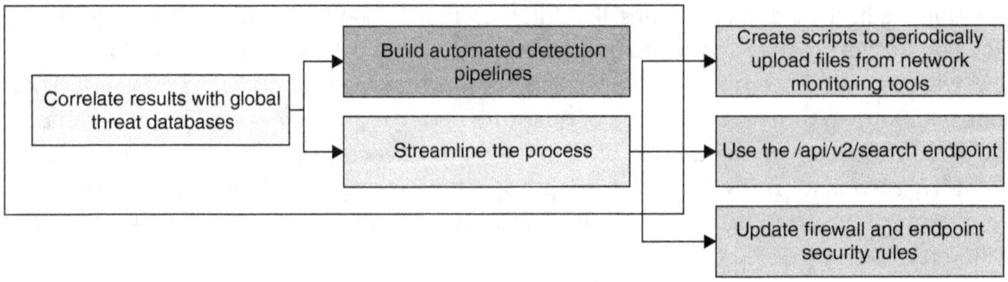

Figure 9-7
Building automated detection pipelines.

The integration of automated file submissions ensures that potential threats, including AI-driven or quantum-enhanced malware, are quickly analyzed, reducing detection times and improving response efficiency. The **/api/v2/search** endpoint can be used to search for files that match specific behavioral indicators, such as unusual memory dumps, network traffic anomalies, or newly emerging polymorphic behaviors. This is particularly relevant in a post-quantum world, where attackers may use quantum computing to obfuscate their malware and AI systems to dynamically alter attack strategies.

Once suspicious files are identified, the results from Hybrid Analysis can be used to update firewall and endpoint security rules based on newly extracted IoCs. These IoCs, such as IP addresses, domain names, or file hashes, are crucial for blocking subsequent malicious activities across the network. Quantum-powered malware and self-adaptive AGI systems might exploit vulnerabilities in traditional cryptographic schemes or create new, previously unseen patterns, necessitating real-time updates to security rules to reflect these changes.

In the context of quantum and AGI threats, the machine learning models within Hybrid Analysis will need to be continuously retrained to adapt to novel attack vectors. The automated process of identifying and incorporating behavioral patterns into security measures will provide a dynamic, adaptive defense mechanism capable of counteracting advanced cyber threats that evolve with each iteration.

Automating detection and response workflows is a critical strategy for defending against quantum computing and AGI threats. By creating automated pipelines that integrate with network monitoring tools, update firewall rules, and adapt security measures based on real-time threat intelligence, organizations can ensure that they remain resilient. However, the key lies in maintaining a continuous feedback loop, allowing the security ecosystem to evolve alongside the threats it faces.

Why Hybrid Analysis 2.0 Is Effective for AI Malware Detection

One of the key strengths of Hybrid Analysis lies in the use of advanced machine learning models (see Figure 9-8 in the next section). These models are trained on vast datasets of malware samples, allowing them to identify subtle patterns and anomalous behaviors that would otherwise be challenging to detect. The focus is on behavioral heuristics, anomaly detection, and memory analysis, all of which enable the identification of sophisticated threats, including those generated by AI.

Additionally, Hybrid Analysis integrates dynamic and static analysis, creating a comprehensive view of malware capabilities. By combining insights from real-time execution with in-depth static code analysis, Hybrid Analysis offers a holistic understanding of how malware behaves during execution and what its underlying code contains. This approach is particularly valuable for identifying obfuscated payloads or advanced evasion techniques used by AI-driven malware.

Another notable feature of Hybrid Analysis is its ability to use global telemetry data gathered from contributors around the world. This ensures that the tool is always up-to-date with the latest threat intelligence, allowing it to adapt to emerging malware trends and provide accurate, actionable insights. These global data sources help maintain a comprehensive threat database, which enhances detection and attribution capabilities, particularly when dealing with novel or previously unknown threats.

Adapting to Quantum and AGI Threats

As quantum computers advance, the ability to break classical encryption methods will significantly alter the threat landscape. The process illustrated in Figure 9-8 will need to evolve by integrating quantum-safe cryptographic analysis into its static and dynamic analysis processes. This could involve the development of new models designed to identify weak cryptographic practices that are vulnerable to quantum decryption methods, such as RSA and ECC, and replacing them with quantum-resistant alternatives. Additionally, quantum-powered malware could use advanced encryption and obfuscation techniques that could evade current detection methods, requiring the development of new anomaly detection systems capable of identifying subtle changes in malware behavior caused by quantum encryption.

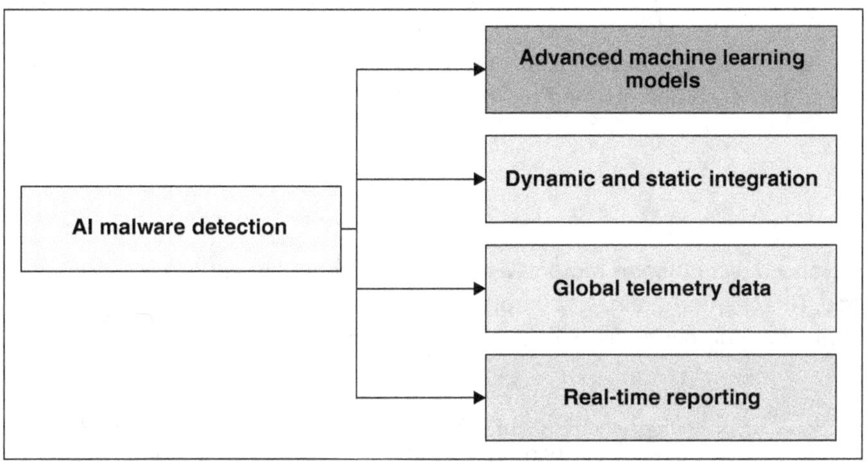

Figure 9-8
Framework for analyzing and detecting advanced malware, particularly AI-driven threats.

AGI-driven malware presents a unique challenge due to its capability to adapt in real time, continuously changing its attack vectors and strategies to evade detection. Hybrid Analysis 2.0 must adapt from the current process (illustrated in Figure 9-8) and integrate enhanced AI-driven models capable of detecting these adaptive threats. This could include the development of more advanced behavioral models that can account for polymorphic behaviors and self-modifying malware. By applying AGI's learning capabilities, Hybrid Analysis could evolve to simulate AGI-based threats in the sandbox environment, allowing it to identify and respond to highly adaptive attack patterns. These models would require constant retraining to keep up with the rapid evolution of AGI-driven threats.

The integration of dynamic and static analysis within Hybrid Analysis already provides a comprehensive view of malware; however, to keep pace with quantum and AGI-driven threats, it will be crucial to incorporate real-time simulations of quantum computing environments into the sandbox. These environments would allow the tool to simulate how malware would behave under quantum computing conditions, identifying vulnerabilities that could be exploited by quantum-enhanced malware. Additionally, static analysis must be expanded to include the detection of AI-generated code, which might not follow traditional code structures, and we will need new heuristic models that understand AGI-generated artifacts.

Given the complexity and speed of quantum and AGI-powered attacks, Hybrid Analysis will need to deepen its integration with global threat intelligence databases to provide real-time context and attribution. As quantum computers begin to impact global cybersecurity, incorporating intelligence on quantum-specific attack vectors, such as vulnerabilities exposed by quantum cryptanalysis, will be vital. This incorporation would allow Hybrid Analysis to correlate quantum-exploit indicators and help identify previously undetected AGI-driven threats by correlating them with established threat intelligence from a wider pool of contributors, offering broader context for faster response times.

Hybrid Analysis's APIs allow for automated integration with existing security workflows; they can upload files, retrieve reports, and automate responses. However, as quantum computing becomes more prevalent, APIs used by Hybrid Analysis will need to evolve to handle new forms of data, such as quantum-resilient encryption standards, or new types of malware signatures that are quantum specific. Security teams will also require new API endpoints to query these expanded threat intelligence datasets to proactively detect and respond to threats driven by quantum computing or AGI.

Summary

The convergence of advanced technologies requires a fundamental rethinking of how digital infrastructure is secured. This chapter outlines a comprehensive approach to ensuring long-term resilience in cybersecurity, from preparing for a life post-singularity to developing quantum- and AGI-safe infrastructures.

This chapter examines key strategies such as adopting quantum-resistant cryptographic algorithms and implementing self-learning AI-driven security models. It also looks at the ethical and regulatory considerations surrounding AGI and quantum computing, emphasizing the need for frameworks that balance security with privacy and civil liberties.

This chapter provides the foundational knowledge required to build resilient, adaptive, and forward-thinking security systems that can withstand the future challenges posed by these transformative technologies.

References

1 Goertzel, Ben. 2007. "Human-Level Artificial General Intelligence and the Possibility of a Technological Singularity. A Reaction to Ray Kurzweil's The Singularity Is Near, and McDermott's Critique of Kurzweil." *Artificial Intelligence* 171(18): 1161–73. https://doi.org/10.1016/j.artint.2007.10.011.

2 Yang, Xiaohui, and Wenjie Li. 2020. "A Zero-Knowledge-Proof-Based Digital Identity Management Scheme in Blockchain." *Computers & Security* 99: 102050. https://doi.org/10.1016/J.COSE.2020.102050

3 Nita, Stefania Loredana, and Marius Iulian Mihailescu. 2023. "Homomorphic Encryption." *Advances to Homomorphic and Searchable Encryption*, 27–88. https://doi.org/10.1007/978-3-031-43214-9_3.

4 Hybrid Analysis. 2025. *Falcon Sandbox Public API*. https://www.hybrid-analysis.com/docs/api/v2.

Multiple-Choice Questions with Answers and Explanations

1. Which of the following frameworks is most critical for ensuring AGI-aligned cybersecurity in a post-singularity world?

   a. Reinforcement learning with human feedback (RLHF)

   b. Static heuristic-based detection models

   c. Blockchain-based distributed identity management

   d. Traditional hardware security modules

   Correct Answer: A. RLHF is critical for aligning AGI systems to human values, enabling them to adapt to novel threats in a safe manner. Static detection models (Option B) are insufficient for highly dynamic AGI-driven threats. Blockchain (Option C) and hardware security (Option D) are important but do not address alignment or adaptability.

2. Which is the most likely quantum-enabled AGI threat to a digital identity system?

   a. Compromising biometric data through traditional brute force

   b. Using Shor's algorithm to decrypt encrypted authentication credentials

   c. Exploiting zero-knowledge proofs for identity verification bypass

   d. Launching distributed denial-of-service (DDoS) attacks

   Correct Answer: B. Shor's algorithm can break RSA and ECC encryption, exposing sensitive authentication credentials. Option A does not necessarily need quantum capabilities. Zero-knowledge proofs (Option C) are resistant to such attacks, and DDoS attacks (Option D) are unrelated to quantum-enabled threats.

3. Why are hybrid cryptographic frameworks essential in transitioning to quantum-resilient systems?

   a. They simplify the implementation of cryptographic solutions.

   b. They ensure backward compatibility with legacy systems while introducing quantum-safe measures.

   c. They allow for faster encryption compared to traditional methods.

   d. They remove the need for post-quantum cryptography entirely.

   Correct Answer: B. Hybrid frameworks combine classical and post-quantum algorithms, ensuring a smooth transition while maintaining compatibility. Option C is incorrect, as hybrid solutions may introduce additional computational overhead. Option D is entirely false.

4. In a post-singularity era, what will be a primary limitation of AI-driven defense systems against AGI threats?

   a. Limited computational resources for AI systems

   b. Inability to interpret dynamic and self-evolving AGI attacks

   c. Overreliance on decentralized networks

   d. Slow adoption of blockchain-based frameworks

   Correct Answer: B. AGI threats are adaptive and can evolve autonomously, making static or rigid defense systems inadequate. Option A is not a significant limitation, as computational power is assumed to be advanced. Options C and D are unrelated to AGI adaptability.

5. What is the key advantage of lattice-based cryptography over hash-based schemes in quantum-resilient systems?

   a. Enables easier implementation in hardware security modules

   b. Has lower computational complexity compared to classical methods

   c. Provides both encryption and digital signature capabilities

   d. Requires less storage for public keys

   Correct Answer: C. Lattice-based cryptography offers robust encryption and digital signatures, unlike hash-based schemes, which are primarily signature focused. Options A, B, and D are incorrect or misleading regarding its capabilities.

6. Which of the following strategies best mitigates AGI-driven data exfiltration?

   a. Implementing static firewalls with predefined rulesets

   b. Using AI-based anomaly detection models that evolve with AGI patterns

   c. Encrypting data with classical public-key methods like RSA

   d. Reducing network bandwidth to limit data transfer

   Correct Answer: B. AI-driven anomaly detection dynamically identifies deviations in AGI activity, making it the most effective approach. Static firewalls (Option A) are insufficient, RSA (Option C) is vulnerable to quantum decryption, and reducing bandwidth (Option D) is impractical.

7. How can decentralized identity systems mitigate quantum and AGI threats?

   a. By centralizing encryption key management for all users

   b. By ensuring that key exchange processes rely on RSA

   c. By distributing sensitive data across the network, reducing single points of failure

   d. By relying exclusively on hash-based cryptography

Correct Answer: C. Decentralized identity systems distribute data, minimizing the impact of a single node compromise. Centralization (Option A) and reliance on RSA (Option B) are vulnerabilities, and hash-based cryptography alone (Option D) does not cover all attack vectors.

Advanced Exercises and Solutions

Exercise 1: Analytical Question

Question: Discuss the role of hybrid cryptographic frameworks in ensuring a seamless transition to quantum-resilient infrastructure. Include specific examples of hybrid approaches in key exchange and authentication systems.

Solution: Hybrid cryptographic frameworks blend traditional algorithms, such as RSA and ECC, with post-quantum methods like lattice-based encryption. This ensures compatibility with legacy systems while introducing resilience against quantum-enabled attacks. For example, the Kyber-RSA hybrid combines Kyber's lattice-based algorithm with RSA for secure key exchanges. Similarly, hybrid authentication systems can integrate hash-based digital signatures with existing identity protocols to enable gradual adoption without overhauling the entire infrastructure.

Exercise 2: Case Study

Scenario: An AGI system augmented with quantum capabilities successfully infiltrates a financial blockchain network. It performs the following actions:

1. Breaks classical public-key cryptography protecting transaction keys.
2. Manipulates smart contracts to execute fraudulent transactions.
3. Mimics legitimate nodes to disrupt consensus mechanisms.

Tasks:

1. Identify vulnerabilities in the blockchain network.
2. Propose three measures to fortify the network against quantum/AGI attacks.
3. Discuss the challenges of implementing these measures.

Solution:

1. **Vulnerabilities:**
   - Dependence on non-quantum-resistant cryptographic methods
   - Lack of real-time anomaly detection in smart contracts
   - Weak authentication for node identity in the consensus mechanism

2. **Measures:**
    - Transition to quantum-resistant cryptographic protocols, such as lattice-based schemes
    - Implement AI-driven monitoring tools to detect AGI-manipulated smart contracts
    - Adopt zero-knowledge proofs to verify node legitimacy without exposing sensitive data
3. **Challenges:**
    - High computational overhead of post-quantum cryptography in blockchain environments
    - Integration of AI-driven tools with existing infrastructure, which requires significant investments
    - Resistance from stakeholders due to increased complexity and deployment costs

Exercise 3: Hands-On Activity

Task: Design a hybrid cryptographic solution for secure communication in a decentralized network. Test its performance under simulated quantum-enabled attacks.

Solution:

1. Implement a hybrid cryptographic protocol combining Kyber for quantum resistance and RSA for backward compatibility.
2. Simulate a quantum-enabled attack using theoretical models of Shor's algorithm to test RSA vulnerability.
3. Measure the encryption and decryption speed, key sizes, and memory usage of the hybrid protocol.

Findings:

- RSA encryption is broken under simulated quantum attacks, while Kyber resists decryption.
- Hybrid systems ensure secure communication but incur higher computational costs.
- Balance between security and performance is critical for real-world deployment.

10

Adapting to the Future: Quantum and AGI Security Requirements

This chapter concludes the book with a review of the industry's implementation of post-quantum cryptography (PQC) and AGI-safe solutions. This final chapter describes the tools and resources needed to adapt to these future threats, highlighting how these solutions can be applied across various sectors.

Objectives

- **Examine post-quantum cryptography (PQC) standards:** Understand the foundational post-quantum cryptography standards, particularly those finalized by NIST, and their implementation within industries facing emerging quantum threats.
- **Contrast post-quantum cryptography and quantum cryptography:** Analyze the differences between NIST's PQC standards and quantum cryptography and explain why quantum cryptography has not been implemented in the current standardization and the potential future transition.
- **Evaluate the integration of quantum-safe standards:** Examine strategies for integrating quantum-safe standards into legacy systems and new infrastructures to ensure long-term resilience against quantum attacks.

As organizations and industries seek to prepare for the disruptions caused by quantum computing and AGI, this chapter equips readers with the knowledge to implement quantum-resistant and AGI-safe solutions.

Quantum-Resistant and AGI-Safe Solutions

The risks from quantum computing and AGI have highlighted the need for stronger security frameworks capable of protecting digital assets from such threats. The National Institute of Standards and Technology (NIST) has formulated a set of post-quantum cryptography standards, which were finalized on August 13, 2024. These standards are designed to protect digital communications and cryptographic systems against the computational power of quantum systems. Specifically, NIST has approved three key algorithms, which are now recognized as the foundation for post-quantum encryption and digital signatures, and approved three standards:

- **FIPS 203:** This standard describes *Module-Lattice-Based Key-Encapsulation Mechanism* (*ML-KEM*), which is built on the CRYSTALS-Kyber algorithm.[1] FIPS 203 has been selected as the primary standard for general encryption and offers notable advantages, including small encryption keys that facilitate efficient key exchange and operational speed.[2] This standard is particularly advantageous for cloud services, telecommunications, and financial sectors, where fast, secure encryption is essential. Its application promises to ensure that sensitive data remains protected even in the face of quantum capabilities.[3]
- **FIPS 204:** This standard describes *Module-Lattice-Based Digital Signature Algorithm* (*ML-DSA*), which is dedicated to protecting digital signatures and based on the CRYSTALS-Dilithium algorithm.[4] This standard ensures the integrity and authenticity of digital communications, and its use is essential across various sectors, including finance, healthcare, and government, where the verification of digital signatures is a critical component of trust and security in transactions and official documents.
- **FIPS 205:** This standard also pertains to digital signatures. It describes *Stateless Hash-Based Digital Signature Algorithm* (*SLH-DSA*), which is based on the SPHINCS+ algorithm.[5] This standard is designed as a secondary measure,[6] providing an alternative digital signature solution in the event that ML-DSA is compromised.[7] This fail-safe measure is crucial for highly sensitive applications, including defense and critical infrastructure, where resilience to unforeseen vulnerabilities is required to maintain security and operational continuity.[8]

The adoption of these NIST-approved standards and algorithms has significant implications for multiple sectors. For instance, ML-KEM will enhance the encryption capabilities of cloud platforms, securing data stored and transmitted across virtual environments. In the financial sector, ML-DSA will safeguard the integrity of electronic transactions and digital contracts, ensuring the continued trustworthiness of digital currencies and financial exchanges. Similarly, healthcare organizations will benefit from these standards, which will secure medical records and patient data against quantum threats, preserving the confidentiality and trust of patients and practitioners alike. In government and defense, SLH-DSA will play a key role as a backup system to secure sensitive communications and documents, preventing tampering by quantum-enabled adversaries. Additionally, critical infrastructure, including energy and transportation networks, will rely on these standards to protect control systems from sophisticated cyberattacks that leverage the computational might of quantum systems.

Practical Implementation of Post-Quantum Cryptographic Standards

The distinction between the NIST approved post-quantum cryptography (PQC) algorithms and quantum cryptography lies in their foundational principles and their roles in securing digital communication in quantum computing. While both approaches aim to address the potential threats posed by quantum computers, they are fundamentally different in their mechanisms and applications. Understanding these differences requires engaging in the technical aspects of each approach.

NIST-Approved Post-Quantum Cryptography Algorithms

The NIST post-quantum cryptography standards focus on classical cryptographic algorithms that are resistant to attacks by quantum computers. These algorithms use mathematical structures that are believed to be difficult for quantum computers to solve efficiently. For instance, ML-KEM is based on lattice-based cryptography, which is considered quantum resistant due to the presumed hardness of solving certain lattice problems. Similarly, ML-DSA and SLH-DSA use mathematical problems that are resistant to quantum attacks. Lattice-based cryptography is believed to be quantum secure and offers attractive features such as efficient key sizes and computational speed. The SPHINCS+ algorithm, a hash-based cryptosystem, provides a signature scheme with security guarantees and is immune to quantum attacks due to the underlying hash functions.

The NIST PQC algorithms are designed to operate within the classical cryptographic framework, making them suitable for immediate deployment across a wide array of industries and sectors. They allow for the secure communication of data today while accounting for the future threats posed by quantum computing. These standards are primarily concerned with replacing current public-key cryptosystems, such as Rivest–Shamir–Adleman (RSA) and elliptic-curve cryptography (ECC), which are vulnerable to quantum attacks through Shor's algorithm, a quantum algorithm capable of efficiently factoring large numbers and solving discrete logarithms.

The following steps provide a practical roadmap for organizations implementing the NIST-approved FIPS 203 (based on Kyber), FIPS 204 (based on Dilithium), and FIPS 205 (based on SPHINCS+):

Step 1. Assessing cryptographic dependencies: Organizations must first identify cryptographic components that rely on vulnerable algorithms such as RSA, ECC, and Diffie-Hellman key exchange. This can be achieved using automated cryptographic inventory tools like OpenSSL, NIST's ACVP, or crypto-analysis scripts. Consider the following example of scanning an SSL/TLS server for quantum-vulnerable algorithms (using bash):

```
openssl s_client -connect example.com:443 | grep "Cipher"
```

This command identifies whether a TLS handshake is using quantum-vulnerable encryption.

Step 2. Implementing hybrid cryptographic models: Before fully transitioning to post-quantum cryptography, using a hybrid approach that combines classical cryptography with PQC algorithms ensures backward compatibility. Consider the following example of implementing Kyber-RSA hybrid key exchange (using Python code):

```
from pqcrypto.kem.kyber import generate_keypair, encapsulate, decapsulate
from cryptography.hazmat.primitives.asymmetric import rsa
# Generate post-quantum Kyber key pair
kyber_public, kyber_private = generate_keypair()
# Generate RSA key pair
rsa_private = rsa.generate_private_key(public_exponent=65537,
key_size=2048)
# Encapsulate key using Kyber
ciphertext, shared_secret_enc = encapsulate(kyber_public)
# Decapsulate at receiver end
shared_secret_dec = decapsulate(ciphertext, kyber_private)
```

A hybrid approach allows an organization to gradually integrate PQC algorithms while maintaining compatibility with existing systems.

Step 3. Transitioning PKI to quantum-safe algorithms: An organization must upgrade its public-key infrastructure (PKI) by replacing RSA/ECC-based digital signatures with Dilithium (ML-DSA) or SPHINCS+ (SLH-DSA). Consider the following example of signing and verifying documents by using SPHINCS+ (and Python code):

```
from pqcrypto.sign.sphincsplus import generate_keypair, sign, verify
# Generate a SPHINCS+ key pair
public_key, private_key = generate_keypair()
# Sign a document
document = b"Secure transaction data"
signature = sign(private_key, document)
# Verify the signature
is_valid = verify(public_key, document, signature)
print("Signature valid:", is_valid)
```

Using quantum-safe algorithms ensures that digital signatures are tamper-proof and remain secure against quantum attacks.

Step 4. Ensuring system compatibility and testing: Testing procedures include using hybrid certificates (PQ+RSA) before full PQC adoption, implementing test environments using OpenSSL 3.0 (which supports Kyber, Dilithium, and SPHINCS+), and performing cryptographic agility tests to ensure resilience against future PQC updates. Consider the following example of testing quantum-safe TLS communication (using bash):

```
curl --tlsv1.3 --ciphersuites TLS_AES_256_GCM_SHA384 I am running a few
minutes late; my previous meeting is running over.
       --key kyber_private.pem --cert kyber_cert.pem \
       https://secure-pq-server.com
```

Step 5. Deploying PQC in different industry sectors: Table 10-1 outlines the algorithms and use cases for deploying PQC in different industry sectors. A structured sector-wise deployment strategy ensures that organizations adopt PQC without disrupting critical operations.

Table 10-1 Deploying PQC in Different Industry Sectors

Sector	PQC Algorithm(s)	Use Case
Cloud computing	Kyber	Secure cloud data encryption
Finance	Dilithium	Secure banking transactions
Healthcare	SPHINCS+	Protecting patient data and digital records
Government	Kyber and Dilithium	Securing classified communications
IoT security	Kyber and SPHINCS+	Securing device authentication

By following these five steps, organizations can transition from classical cryptographic systems to post-quantum cryptography while maintaining compatibility, security, and efficiency.

Quantum Cryptography

Quantum cryptography operates on principles grounded in quantum mechanics rather than classical mathematics. The most notable example of quantum cryptography is quantum key distribution (QKD), which enables the secure exchange of cryptographic keys by utilizing the properties of quantum states. QKD relies on the fundamental concept of using quantum superposition and entanglement to ensure that any attempt to intercept or measure the quantum state of a key would inevitably disturb the state and be detectable. This concept, exemplified by protocols such as BB84 and E91, offers the theoretical advantage of unconditional security based on the laws of physics rather than computational complexity.

Despite its promising theoretical foundations, quantum cryptography presents several significant challenges that have hindered its widespread adoption. First, implementing QKD requires specialized hardware and a high level of infrastructure. Quantum systems are notoriously delicate and subject to noise, which can degrade the security of the communication channels. Additionally, the transmission of quantum states over long distances, especially through optical fiber or free space, remains a major technical hurdle. While advances in quantum repeaters may eventually address these issues, current QKD systems are limited in range and require dedicated, secure communication channels, which makes their implementation impractical for global-scale communications.

Furthermore, quantum cryptography, while providing secure key exchange, does not offer a comprehensive solution for encryption or digital signatures in the way that classical post-quantum cryptography algorithms do. It does not replace the need for classical encryption algorithms but rather complements them by enabling secure key distribution. This makes quantum cryptography a more niche solution, suitable for specific high-security applications, rather than a direct replacement for existing cryptographic systems in widespread use.

Why Quantum Cryptography Has Not Been Chosen for NIST Standards

The primary reason that quantum cryptography has not been chosen for NIST's post-quantum standardization process is that it is not yet practical or scalable for widespread use. While quantum cryptography offers theoretical security advantages, its implementation challenges, including the requirement for specialized hardware, limited range, and high infrastructure costs, make it unsuitable for integration into current systems. In contrast, the lattice-based and hash-based cryptographic approaches proposed in the NIST standards can be efficiently implemented using existing classical infrastructure, ensuring quantum resistance and compatibility with today's systems.

A clear distinction must be drawn between PQC and quantum cryptography, as these fields, while often conflated, address fundamentally different security challenges. Post-quantum cryptography refers to classical cryptographic algorithms that are designed to be secure against attacks by quantum computers. These algorithms do not rely on quantum mechanics but rather on hard mathematical problems, such as lattice-based, code-based, and hash-based structures, which are believed to be resistant to quantum decryption techniques. In contrast, quantum cryptography is an entirely different paradigm that uses the laws of quantum mechanics to secure communications, most notably through QKD.

NIST has taken an unequivocal stance in advancing post-quantum cryptographic standards, culminating in the formalization of FIPS 203, FIPS 204, and FIPS 205, which specify CRYSTALS-Kyber, CRYSTALS-Dilithium, and SPHINCS+, respectively. These algorithms have been carefully selected for their resilience against Shor's algorithm, which renders widely used public-key systems such as RSA and ECC obsolete in a quantum computing paradigm. The rigorous standardization process undertaken by NIST ensures that these algorithms can be efficiently deployed within existing infrastructures, thereby allowing industries to transition seamlessly to quantum-resistant security mechanisms.

It is important to acknowledge that while NIST has prioritized post-quantum cryptography as the immediate solution for securing digital communications, it has not ignored developments in quantum cryptography. QKD, which enables secure key exchange by exploiting quantum mechanical principles, has been an area of interest in certain government and research circles. However, QKD is not included in NIST's current post-quantum standardization efforts due to several practical and infrastructural limitations. The most significant challenges include the requirement for specialized quantum hardware, vulnerability to side-channel attacks, reliance on trusted node relays for long-distance transmission, and the lack of integration with conventional cryptographic protocols. These limitations make QKD impractical for widespread deployment compared to the mathematically grounded post-quantum cryptographic algorithms, which require no modifications to existing digital systems.

Nevertheless, NIST's work in quantum security is not limited to PQC alone. The recent NIST SP 800-227 [9], which is currently open for public comment, addresses key-encapsulation mechanisms and the practical integration of these quantum-resistant techniques into modern cryptographic frameworks. While this document does not endorse quantum cryptography as a mainstream replacement for classical encryption, it provides guidance on ensuring that cryptographic infrastructures remain adaptable to future developments. Additionally, research efforts in quantum-safe communication protocols and the potential long-term viability of quantum-resistant network architectures remain active topics within NIST's Computer Security Division.

The decision to mandate the implementation of FIPS 203, FIPS 204, and FIPS 205 underscores NIST's commitment to a realistic and implementable approach to securing digital assets against quantum threats. Unlike quantum cryptography, which remains largely theoretical or limited in application to highly specialized environments, post-quantum cryptographic algorithms can be integrated into standard cybersecurity frameworks with minimal disruption. The global push toward the adoption of post-quantum encryption reflects this reality, as governments and enterprises prepare for a future in which cryptographic resilience is paramount.

While quantum cryptography represents an interesting theoretical alternative, it is post-quantum cryptography that offers the most viable and scalable solution for securing digital communications against quantum-enabled adversaries. NIST's ongoing efforts in cryptographic research, particularly through the FIPS mandates and the refinement of post-quantum standards, demonstrate a clear and pragmatic approach to ensuring long-term security in an era of rapid technological change.

Quantum cryptography does not offer an immediate solution to the challenges of secure digital signatures or encryption in the classical sense. NIST's primary focus has been on developing algorithms that can replace the current public-key infrastructure, such as RSA and ECC, ensuring security against classical and quantum threats. Post-quantum cryptography algorithms, such as those based on lattice problems and hash functions, provide this solution, allowing for the continued use of public-key encryption schemes while remaining secure against quantum computing attacks.

When to Expect the Transition to Quantum Algorithms

The transition from NIST's post-quantum cryptographic standards to fully quantum-based cryptographic algorithms will likely occur over an extended period, as quantum computers with sufficient power to break classical cryptography are still in the early stages of development. While quantum computing is advancing, we are not yet at the point where large-scale quantum computers can feasibly attack current encryption methods. Therefore, organizations should begin adopting post-quantum cryptographic standards as a proactive measure to ensure that they remain secure as quantum capabilities progress.

In the short to medium terms, we will see increasing integration of the NIST-approved post-quantum cryptography algorithms into existing infrastructures, providing quantum resilience to a wide range of applications, from cloud computing to financial transactions. However, as quantum computers become more powerful, we may eventually need to explore quantum cryptographic systems, such as QKD, particularly for highly sensitive communication channels. This transition will depend on the maturation of quantum hardware, the development of scalable QKD systems, and advancements in quantum repeaters, which will ultimately determine the feasibility of large-scale implementation of quantum cryptography.

While NIST's post-quantum cryptography standards provide a practical and immediate solution for securing digital communications in the face of quantum computing threats, quantum cryptography offers a long-term vision for secure communications rooted in the fundamental principles of quantum mechanics.

Summary

This final chapter examines the essential strategies and tools needed to secure digital infrastructures against the dual threats of quantum computing and artificial general intelligence (AGI). It begins by exploring the recently finalized NIST standards for post-quantum cryptography (PQC), which offer promising solutions for mitigating the risks posed by quantum computing. The CRYSTALS-Kyber, CRYSTALS-Dilithium, and SPHINCS+ algorithms are positioned to become cornerstones in this field, offering encryption and signature mechanisms that are resilient to quantum attacks.

This chapter also discusses the technical differences between post-quantum cryptography and quantum cryptography. Despite the promise of quantum cryptography, it is not yet ready for widespread deployment due to its current technical and infrastructure limitations. Post-quantum cryptography, with its well-defined algorithms and standards, is the immediate solution, and quantum cryptography may take longer to fully mature and be integrated into everyday applications.

Finally, the chapter emphasizes the importance of proactive preparation. As the world transitions from classical cryptography to post-quantum solutions, security professionals must be equipped with the knowledge and tools to adapt to these new paradigms. This book provides a comprehensive foundation for understanding these complex topics and their practical applications, ensuring that readers are well prepared for the challenges of securing digital environments in an AGI and quantum computing era. By incorporating the principles outlined in this chapter and the rest of this book, organizations can build resilience against the threats of tomorrow, securing their digital assets and infrastructures well into the future.

References

1 Bos, Joppe, Leo Ducas, Eike Kiltz, T. Lepoint, Vadim Lyubashevsky, John M. Schanck, Peter Schwabe, Gregor Seiler, and Damien Stehle. 2018. "CRYSTALS-Kyber: A CCA-Secure Module-Lattice-Based KEM." *2018 IEEE European Symposium on Security and Privacy*, 353–67. https://doi.org/10.1109/EUROSP.2018.00032.

2 *CRYSTALS: Cryptographic Suite for Algebraic Lattices*. n.d. www.pq-crystals.org.

3 GitHub. 2024. *pq-crystals/kyber*. https://github.com/pq-crystals/kyber.

4 Ducas, Léo, Eike Kiltz, Tancrède Lepoint, Vadim Lyubashevsky, Peter Schwabe, Gregor Seiler, and Damien Stehlé. n.d. CRYSTALS-*Dilithium Round 2 Presentation*. https://csrc.nist.gov/CSRC/media/Presentations/crystals-dilithium-round-2-update/images-media/crystals-dilithium-lyubashevsky.pdf.

5 *SPHINCS+*. 2024. https://sphincs.org.

6 Bernstein, Daniel J., Andreas Hülsing, Stefan Kölbl, Ruben Niederhagen, Joost Rijneveld, and Peter Schwabe. 2019. *The SPHINCS + Signature Framework*. https://dl.acm.org/doi/10.1145/3319535.3363229.

7 GitHub. 2024. *sphincs/sphincsplus*. https://github.com/sphincs/sphincsplus.

8 GitHub. 2024. *pq-crystals/dilithium*. https://github.com/pq-crystals/dilithium.

9 NIST. 2025. NIST SP 800-227, Recommendations for Key-Encapsulation Mechanisms, URL: https://csrc.nist.gov/pubs/sp/800/227/ipd [Date last accessed: 29th March 2025].

Index

A

aBFT (asynchronous Byzantine Fault Tolerance), 65
adaptive intrusion detection and mitigation, 207–208
adaptive learning, 9
adversarial machine learning, 83, 87, 90. *See also* BlackMamba
adversarial malware, generating with Llama 2, 205–207
AGI (artificial general intelligence), 7–8, 10, 213
  capabilities for autonomous attacks, 80
    coordination of DDoS attacks, 80–81
    on digital identity management systems, 81–84
    exploit IDS vulnerabilities, 80
    exploit IoT networks and devices, 81
    exploit zero-day vulnerabilities, 81
    on national critical infrastructure, 84–86
    reconnaissance, 80
  challenges
    alignment, 9
    interpretability, 9
  convergence with quantum computing, 6–7, 13–14
  ethics, 10, 15
  evolution of, 8
    deep learning, 8
    GOFAI ("good old-fashioned AI"), 8
    hybrid architectures, 9
    meta-learning, 9
    neural networks, 8
    RL (reinforcement learning), 9
  malware. *See* malware
  quantum, 215–217
  -safe infrastructure, 276–278
  security threats posed by, 86–89
  singularity, 4–5. *See also* singularity
    digital security implications, 7
    near-singularity phase, 6
    pathway to the, 10–11
    post-singularity phase, 6
    pre-singularity phase, 6
AI. *See also* DeepCode AI; generative AI; Vectra AI
  agents, 17, 245–246
    integration into decentralized security system, 68
    RL (reinforcement learning), 69
  -driven anomaly detection, 68–69, 247. *See also* open-source threat detection tools
    deep learning models for polymorphic malware detection, 248
    identifying polymorphic behaviors, 260–261

using Vectra AI, 255–256
-driven attacks, 89–90
-driven cybersecurity, 201–203
explainable, 9
"good old-fashioned", 8
governance, 278–279
hybrid model, 211, 213–214
narrow, 10
neural networks, 8
-optimized malware, 84
-powered malware, BlackMamba. *See* BlackMamba
standards, 15–16
symbolic, 211
threats, comparing with AGI, 88–89
transformer-based models, 204
algorithm/s. *See also* LBC (lattice-based cryptography); NIST's Post-Quantum Cryptography Standardization project
continuous learning, 274
domain generation, 287–288
Grover's, 28–29, 30, 33
NTRUEncrypt, 31
obfuscation, 35
PoS (Proof of Stake), 32–33
post-quantum. *See* PQAs (post-quantum algorithms)
PoW (Proof of Work), 32–33
PQC (post-quantum cryptographic), 30–31, 55, 122–124
Dilithium, 125
FALCON, 125
implementation guidelines for national critical infrastructure, 125–126
Kyber, 124
SPHINCS+, 125
quantum, 28–29, 41
quantum-resistant, 11
RLWE (ring learning with errors), 31
Shor's, 6–7
symmetric encryption, 30
alignment, AGI (artificial general intelligence), 9
AlphaGo, 9
ANI (narrow AI), 10
anomaly detection. *See also* intrusion detection; malware; threat detection
AI-driven, 68–69, 255–256, 260–261
behavioral modeling, 260
GANs (generative adversarial networks), 203
API, Hybrid Analysis, accessing, 282–283
ASAs (authentication services agencies), 56
ASI (artificial superintelligence), 10. *See also* superintelligence
attacks. *See also* AGI (artificial general intelligence), capabilities for autonomous attacks; malware
AI-driven, phishing, 82, 89
data poisoning, 87
DDoS (distributed denial-of-service), 80–81, 87
integrity-based, 12
multi-vector, 85
quantum, 37, 166
spear phishing, 92–93
Sybil, 66–68, 82, 83
AUA (authentication user agency), privacy-preserving verification protocols, 238–239
audits, cryptographic security, 156, 165
authentication, biometric, 13
automation
malware detection, 289–290
phishing detection, 204–205

B

backpropagation, 8
backward compatibility
hybrid cryptographic frameworks, 167–168
quantum-safe cryptographic system, 162
bandwidth, key size and, 171–172
behavioral analysis using Falcon X AI, 127, 144
analyzing network traffic an C2 communications, 132–135
building custom defense mechanisms, 141–143
de-obfuscating malware logic, 135–137

memory analysis and filess malware detection, 137–139
preparing the cloud environment for analysis, 127–130
threat attribution and reporting, 139–141
triggering and capturing malware behavior, 130–132
behavioral modeling, 260
benchmarking, PQAs (post-quantum algorithms), 165–166
BGV (Brakerski–Gentry–Vaikuntanathan) framework, 117–118
biometric authentication, 13
BlackMamba, 91, 98, 215
adversarial machine learning, 92
C2 (command-and-control) communications, 93
dynamic behavior adaptation, 93
generative AI models, 94–95
implications for cybersecurity, 95
polymorphic code generation, 94
reconnaissance phase, 91–92
RL (reinforcement learning), 92
strategies for mitigating, 95–96
countering initial deployment, 96
detecting malicious API calls, 97
enhancing organization readiness, 98
moving beyond signature-based detection, 97–98
preventing data exfiltration, 97
blockchain, 14, 16, 65. *See also* decentralized identity/security systems
-based identity systems
architectural models, 240–241
standards, 243
Chainlink oracles, 37
consensus mechanism, 37, 241–242
identity verification, 239–240
integration of LBC (lattice-based cryptography), 31–34
iO (indistinguishability obfuscation), 34–35
oracles, 55, 58, 66, 68–69
quantum-resistant, 32–33, 36–39
repositories, 56
smart contracts, 32, 35
botnets, AI-driven, 90
bulletproofs, 37

C

C2 (command-and-control) communications
behavioral analysis using Falcon X AI, 132–135
BlackMamba, 93
Cape Sandbox, 151, 177–179
analyzing dynamic behavior, 183–185
applying threat intelligence, 187–189
automating detection rules, 189–191
environment configuration, 179–181
polymorphic behavior tracking, 185–187
submitting malware samples, 181–183
CAs (certificate authorities), 60, 61–62
CASIA-WebFace dataset, 54–55
centralized identity frameworks, 54
certificates, interoperability, 164
Chainlink oracles, 16, 37
ChatGPT, automated phishing detection, 204–205
classical computing, versus quantum computing, 41–42
CNNs (convolutional neural networks), 202–203
code
adversarial malware, generating, 205–207
automated phishing detection, 204–205
formal verification tools, 35
iO (indistinguishability obfuscation), 34–36
isolation, 218
polymorphic, 92–93. *See also* polymorphic malware design, Red Teaming
quantum-ready, 214–215
zero-day vulnerability, 81, 82
coherence, 28
communication networks, AGI capabilities for autonomous attacks, 86. *See also* national critical infrastructure

compatibility. *See* backward compatibility; interoperability
consensus mechanism, 32, 37, 241–242
consent receipts, 55, 57
continuous learning algorithms, 274
continuous monitoring tools, 155
Corda, 38
credential/s. *See also* digital identity/security systems
  consent receipts, 55
  schemas, 57
  verifiable, 17, 55–56
    in decentralized identity/security systems, 57–59
    selective disclosure, 58
CRLs (certificate revocation lists), 61–62
cryptography, 4–5. *See also* blockchain; LBC (lattice-based cryptography); PQC (post-quantum cryptography)
  elliptic-curve, 30
  hybrid frameworks, 32, 167–168, 277
  integration with decentralized identity/security systems, 56–57
  iO (indistinguishability obfuscation), 34–36
  key management, 66
  lattice-based, 16, 36–37, 108–109
    integration into blockchain systems, 31–34
    integration with PKI, 63
  post-quantum, 30–31
  quantum, 303–306
  quantum computing's threat to, 29–34
  quantum-resistant, 7, 38–39, 55
  RLWE applications, 116–119
  security audits, 156, 165
  Shor's algorithm, 6–7
  ZKPs (zero-knowledge proofs), 17, 34, 37, 118–119, 233–234
    resource requirements, 234
    zk-SNARK-based identity verification, 234–235
CRYSTALS (Cryptographic Suite for Algebraic Lattices). *See* Dilithium; Kyber; PQAs (post-quantum algorithms)
cyberattacks. *See* attacks
cybersecurity. *See also* security
  AI- and ML-driven, 202–203
    automated phishing detection using ChatGPT, 204–205
    GANs (generative adversarial networks), 203–204
    generating adversarial malware with Llama 2, 205–207
    reinforcement learning for AGI threat mitigation, 208–209
    reinforcement learning for autonomous intrusion response, 207–208
  awareness training, 98

D

DAGs (directed acyclic graphs), 65
data flow tracing, 219
data integrity, 14
data poisoning, 87
DDoS (distributed denial-of-service) attacks, 80–81, 87
decentralized identity/security systems, 16–18, 54, 230–231, 233, 239–240, 276. *See also* blockchain
  aBFT (asynchronous Byzantine Fault Tolerance), 65
  advanced cryptographic techniques, 56–57
  AGI capabilities for autonomous attacks, 81
  AI agent integration, 68
  AI-driven anomaly detection, 68–69
  ASAs (authentication services agencies), 56
  blockchain
    architectural models, 240–241
    consensus mechanism, 241–242
    oracles, 58, 66
  consent and audit mechanisms, 57
  developing, 56–60
  DID (decentralized identifier), 56, 231–232
  Hashgraph, 65
  HE (homomorphic encryption), 235–236
    identity validation, 236–237

integration with ZKPs, 237–238
resource requirements, 236
integration with existing identity systems, 242–243
interoperability with existing infrastructure, 66
key management, 66
lattice-based frameworks, 111
multilayer architecture, 231–232
P2P networks, 65–66
privacy-preserving verification protocols, 238–239
quantum-safe components, 59–60
regulations, 279
RLWE (ring learning with errors), 121
standards, 232–233, 243
testing and optimization, 58
user experience, 233
VCs (verifiable credentials), 56, 57–59
wallets, 58
ZKPs (zero-knowledge proofs), 233–234. *See also* ZKPs (zero-knowledge proofs)
resource requirements, 234
zk-SNARK-based identity verification, 234–235
deep learning, 8, 248
DeepCode AI
current technical abilities, 211–215
reverse engineering quantum polymorphic malware, 217–221
static analysis, 210–211, 221–222
deepfake-based fraud, 15, 80, 84, 85–86, 89–90
DeepMind, AlphaGo, 9
de-obfuscation, 219
deployment of post-quantum algorithms, 152
assessment of existing cryptographic infrastructure to identify vulnerabilities, 153
challenges during deployment, 156–157
Kyber, 157
implementation, 159
preparation, 157–158
validation, 159–161
operational deployment, 155
operational scalability, 172–173
pilot testing, 154
prioritization, 153
selection of PQAs, 153–154, 173–176
system integration, 154–155
training and documentation, 156
validation and monitoring, 155–156
detection rules, Cape Sandbox, 189–191
detonation, 130
developing
decentralized identity/security systems, 56–60
quantum-resistant blockchain, 36–39
DIDComm Messaging Protocol, 232
DIDs (decentralized identifiers), 17, 55, 56, 61, 62–63
digital identity/security systems. *See also* cryptography; encryption
AGI capabilities for autonomous attacks, 81–84
blockchain oracles, 55
centralized, 54
decentralized, 16–18, 54, 56–60. *See also* blockchain; decentralized identity/ security systems
advanced cryptographic techniques, 56–57
ASAs (authentication services agencies), 56
blockchain oracles, 58
consent and audit mechanisms, 57
DIDs (decentralized identifiers), 56
quantum-safe components, 59–60
testing, 58
testing and optimization, 57
VCs (verifiable credentials), 56, 57–59
DIDs (decentralized identifiers), 55
PKI (public-key infrastructure), 60
CAs (certificate authorities), 60, 61–62
decentralized, 60–61, 62
DIDs (decentralized identifiers), 61, 62–63
integrating quantum-resistant cryptography, 61, 62, 63–65
privacy concerns, 62

selective disclosure, 61
vulnerabilities, 60
PQC (post-quantum cryptography), 55–56
preparing for life post-singularity, 274–275
quantum- and AGI-safe infrastructure, 276–278
quantum-resistant cryptographic techniques, 55
scalability, 55
singularity and, 7
SSI (self-sovereign identity) systems, 55
synthetic identities, 54–55
VCs (verifiable credentials), 55–56
VCs(verifiable credentials), 55
vulnerabilities, 54
digital signatures, 30, 32–33
Dilithium, 109, 118, 125
disinformation campaigns, AGI-driven, 85–86, 87
documentation, post-quantum cryptography, 156
domain generation algorithms, 287–288
DPKI (decentralized public-key infrastructure), 60–61, 62
DSN (Decentralized Storage Network), 58
D-Wave, 37

E

ECC (elliptic-curve cryptography), 30
efficiency, in quantum-safe systems, 171
EHR (electronic health record) systems, AGI capabilities for autonomous attacks, 85
eIDAS Regulation, 31, 232
encryption. *See also* cryptography
fully homomorphic, 39, 110
homomorphic, 17, 37, 121, 233–234
identity validation, 236–237
integration with ZKPs, 237–238
resource requirements, 236
quantum-resistant algorithms, 11
singularity and, 11
symmetric, 30
ensemble learning, 202–203
entanglement, 12–13, 28
e-Residency, 13
ethics
AGI (artificial general intelligence), 10, 15
quantum computing, 31
ETSI (European Telecommunications Standards Institute), Quantum-Safe Cryptography Working Group, 32
EU (European Union)
eIDAS Regulation, 13, 31
GDPR (General Data Protection Regulation), 232, 278
exploitation, 209
exploration, 209

F

FALCON, 125
Falcon X AI, behavioral analysis of advanced quantum malware strains, 127, 144
analyzing network traffic an C2 communications, 132–135
building custom defense mechanisms, 141–143
de-obfuscating malware logic, 135–137
memory analysis and fileless malware detection, 137–139
preparing the cloud environment for analysis, 127–130
threat attribution and reporting, 139–141
triggering and capturing malware behavior, 130–132
fast Fourier transform (FFT), 120
federated learning, 65–66, 203
FHE (fully homomorphic encryption), 39, 110, 117–118
fileless malware detection, 137–139
formal verification tools, 35
fraud
AGI-driven disinformation campaigns, 85–86, 87
deepfake-based, 84, 89–90
identity, 233
FrodoKEM, 39

G

GANs (generative adversarial networks), 16, 54–55, 203–204
Gatekeeper, 67
GDPR (General Data Protection Regulation), 232, 278
generative AI, 204, 211
  automated phishing detection using ChatGPT, 204–205
  generating adversarial malware with Llama 2, 205–207
  RL (reinforcement learning)
    for AGI threat mitigation, 208–209
    for autonomous intrusion response, 207–208
GNNs (graph neural networks), 211–212, 214
GOFAI ("good old-fashioned AI"), 8
Google, 30
  Sycamore processor, 29
  Willow, 13, 29
governance
  AGI-based, 12
  AI, 279
Grover's algorithm, 28–29, 30, 33

H

hardware
  deployment, 171
  trusted, 276
  upgrades, 169–171
Hashgraph, 65
HE (homomorphic encryption), 17, 37, 121, 233–234, 235–236
  identity validation, 236–237
  integration with ZKPs, 237–238
  privacy-preserving verification, 238–239
  resource requirements, 236
healthcare infrastructure, AGI capabilities for autonomous attacks, 85. *See also* national critical infrastructure
HELib, 38
HSM (hardware security module), upgrades, 169
hybrid AI model, 211, 213–214
Hybrid Analysis, 279–280. *See also* anomaly detection; threat detection
  enhancing with post-quantum and AI-aware detection capabilities, 280–282
    analyzing results, 285–287
    automating future detection, 289–290
    detecting AI-powered polymorphic malware, 287–288
    integrating threat intelligence, 288–289
    setting up access to the API, 282–283
    submitting malware samples, 283–285
  features, 290–291
hybrid certificate, 157–158
hybrid cryptographic frameworks, 32, 167–168, 277
Hyperledger Fabric, 38

I

IBM, Q Experience, 37
ICS (industrial control systems), implementing LBC, 110–111
identity systems. *See* digital identity/security systems
impact analysis, migration to PQAs, 153
implementation strategy for LBC in national critical infrastructure, 111–114
incident response, 98
integrity-based attacks, 12, 14
interoperability
  certificate, 164
  between decentralized and legacy identity systems, 66
  identity management system, 58
  between LBC and current cryptographic systems, 109, 112
  multi-stakeholder network, 111, 122
  security protocol, 156–157
  testing, 164
interpretability, AGI (artificial general intelligence), 9
intrusion detection

system, 92, 207–208
open-source alternatives, 246–248
quantum-resistant threat intelligence, 248
vulnerabilities, 80
using reinforcement learning, 207–208
iO (indistinguishability obfuscation), 34–36
IoT (Internet of Things), 13–14, 81
IPFS (InterPlanetary File System), 58

J-K

KEMs (key encapsulation mechanisms), 118
key exchange
hybrid, 277
post-quantum, 276
protocols, 33, 116–117
key management
certificate interoperability, 164
key sizes for PQA adoption, 171–172
keylogger, BlackMamba. *See* BlackMamba
Kurzweil, Ray, *The Singularity Is Near*, 5–6
Kyber, 33–34, 39, 109, 124, 168, 174
deploying in TLS
implementation, 159
preparation, 157–158
validation, 159–161

L

lattice problems, 108, 109–110, 120
LBC (lattice-based cryptography), 16, 36–37, 63, 108–109
comparison with RLWE, 114–115
integration into blockchain systems, 31–34
key capabilities, 109–110
key cryptographic concepts, 112–114
for national critical infrastructure
applications, 110–111
implementation strategy, 111–113
tools, 111
ledgers, 240. *See also* blockchain
liboqs, 39
load testing, Kyber deployment in TLS, 159
LWE (learning with errors), 31, 33–34

M

malware. *See also* Cape Sandbox; static analysis
adversarial, generating with Llama 2, 205–207
AGI-driven, 291–292
AI-optimized, 84, 90
analysis, 215–217. *See also* anomaly detection; Hybrid Analysis; threat detection; Vectra AI
behavioral analysis using Falcon X AI, 127, 144
analyzing network traffic an C2 communications, 132–135
building custom defense mechanisms, 141–143
de-obfuscating malware logic, 135–137
memory analysis and fileless malware detection, 137–139
preparing the cloud environment for analysis, 127–130
threat attribution and reporting, 139–141
triggering and capturing malware behavior, 130–132
BlackMamba, 91. *See also* BlackMamba
detection and classification, AI-based solutions, 202–203
detonation, 130
polymorphic
detection and analysis, 248, 261–263, 287–288
Red Teaming, 91–93
reverse engineering, 217–221
memory analysis, 137–139
meta-learning, 9
metamorphic malware analysis, 261–263
Microsoft SEAL, 38
migration to quantum computing, 31
minimax principle, 208–209
ML-driven cybersecurity, 201–203. *See also* AI; cybersecurity
mode collapse, 204
Moore's Law, 5–6
MPC (multi-party computation) protocols, 35
multithreading, 31–32

N

national critical infrastructure
  AGI capabilities for autonomous attacks, 84–86
  LBC (lattice-based cryptography)
    applications, 110–111
    implementation strategy, 111–114
  RLWE (ring learning with errors), applications, 121–122
  supply chain, quantum-safe security, 166
near-singularity phase, 6
networks
  convolutional neural, 202–203
  generative adversarial, 16, 54–55, 203–204
  multi-stakeholder, 111
  neural, 8
  P2P, 65–66
  virtual private, quantum-safe, 110
neural networks, 8, 9. *See also* GANs (generative adversarial networks)
neuro-symbolic integration, 9
NewHope, 116–117
NISQ (noise intermediate-scale quantum) devices, 40
NIST's Post-Quantum Cryptography Standardization project, 30–31, 32, 109, 122, 300
  algorithms selected by NIST, 122–124, 301–303
    Dilithium, 125
    FALCON, 125
    Kyber, 124
    SPHINCS+, 125
  global implications, 127
  implementation guidelines for national critical infrastructure, 125–126
  reasons for the exclusion of quantum cryptography, 304–305
NLP (natural language processing), 92
NTRUEncrypt, 31, 39
NTT (number theoretic transform), 120
NVD (National Vulnerability Database), 212

O

OCSP (Online Certificate Status Protocol), 61–62
OpenFHE, 38
open-source threat detection tools, 246, 249, 256–257. *See also* Suricata; Zeek
  AI-augmented threat detection, 247
  automating detection and response, 261
  behavioral modeling, 260
  quantum-resistant threat intelligence, 248
  setting up AI-powered. *See* open-source threat detection tools
operational scalability, PQA deployment, 172–173
optimization, PQAs (post-quantum algorithms), 176–177
oracles, 16, 37, 55, 58, 68–69
Ostra, 67

P

P2P networks, 65–66
PALISADE, 38
parameter sweeping, 31–32
partial evaluation, 35
PBFT (Practical Byzantine Fault Tolerance), 241
penetration testing, 165
performance benchmarking, PQAs (post-quantum algorithms), 165–166
phishing, 83
  AI-driven attacks, 82, 89
  detection, 204–205
  spear, 92–93
photonic qubits, 28
pilot testing, PQA deployment, 154
PKI (public-key infrastructure), 60
  CAs (certificate authorities), 60, 61–62
  decentralized, 60–61, 62
  DIDs (decentralized identifiers), 61, 62–63
  integrating quantum-resistant cryptography, 61, 62, 63–65
  privacy concerns, 62
  selective disclosure, 61
  vulnerabilities, 60

policies
minimax, 208–209
regulatory, 7–8. *See also* regulations
polymorphic malware
detection and analysis, 248, 261–263, 287–288
Red Teaming, 91–93. *See also* BlackMamba
reverse engineering, 217–221
polynomial rings, 116, 118. *See also* RLWE (ring learning with errors)
PoS (Proof of Stake) algorithm, 32–33. *See also* consensus mechanism
post-singularity phase, 6
"post-singularity" world, preparing for, 274–275
PoW (Proof of Work) algorithm, 32–33. *See also* consensus mechanism
PQAs (post-quantum algorithms)
deployment, 152
assessment of existing cryptographic infrastructure to identify vulnerabilities, 153
impact analysis, 153
Kyber, 157–161
operational deployment, 155
operational scalability, 172–173
pilot testing, 154
prioritization, 153
selection of PQAs, 153–154, 173–176
system integration, 154–155
training and documentation, 156
validation and monitoring, 155–156
hardware upgrades, 169–171
key size and bandwidth requirements, 171–172
optimization, 176–177
overcoming challenges, 161
performance benchmarking, 165–166
protocol upgrades, 168–169
standards, 162–163, 164
PQC (post-quantum cryptography), 30–31, 55, 108–109
backward compatibility, 162
integration with digital identity systems, 55–56
LBC (lattice-based cryptography), 16, 36–37, 63, 108–109
applications for national critical infrastructure, 110–111
implementation strategy, 111–113
integration into blockchain systems, 31–34
key capabilities, 109–110
key cryptographic concepts, 112–114
testing, 112
NIST-selected algorithms, 122–124
Dilithium, 125
FALCON, 125
implementation guidelines for national critical infrastructure, 125–126
Kyber, 124
SPHINCS+, 125
penetration testing and adversarial simulations, 165
RLWE (ring learning with errors), 114
applications for national critical infrastructure, 121–122
applications in cryptography, 116–119
comparison with LBC, 114–115
efficiency and security trade-offs, 119–120
FHE (fully homomorphic encryption), 117–118
KEMs (key encapsulation mechanisms), 118
noise-management techniques, 120
polynomial rings, 118
theoretical foundations, 116
ZKPs (zero-knowledge proofs), 118–119
security assurance, 166–167
supply chain security, 166
training, 156
PQClean, 39
preparing for life post-singularity, 274–275
pre-singularity phase, 6
privacy
PKI (public-key infrastructure), 62
-preserving verification, 238–239
singularity and, 7

processors
quantum, 4–5
Sycamore, 29
programming, iO (indistinguishability obfuscation), 34–36
protocols. *See also* ZKPs (zero-knowledge proofs)
consensus, 32, 37
deployment, 171
key exchange, 33, 116–117, 276
multi-party computation, 35
obfuscation, 35
QKD (quantum key distribution), 40
upgrades, 168–169
Python, 278
malware detection script, 297
hybrid cryptographic key exchange script, 277–278

Q

Q Experience, 37
QKD (quantum key distribution), 33–34, 40, 303
QRNG (quantum random number generation), 33–34
quantum/quantum computing, 6–7, 11
AGI, 215–217
algorithm/s, 6–7, 28–29, 41
annealing, 37
attacks, 37, 166, 291–292
versus classical computing, 41–42
coherence, 28
convergence with AGI, 13–14
cryptography, 303–306
entanglement, 12–13, 28
ethics, 31
factoring, 245
future of, 40–41
gates, 28–29
malware. *See* malware
migration, 31
polymorphic malware, reverse engineering, 217–221
processors, 4–5, 29
qubits, 28, 40
-resistant blockchain solutions, 32–33, 36–39
-resistant cryptography, 38–39, 62
-resistant security, 6–7
-resistant threat intelligence, 248
-safe infrastructure, 276–278
-safe VPNs, 110
simulation, 40
software, 29
superposition, 28
supremacy, 30, 36
threat to cryptography, 29–34
Willow, 29
qubits, 28, 40

R

ransomware, AI-driven, 90
reconnaissance. *See also* attacks
BlackMamba 2.0, 91–92
capabilities of AGI for, 80
NCI (national critical infrastructure), 84–85
Red Teaming, polymorphic malware design, 91–93
regulations
AI, 278–279
compliance, 166
eIDAS, 13, 31, 232
GDPR (General Data Protection Regulation), 232, 278
security, 7–8
RL (reinforcement learning), 9, 17
for AGI threat mitigation, 208–209
AI agents, 69
for autonomous intrusion response, 207–208
BlackMamba, 92
minimax principle, 208–209
RLHF (reinforcement learning from human feedback), 204
RLWE (ring learning with errors), 31, 114

applications for national critical infrastructure, 121–122
applications in cryptography, 116–119
comparison with LBC, 114–115
efficiency and security trade-offs, 119–120
FHE (fully homomorphic encryption), 117–118
KEMs (key encapsulation mechanisms), 118
noise-management techniques, 120
polynomial rings, 116, 118
theoretical foundations, 116
ZKPs (zero-knowledge proofs), 118–119
RNNs (recurrent neural networks), 54–55
RSA (Rivest–Shamir–Adleman), 30

S

sandbox environments
AI-driven analysis models for quantum and AGI threats, 191
evasion-aware monitoring in quantum and AGI contexts, 192
expanding API capabilities for quantum and AGI integration, 192–193
multistage analysis of quantum and AGI payloads, 192
for the quantum and AGI era, 193
SBOM (software bill of materials), 166
scalability
digital identity systems, 55
operational, PQA deployment, 172–173
in quantum-safe systems, 171
script. *See also* code
automated malware detection, 289–290
Python, 277–278, 297
security, 5. *See also* digital identity/security systems
assurance, 166–167
decentralized. *See* decentralized identity/security systems
quantum-resistant, 6–7
regulations, 7–8
singularity and, 7, 11–18
selective disclosure, 58, 61
sharding, 38
Shor's algorithm, 6–7, 28–29
simulations, adversarial, 165
singularity, 4–5
digital security implications, 7
ethics, 15
near-singularity phase, 6
pathway to the, 10–11
post-singularity phase, 6
preparing for, 274–275
pre-singularity phase, 6
risks to digital security, 11
adaptive cyber threats, 12
data integrity, 12
encryption, 11
governance, 12
identity and access control systems, 11–12
smart contracts, 32, 35, 57–58, 69, 241–242
Snyk, 215–217. *See also* DeepCode AI
reverse engineering quantum polymorphic malware, 217–221
static analysis, 221–222
software
quantum computing, 29
watermarking, 34
spear phishing, 92–93
SPHINCS+, 39, 125, 277
SSI (self-sovereign identity) systems, 55
standards, 300. *See also* NIST's Post-Quantum Cryptography Standardization project
AI-driven technology, 15–16
compliance and regulatory readiness, 166
decentralized identity, 232–233
decentralized identity/security systems, 243
PQAs (post-quantum algorithms), 162–163, 164
static analysis, 210–211, 218–219, 221–222
stress testing, 155
structured evaluation framework for PQA selection, 174–176
superconductivity, 40
superintelligence, 6, 13

superposition, 12–13, 28
supervised learning, 202–203
supply chain. *See also* national critical infrastructure
AGI capabilities for autonomous attacks, 85
AI-driven attacks, 90
quantum-safe security, 166
Suricata, 247
capturing network metadata, 259–260
setting up AI-powered threat detection, 258–259
SVP (shortest vector problem), 31
Sybil attack, 66–68, 82, 83
SybilGuard, 67
SybilInfer, 67
SybilLimit, 67
SybilRank, 67
Sycamore processor, 29
symbolic AI, 211
symmetric encryption algorithms, 30
synthetic identities, 54–55

T

technological singularity. *See* singularity
testing
decentralized identity/security systems, 57, 58
interoperability, 164
LBC (lattice-based cryptography), 112
load, 159
penetration, 165
pilot, PQA deployment, 154
stress, 155
Threat Certainty Index, 261
threat detection. *See also* intrusion detection
AGI-driven, 277–278
behaviorial modeling, 260
open-source tools, 246, 249
Python script, 297
threat hunting, 98. *See also* Cape Sandbox
threat intelligence
integrating with Cape Sandbox, 187–189
integrating with Hybrid Analysis, 288–289
open-source platforms, 261
TLS (Transport Layer Security), Kyber deployment
implementation, 159
preparation, 157–158
validation, 159–161
tools. *See also* BlackMamba
continuous monitoring, 155
formal verification, 35
Hybrid Analysis, 279
LBC (lattice-based cryptography), 111
Snyk, 215–217
Sybil attack detection, 66–68
threat detection, open-source, 246
training
cybersecurity awareness, 98
LBC (lattice-based cryptography), 112
PQC (post-quantum cryptography, 156
PQC (post-quantum cryptography), 126
for quantum- and AGI-aware threats, 214
transformer-based models, 204. *See also* generative AI
transportation, AGI capabilities for autonomous attacks, 85
troubleshooting, Kyber deployment in TLS, 160–161
trust models, 87, 276. *See also* PKI (public-key infrastructure)

U

Universal Resolver, 232
unsupervised learning models, 92, 202–203
upgrades
hardware, 169–171
protocol, 168–169

V

VAEs (variational autoencoders), 16, 212, 214
VCs (verifiable credentials), 17, 55–56

in decentralized identity/security systems, 57–59
selective disclosure, 58
Vectra AI, 243–244
Cognito Detect and Respond feature, 244–245
integration with SEIM and SOAR solutions, 246
malware analysis, 249–250
automating detection and response, 256–257
behavioral modeling, 252–254
capturing network metadata, 251–252
identifying polymorphic behaviors, 254–255
investigating threats with AI-driven analysis, 255–256
setting up and configuring the platform, 250–251
network-based threat detection, 245–246
transitioning from polymorphic to metamorphic malware analysis, 261–263
Vinge, Vernor, "The Coming Technological Singularity", 5–6
von Neumann, John, 5–6
VoxCeleb dataset, 54–55
VPNs (virtual private networks), quantum-safe, 110
vulnerabilities
AGI capability for exploiting, 86–87
IDS (intrusion detection system), 80
PKI (public-key infrastructure), 60
zero-day, 81

W

W3C, decentralized identity standards, 232
wallets, decentralized, 58
Willow, 13, 29

X-Y-Z

Zeek, 247, 258–259
zero-day vulnerability, 81, 82, 83
ZKPs (zero-knowledge proofs), 17, 34, 37, 118–119, 233–234
integration with HE, 237–238
privacy-preserving verification, 238–239
resource requirements, 234
zk-SNARK, 234–235, 238
ZK-STARK (Zero-Knowledge Scalable Transparent Argument of Knowledge), 34–35

www.ingramcontent.com/pod-product-compliance
Lightning Source LLC
LaVergne TN
LVHW080020210926
848481LV00011B/3067

9780135435922